A Quintet of Shakespeare Tragedies

Start Publishing PD LLC
Copyright © 2024 by Start Publishing PD LLC

All rights reserved, including the right to reproduce this book or portions thereof in any form whatsoever.

Start Publishing PD is a registered trademark of Start Publishing PD LLC
Manufactured in the United States of America

Cover art: Shutterstock/Taisiya Kozorez

Cover design: Jennifer Do

10 9 8 7 6 5 4 3 2 1

ISBN 979-8-8809-1143-1

A Quintet of Shakespeare Tragedies
(Romeo and Juliet, Hamlet, Macbeth, Othello, and King Lear)

by William Shakespeare

Romeo and Juliet

Dramatis Personae

CHORUS.
ESCALUS, Prince of Verona.
PARIS, a young Count, kinsman to the Prince.
MONTAGUE, heads of two houses at variance with each other.
CAPULET, heads of two houses at variance with each other.
AN OLD MAN, of the Capulet family.
ROMEO, son to Montague.
TYBALT, nephew to Lady Capulet.
MERCUTIO, kinsman to the Prince and friend to Romeo.
BENVOLIO, nephew to Montague, and friend to Romeo
TYBALT, nephew to Lady Capulet.
FRIAR LAURENCE, Franciscan.
FRIAR JOHN, Franciscan.
BALTHASAR, servant to Romeo.
ABRAM, servant to Montague.
SAMPSON, servant to Capulet.
GREGORY, servant to Capulet.
PETER, servant to Juliet's nurse.
AN APOTHECARY.
THREE MUSICIANS.
AN OFFICER.
LADY MONTAGUE, wife to Montague.
LADY CAPULET, wife to Capulet.
JULIET, daughter to Capulet.
NURSE TO JULIET.
Citizens of Verona; Gentlemen and Gentlewomen of both houses; Maskers, Torchbearers, Pages, Guards, Watchmen, Servants, and Attendants.

SCENE.: *Verona; Mantua.*

THE PROLOGUE

Enter Chorus.

CHORUS: Two households, both alike in dignity,
In fair Verona, where we lay our scene,
From ancient grudge break to new mutiny,
Where civil blood makes civil hands unclean.
From forth the fatal loins of these two foes
A pair of star-cross'd lovers take their life;
Whose misadventur'd piteous overthrows
Doth with their death bury their parents' strife.
The fearful passage of their death-mark'd love,
And the continuance of their parents' rage,
Which, but their children's end, naught could remove,
Is now the two hours' traffic of our stage;
The which if you with patient ears attend,
What here shall miss, our toil shall strive to mend.
  Exit.

ACT I. SCENE I. Verona. A Public Place.

Enter Sampson and Gregory (With Swords and Bucklers) of the House of Capulet.

SAMPSON: Gregory, on my word, we'll not carry coals.

GREGORY: No, for then we should be colliers.

SAMPSON: I mean, an we be in choler, we'll draw.

GREGORY: Ay, while you live, draw your neck out of collar.

SAMPSON: I strike quickly, being moved.

GREGORY: But thou art not quickly moved to strike.

SAMPSON: A dog of the house of Montague moves me.

GREGORY: To move is to stir, and to be valiant is to stand. Therefore, if thou art moved, thou runn'st away.

SAMPSON: A dog of that house shall move me to stand. I will take the wall of any man or maid of Montague's.

GREGORY: That shows thee a weak slave; for the weakest goes to the wall.

SAMPSON: 'Tis true; and therefore women, being the weaker vessels, are ever thrust to the wall. Therefore I will push Montague's men from the wall and thrust his maids to the wall.

GREGORY: The quarrel is between our masters and us their men.

SAMPSON: 'Tis all one. I will show myself a tyrant. When I have fought with the men, I will be cruel with the maids- I will cut off their heads.

GREGORY: The heads of the maids?

SAMPSON: Ay, the heads of the maids, or their maidenheads. Take it in what sense thou wilt.

GREGORY: They must take it in sense that feel it.

SAMPSON: Me they shall feel while I am able to stand; and 'tis known I am a pretty piece of flesh.

GREGORY: 'Tis well thou art not fish; if thou hadst, thou hadst been poor-John. Draw thy tool! Here comes two of the house of Montagues.
Enter Two Other Servingmen Abram and Balthasar.

SAMPSON: My naked weapon is out. Quarrel! I will back thee.

GREGORY: How? turn thy back and run?

SAMPSON: Fear me not.

GREGORY: No, marry. I fear thee!

SAMPSON: Let us take the law of our sides; let them begin.

GREGORY: I will frown as I pass by, and let them take it as they list.

SAMPSON: Nay, as they dare. I will bite my thumb at them; which is disgrace to them, if they bear it.

ABRAM: Do you bite your thumb at us, sir?

SAMPSON: I do bite my thumb, sir.

ABRAM: Do you bite your thumb at us, sir?

SAMPSON: *Aside to Gregory* Is the law of our side if I say ay?

GREGORY: *Aside to Sampson* No.

SAMPSON: No, sir, I do not bite my thumb at you, sir; but I bite my thumb, sir.

GREGORY: Do you quarrel, sir?

ABRAM: Quarrel, sir? No, sir.

SAMPSON: But if you do, sir, am for you. I serve as good a man as you.

ABRAM: No better.

SAMPSON: Well, sir.
   Enter Benvolio.

GREGORY: *Aside to Sampson* Say 'better.' Here comes one of my master's kinsmen.

SAMPSON: Yes, better, sir.

ABRAM: You lie.

SAMPSON: Draw, if you be men. Gregory, remember thy swashing blow.
They fight.

BENVOLIO: Part, fools! *Beats down Their Swords.*
Put up your swords. You know not what you do.
Enter Tybalt.

TYBALT: What, art thou drawn among these heartless hinds?
Turn thee Benvolio! look upon thy death.

BENVOLIO: I do but keep the peace. Put up thy sword,
Or manage it to part these men with me.

TYBALT: What, drawn, and talk of peace? I hate the word
As I hate hell, all Montagues, and thee.
Have at thee, coward! They fight.
Enter an Officer, and Three or Four Citizens with Clubs or Partisans.

OFFICER: Clubs, bills, and partisans! Strike! beat them down!

CITIZENS: Down with the Capulets! Down with the Montagues!
Enter Old Capulet in His Gown, and His Wife.

CAPULET: What noise is this? Give me my long sword, ho!

WIFE: A crutch, a crutch! Why call you for a sword?

CAPULET: My sword, I say! Old Montague is come
And flourishes his blade in spite of me.
Enter Old Montague and His Wife.

MONTAGUE: Thou villain Capulet!- Hold me not, let me go.

MONTAGUE'S WIFE: Thou shalt not stir one foot to seek a foe.
Enter Prince Escalus, with His Train.

PRINCE: Rebellious subjects, enemies to peace,
Profaners of this neighbour-stained steel-
Will they not hear? What, ho! you men, you beasts,
That quench the fire of your pernicious rage
With purple fountains issuing from your veins!
On pain of torture, from those bloody hands
Throw your mistempered weapons to the ground
And hear the sentence of your moved prince.
Three civil brawls, bred of an airy word
By thee, old Capulet, and Montague,
Have thrice disturb'd the quiet of our streets
And made Verona's ancient citizens
Cast by their grave beseeming ornaments
To wield old partisans, in hands as old,
Cank'red with peace, to part your cank'red hate.
If ever you disturb our streets again,
Your lives shall pay the forfeit of the peace.
For this time all the rest depart away.
You, Capulet, shall go along with me;
And, Montague, come you this afternoon,
To know our farther pleasure in this case,
To old Freetown, our common judgment place.
Once more, on pain of death, all men depart.
Exeunt All but Montague, His Wife, and Benvolio.

MONTAGUE: Who set this ancient quarrel new abroach?
Speak, nephew, were you by when it began?

BENVOLIO: Here were the servants of your adversary
And yours, close fighting ere I did approach.
I drew to part them. In the instant came
The fiery Tybalt, with his sword prepar'd;
Which, as he breath'd defiance to my ears,
He swung about his head and cut the winds,
Who, nothing hurt withal, hiss'd him in scorn.

While we were interchanging thrusts and blows,
Came more and more, and fought on part and part,
Till the Prince came, who parted either part.

MONTAGUE'S WIFE: O, where is Romeo? Saw you him to-day?
Right glad I am he was not at this fray.

BENVOLIO: Madam, an hour before the worshipp'd sun
Peer'd forth the golden window of the East,
A troubled mind drave me to walk abroad;
Where, underneath the grove of sycamore
That westward rooteth from the city's side,
So early walking did I see your son.
Towards him I made; but he was ware of me
And stole into the covert of the wood.
I- measuring his affections by my own,
Which then most sought where most might not be found,
Being one too many by my weary self-
Pursu'd my humour, not Pursuing his,
And gladly shunn'd who gladly fled from me.

MONTAGUE: Many a morning hath he there been seen,
With tears augmenting the fresh morning's dew,
Adding to clouds more clouds with his deep sighs;
But all so soon as the all-cheering sun
Should in the farthest East bean to draw
The shady curtains from Aurora's bed,
Away from light steals home my heavy son
And private in his chamber pens himself,
Shuts up his windows, locks fair daylight
And makes himself an artificial night.
Black and portentous must this humour prove
Unless good counsel may the cause remove.

BENVOLIO: My noble uncle, do you know the cause?

MONTAGUE: I neither know it nor can learn of him

BENVOLIO: Have you importun'd him by any means?

MONTAGUE: Both by myself and many other friend;
But he, his own affections' counsellor,
Is to himself- I will not say how true-
But to himself so secret and so close,
So far from sounding and discovery,
As is the bud bit with an envious worm
Ere he can spread his sweet leaves to the air
Or dedicate his beauty to the sun.
Could we but learn from whence his sorrows grow,
We would as willingly give cure as know.
   Enter Romeo.

BENVOLIO: See, where he comes. So please you step aside,
I'll know his grievance, or be much denied.

MONTAGUE: I would thou wert so happy by thy stay
To hear true shrift. Come, madam, let's away,
   Exeunt Montague and Wife.

BENVOLIO: Good morrow, cousin.

ROMEO: Is the day so young?

BENVOLIO: But new struck nine.

ROMEO: Ay me! sad hours seem long.
Was that my father that went hence so fast?

BENVOLIO: It was. What sadness lengthens Romeo's hours?

ROMEO: Not having that which having makes them short.

BENVOLIO: In love?

ROMEO: Out-

BENVOLIO: Of love?

ROMEO: Out of her favour where I am in love.

BENVOLIO: Alas that love, so gentle in his view,
Should be so tyrannous and rough in proof!

ROMEO: Alas that love, whose view is muffled still,
Should without eyes see pathways to his will!
Where shall we dine? O me! What fray was here?
Yet tell me not, for I have heard it all.
Here's much to do with hate, but more with love.
Why then, O brawling love! O loving hate!
O anything, of nothing first create!
O heavy lightness! serious vanity!
Misshapen chaos of well-seeming forms!
Feather of lead, bright smoke, cold fire, sick health!
Still-waking sleep, that is not what it is
This love feel I, that feel no love in this.
Dost thou not laugh?

BENVOLIO: No, coz, I rather weep.

ROMEO: Good heart, at what?

BENVOLIO: At thy good heart's oppression.

ROMEO: Why, such is love's transgression.
Griefs of mine own lie heavy in my breast,
Which thou wilt propagate, to have it prest
With more of thine. This love that thou hast shown
Doth add more grief to too much of mine own.
Love is a smoke rais'd with the fume of sighs;
Being purg'd, a fire sparkling in lovers' eyes;
Being vex'd, a sea nourish'd with lovers' tears.
What is it else? A madness most discreet,
A choking gall, and a preserving sweet.

Farewell, my coz.

BENVOLIO: Soft! I will go along.
An if you leave me so, you do me wrong.

ROMEO: Tut! I have lost myself; I am not here:
This is not Romeo, he's some other where.

BENVOLIO: Tell me in sadness, who is that you love?

ROMEO: What, shall I groan and tell thee?

BENVOLIO: Groan? Why, no;
But sadly tell me who.

ROMEO: Bid a sick man in sadness make his will.
Ah, word ill urg'd to one that is so ill!
In sadness, cousin, I do love a woman.

BENVOLIO: I aim'd so near when I suppos'd you lov'd.

ROMEO: A right good markman! And she's fair I love.

BENVOLIO: A right fair mark, fair coz, is soonest hit.

ROMEO: Well, in that hit you miss. She'll not be hit
With Cupid's arrow. She hath Dian's wit,
And, in strong proof of chastity well arm'd,
From Love's weak childish bow she lives unharm'd.
She will not stay the siege of loving terms,
Nor bide th' encounter of assailing eyes,
Nor ope her lap to saint-seducing gold.
O, she's rich in beauty; only poor
That, when she dies, with beauty dies her store.

BENVOLIO: Then she hath sworn that she will still live chaste?

ROMEO: She hath, and in that sparing makes huge waste;
For beauty, starv'd with her severity,
Cuts beauty off from all posterity.
She is too fair, too wise, wisely too fair,
To merit bliss by making me despair.
She hath forsworn to love, and in that vow
Do I live dead that live to tell it now.

BENVOLIO: Be rul'd by me: forget to think of her.

ROMEO: O, teach me how I should forget to think!

BENVOLIO: By giving liberty unto thine eyes.
Examine other beauties.

ROMEO: 'Tis the way
To call hers (exquisite) in question more.
These happy masks that kiss fair ladies' brows,
Being black puts us in mind they hide the fair.
He that is strucken blind cannot forget
The precious treasure of his eyesight lost.
Show me a mistress that is passing fair,
What doth her beauty serve but as a note
Where I may read who pass'd that passing fair?
Farewell. Thou canst not teach me to forget.

BENVOLIO: I'll pay that doctrine, or else die in debt.
Exeunt.

ACT I. SCENE II. A Street.
Enter Capulet, County Paris, and Servant -the Clown.

CAPULET: But Montague is bound as well as I,
In penalty alike; and 'tis not hard, I think,
For men so old as we to keep the peace.

PARIS: Of honourable reckoning are you both,

And pity 'tis you liv'd at odds so long.
But now, my lord, what say you to my suit?

CAPULET: But saying o'er what I have said before:
My child is yet a stranger in the world,
She hath not seen the change of fourteen years;
Let two more summers wither in their pride
Ere we may think her ripe to be a bride.

PARIS: Younger than she are happy mothers made.

CAPULET: And too soon marr'd are those so early made.
The earth hath swallowed all my hopes but she;
She is the hopeful lady of my earth.
But woo her, gentle Paris, get her heart;
My will to her consent is but a part.
An she agree, within her scope of choice
Lies my consent and fair according voice.
This night I hold an old accustom'd feast,
Whereto I have invited many a guest,
Such as I love; and you among the store,
One more, most welcome, makes my number more.
At my poor house look to behold this night
Earth-treading stars that make dark heaven light.
Such comfort as do lusty young men feel
When well apparell'd April on the heel
Of limping Winter treads, even such delight
Among fresh female buds shall you this night
Inherit at my house. Hear all, all see,
And like her most whose merit most shall be;
Which, on more view of many, mine, being one,
May stand in number, though in reck'ning none.
Come, go with me.
  To Servant, Giving Him a Paper Go, sirrah,
Trudge about through fair Verona; find those persons out
Whose names are written there, and to them say,
My house and welcome on their pleasure stay-
  Exeunt Capulet and Paris.

SERVANT: Find them out whose names are written here? It is written that the shoemaker should meddle with his yard and the tailor with his last, the fisher with his pencil and the painter with his nets; but I am sent to find those persons whose names are here writ, and can never find what names the writing person hath here writ. I must to the learned. In good time!
Enter Benvolio and Romeo.

BENVOLIO: Tut, man, one fire burns out another's burning;
One pain is lessoned by another's anguish;
Turn giddy, and be holp by backward turning;
One desperate grief cures with another's languish.
Take thou some new infection to thy eye,
And the rank poison of the old will die.

ROMEO: Your plantain leaf is excellent for that.

BENVOLIO: For what, I pray thee?

ROMEO: For your broken shin.

BENVOLIO: Why, Romeo, art thou mad?

ROMEO: Not mad, but bound more than a madman is;
Shut up in Prison, kept without my food,
Whipp'd and tormented and- God-den, good fellow.

SERVANT: God gi' go-den. I pray, sir, can you read?

ROMEO: Ay, mine own fortune in my misery.

SERVANT: Perhaps you have learned it without book. But I pray, can you read anything you see?

ROMEO: Ay, If I know the letters and the language.

SERVANT: Ye say honestly. Rest you merry!

ROMEO: Stay, fellow; I can read. *He reads.*

> 'Signior Martino and his wife and daughters;
> County Anselmo and his beauteous sisters;
> The lady widow of Vitruvio;
> Signior Placentio and His lovely nieces;
> Mercutio and his brother Valentine;
> Mine uncle Capulet, his wife, and daughters;
> My fair niece Rosaline and Livia;
> Signior Valentio and His cousin Tybalt;
> Lucio and the lively Helena.'
> *Gives Back the Paper.* A fair assembly. Whither should they come?

SERVANT: Up.

ROMEO: Whither?

SERVANT: To supper, to our house.

ROMEO: Whose house?

SERVANT: My master's.

ROMEO: Indeed I should have ask'd you that before.

SERVANT: Now I'll tell you without asking. My master is the great rich Capulet; and if you be not of the house of Montagues, I pray come and crush a cup of wine. Rest you merry!
   Exit.

BENVOLIO: At this same ancient feast of Capulet's
Sups the fair Rosaline whom thou so lov'st;
With all the admired beauties of Verona.
Go thither, and with unattainted eye
Compare her face with some that I shall show,

And I will make thee think thy swan a crow.

ROMEO: When the devout religion of mine eye
Maintains such falsehood, then turn tears to fires;
And these, who, often drown'd, could never die,
Transparent heretics, be burnt for liars!
One fairer than my love? The all-seeing sun
Ne'er saw her match since first the world begun.

BENVOLIO: Tut! you saw her fair, none else being by,
Herself pois'd with herself in either eye;
But in that crystal scales let there be weigh'd
Your lady's love against some other maid
That I will show you shining at this feast,
And she shall scant show well that now seems best.

ROMEO: I'll go along, no such sight to be shown,
But to rejoice in splendour of my own.
   Exeunt.

ACT I. SCENE III. Capulet's House.
Enter Capulet's Wife, and Nurse.

WIFE: Nurse, where's my daughter? Call her forth to me.

NURSE: Now, by my maidenhead at twelve year old,
I bade her come. What, lamb! what ladybird!
God forbid! Where's this girl? What, Juliet!
   Enter Juliet.

JULIET: How now? Who calls?

NURSE: Your mother.

JULIET: Madam, I am here.
What is your will?

WIFE: This is the matter- Nurse, give leave awhile,
We must talk in secret. Nurse, come back again;
I have rememb'red me, thou's hear our counsel.
Thou knowest my daughter's of a pretty age.

NURSE: Faith, I can tell her age unto an hour.

WIFE: She's not fourteen.

NURSE: I'll lay fourteen of my teeth-
And yet, to my teen be it spoken, I have but four-
She is not fourteen. How long is it now
To Lammastide?

WIFE: A fortnight and odd days.

NURSE: Even or odd, of all days in the year,
Come Lammas Eve at night shall she be fourteen.
Susan and she (God rest all Christian souls!)
Were of an age. Well, Susan is with God;
She was too good for me. But, as I said,
On Lammas Eve at night shall she be fourteen;
That shall she, marry; I remember it well.
'Tis since the earthquake now eleven years;
And she was wean'd (I never shall forget it),
Of all the days of the year, upon that day;
For I had then laid wormwood to my dug,
Sitting in the sun under the dovehouse wall.
My lord and you were then at Mantua.
Nay, I do bear a brain. But, as I said,
When it did taste the wormwood on the nipple
Of my dug and felt it bitter, pretty fool,
To see it tetchy and fall out with the dug!
Shake, quoth the dovehouse! 'Twas no need, I trow,
To bid me trudge.
And since that time it is eleven years,
For then she could stand high-lone; nay, by th' rood,
She could have run and waddled all about;

For even the day before, she broke her brow;
And then my husband (God be with his soul!
'A was a merry man) took up the child.
'Yea,' quoth he, 'dost thou fall upon thy face?
Thou wilt fall backward when thou hast more wit;
Wilt thou not, Jule?' and, by my holidam,
The pretty wretch left crying, and said 'Ay.'
To see now how a jest shall come about!
I warrant, an I should live a thousand yeas,
I never should forget it. 'Wilt thou not, Jule?' quoth he,
And, pretty fool, it stinted, and said 'Ay.'

WIFE: Enough of this. I pray thee hold thy peace.

NURSE: Yes, madam. Yet I cannot choose but laugh
To think it should leave crying and say 'Ay.'
And yet, I warrant, it bad upon it brow
A bump as big as a young cock'rel's stone;
A perilous knock; and it cried bitterly.
'Yea,' quoth my husband, 'fall'st upon thy face?
Thou wilt fall backward when thou comest to age;
Wilt thou not, Jule?' It stinted, and said 'Ay.'

JULIET: And stint thou too, I pray thee, nurse, say I.

NURSE: Peace, I have done. God mark thee to his grace!
Thou wast the prettiest babe that e'er I nurs'd.
An I might live to see thee married once, I have my wish.

WIFE: Marry, that 'marry' is the very theme
I came to talk of. Tell me, daughter Juliet,
How stands your disposition to be married?

JULIET: It is an honour that I dream not of.

NURSE: An honour? Were not I thine only nurse,
I would say thou hadst suck'd wisdom from thy teat.

WIFE: Well, think of marriage now. Younger than you,
Here in Verona, ladies of esteem,
Are made already mothers. By my count,
I was your mother much upon these years
That you are now a maid. Thus then in brief:
The valiant Paris seeks you for his love.

NURSE: A man, young lady! lady, such a man
As all the world- why he's a man of wax.

WIFE: Verona's summer hath not such a flower.

NURSE: Nay, he's a flower, in faith- a very flower.

WIFE: What say you? Can you love the gentleman?
This night you shall behold him at our feast.
Read o'er the volume of young Paris' face,
And find delight writ there with beauty's pen;
Examine every married lineament,
And see how one another lends content;
And what obscur'd in this fair volume lies
Find written in the margent of his eyes,
This precious book of love, this unbound lover,
To beautify him only lacks a cover.
The fish lives in the sea, and 'tis much pride
For fair without the fair within to hide.
That book in many's eyes doth share the glory,
That in gold clasps locks in the golden story;
So shall you share all that he doth possess,
By having him making yourself no less.

NURSE: No less? Nay, bigger! Women grow by men

WIFE: Speak briefly, can you like of Paris' love?

JULIET: I'll look to like, if looking liking move;
But no more deep will I endart mine eye

Than your consent gives strength to make it fly.
Enter Servingman.

SERVANT: Madam, the guests are come, supper serv'd up, you call'd, my young lady ask'd for, the nurse curs'd in the pantry, and everything in extremity. I must hence to wait. I beseech you follow straight.

WIFE: We follow thee.
Exit Servingman. Juliet, the County stays.

NURSE: Go, girl, seek happy nights to happy days.
Exeunt.

ACT I. SCENE IV. A Street.

Enter Romeo, Mercutio, Benvolio, with Five or Six Other Maskers; Torchbearers.

ROMEO: What, shall this speech be spoke for our excuse?
Or shall we on without apology?

BENVOLIO: The date is out of such prolixity.
We'll have no Cupid hoodwink'd with a scarf,
Bearing a Tartar's painted bow of lath,
Scaring the ladies like a crowkeeper;
Nor no without-book prologue, faintly spoke
After the prompter, for our entrance;
But, let them measure us by what they will,
We'll measure them a measure, and be gone.

ROMEO: Give me a torch. I am not for this ambling.
Being but heavy, I will bear the light.

MERCUTIO: Nay, gentle Romeo, we must have you dance.

ROMEO: Not I, believe me. You have dancing shoes
With nimble soles; I have a soul of lead
So stakes me to the ground I cannot move.

MERCUTIO: You are a lover. Borrow Cupid's wings
And soar with them above a common bound.

ROMEO: I am too sore enpierced with his shaft
To soar with his light feathers; and so bound
I cannot bound a pitch above dull woe.
Under love's heavy burthen do I sink.

MERCUTIO: And, to sink in it, should you burthen love-
Too great oppression for a tender thing.

ROMEO: Is love a tender thing? It is too rough,
Too rude, too boist'rous, and it pricks like thorn.

MERCUTIO: If love be rough with you, be rough with love.
Prick love for pricking, and you beat love down.
Give me a case to put my visage in.
A visor for a visor! What care I
What curious eye doth quote deformities?
Here are the beetle brows shall blush for me.

BENVOLIO: Come, knock and enter; and no sooner in
But every man betake him to his legs.

ROMEO: A torch for me! Let wantons light of heart
Tickle the senseless rushes with their heels;
For I am proverb'd with a grandsire phrase,
I'll be a candle-holder and look on;
The game was ne'er so fair, and I am done.

MERCUTIO: Tut! dun's the mouse, the constable's own word!
If thou art Dun, we'll draw thee from the mire
Of this sir-reverence love, wherein thou stick'st
Up to the ears. Come, we burn daylight, ho!

ROMEO: Nay, that's not so.

MERCUTIO: I mean, sir, in delay
We waste our lights in vain, like lamps by day.
Take our good meaning, for our judgment sits
Five times in that ere once in our five wits.

ROMEO: And we mean well, in going to this masque;
But 'tis no wit to go.

MERCUTIO: Why, may one ask?

ROMEO: I dreamt a dream to-night.

MERCUTIO: And so did I.

ROMEO: Well, what was yours?

MERCUTIO: That dreamers often lie.

ROMEO: In bed asleep, while they do dream things true.

MERCUTIO: O, then I see Queen Mab hath been with you.
She is the fairies' midwife, and she comes
In shape no bigger than an agate stone
On the forefinger of an alderman,
Drawn with a team of little atomies
Athwart men's noses as they lie asleep;
Her wagon spokes made of long spinners' legs,
The cover, of the wings of grasshoppers;
Her traces, of the smallest spider's web;
Her collars, of the moonshine's wat'ry beams;
Her whip, of cricket's bone; the lash, of film;
Her wagoner, a small grey-coated gnat,
Not half so big as a round little worm
Prick'd from the lazy finger of a maid;
Her chariot is an empty hazelnut,
Made by the joiner squirrel or old grub,
Time out o' mind the fairies' coachmakers.

And in this state she 'gallops night by night
Through lovers' brains, and then they dream of love;
O'er courtiers' knees, that dream on cursies straight;
O'er lawyers' fingers, who straight dream on fees;
O'er ladies' lips, who straight on kisses dream,
Which oft the angry Mab with blisters plagues,
Because their breaths with sweetmeats tainted are.
Sometime she gallops o'er a courtier's nose,
And then dreams he of smelling out a suit;
And sometime comes she with a tithe-pig's tail
Tickling a parson's nose as 'a lies asleep,
Then dreams he of another benefice.
Sometimes she driveth o'er a soldier's neck,
And then dreams he of cutting foreign throats,
Of breaches, ambuscadoes, Spanish blades,
Of healths five fadom deep; and then anon
Drums in his ear, at which he starts and wakes,
And being thus frighted, swears a prayer or two
And sleeps again. This is that very Mab
That plats the manes of horses in the night
And bakes the elflocks in foul sluttish, hairs,
Which once untangled much misfortune bodes
This is the hag, when maids lie on their backs,
That presses them and learns them first to bear,
Making them women of good carriage.
This is she-

ROMEO: Peace, peace, Mercutio, peace!
Thou talk'st of nothing.

MERCUTIO: True, I talk of dreams;
Which are the children of an idle brain,
Begot of nothing but vain fantasy;
Which is as thin of substance as the air,
And more inconstant than the wind, who wooes
Even now the frozen bosom of the North
And, being anger'd, puffs away from thence,
Turning his face to the dew-dropping South.

BENVOLIO: This wind you talk of blows us from ourselves.
Supper is done, and we shall come too late.

ROMEO: I fear, too early; for my mind misgives
Some consequence, yet hanging in the stars,
Shall bitterly begin his fearful date
With this night's revels and expire the term
Of a despised life, clos'd in my breast,
By some vile forfeit of untimely death.
But he that hath the steerage of my course
Direct my sail! On, lusty gentlemen!

BENVOLIO: Strike, drum.
They March about the Stage. Exeunt.

ACT I. SCENE V. Capulet's House.
Servingmen come forth with napkins.

FIRST SERVANT: Where's Potpan, that he helps not to take away?
He shift a trencher! he scrape a trencher!

SECOND SERVANT: When good manners shall lie all in one or two men's hands, and they unwash'd too, 'tis a foul thing.

FIRST SERVANT: Away with the join-stools, remove the court-cubbert, look to the plate. Good thou, save me a piece of marchpane and, as thou loves me, let the porter let in Susan Grindstone and Nell. Anthony, and Potpan!

SECOND SERVANT: Ay, boy, ready.

FIRST SERVANT: You are look'd for and call'd for, ask'd for and sought for, in the great chamber.

THIRD SERVANT: We cannot be here and there too. Cheerly, boys!
Be brisk awhile, and the longer liver take all.
Exeunt.

Enter the Maskers; Enter, With Servants, Capulet, His Wife, Juliet, Tybalt, and All the Guests and Gentlewomen to the Maskers.

CAPULET: Welcome, gentlemen! Ladies that have their toes
Unplagu'd with corns will have a bout with you.
Ah ha, my mistresses! which of you all
Will now deny to dance? She that makes dainty,
She I'll swear hath corns. Am I come near ye now?
Welcome, gentlemen! I have seen the day
That I have worn a visor and could tell
A whispering tale in a fair lady's ear,
Such as would please. 'Tis gone, 'tis gone, 'tis gone!
You are welcome, gentlemen! Come, musicians, play.
A hall, a hall! give room! and foot it, girls.
   Music Plays, and They Dance.
More light, you knaves! and turn the tables up,
And quench the fire, the room is grown too hot.
Ah, sirrah, this unlook'd-for sport comes well.
Nay, sit, nay, sit, good cousin Capulet,
For you and I are past our dancing days.
How long is't now since last yourself and I
Were in a mask?

SECOND CAPULET: By'r Lady, thirty years.

CAPULET: What, man? 'Tis not so much, 'tis not so much!
'Tis since the nuptial of Lucentio,
Come Pentecost as quickly as it will,
Some five-and-twenty years, and then we mask'd.

SECOND CAPULET: 'Tis more, 'tis more! His son is elder, sir;
His son is thirty.

CAPULET: Will you tell me that?
His son was but a ward two years ago.

ROMEO: *To a Servingman* What lady's that, which doth enrich the hand
Of yonder knight?

SERVANT: I know not, sir.

ROMEO: O, she doth teach the torches to burn bright!
It seems she hangs upon the cheek of night
Like a rich jewel in an Ethiop's ear-
Beauty too rich for use, for earth too dear!
So shows a snowy dove trooping with crows
As yonder lady o'er her fellows shows.
The measure done, I'll watch her place of stand
And, touching hers, make blessed my rude hand.
Did my heart love till now? Forswear it, sight!
For I ne'er saw true beauty till this night.

TYBALT: This, by his voice, should be a Montague.
Fetch me my rapier, boy. What, dares the slave
Come hither, cover'd with an antic face,
To fleer and scorn at our solemnity?
Now, by the stock and honour of my kin,
To strike him dead I hold it not a sin.

CAPULET: Why, how now, kinsman? Wherefore storm you so?

TYBALT: Uncle, this is a Montague, our foe;
A villain, that is hither come in spite
To scorn at our solemnity this night.

CAPULET: Young Romeo is it?

TYBALT: 'Tis he, that villain Romeo.

CAPULET: Content thee, gentle coz, let him alone.
'A bears him like a portly gentleman,
And, to say truth, Verona brags of him
To be a virtuous and well-govern'd youth.
I would not for the wealth of all this town
Here in my house do him disparagement.
Therefore be patient, take no note of him.

It is my will; the which if thou respect,
Show a fair presence and put off these frowns,
An ill-beseeming semblance for a feast.

TYBALT: It fits when such a villain is a guest.
I'll not endure him.

CAPULET: He shall be endur'd.
What, goodman boy? I say he shall. Go to!
Am I the master here, or you? Go to!
You'll not endure him? God shall mend my soul!
You'll make a mutiny among my guests!
You will set cock-a-hoop! you'll be the man!

TYBALT: Why, uncle, 'tis a shame.

CAPULET: Go to, go to!
You are a saucy boy. Is't so, indeed?
This trick may chance to scathe you. I know what.
You must contrary me! Marry, 'tis time.-
Well said, my hearts!- You are a princox- go!
Be quiet, or- More light, more light!- For shame!
I'll make you quiet; what!- Cheerly, my hearts!

TYBALT: Patience perforce with wilful choler meeting
Makes my flesh tremble in their different greeting.
I will withdraw; but this intrusion shall,
Now seeming sweet, convert to bitt'rest gall.
   Exit.

ROMEO: If I profane with my unworthiest hand
This holy shrine, the gentle fine is this:
My lips, two blushing pilgrims, ready stand
To smooth that rough touch with a tender kiss.

JULIET: Good pilgrim, you do wrong your hand too much,
Which mannerly devotion shows in this;

For saints have hands that pilgrims' hands do touch,
And palm to palm is holy palmers' kiss.

ROMEO: Have not saints lips, and holy palmers too?

JULIET: Ay, pilgrim, lips that they must use in pray'r.

ROMEO: O, then, dear saint, let lips do what hands do!
They pray; grant thou, lest faith turn to despair.

JULIET: Saints do not move, though grant for prayers' sake.

ROMEO: Then move not while my prayer's effect I take.
Thus from my lips, by thine my sin is purg'd. *Kisses Her.*

JULIET: Then have my lips the sin that they have took.

ROMEO: Sin from my lips? O trespass sweetly urg'd!
Give me my sin again. *Kisses Her.*

JULIET: You kiss by th' book.

NURSE: Madam, your mother craves a word with you.

ROMEO: What is her mother?

NURSE: Marry, bachelor,
Her mother is the lady of the house.
And a good lady, and a wise and virtuous.
I nurs'd her daughter that you talk'd withal.
I tell you, he that can lay hold of her
Shall have the chinks.

ROMEO: Is she a Capulet?
O dear account! my life is my foe's debt.

BENVOLIO: Away, be gone; the sport is at the best.

ROMEO: Ay, so I fear; the more is my unrest.

CAPULET: Nay, gentlemen, prepare not to be gone;
We have a trifling foolish banquet towards.
Is it e'en so? Why then, I thank you all.
I thank you, honest gentlemen. Good night.
More torches here!
   Exeunt Maskers.
Come on then, let's to bed.
Ah, sirrah, by my fay, it waxes late;
I'll to my rest.
   Exeunt All but Juliet and Nurse.

JULIET: Come hither, nurse. What is yond gentleman?

NURSE: The son and heir of old Tiberio.

JULIET: What's he that now is going out of door?

NURSE: Marry, that, I think, be young Petruchio.

JULIET: What's he that follows there, that would not dance?

NURSE: I know not.

JULIET: Go ask his name.- If he be married,
My grave is like to be my wedding bed.

NURSE: His name is Romeo, and a Montague,
The only son of your great enemy.

JULIET: My only love, sprung from my only hate!
Too early seen unknown, and known too late!
Prodigious birth of love it is to me
That I must love a loathed enemy.

NURSE: What's this? what's this?

JULIET: A rhyme I learnt even now
Of one I danc'd withal.
  One Calls Within, 'Juliet.'

NURSE: Anon, anon!
Come, let's away; the strangers all are gone. *Exeunt.*

PROLOGUE
Enter Chorus.

CHORUS: Now old desire doth in his deathbed lie,
And young affection gapes to be his heir;
That fair for which love groan'd for and would die,
With tender Juliet match'd, is now not fair.
Now Romeo is belov'd, and loves again,
Alike bewitched by the charm of looks;
But to his foe suppos'd he must complain,
And she steal love's sweet bait from fearful hooks.
Being held a foe, he may not have access
To breathe such vows as lovers use to swear,
And she as much in love, her means much less
To meet her new beloved anywhere;
But passion lends them power, time means, to meet,
Temp'ring extremities with extreme sweet.
  Exit.

ACT II. SCENE I. A Lane by the Wall of Capulet's Orchard.
Enter Romeo alone.

ROMEO: Can I go forward when my heart is here?
Turn back, dull earth, and find thy centre out.
  Climbs the Wall and Leaps down Within It.
  Enter Benvolio with Mercutio.

BENVOLIO: Romeo! my cousin Romeo! Romeo!

MERCUTIO: He is wise,

And, on my life, hath stol'n him home to bed.

BENVOLIO: He ran this way, and leapt this orchard wall.
Call, good Mercutio.

MERCUTIO: Nay, I'll conjure too.
Romeo! humours! madman! passion! lover!
Appear thou in the likeness of a sigh;
Speak but one rhyme, and I am satisfied!
Cry but 'Ay me!' pronounce but 'love' and 'dove';
Speak to my gossip Venus one fair word,
One nickname for her purblind son and heir,
Young Adam Cupid, he that shot so trim
When King Cophetua lov'd the beggar maid!
He heareth not, he stirreth not, be moveth not;
The ape is dead, and I must conjure him.
I conjure thee by Rosaline's bright eyes.
By her high forehead and her scarlet lip,
By her fine foot, straight leg, and quivering thigh,
And the demesnes that there adjacent lie,
That in thy likeness thou appear to us!

BENVOLIO: An if he hear thee, thou wilt anger him.

MERCUTIO: This cannot anger him. 'Twould anger him
To raise a spirit in his mistress' circle
Of some strange nature, letting it there stand
Till she had laid it and conjur'd it down.
That were some spite; my invocation
Is fair and honest: in his mistress' name,
I conjure only but to raise up him.

BENVOLIO: Come, he hath hid himself among these trees
To be consorted with the humorous night.
Blind is his love and best befits the dark.

MERCUTIO: If love be blind, love cannot hit the mark.

Now will he sit under a medlar tree
And wish his mistress were that kind of fruit
As maids call medlars when they laugh alone.
O, Romeo, that she were, O that she were
An open et cetera, thou a pop'rin pear!
Romeo, good night. I'll to my truckle-bed;
This field-bed is too cold for me to sleep.
Come, shall we go?

BENVOLIO: Go then, for 'tis in vain
'To seek him here that means not to be found.
    Exeunt.

ACT II. SCENE II. Capulet's Orchard.

Enter Romeo.

ROMEO: He jests at scars that never felt a wound.
    Enter Juliet above at a window.

But soft! What light through yonder window breaks?
It is the East, and Juliet is the sun!
Arise, fair sun, and kill the envious moon,
Who is already sick and pale with grief
That thou her maid art far more fair than she.
Be not her maid, since she is envious.
Her vestal livery is but sick and green,
And none but fools do wear it. Cast it off.
It is my lady; O, it is my love!
O that she knew she were!
She speaks, yet she says nothing. What of that?
Her eye discourses; I will answer it.
I am too bold; 'tis not to me she speaks.
Two of the fairest stars in all the heaven,
Having some business, do entreat her eyes
To twinkle in their spheres till they return.
What if her eyes were there, they in her head?
The brightness of her cheek would shame those stars
As daylight doth a lamp; her eyes in heaven

Would through the airy region stream so bright
That birds would sing and think it were not night.
See how she leans her cheek upon her hand!
O that I were a glove upon that hand,
That I might touch that cheek!

JULIET: Ay me!

ROMEO: She speaks.
O, speak again, bright angel! for thou art
As glorious to this night, being o'er my head,
As is a winged messenger of heaven
Unto the white-upturned wond'ring eyes
Of mortals that fall back to gaze on him
When he bestrides the lazy-pacing clouds
And sails upon the bosom of the air.

JULIET: O Romeo, Romeo! wherefore art thou Romeo?
Deny thy father and refuse thy name!
Or, if thou wilt not, be but sworn my love,
And I'll no longer be a Capulet.

ROMEO: *Aside* Shall I hear more, or shall I speak at this?

JULIET: 'Tis but thy name that is my enemy.
Thou art thyself, though not a Montague.
What's Montague? it is nor hand, nor foot,
Nor arm, nor face, nor any other part
Belonging to a man. O, be some other name!
What's in a name? That which we call a rose
By any other name would smell as sweet.
So Romeo would, were he not Romeo call'd,
Retain that dear perfection which he owes
Without that title. Romeo, doff thy name;
And for that name, which is no part of thee,
Take all myself.

ROMEO: I take thee at thy word.

Call me but love, and I'll be new baptiz'd;
Henceforth I never will be Romeo.

JULIET: What man art thou that, thus bescreen'd in night,
So stumblest on my counsel?

ROMEO: By a name
I know not how to tell thee who I am.
My name, dear saint, is hateful to myself,
Because it is an enemy to thee.
Had I it written, I would tear the word.

JULIET: My ears have yet not drunk a hundred words
Of that tongue's utterance, yet I know the sound.
Art thou not Romeo, and a Montague?

ROMEO: Neither, fair saint, if either thee dislike.

JULIET: How cam'st thou hither, tell me, and wherefore?
The orchard walls are high and hard to climb,
And the place death, considering who thou art,
If any of my kinsmen find thee here.

ROMEO: With love's light wings did I o'erperch these walls;
For stony limits cannot hold love out,
And what love can do, that dares love attempt.
Therefore thy kinsmen are no let to me.

JULIET: If they do see thee, they will murther thee.

ROMEO: Alack, there lies more peril in thine eye
Than twenty of their swords! Look thou but sweet,
And I am proof against their enmity.

JULIET: I would not for the world they saw thee here.

ROMEO: I have night's cloak to hide me from their sight;

And but thou love me, let them find me here.
My life were better ended by their hate
Than death prorogued, wanting of thy love.

JULIET: By whose direction found'st thou out this place?

ROMEO: By love, that first did prompt me to enquire.
He lent me counsel, and I lent him eyes.
I am no pilot; yet, wert thou as far
As that vast shore wash'd with the farthest sea,
I would adventure for such merchandise.

JULIET: Thou knowest the mask of night is on my face;
Else would a maiden blush bepaint my cheek
For that which thou hast heard me speak to-night.
Fain would I dwell on form- fain, fain deny
What I have spoke; but farewell compliment!
Dost thou love me, I know thou wilt say 'Ay';
And I will take thy word. Yet, if thou swear'st,
Thou mayst prove false. At lovers' perjuries,
They say Jove laughs. O gentle Romeo,
If thou dost love, pronounce it faithfully.
Or if thou thinkest I am too quickly won,
I'll frown, and be perverse, and say thee nay,
So thou wilt woo; but else, not for the world.
In truth, fair Montague, I am too fond,
And therefore thou mayst think my haviour light;
But trust me, gentleman, I'll prove more true
Than those that have more cunning to be strange.
I should have been more strange, I must confess,
But that thou overheard'st, ere I was ware,
My true-love passion. Therefore pardon me,
And not impute this yielding to light love,
Which the dark night hath so discovered.

ROMEO: Lady, by yonder blessed moon I swear,
That tips with silver all these fruit-tree tops-

JULIET: O, swear not by the moon, th' inconstant moon,
That monthly changes in her circled orb,
Lest that thy love prove likewise variable.

ROMEO: What shall I swear by?

JULIET: Do not swear at all;
Or if thou wilt, swear by thy gracious self,
Which is the god of my idolatry,
And I'll believe thee.

ROMEO: If my heart's dear love—

JULIET: Well, do not swear. Although I joy in thee,
I have no joy of this contract to-night.
It is too rash, too unadvis'd, too sudden;
Too like the lightning, which doth cease to be
Ere one can say 'It lightens.' Sweet, good night!
This bud of love, by summer's ripening breath,
May prove a beauteous flow'r when next we meet.
Good night, good night! As sweet repose and rest
Come to thy heart as that within my breast!

ROMEO: O, wilt thou leave me so unsatisfied?

JULIET: What satisfaction canst thou have to-night?

ROMEO: Th' exchange of thy love's faithful vow for mine.

JULIET: I gave thee mine before thou didst request it;
And yet I would it were to give again.

ROMEO: Would'st thou withdraw it? For what purpose, love?

JULIET: But to be frank and give it thee again.
And yet I wish but for the thing I have.
My bounty is as boundless as the sea,

My love as deep; the more I give to thee,
The more I have, for both are infinite.
I hear some noise within. Dear love, adieu!
   Nurse Calls Within.
Anon, good nurse! Sweet Montague, be true.
Stay but a little, I will come again.
   Exit.

ROMEO: O blessed, blessed night! I am afeard,
Being in night, all this is but a dream,
Too flattering-sweet to be substantial.
   Enter Juliet Above.

JULIET: Three words, dear Romeo, and good night indeed.
If that thy bent of love be honourable,
Thy purpose marriage, send me word to-morrow,
By one that I'll procure to come to thee,
Where and what time thou wilt perform the rite;
And all my fortunes at thy foot I'll lay
And follow thee my lord throughout the world.

NURSE: (within) Madam!

JULIET: I come, anon.- But if thou meanest not well,
I do beseech thee-

NURSE: (within) Madam!

JULIET: By-and-by I come.-
To cease thy suit and leave me to my grief.
To-morrow will I send.

ROMEO: So thrive my soul-

JULIET: A thousand times good night!
   Exit.

ROMEO: A thousand times the worse, to want thy light!
Love goes toward love as schoolboys from their books;
But love from love, towards school with heavy looks.
   Enter Juliet Again, Above.

JULIET: Hist! Romeo, hist! O for a falconer's voice
To lure this tassel-gentle back again!
Bondage is hoarse and may not speak aloud;
Else would I tear the cave where Echo lies,
And make her airy tongue more hoarse than mine
With repetition of my Romeo's name.
Romeo!

ROMEO: It is my soul that calls upon my name.
How silver-sweet sound lovers' tongues by night,
Like softest music to attending ears!

JULIET: Romeo!

ROMEO: My dear?

JULIET: At what o'clock to-morrow
Shall I send to thee?

ROMEO: By the hour of nine.

JULIET: I will not fail. 'Tis twenty years till then.
I have forgot why I did call thee back.

ROMEO: Let me stand here till thou remember it.

JULIET: I shall forget, to have thee still stand there,
Rememb'ring how I love thy company.

ROMEO: And I'll still stay, to have thee still forget,
Forgetting any other home but this.

JULIET: 'Tis almost morning. I would have thee gone-
And yet no farther than a wanton's bird,
That lets it hop a little from her hand,
Like a poor prisoner in his twisted gyves,
And with a silk thread plucks it back again,
So loving-jealous of his liberty.

ROMEO: I would I were thy bird.

JULIET: Sweet, so would I.
Yet I should kill thee with much cherishing.
Good night, good night! Parting is such sweet sorrow,
That I shall say good night till it be morrow.
  Exit.

ROMEO: Sleep dwell upon thine eyes, peace in thy breast!
Would I were sleep and peace, so sweet to rest!
Hence will I to my ghostly father's cell,
His help to crave and my dear hap to tell.
  Exit

ACT II. SCENE III. Friar Laurence's Cell.
Enter Friar Laurence Alone, with a Basket.

FRIAR: The grey-ey'd morn smiles on the frowning night,
Check'ring the Eastern clouds with streaks of light;
And flecked darkness like a drunkard reels
From forth day's path and Titan's fiery wheels.
Non, ere the sun advance his burning eye
The day to cheer and night's dank dew to dry,
I must up-fill this osier cage of ours
With baleful weeds and precious-juiced flowers.
The earth that's nature's mother is her tomb.
What is her burying gave, that is her womb;
And from her womb children of divers kind
We sucking on her natural bosom find;
Many for many virtues excellent,
None but for some, and yet all different.

O, mickle is the powerful grace that lies
In plants, herbs, stones, and their true qualities;
For naught so vile that on the earth doth live
But to the earth some special good doth give;
Nor aught so good but, strain'd from that fair use,
Revolts from true birth, stumbling on abuse.
Virtue itself turns vice, being misapplied,
And vice sometime's by action dignified.
Within the infant rind of this small flower
Poison hath residence, and medicine power;
For this, being smelt, with that part cheers each part;
Being tasted, slays all senses with the heart.
Two such opposed kings encamp them still
In man as well as herbs- grace and rude will;
And where the worser is predominant,
Full soon the canker death eats up that plant.
   Enter Romeo.

ROMEO: Good morrow, father.

FRIAR: Benedicite!
What early tongue so sweet saluteth me?
Young son, it argues a distempered head
So soon to bid good morrow to thy bed.
Care keeps his watch in every old man's eye,
And where care lodges sleep will never lie;
But where unbruised youth with unstuff'd brain
Doth couch his limbs, there golden sleep doth reign.
Therefore thy earliness doth me assure
Thou art uprous'd with some distemp'rature;
Or if not so, then here I hit it right-
Our Romeo hath not been in bed to-night.

ROMEO: That last is true-the sweeter rest was mine.

FRIAR: God pardon sin! Wast thou with Rosaline?

ROMEO: With Rosaline, my ghostly father? No.

I have forgot that name, and that name's woe.

FRIAR: That's my good son! But where hast thou been then?

ROMEO: I'll tell thee ere thou ask it me again.
I have been feasting with mine enemy,
Where on a sudden one hath wounded me
That's by me wounded. Both our remedies
Within thy help and holy physic lies.
I bear no hatred, blessed man, for, lo,
My intercession likewise steads my foe.

FRIAR: Be plain, good son, and homely in thy drift
Riddling confession finds but riddling shrift.

ROMEO: Then plainly know my heart's dear love is set
On the fair daughter of rich Capulet;
As mine on hers, so hers is set on mine,
And all combin'd, save what thou must combine
By holy marriage. When, and where, and how
We met, we woo'd, and made exchange of vow,
I'll tell thee as we pass; but this I pray,
That thou consent to marry us to-day.

FRIAR: Holy Saint Francis! What a change is here!
Is Rosaline, that thou didst love so dear,
So soon forsaken? Young men's love then lies
Not truly in their hearts, but in their eyes.
Jesu Maria! What a deal of brine
Hath wash'd thy sallow cheeks for Rosaline!
How much salt water thrown away in waste,
To season love, that of it doth not taste!
The sun not yet thy sighs from heaven clears,
Thy old groans ring yet in mine ancient ears.
Lo, here upon thy cheek the stain doth sit
Of an old tear that is not wash'd off yet.
If e'er thou wast thyself, and these woes thine,
Thou and these woes were all for Rosaline.

And art thou chang'd? Pronounce this sentence then:
Women may fall when there's no strength in men.

ROMEO: Thou chid'st me oft for loving Rosaline.

FRIAR: For doting, not for loving, pupil mine.

ROMEO: And bad'st me bury love.

FRIAR: Not in a grave
To lay one in, another out to have.

ROMEO: I pray thee chide not. She whom I love now
Doth grace for grace and love for love allow.
The other did not so.

FRIAR: O, she knew well
Thy love did read by rote, that could not spell.
But come, young waverer, come go with me.
In one respect I'll thy assistant be;
For this alliance may so happy prove
To turn your households' rancour to pure love.

ROMEO: O, let us hence! I stand on sudden haste.

FRIAR: Wisely, and slow. They stumble that run fast.
Exeunt.

ACT II. SCENE IV. A Street.

Enter Benvolio and Mercutio.

MERCUTIO: Where the devil should this Romeo be?
Came he not home to-night?

BENVOLIO: Not to his father's. I spoke with his man.

MERCUTIO: Why, that same pale hard-hearted wench, that Rosaline,

Torments him so that he will sure run mad.

BENVOLIO: Tybalt, the kinsman to old Capulet,
Hath sent a letter to his father's house.

MERCUTIO: A challenge, on my life.

BENVOLIO: Romeo will answer it.

MERCUTIO: Any man that can write may answer a letter.

BENVOLIO: Nay, he will answer the letter's master, how he dares, being dared.

MERCUTIO: Alas, poor Romeo, he is already dead! stabb'd with a white wench's black eye; shot through the ear with a love song; the very pin of his heart cleft with the blind bow-boy's butt-shaft; and is he a man to encounter Tybalt?

BENVOLIO: Why, what is Tybalt?

MERCUTIO: More than Prince of Cats, I can tell you. O, he's the courageous captain of compliments. He fights as you sing pricksong-keeps time, distance, and proportion; rests me his minim rest, one, two, and the third in your bosom! the very butcher of a silk button, a duellist, a duellist! a gentleman of the very first house, of the first and second cause. Ah, the immortal passado! the punto reverse! the hay.

BENVOLIO: The what?

MERCUTIO: The pox of such antic, lisping, affecting fantasticoes- these new tuners of accent! 'By Jesu, a very good blade! a very tall man! a very good whore!' Why, is not this a lamentable thing, grandsir, that we should be thus afflicted with these strange flies, these fashion-mongers, these pardona-mi's, who stand so much on the new form that they cannot sit at ease on the old

bench? O, their bones, their bones!
Enter Romeo.

BENVOLIO: Here comes Romeo! here comes Romeo!

MERCUTIO: Without his roe, like a dried herring. O flesh, flesh, how art thou fishified! Now is he for the numbers that Petrarch flowed in. Laura, to his lady, was but a kitchen wench (marry, she had a better love to berhyme her), Dido a dowdy, Cleopatra a gypsy, Helen and Hero hildings and harlots, This be a gray eye or so, but not to the purpose. Signior Romeo, bon jour! There's a French salutation to your French slop. You gave us the counterfeit fairly last night.

ROMEO: Good morrow to you both. What counterfeit did I give you?

MERCUTIO: The slip, sir, the slip. Can you not conceive?

ROMEO: Pardon, good Mercutio. My business was great, and in such a case as mine a man may strain courtesy.

MERCUTIO: That's as much as to say, such a case as yours constrains a man to bow in the hams.

ROMEO: Meaning, to cursy.

MERCUTIO: Thou hast most kindly hit it.

ROMEO: A most courteous exposition.

MERCUTIO: Nay, I am the very pink of courtesy.

ROMEO: Pink for flower.

MERCUTIO: Right.

ROMEO: Why, then is my pump well-flower'd.

MERCUTIO: Well said! Follow me this jest now till thou hast worn out thy pump, that, when the single sole of it is worn, the jest may remain, after the wearing, solely singular.

ROMEO: O single-sold jest, solely singular for the singleness!

MERCUTIO: Come between us, good Benvolio! My wits faint.

ROMEO: Swits and spurs, swits and spurs! or I'll cry a match.

MERCUTIO: Nay, if our wits run the wild-goose chase, I am done; for thou hast more of the wild goose in one of thy wits than, I am sure, I have in my whole five. Was I with you there for the goose?

ROMEO: Thou wast never with me for anything when thou wast not there for the goose.

MERCUTIO: I will bite thee by the ear for that jest.

ROMEO: Nay, good goose, bite not!

MERCUTIO: Thy wit is a very bitter sweeting; it is a most sharp sauce.

ROMEO: And is it not, then, well serv'd in to a sweet goose?

MERCUTIO: O, here's a wit of cheveril, that stretches from an inch narrow to an ell broad!

ROMEO: I stretch it out for that word 'broad,' which, added to the goose, proves thee far and wide a broad goose.

MERCUTIO: Why, is not this better now than groaning for love? Now art thou sociable, now art thou Romeo; now art thou what thou art, by art as well as by nature. For this drivelling love is like a great natural that runs lolling up and down to hide his bauble in a hole.

BENVOLIO: Stop there, stop there!

MERCUTIO: Thou desirest me to stop in my tale against the hair.

BENVOLIO: Thou wouldst else have made thy tale large.

MERCUTIO: O, thou art deceiv'd! I would have made it short; for I was come to the whole depth of my tale, and meant indeed to occupy the argument no longer.

ROMEO: Here's goodly gear!
  Enter Nurse and Her Man Peter.

MERCUTIO: A sail, a sail!

BENVOLIO: Two, two! a shirt and a smock.

NURSE: Peter!

PETER: Anon.

NURSE: My fan, Peter.

MERCUTIO: Good Peter, to hide her face; for her fan's the fairer face of the two.

NURSE: God ye good morrow, gentlemen.

MERCUTIO: God ye good-den, fair gentlewoman.

NURSE: Is it good-den?

MERCUTIO: 'Tis no less, I tell ye; for the bawdy hand of the dial is now upon the prick of noon.

NURSE: Out upon you! What a man are you!

ROMEO: One, gentlewoman, that God hath made for himself to mar.

NURSE: By my troth, it is well said. 'For himself to mar,' quoth 'a? Gentlemen, can any of you tell me where I may find the young Romeo?

ROMEO: I can tell you; but young Romeo will be older when you have found him than he was when you sought him. I am the youngest of that name, for fault of a worse.

NURSE: You say well.

MERCUTIO: Yea, is the worst well? Very well took, i' faith! wisely, wisely.

NURSE: If you be he, sir, I desire some confidence with you.

BENVOLIO: She will endite him to some supper.

MERCUTIO: A bawd, a bawd, a bawd! So ho!

ROMEO: What hast thou found?

MERCUTIO: No hare, sir; unless a hare, sir, in a lenten pie, that is something stale and hoar ere it be spent
  He Walks by Them and Sings.

> An old hare hoar,
> And an old hare hoar,
> Is very good meat in Lent;
> But a hare that is hoar
> Is too much for a score
> When it hoars ere it be spent.

Romeo, will you come to your father's? We'll to dinner thither.

ROMEO: I will follow you.

MERCUTIO: Farewell, ancient lady. Farewell,
Sings lady, lady, lady.
  Exeunt Mercutio, Benvolio.

NURSE: Marry, farewell! I Pray you, Sir, what saucy merchant was this that was so full of his ropery?

ROMEO: A gentleman, nurse, that loves to hear himself talk and will speak more in a minute than he will stand to in a month.

NURSE: An 'a speak anything against me, I'll take him down, an 'a were lustier than he is, and twenty such jacks; and if I cannot, I'll find those that shall. Scurvy knave! I am none of his flirt-gills; I am none of his skains-mates. And thou must stand by too, and suffer every knave to use me at his pleasure!

PETER: I saw no man use you at his pleasure. If I had, my weapon should quickly have been out, I warrant you. I dare draw as soon as another man, if I see occasion in a good quarrel, and the law on my side.

NURSE: Now, afore God, I am so vexed that every part about me quivers. Scurvy knave! Pray you, sir, a word; and, as I told you, my young lady bid me enquire you out. What she bid me say, I will keep to myself; but first let me tell ye, if ye should lead her into a fool's paradise, as they say, it were a very gross kind of behaviour, as they say; for the gentlewoman is young; and therefore, if you should deal double with her, truly it were an ill thing to be off'red to any gentlewoman, and very weak dealing.

ROMEO: Nurse, commend me to thy lady and mistress. I protest unto thee-

NURSE: Good heart, and I faith I will tell her as much. Lord, Lord! she will be a joyful woman.

ROMEO: What wilt thou tell her, nurse? Thou dost not mark me.

NURSE: I will tell her, sir, that you do protest, which, as I take it, is a gentlemanlike offer.

ROMEO: Bid her devise
Some means to come to shrift this afternoon;
And there she shall at Friar Laurence' cell
Be shriv'd and married. Here is for thy pains.

NURSE: No, truly, sir; not a penny.

ROMEO: Go to! I say you shall.

NURSE: This afternoon, sir? Well, she shall be there.

ROMEO: And stay, good nurse, behind the abbey wall.
Within this hour my man shall be with thee
And bring thee cords made like a tackled stair,
Which to the high topgallant of my joy
Must be my convoy in the secret night.
Farewell. Be trusty, and I'll quit thy pains.
Farewell. Commend me to thy mistress.

NURSE: Now God in heaven bless thee! Hark you, sir.

ROMEO: What say'st thou, my dear nurse?

NURSE: Is your man secret? Did you ne'er hear say,
Two may keep counsel, putting one away?

ROMEO: I warrant thee my man's as true as steel.

NURSE: Well, sir, my mistress is the sweetest lady. Lord, Lord! when 'twas a little prating thing- O, there is a nobleman in town, one Paris, that would fain lay knife aboard; but she, good soul, had as lieve see a toad, a very toad, as see him. I anger her sometimes, and tell her that Paris is the properer man; but I'll warrant you, when I say so, she looks as pale as any clout

in the versal world. Doth not rosemary and Romeo begin both with
a letter?

ROMEO: Ay, nurse; what of that? Both with an R.

NURSE: Ah, mocker! that's the dog's name. R is for the- No; I know
it begins with some other letter; and she hath the prettiest
sententious of it, of you and rosemary, that it would do you good
to hear it.

ROMEO: Commend me to thy lady.

NURSE: Ay, a thousand times.
  Exit Romeo. Peter!

PETER: Anon.

NURSE: Peter, take my fan, and go before, and apace.
  Exeunt.

ACT II. SCENE V. Capulet's Orchard.

Enter Juliet.

JULIET: The clock struck nine when I did send the nurse;
In half an hour she 'promis'd to return.
Perchance she cannot meet him. That's not so.
O, she is lame! Love's heralds should be thoughts,
Which ten times faster glide than the sun's beams
Driving back shadows over low'ring hills.
Therefore do nimble-pinion'd doves draw Love,
And therefore hath the wind-swift Cupid wings.
Now is the sun upon the highmost hill
Of this day's journey, and from nine till twelve
Is three long hours; yet she is not come.
Had she affections and warm youthful blood,
She would be as swift in motion as a ball;
My words would bandy her to my sweet love,

And his to me,
But old folks, many feign as they were dead-
Unwieldy, slow, heavy and pale as lead.
   Enter Nurse and Peter.

O God, she comes! O honey nurse, what news?
Hast thou met with him? Send thy man away.

NURSE: Peter, stay at the gate.
   Exit Peter.

JULIET: Now, good sweet nurse- O Lord, why look'st thou sad?
Though news be sad, yet tell them merrily;
If good, thou shamest the music of sweet news
By playing it to me with so sour a face.

NURSE: I am aweary, give me leave awhile.
Fie, how my bones ache! What a jaunce have I had!

JULIET: I would thou hadst my bones, and I thy news.
Nay, come, I pray thee speak. Good, good nurse, speak.

NURSE: Jesu, what haste! Can you not stay awhile?
Do you not see that I am out of breath?

JULIET: How art thou out of breath when thou hast breath
To say to me that thou art out of breath?
The excuse that thou dost make in this delay
Is longer than the tale thou dost excuse.
Is thy news good or bad? Answer to that.
Say either, and I'll stay the circumstance.
Let me be satisfied, is't good or bad?

NURSE: Well, you have made a simple choice; you know not how to choose a man. Romeo? No, not he. Though his face be better than any man's, yet his leg excels all men's; and for a hand and a foot, and a body, though they be not to be talk'd on, yet they

are past compare. He is not the flower of courtesy, but, I'll
warrant him, as gentle as a lamb. Go thy ways, wench; serve God.
What, have you din'd at home?

JULIET: No, no. But all this did I know before.
What says he of our marriage? What of that?

NURSE: Lord, how my head aches! What a head have I!
It beats as it would fall in twenty pieces.
My back o' t' other side,- ah, my back, my back!
Beshrew your heart for sending me about
To catch my death with jauncing up and down!

JULIET: I' faith, I am sorry that thou art not well.
Sweet, sweet, Sweet nurse, tell me, what says my love?

NURSE: Your love says, like an honest gentleman, and a courteous,
and a kind, and a handsome; and, I warrant, a virtuous- Where is
your mother?

JULIET: Where is my mother? Why, she is within.
Where should she be? How oddly thou repliest!
'Your love says, like an honest gentleman,
"Where is your mother?"'

NURSE: O God's Lady dear!
Are you so hot? Marry come up, I trow.
Is this the poultice for my aching bones?
Henceforward do your messages yourself.

JULIET: Here's such a coil! Come, what says Romeo?

NURSE: Have you got leave to go to shrift to-day?

JULIET: I have.

NURSE: Then hie you hence to Friar Laurence' cell;

There stays a husband to make you a wife.
Now comes the wanton blood up in your cheeks:
They'll be in scarlet straight at any news.
Hie you to church; I must another way,
To fetch a ladder, by the which your love
Must climb a bird's nest soon when it is dark.
I am the drudge, and toil in your delight;
But you shall bear the burthen soon at night.
Go; I'll to dinner; hie you to the cell.

JULIET: Hie to high fortune! Honest nurse, farewell.
Exeunt.

ACT II. SCENE VI. Friar Laurence's Cell.
Enter Friar Laurence and Romeo.

FRIAR: So smile the heavens upon this holy act
That after-hours with sorrow chide us not!

ROMEO: Amen, amen! But come what sorrow can,
It cannot countervail the exchange of joy
That one short minute gives me in her sight.
Do thou but close our hands with holy words,
Then love-devouring death do what he dare-
It is enough I may but call her mine.

FRIAR: These violent delights have violent ends
And in their triumph die, like fire and powder,
Which, as they kiss, consume. The sweetest honey
Is loathsome in his own deliciousness
And in the taste confounds the appetite.
Therefore love moderately: long love doth so;
Too swift arrives as tardy as too slow.
   Enter Juliet.
Here comes the lady. O, so light a foot
Will ne'er wear out the everlasting flint.
A lover may bestride the gossamer

That idles in the wanton summer air,
And yet not fall; so light is vanity.

JULIET: Good even to my ghostly confessor.

FRIAR: Romeo shall thank thee, daughter, for us both.

JULIET: As much to him, else is his thanks too much.

ROMEO: Ah, Juliet, if the measure of thy joy
Be heap'd like mine, and that thy skill be more
To blazon it, then sweeten with thy breath
This neighbour air, and let rich music's tongue
Unfold the imagin'd happiness that both
Receive in either by this dear encounter.

JULIET: Conceit, more rich in matter than in words,
Brags of his substance, not of ornament.
They are but beggars that can count their worth;
But my true love is grown to such excess
cannot sum up sum of half my wealth.

FRIAR: Come, come with me, and we will make short work;
For, by your leaves, you shall not stay alone
Till Holy Church incorporate two in one.
  Exeunt.

ACT III. SCENE I. A Public Place.
Enter Mercutio, Benvolio, and Men.

BENVOLIO: I pray thee, good Mercutio, let's retire.
The day is hot, the Capulets abroad.
And if we meet, we shall not scape a brawl,
For now, these hot days, is the mad blood stirring.

MERCUTIO: Thou art like one of these fellows that, when he enters the confines of a tavern, claps me his sword upon the table and says

'God send me no need of thee!' and by the operation of the second cup draws him on the drawer, when indeed there is no need.

BENVOLIO: Am I like such a fellow?

MERCUTIO: Come, come, thou art as hot a jack in thy mood as any in Italy; and as soon moved to be moody, and as soon moody to be moved.

BENVOLIO: And what to?

MERCUTIO: Nay, an there were two such, we should have none shortly, for one would kill the other. Thou! why, thou wilt quarrel with a man that hath a hair more or a hair less in his beard than thou hast. Thou wilt quarrel with a man for cracking nuts, having no other reason but because thou hast hazel eyes. What eye but such an eye would spy out such a quarrel? Thy head is as full of quarrels as an egg is full of meat; and yet thy head hath been beaten as addle as an egg for quarrelling. Thou hast quarrell'd with a man for coughing in the street, because he hath wakened thy dog that hath lain asleep in the sun. Didst thou not fall out with a tailor for wearing his new doublet before Easter, with another for tying his new shoes with an old riband? And yet thou wilt tutor me from quarrelling!

BENVOLIO: An I were so apt to quarrel as thou art, any man should buy the fee simple of my life for an hour and a quarter.

MERCUTIO: The fee simple? O simple!
   Enter Tybalt and Others.

BENVOLIO: By my head, here come the Capulets.

MERCUTIO: By my heel, I care not.

TYBALT: Follow me close, for I will speak to them.
Gentlemen, good den. A word with one of you.

MERCUTIO: And but one word with one of us?
Couple it with something; make it a word and a blow.

TYBALT: You shall find me apt enough to that, sir, an you will give me occasion.

MERCUTIO: Could you not take some occasion without giving

TYBALT: Mercutio, thou consortest with Romeo.

MERCUTIO: Consort? What, dost thou make us minstrels? An thou make minstrels of us, look to hear nothing but discords. Here's my fiddlestick; here's that shall make you dance. Zounds, consort!

BENVOLIO: We talk here in the public haunt of men.
Either withdraw unto some private place
And reason coldly of your grievances,
Or else depart. Here all eyes gaze on us.

MERCUTIO: Men's eyes were made to look, and let them gaze.
I will not budge for no man's pleasure,
   Enter Romeo.

TYBALT: Well, peace be with you, sir. Here comes my man.

MERCUTIO: But I'll be hang'd, sir, if he wear your livery.
Marry, go before to field, he'll be your follower!
Your worship in that sense may call him man.

TYBALT: Romeo, the love I bear thee can afford
No better term than this: thou art a villain.

ROMEO: Tybalt, the reason that I have to love thee
Doth much excuse the appertaining rage
To such a greeting. Villain am I none.
Therefore farewell. I see thou knowest me not.

TYBALT: Boy, this shall not excuse the injuries
That thou hast done me; therefore turn and draw.

ROMEO: I do protest I never injur'd thee,
But love thee better than thou canst devise
Till thou shalt know the reason of my love;
And so good Capulet, which name I tender
As dearly as mine own, be satisfied.

MERCUTIO: O calm, dishonourable, vile submission!
Alla stoccata carries it away. *Draws.*
Tybalt, you ratcatcher, will you walk?

TYBALT: What wouldst thou have with me?

MERCUTIO: Good King of Cats, nothing but one of your nine lives. That I mean to make bold withal, and, as you shall use me hereafter, dry-beat the rest of the eight. Will you pluck your sword out of his pitcher by the ears? Make haste, lest mine be about your ears ere it be out.

TYBALT: I am for you.
Draws.

ROMEO: Gentle Mercutio, put thy rapier up.

MERCUTIO: Come, sir, your passado!
They Fight.

ROMEO: Draw, Benvolio; beat down their weapons.
Gentlemen, for shame! forbear this outrage!
Tybalt, Mercutio, the Prince expressly hath
Forbid this bandying in Verona streets.
Hold, Tybalt! Good Mercutio!
Tybalt under Romeo's arm thrusts Mercutio in, and flies With His Followers.

MERCUTIO: I am hurt.

A plague o' both your houses! I am sped.
Is he gone and hath nothing?

BENVOLIO: What, art thou hurt?

MERCUTIO: Ay, ay, a scratch, a scratch. Marry, 'tis enough.
Where is my page? Go, villain, fetch a surgeon.
 Exit Page.

ROMEO: Courage, man. The hurt cannot be much.

MERCUTIO: No, 'tis not so deep as a well, nor so wide as a church door; but 'tis enough, 'twill serve. Ask for me to-morrow, and you shall find me a grave man. I am peppered, I warrant, for this world. A plague o' both your houses! Zounds, a dog, a rat, a mouse, a cat, to scratch a man to death! a braggart, a rogue, a villain, that fights by the book of arithmetic! Why the devil came you between us? I was hurt under your arm.

ROMEO: I thought all for the best.

MERCUTIO: Help me into some house, Benvolio,
Or I shall faint. A plague o' both your houses!
They have made worms' meat of me. I have it,
And soundly too. Your houses!
 Exit. Supported by Benvolio.

ROMEO: This gentleman, the Prince's near ally,
My very friend, hath got this mortal hurt
In my behalf- my reputation stain'd
With Tybalt's slander- Tybalt, that an hour
Hath been my kinsman. O sweet Juliet,
Thy beauty hath made me effeminate
And in my temper soft'ned valour's steel
 Enter Benvolio.

BENVOLIO: O Romeo, Romeo, brave Mercutio's dead!

That gallant spirit hath aspir'd the clouds,
Which too untimely here did scorn the earth.

ROMEO: This day's black fate on moe days doth depend;
This but begins the woe others must end.
  Enter Tybalt.

BENVOLIO: Here comes the furious Tybalt back again.

ROMEO: Alive in triumph, and Mercutio slain?
Away to heaven respective lenity,
And fire-ey'd fury be my conduct now!
Now, Tybalt, take the 'villain' back again
That late thou gavest me; for Mercutio's soul
Is but a little way above our heads,
Staying for thine to keep him company.
Either thou or I, or both, must go with him.

TYBALT: Thou, wretched boy, that didst consort him here,
Shalt with him hence.

ROMEO: This shall determine that.
  They Fight. Tybalt Falls.

BENVOLIO: Romeo, away, be gone!
The citizens are up, and Tybalt slain.
Stand not amaz'd. The Prince will doom thee death
If thou art taken. Hence, be gone, away!

ROMEO: O, I am fortune's fool!

BENVOLIO: Why dost thou stay?
  Exit Romeo.
  Enter Citizens.

CITIZEN: Which way ran he that kill'd Mercutio?
Tybalt, that murtherer, which way ran he?

William Shakespeare

BENVOLIO: There lies that Tybalt.

CITIZEN: Up, sir, go with me.
I charge thee in the Prince's name obey.
Enter Prince attended, Old Montague, Capulet, their Wives, and others.

PRINCE: Where are the vile beginners of this fray?

BENVOLIO: O noble Prince. I can discover all
The unlucky manage of this fatal brawl.
There lies the man, slain by young Romeo,
That slew thy kinsman, brave Mercutio.

CAPULET: Wife. Tybalt, my cousin! O my brother's child!
O Prince! O husband! O, the blood is spill'd
Of my dear kinsman! Prince, as thou art true,
For blood of ours shed blood of Montague.
O cousin, cousin!

PRINCE: Benvolio, who began this bloody fray?

BENVOLIO: Tybalt, here slain, whom Romeo's hand did stay.
Romeo, that spoke him fair, bid him bethink
How nice the quarrel was, and urg'd withal
Your high displeasure. All this- uttered
With gentle breath, calm look, knees humbly bow'd-
Could not take truce with the unruly spleen
Of Tybalt deaf to peace, but that he tilts
With piercing steel at bold Mercutio's breast;
Who, all as hot, turns deadly point to point,
And, with a martial scorn, with one hand beats
Cold death aside and with the other sends
It back to Tybalt, whose dexterity
Retorts it. Romeo he cries aloud,
'Hold, friends! friends, part!' and swifter than his tongue,
His agile arm beats down their fatal points,
And 'twixt them rushes; underneath whose arm

An envious thrust from Tybalt hit the life
Of stout Mercutio, and then Tybalt fled;
But by-and-by comes back to Romeo,
Who had but newly entertain'd revenge,
And to't they go like lightning; for, ere I
Could draw to part them, was stout Tybalt slain;
And, as he fell, did Romeo turn and fly.
This is the truth, or let Benvolio die.

CAPULET: Wife. He is a kinsman to the Montague;
Affection makes him false, he speaks not true.
Some twenty of them fought in this black strife,
And all those twenty could but kill one life.
I beg for justice, which thou, Prince, must give.
Romeo slew Tybalt; Romeo must not live.

PRINCE: Romeo slew him; he slew Mercutio.
Who now the price of his dear blood doth owe?

MONTAGUE: Not Romeo, Prince; he was Mercutio's friend;
His fault concludes but what the law should end,
The life of Tybalt.

PRINCE: And for that offence
Immediately we do exile him hence.
I have an interest in your hate's proceeding,
My blood for your rude brawls doth lie a-bleeding;
But I'll amerce you with so strong a fine
That you shall all repent the loss of mine.
I will be deaf to pleading and excuses;
Nor tears nor prayers shall purchase out abuses.
Therefore use none. Let Romeo hence in haste,
Else, when he is found, that hour is his last.
Bear hence this body, and attend our will.
Mercy but murders, pardoning those that kill.
   Exeunt.

William Shakespeare

ACT III. SCENE II. Capulet's Orchard.

Enter Juliet alone.

JULIET: Gallop apace, you fiery-footed steeds,
Towards Phoebus' lodging! Such a wagoner
As Phaeton would whip you to the West
And bring in cloudy night immediately.
Spread thy close curtain, love-performing night,
That runaway eyes may wink, and Romeo
Leap to these arms untalk'd of and unseen.
Lovers can see to do their amorous rites
By their own beauties; or, if love be blind,
It best agrees with night. Come, civil night,
Thou sober-suited matron, all in black,
And learn me how to lose a winning match,
Play'd for a pair of stainless maidenhoods.
Hood my unmann'd blood, bating in my cheeks,
With thy black mantle till strange love, grown bold,
Think true love acted simple modesty.
Come, night; come, Romeo; come, thou day in night;
For thou wilt lie upon the wings of night
Whiter than new snow upon a raven's back.
Come, gentle night; come, loving, black-brow'd night;
Give me my Romeo; and, when he shall die,
Take him and cut him out in little stars,
And he will make the face of heaven so fine
That all the world will be in love with night
And pay no worship to the garish sun.
O, I have bought the mansion of a love,
But not possess'd it; and though I am sold,
Not yet enjoy'd. So tedious is this day
As is the night before some festival
To an impatient child that hath new robes
And may not wear them. O, here comes my nurse,
  Enter Nurse, with Cords.

And she brings news; and every tongue that speaks
But Romeo's name speaks heavenly eloquence.

Now, nurse, what news? What hast thou there? the cords
That Romeo bid thee fetch?

NURSE: Ay, ay, the cords.
   Throws Them Down.

JULIET: Ay me! what news? Why dost thou wring thy hands

NURSE: Ah, weraday! he's dead, he's dead, he's dead!
We are undone, lady, we are undone!
Alack the day! he's gone, he's kill'd, he's dead!

JULIET: Can heaven be so envious?

NURSE: Romeo can,
Though heaven cannot. O Romeo, Romeo!
Who ever would have thought it? Romeo!

JULIET: What devil art thou that dost torment me thus?
This torture should be roar'd in dismal hell.
Hath Romeo slain himself? Say thou but 'I,'
And that bare vowel 'I' shall poison more
Than the death-darting eye of cockatrice.
I am not I, if there be such an 'I';
Or those eyes shut that make thee answer 'I.'
If be be slain, say 'I'; or if not, 'no.'
Brief sounds determine of my weal or woe.

NURSE: I saw the wound, I saw it with mine eyes,
(God save the mark!) here on his manly breast.
A piteous corse, a bloody piteous corse;
Pale, pale as ashes, all bedaub'd in blood,
All in gore-blood. I swounded at the sight.

JULIET: O, break, my heart! poor bankrout, break at once!
To prison, eyes; ne'er look on liberty!
Vile earth, to earth resign; end motion here,

And thou and Romeo press one heavy bier!

NURSE: O Tybalt, Tybalt, the best friend I had!
O courteous Tybalt! honest gentleman
That ever I should live to see thee dead!

JULIET: What storm is this that blows so contrary?
Is Romeo slaught'red, and is Tybalt dead?
My dear-lov'd cousin, and my dearer lord?
Then, dreadful trumpet, sound the general doom!
For who is living, if those two are gone?

NURSE: Tybalt is gone, and Romeo banished;
Romeo that kill'd him, he is banished.

JULIET: O God! Did Romeo's hand shed Tybalt's blood?

NURSE: It did, it did! alas the day, it did!

JULIET: O serpent heart, hid with a flow'ring face!
Did ever dragon keep so fair a cave?
Beautiful tyrant! fiend angelical!
Dove-feather'd raven! wolvish-ravening lamb!
Despised substance of divinest show!
Just opposite to what thou justly seem'st-
A damned saint, an honourable villain!
O nature, what hadst thou to do in hell
When thou didst bower the spirit of a fiend
In mortal paradise of such sweet flesh?
Was ever book containing such vile matter
So fairly bound? O, that deceit should dwell
In such a gorgeous palace!

NURSE: There's no trust,
No faith, no honesty in men; all perjur'd,
All forsworn, all naught, all dissemblers.
Ah, where's my man? Give me some aqua vitae.

These griefs, these woes, these sorrows make me old.
Shame come to Romeo!

JULIET: Blister'd be thy tongue
For such a wish! He was not born to shame.
Upon his brow shame is asham'd to sit;
For 'tis a throne where honour may be crown'd
Sole monarch of the universal earth.
O, what a beast was I to chide at him!

NURSE: Will you speak well of him that kill'd your cousin?

JULIET: Shall I speak ill of him that is my husband?
Ah, poor my lord, what tongue shall smooth thy name
When I, thy three-hours wife, have mangled it?
But wherefore, villain, didst thou kill my cousin?
That villain cousin would have kill'd my husband.
Back, foolish tears, back to your native spring!
Your tributary drops belong to woe,
Which you, mistaking, offer up to joy.
My husband lives, that Tybalt would have slain;
And Tybalt's dead, that would have slain my husband.
All this is comfort; wherefore weep I then?
Some word there was, worser than Tybalt's death,
That murd'red me. I would forget it fain;
But O, it presses to my memory
Like damned guilty deeds to sinners' minds!
'Tybalt is dead, and Romeo- banished.'
That 'banished,' that one word 'banished,'
Hath slain ten thousand Tybalts. Tybalt's death
Was woe enough, if it had ended there;
Or, if sour woe delights in fellowship
And needly will be rank'd with other griefs,
Why followed not, when she said 'Tybalt's dead,'
Thy father, or thy mother, nay, or both,
Which modern lamentation might have mov'd?
But with a rearward following Tybalt's death,
'Romeo is banished'- to speak that word

Is father, mother, Tybalt, Romeo, Juliet,
All slain, all dead. 'Romeo is banished'-
There is no end, no limit, measure, bound,
In that word's death; no words can that woe sound.
Where is my father and my mother, nurse?

NURSE: Weeping and wailing over Tybalt's corse.
Will you go to them? I will bring you thither.

JULIET: Wash they his wounds with tears? Mine shall be spent,
When theirs are dry, for Romeo's banishment.
Take up those cords. Poor ropes, you are beguil'd,
Both you and I, for Romeo is exil'd.
He made you for a highway to my bed;
But I, a maid, die maiden-widowed.
Come, cords; come, nurse. I'll to my wedding bed;
And death, not Romeo, take my maidenhead!

NURSE: Hie to your chamber. I'll find Romeo
To comfort you. I wot well where he is.
Hark ye, your Romeo will be here at night.
I'll to him; he is hid at Laurence' cell.

JULIET: O, find him! give this ring to my true knight
And bid him come to take his last farewell.
Exeunt.

ACT III. SCENE III. Friar Laurence's Cell.

Enter Friar Laurence.

FRIAR: Romeo, come forth; come forth, thou fearful man.
Affliction is enanmour'd of thy parts,
And thou art wedded to calamity.
Enter Romeo.

ROMEO: Father, what news? What is the Prince's doom
What sorrow craves acquaintance at my hand

That I yet know not?

FRIAR: Too familiar
Is my dear son with such sour company.
I bring thee tidings of the Prince's doom.

ROMEO: What less than doomsday is the Prince's doom?

FRIAR: A gentler judgment vanish'd from his lips-
Not body's death, but body's banishment.

ROMEO: Ha, banishment? Be merciful, say 'death';
For exile hath more terror in his look,
Much more than death. Do not say 'banishment.'

FRIAR: Hence from Verona art thou banished.
Be patient, for the world is broad and wide.

ROMEO: There is no world without Verona walls,
But purgatory, torture, hell itself.
Hence banished is banish'd from the world,
And world's exile is death. Then 'banishment'
Is death misterm'd. Calling death 'banishment,'
Thou cut'st my head off with a golden axe
And smilest upon the stroke that murders me.

FRIAR: O deadly sin! O rude unthankfulness!
Thy fault our law calls death; but the kind Prince,
Taking thy part, hath rush'd aside the law,
And turn'd that black word death to banishment.
This is dear mercy, and thou seest it not.

ROMEO: 'Tis torture, and not mercy. Heaven is here,
Where Juliet lives; and every cat and dog
And little mouse, every unworthy thing,
Live here in heaven and may look on her;
But Romeo may not. More validity,

More honourable state, more courtship lives
In carrion flies than Romeo. They may seize
On the white wonder of dear Juliet's hand
And steal immortal blessing from her lips,
Who, even in pure and vestal modesty,
Still blush, as thinking their own kisses sin;
But Romeo may not- he is banished.
This may flies do, when I from this must fly;
They are free men, but I am banished.
And sayest thou yet that exile is not death?
Hadst thou no poison mix'd, no sharp-ground knife,
No sudden mean of death, though ne'er so mean,
But 'banished' to kill me- 'banished'?
O friar, the damned use that word in hell;
Howling attends it! How hast thou the heart,
Being a divine, a ghostly confessor,
A sin-absolver, and my friend profess'd,
To mangle me with that word 'banished'?

FRIAR: Thou fond mad man, hear me a little speak.

ROMEO: O, thou wilt speak again of banishment.

FRIAR: I'll give thee armour to keep off that word;
Adversity's sweet milk, philosophy,
To comfort thee, though thou art banished.

ROMEO: Yet 'banished'? Hang up philosophy!
Unless philosophy can make a Juliet,
Displant a town, reverse a prince's doom,
It helps not, it prevails not. Talk no more.

FRIAR: O, then I see that madmen have no ears.

ROMEO: How should they, when that wise men have no eyes?

FRIAR: Let me dispute with thee of thy estate.

ROMEO: Thou canst not speak of that thou dost not feel.
Wert thou as young as I, Juliet thy love,
An hour but married, Tybalt murdered,
Doting like me, and like me banished,
Then mightst thou speak, then mightst thou tear thy hair,
And fall upon the ground, as I do now,
Taking the measure of an unmade grave.
  Knock Within.

FRIAR: Arise; one knocks. Good Romeo, hide thyself.

ROMEO: Not I; unless the breath of heartsick groans,
Mist-like infold me from the search of eyes. Knock.

FRIAR: Hark, how they knock! Who's there? Romeo, arise;
Thou wilt be taken.- Stay awhile!- Stand up; Knock.
Run to my study.- By-and-by!- God's will,
What simpleness is this.- I come, I come! Knock.
Who knocks so hard? Whence come you? What's your will

NURSE: *Within* Let me come in, and you shall know my errand.
I come from Lady Juliet.

FRIAR: Welcome then.
  Enter Nurse.

NURSE: O holy friar, O, tell me, holy friar
Where is my lady's lord, where's Romeo?

FRIAR: There on the ground, with his own tears made drunk.

NURSE: O, he is even in my mistress' case,
Just in her case!

FRIAR: O woeful sympathy!
Piteous predicament!

NURSE: Even so lies she,
Blubb'ring and weeping, weeping and blubbering.
Stand up, stand up! Stand, an you be a man.
For Juliet's sake, for her sake, rise and stand!
Why should you fall into so deep an O?

ROMEO: (rises) Nurse–

NURSE: Ah sir! ah sir! Well, death's the end of all.

ROMEO: Spakest thou of Juliet? How is it with her?
Doth not she think me an old murtherer,
Now I have stain'd the childhood of our joy
With blood remov'd but little from her own?
Where is she? and how doth she! and what says
My conceal'd lady to our cancell'd love?

NURSE: O, she says nothing, sir, but weeps and weeps;
And now falls on her bed, and then starts up,
And Tybalt calls; and then on Romeo cries,
And then down falls again.

ROMEO: As if that name,
Shot from the deadly level of a gun,
Did murther her; as that name's cursed hand
Murder'd her kinsman. O, tell me, friar, tell me,
In what vile part of this anatomy
Doth my name lodge? Tell me, that I may sack
The hateful mansion.
   Draws His Dagger.

FRIAR: Hold thy desperate hand.
Art thou a man? Thy form cries out thou art;
Thy tears are womanish, thy wild acts denote
The unreasonable fury of a beast.
Unseemly woman in a seeming man!
Or ill-beseeming beast in seeming both!

Thou hast amaz'd me. By my holy order,
I thought thy disposition better temper'd.
Hast thou slain Tybalt? Wilt thou slay thyself?
And slay thy lady that in thy life lives,
By doing damned hate upon thyself?
Why railest thou on thy birth, the heaven, and earth?
Since birth and heaven and earth, all three do meet
In thee at once; which thou at once wouldst lose.
Fie, fie, thou shamest thy shape, thy love, thy wit,
Which, like a usurer, abound'st in all,
And usest none in that true use indeed
Which should bedeck thy shape, thy love, thy wit.
Thy noble shape is but a form of wax
Digressing from the valour of a man;
Thy dear love sworn but hollow perjury,
Killing that love which thou hast vow'd to cherish;
Thy wit, that ornament to shape and love,
Misshapen in the conduct of them both,
Like powder in a skilless soldier's flask,
is get afire by thine own ignorance,
And thou dismemb'red with thine own defence.
What, rouse thee, man! Thy Juliet is alive,
For whose dear sake thou wast but lately dead.
There art thou happy. Tybalt would kill thee,
But thou slewest Tybalt. There art thou happy too.
The law, that threat'ned death, becomes thy friend
And turns it to exile. There art thou happy.
A pack of blessings light upon thy back;
Happiness courts thee in her best array;
But, like a misbhav'd and sullen wench,
Thou pout'st upon thy fortune and thy love.
Take heed, take heed, for such die miserable.
Go get thee to thy love, as was decreed,
Ascend her chamber, hence and comfort her.
But look thou stay not till the watch be set,
For then thou canst not pass to Mantua,
Where thou shalt live till we can find a time
To blaze your marriage, reconcile your friends,

Beg pardon of the Prince, and call thee back
With twenty hundred thousand times more joy
Than thou went'st forth in lamentation.
Go before, nurse. Commend me to thy lady,
And bid her hasten all the house to bed,
Which heavy sorrow makes them apt unto.
Romeo is coming.

NURSE: O Lord, I could have stay'd here all the night
To hear good counsel. O, what learning is!
My lord, I'll tell my lady you will come.

ROMEO: Do so, and bid my sweet prepare to chide.

NURSE: Here is a ring she bid me give you, sir.
Hie you, make haste, for it grows very late.
   Exit.

ROMEO: How well my comfort is reviv'd by this!

FRIAR: Go hence; good night; and here stands all your state:
Either be gone before the watch be set,
Or by the break of day disguis'd from hence.
Sojourn in Mantua. I'll find out your man,
And he shall signify from time to time
Every good hap to you that chances here.
Give me thy hand. 'Tis late. Farewell; good night.

ROMEO: But that a joy past joy calls out on me,
It were a grief so brief to part with thee.
Farewell.
   Exeunt.

ACT III. SCENE IV. Capulet's House
Enter Old Capulet, His Wife, and Paris.

CAPULET: Things have fall'n out, sir, so unluckily

That we have had no time to move our daughter.
Look you, she lov'd her kinsman Tybalt dearly,
And so did I. Well, we were born to die.
'Tis very late; she'll not come down to-night.
I promise you, but for your company,
I would have been abed an hour ago.

PARIS: These times of woe afford no tune to woo.
Madam, good night. Commend me to your daughter.

LADY: I will, and know her mind early to-morrow;
To-night she's mew'd up to her heaviness.

CAPULET: Sir Paris, I will make a desperate tender
Of my child's love. I think she will be rul'd
In all respects by me; nay more, I doubt it not.
Wife, go you to her ere you go to bed;
Acquaint her here of my son Paris' love
And bid her (mark you me?) on Wednesday next-
But, soft! what day is this?

PARIS: Monday, my lord.

CAPULET: Monday! ha, ha! Well, Wednesday is too soon.
Thursday let it be- a Thursday, tell her
She shall be married to this noble earl.
Will you be ready? Do you like this haste?
We'll keep no great ado- a friend or two;
For hark you, Tybalt being slain so late,
It may be thought we held him carelessly,
Being our kinsman, if we revel much.
Therefore we'll have some half a dozen friends,
And there an end. But what say you to Thursday?

PARIS: My lord, I would that Thursday were to-morrow.

CAPULET: Well, get you gone. A Thursday be it then.

Go you to Juliet ere you go to bed;
Prepare her, wife, against this wedding day.
Farewell, My lord.- Light to my chamber, ho!
Afore me, It is so very very late
That we may call it early by-and-by.
Good night.
    Exeunt

ACT III. SCENE V. Capulet's Orchard.

Enter Romeo and Juliet Aloft, at the Window.

JULIET: Wilt thou be gone? It is not yet near day.
It was the nightingale, and not the lark,
That pierc'd the fearful hollow of thine ear.
Nightly she sings on yond pomegranate tree.
Believe me, love, it was the nightingale.

ROMEO: It was the lark, the herald of the morn;
No nightingale. Look, love, what envious streaks
Do lace the severing clouds in yonder East.
Night's candles are burnt out, and jocund day
Stands tiptoe on the misty mountain tops.
I must be gone and live, or stay and die.

JULIET: Yond light is not daylight; I know it, I.
It is some meteor that the sun exhales
To be to thee this night a torchbearer
And light thee on the way to Mantua.
Therefore stay yet; thou need'st not to be gone.

ROMEO: Let me be ta'en, let me be put to death.
I am content, so thou wilt have it so.
I'll say yon grey is not the morning's eye,
'Tis but the pale reflex of Cynthia's brow;
Nor that is not the lark whose notes do beat
The vaulty heaven so high above our heads.
I have more care to stay than will to go.
Come, death, and welcome! Juliet wills it so.

How is't, my soul? Let's talk; it is not day.

JULIET: It is, it is! Hie hence, be gone, away!
It is the lark that sings so out of tune,
Straining harsh discords and unpleasing sharps.
Some say the lark makes sweet division;
This doth not so, for she divideth us.
Some say the lark and loathed toad chang'd eyes;
O, now I would they had chang'd voices too,
Since arm from arm that voice doth us affray,
Hunting thee hence with hunt's-up to the day!
O, now be gone! More light and light it grows.

ROMEO: More light and light- more dark and dark our woes!
Enter Nurse.

NURSE: Madam!

JULIET: Nurse?

NURSE: Your lady mother is coming to your chamber.
The day is broke; be wary, look about.

JULIET: Then, window, let day in, and let life out.
Exit.

ROMEO: Farewell, farewell! One kiss, and I'll descend.
He Goeth Down.

JULIET: Art thou gone so, my lord, my love, my friend?
I must hear from thee every day in the hour,
For in a minute there are many days.
O, by this count I shall be much in years
Ere I again behold my Romeo!

ROMEO: Farewell!
I will omit no opportunity

That may convey my greetings, love, to thee.

JULIET: O, think'st thou we shall ever meet again?

ROMEO: I doubt it not; and all these woes shall serve
For sweet discourses in our time to come.

JULIET: O God, I have an ill-divining soul!
Methinks I see thee, now thou art below,
As one dead in the bottom of a tomb.
Either my eyesight fails, or thou look'st pale.

ROMEO: And trust me, love, in my eye so do you.
Dry sorrow drinks our blood. Adieu, adieu!
   Exit.

JULIET: O Fortune, Fortune! all men call thee fickle.
If thou art fickle, what dost thou with him
That is renown'd for faith? Be fickle, Fortune,
For then I hope thou wilt not keep him long
But send him back.

LADY: *Within* Ho, daughter! are you up?

JULIET: Who is't that calls? It is my lady mother.
Is she not down so late, or up so early?
What unaccustom'd cause procures her hither?
   Enter Mother.

LADY: Why, how now, Juliet?

JULIET: Madam, I am not well.

LADY: Evermore weeping for your cousin's death?
What, wilt thou wash him from his grave with tears?
An if thou couldst, thou couldst not make him live.
Therefore have done. Some grief shows much of love;

But much of grief shows still some want of wit.

JULIET: Yet let me weep for such a feeling loss.

LADY: So shall you feel the loss, but not the friend
Which you weep for.

JULIET: Feeling so the loss,
I cannot choose but ever weep the friend.

LADY: Well, girl, thou weep'st not so much for his death
As that the villain lives which slaughter'd him.

JULIET: What villain, madam?

LADY: That same villain Romeo.

JULIET: *Aside* Villain and he be many miles asunder.-
God pardon him! I do, with all my heart;
And yet no man like he doth grieve my heart.

LADY: That is because the traitor murderer lives.

JULIET: Ay, madam, from the reach of these my hands.
Would none but I might venge my cousin's death!

LADY: We will have vengeance for it, fear thou not.
Then weep no more. I'll send to one in Mantua,
Where that same banish'd runagate doth live,
Shall give him such an unaccustom'd dram
That he shall soon keep Tybalt company;
And then I hope thou wilt be satisfied.

JULIET: Indeed I never shall be satisfied
With Romeo till I behold him- dead-
Is my poor heart so for a kinsman vex'd.
Madam, if you could find out but a man

To bear a poison, I would temper it;
That Romeo should, upon receipt thereof,
Soon sleep in quiet. O, how my heart abhors
To hear him nam'd and cannot come to him,
To wreak the love I bore my cousin Tybalt
Upon his body that hath slaughter'd him!

LADY: Find thou the means, and I'll find such a man.
But now I'll tell thee joyful tidings, girl.

JULIET: And joy comes well in such a needy time.
What are they, I beseech your ladyship?

LADY: Well, well, thou hast a careful father, child;
One who, to put thee from thy heaviness,
Hath sorted out a sudden day of joy
That thou expects not nor I look'd not for.

JULIET: Madam, in happy time! What day is that?

LADY: Marry, my child, early next Thursday morn
The gallant, young, and noble gentleman,
The County Paris, at Saint Peter's Church,
Shall happily make thee there a joyful bride.

JULIET: Now by Saint Peter's Church, and Peter too,
He shall not make me there a joyful bride!
I wonder at this haste, that I must wed
Ere he that should be husband comes to woo.
I pray you tell my lord and father, madam,
I will not marry yet; and when I do, I swear
It shall be Romeo, whom you know I hate,
Rather than Paris. These are news indeed!

LADY: Here comes your father. Tell him so yourself,
And see how be will take it at your hands.
    Enter Capulet and Nurse.

CAPULET: When the sun sets the air doth drizzle dew,
But for the sunset of my brother's son
It rains downright.
How now? a conduit, girl? What, still in tears?
Evermore show'ring? In one little body
Thou counterfeit'st a bark, a sea, a wind:
For still thy eyes, which I may call the sea,
Do ebb and flow with tears; the bark thy body is
Sailing in this salt flood; the winds, thy sighs,
Who, raging with thy tears and they with them,
Without a sudden calm will overset
Thy tempest-tossed body. How now, wife?
Have you delivered to her our decree?

LADY: Ay, sir; but she will none, she gives you thanks.
I would the fool were married to her grave!

CAPULET: Soft! take me with you, take me with you, wife.
How? Will she none? Doth she not give us thanks?
Is she not proud? Doth she not count her blest,
Unworthy as she is, that we have wrought
So worthy a gentleman to be her bridegroom?

JULIET: Not proud you have, but thankful that you have.
Proud can I never be of what I hate,
But thankful even for hate that is meant love.

CAPULET: How, how, how, how, choplogic? What is this?
'Proud'- and 'I thank you'- and 'I thank you not'-
And yet 'not proud'? Mistress minion you,
Thank me no thankings, nor proud me no prouds,
But fettle your fine joints 'gainst Thursday next
To go with Paris to Saint Peter's Church,
Or I will drag thee on a hurdle thither.
Out, you green-sickness carrion I out, you baggage!
You tallow-face!

LADY: Fie, fie! what, are you mad?

JULIET: Good father, I beseech you on my knees,
Hear me with patience but to speak a word.

CAPULET: Hang thee, young baggage! disobedient wretch!
I tell thee what- get thee to church a Thursday
Or never after look me in the face.
Speak not, reply not, do not answer me!
My fingers itch. Wife, we scarce thought us blest
That God had lent us but this only child;
But now I see this one is one too much,
And that we have a curse in having her.
Out on her, hilding!

NURSE: God in heaven bless her!
You are to blame, my lord, to rate her so.

CAPULET: And why, my Lady Wisdom? Hold your tongue,
Good Prudence. Smatter with your gossips, go!

NURSE: I speak no treason.

CAPULET: O, God-i-god-en!

NURSE: May not one speak?

CAPULET: Peace, you mumbling fool!
Utter your gravity o'er a gossip's bowl,
For here we need it not.

LADY: You are too hot.

CAPULET: God's bread I it makes me mad. Day, night, late, early,
At home, abroad, alone, in company,
Waking or sleeping, still my care hath been
To have her match'd; and having now provided

A gentleman of princely parentage,
Of fair demesnes, youthful, and nobly train'd,
Stuff'd, as they say, with honourable parts,
Proportion'd as one's thought would wish a man-
And then to have a wretched puling fool,
A whining mammet, in her fortune's tender,
To answer 'I'll not wed, I cannot love;
I am too young, I pray you pardon me'!
But, an you will not wed, I'll pardon you.
Graze where you will, you shall not house with me.
Look to't, think on't; I do not use to jest.
Thursday is near; lay hand on heart, advise:
An you be mine, I'll give you to my friend;
An you be not, hang, beg, starve, die in the streets,
For, by my soul, I'll ne'er acknowledge thee,
Nor what is mine shall never do thee good.
Trust to't. Bethink you. I'll not be forsworn.
   Exit.

JULIET: Is there no pity sitting in the clouds
That sees into the bottom of my grief?
O sweet my mother, cast me not away!
Delay this marriage for a month, a week;
Or if you do not, make the bridal bed
In that dim monument where Tybalt lies.

LADY: Talk not to me, for I'll not speak a word.
Do as thou wilt, for I have done with thee.
   Exit.

JULIET: O God!- O nurse, how shall this be prevented?
My husband is on earth, my faith in heaven.
How shall that faith return again to earth
Unless that husband send it me from heaven
By leaving earth? Comfort me, counsel me.
Alack, alack, that heaven should practise stratagems
Upon so soft a subject as myself!
What say'st thou? Hast thou not a word of joy?

Some comfort, nurse.

NURSE: Faith, here it is.
Romeo is banish'd; and all the world to nothing
That he dares ne'er come back to challenge you;
Or if he do, it needs must be by stealth.
Then, since the case so stands as now it doth,
I think it best you married with the County.
O, he's a lovely gentleman!
Romeo's a dishclout to him. An eagle, madam,
Hath not so green, so quick, so fair an eye
As Paris hath. Beshrew my very heart,
I think you are happy in this second match,
For it excels your first; or if it did not,
Your first is dead- or 'twere as good he were
As living here and you no use of him.

JULIET: Speak'st thou this from thy heart?

NURSE: And from my soul too; else beshrew them both.

JULIET: Amen!

NURSE: What?

JULIET: Well, thou hast comforted me marvellous much.
Go in; and tell my lady I am gone,
Having displeas'd my father, to Laurence' cell,
To make confession and to be absolv'd.

NURSE: Marry, I will; and this is wisely done.
   Exit.

JULIET: Ancient damnation! O most wicked fiend!
Is it more sin to wish me thus forsworn,
Or to dispraise my lord with that same tongue
Which she hath prais'd him with above compare

So many thousand times? Go, counsellor!
Thou and my bosom henceforth shall be twain.
I'll to the friar to know his remedy.
If all else fail, myself have power to die.
  Exit.

ACT IV. SCENE I. Friar Laurence's Cell.
Enter Friar, Laurence and County Paris.

FRIAR: On Thursday, sir? The time is very short.

PARIS: My father Capulet will have it so,
And I am nothing slow to slack his haste.

FRIAR: You say you do not know the lady's mind.
Uneven is the course; I like it not.

PARIS: Immoderately she weeps for Tybalt's death,
And therefore have I little talk'd of love;
For Venus smiles not in a house of tears.
Now, sir, her father counts it dangerous
That she do give her sorrow so much sway,
And in his wisdom hastes our marriage
To stop the inundation of her tears,
Which, too much minded by herself alone,
May be put from her by society.
Now do you know the reason of this haste.

FRIAR: *Aside* I would I knew not why it should be slow'd.-
Look, sir, here comes the lady toward my cell.
  Enter Juliet.

PARIS: Happily met, my lady and my wife!

JULIET: That may be, sir, when I may be a wife.

PARIS: That may be must be, love, on Thursday next.

JULIET: What must be shall be.

FRIAR: That's a certain text.

PARIS: Come you to make confession to this father?

JULIET: To answer that, I should confess to you.

PARIS: Do not deny to him that you love me.

JULIET: I will confess to you that I love him.

PARIS: So will ye, I am sure, that you love me.

JULIET: If I do so, it will be of more price,
Being spoke behind your back, than to your face.

PARIS: Poor soul, thy face is much abus'd with tears.

JULIET: The tears have got small victory by that,
For it was bad enough before their spite.

PARIS: Thou wrong'st it more than tears with that report.

JULIET: That is no slander, sir, which is a truth;
And what I spake, I spake it to my face.

PARIS: Thy face is mine, and thou hast sland'red it.

JULIET: It may be so, for it is not mine own.
Are you at leisure, holy father, now,
Or shall I come to you at evening mass

FRIAR: My leisure serves me, pensive daughter, now.
My lord, we must entreat the time alone.

PARIS: God shield I should disturb devotion!

Juliet, on Thursday early will I rouse ye.
Till then, adieu, and keep this holy kiss.
  Exit.

JULIET: O, shut the door! and when thou hast done so,
Come weep with me- past hope, past cure, past help!

FRIAR: Ah, Juliet, I already know thy grief;
It strains me past the compass of my wits.
I hear thou must, and nothing may prorogue it,
On Thursday next be married to this County.

JULIET: Tell me not, friar, that thou hear'st of this,
Unless thou tell me how I may prevent it.
If in thy wisdom thou canst give no help,
Do thou but call my resolution wise
And with this knife I'll help it presently.
God join'd my heart and Romeo's, thou our hands;
And ere this hand, by thee to Romeo's seal'd,
Shall be the label to another deed,
Or my true heart with treacherous revolt
Turn to another, this shall slay them both.
Therefore, out of thy long-experienc'd time,
Give me some present counsel; or, behold,
'Twixt my extremes and me this bloody knife
Shall play the empire, arbitrating that
Which the commission of thy years and art
Could to no issue of true honour bring.
Be not so long to speak. I long to die
If what thou speak'st speak not of remedy.

FRIAR: Hold, daughter. I do spy a kind of hope,
Which craves as desperate an execution
As that is desperate which we would prevent.
If, rather than to marry County Paris
Thou hast the strength of will to slay thyself,
Then is it likely thou wilt undertake
A thing like death to chide away this shame,

That cop'st with death himself to scape from it;
And, if thou dar'st, I'll give thee remedy.

JULIET: O, bid me leap, rather than marry Paris,
From off the battlements of yonder tower,
Or walk in thievish ways, or bid me lurk
Where serpents are; chain me with roaring bears,
Or shut me nightly in a charnel house,
O'ercover'd quite with dead men's rattling bones,
With reeky shanks and yellow chapless skulls;
Or bid me go into a new-made grave
And hide me with a dead man in his shroud-
Things that, to hear them told, have made me tremble-
And I will do it without fear or doubt,
To live an unstain'd wife to my sweet love.

FRIAR: Hold, then. Go home, be merry, give consent
To marry Paris. Wednesday is to-morrow.
To-morrow night look that thou lie alone;
Let not the nurse lie with thee in thy chamber.
Take thou this vial, being then in bed,
And this distilled liquor drink thou off;
When presently through all thy veins shall run
A cold and drowsy humour; for no pulse
Shall keep his native progress, but surcease;
No warmth, no breath, shall testify thou livest;
The roses in thy lips and cheeks shall fade
To paly ashes, thy eyes' windows fall
Like death when he shuts up the day of life;
Each part, depriv'd of supple government,
Shall, stiff and stark and cold, appear like death;
And in this borrowed likeness of shrunk death
Thou shalt continue two-and-forty hours,
And then awake as from a pleasant sleep.
Now, when the bridegroom in the morning comes
To rouse thee from thy bed, there art thou dead.
Then, as the manner of our country is,
In thy best robes uncovered on the bier

Thou shalt be borne to that same ancient vault
Where all the kindred of the Capulets lie.
In the mean time, against thou shalt awake,
Shall Romeo by my letters know our drift;
And hither shall he come; and he and I
Will watch thy waking, and that very night
Shall Romeo bear thee hence to Mantua.
And this shall free thee from this present shame,
If no inconstant toy nor womanish fear
Abate thy valour in the acting it.

JULIET: Give me, give me! O, tell not me of fear!

FRIAR: Hold! Get you gone, be strong and prosperous
In this resolve. I'll send a friar with speed
To Mantua, with my letters to thy lord.

JULIET: Love give me strength! and strength shall help afford.
Farewell, dear father.
  Exeunt.

ACT IV. SCENE II. Capulet's House.

Enter Father Capulet, Mother, Nurse, and Servingmen, two or three.

CAPULET: So many guests invite as here are writ.
  Exit a Servingman.
Sirrah, go hire me twenty cunning cooks.

SERVANT: You shall have none ill, sir; for I'll try if they can lick their fingers.

CAPULET: How canst thou try them so?

SERVANT: Marry, sir, 'tis an ill cook that cannot lick his own fingers. Therefore he that cannot lick his fingers goes not with me.

CAPULET: Go, begone.

Exit Servingman.
We shall be much unfurnish'd for this time.
What, is my daughter gone to Friar Laurence?

NURSE: Ay, forsooth.

CAPULET: Well, be may chance to do some good on her.
A peevish self-will'd harlotry it is.
   Enter Juliet.

NURSE: See where she comes from shrift with merry look.

CAPULET: How now, my headstrong? Where have you been gadding?

JULIET: Where I have learnt me to repent the sin
Of disobedient opposition
To you and your behests, and am enjoin'd
By holy Laurence to fall prostrate here
To beg your pardon. Pardon, I beseech you!
Henceforward I am ever rul'd by you.

CAPULET: Send for the County. Go tell him of this.
I'll have this knot knit up to-morrow morning.

JULIET: I met the youthful lord at Laurence' cell
And gave him what becomed love I might,
Not stepping o'er the bounds of modesty.

CAPULET: Why, I am glad on't. This is well. Stand up.
This is as't should be. Let me see the County.
Ay, marry, go, I say, and fetch him hither.
Now, afore God, this reverend holy friar,
All our whole city is much bound to him.

JULIET: Nurse, will you go with me into my closet
To help me sort such needful ornaments
As you think fit to furnish me to-morrow?

MOTHER: No, not till Thursday. There is time enough.

CAPULET: Go, nurse, go with her. We'll to church to-morrow.
Exeunt Juliet and Nurse.

MOTHER: We shall be short in our provision.
'Tis now near night.

CAPULET: Tush, I will stir about,
And all things shall be well, I warrant thee, wife.
Go thou to Juliet, help to deck up her.
I'll not to bed to-night; let me alone.
I'll play the housewife for this once. What, ho!
They are all forth; well, I will walk myself
To County Paris, to prepare him up
Against to-morrow. My heart is wondrous light,
Since this same wayward girl is so reclaim'd.
Exeunt.

ACT IV. SCENE III. Juliet's Chamber.
Enter Juliet and Nurse.

JULIET: Ay, those attires are best; but, gentle nurse,
I pray thee leave me to myself to-night;
For I have need of many orisons
To move the heavens to smile upon my state,
Which, well thou knowest, is cross and full of sin.
Enter Mother.

MOTHER: What, are you busy, ho? Need you my help?

JULIET: No, madam; we have cull'd such necessaries
As are behooffull for our state to-morrow.
So please you, let me now be left alone,
And let the nurse this night sit up with you;
For I am sure you have your hands full all
In this so sudden business.

MOTHER: Good night.
Get thee to bed, and rest; for thou hast need.
  Exeunt Mother and Nurse.

JULIET: Farewell! God knows when we shall meet again.
I have a faint cold fear thrills through my veins
That almost freezes up the heat of life.
I'll call them back again to comfort me.
Nurse!- What should she do here?
My dismal scene I needs must act alone.
Come, vial.
What if this mixture do not work at all?
Shall I be married then to-morrow morning?
No, No! This shall forbid it. Lie thou there.
  Lays down a Dagger.
What if it be a poison which the friar
Subtilly hath minist'red to have me dead,
Lest in this marriage he should be dishonour'd
Because he married me before to Romeo?
I fear it is; and yet methinks it should not,
For he hath still been tried a holy man.
I will not entertain so bad a thought.
How if, when I am laid into the tomb,
I wake before the time that Romeo
Come to redeem me? There's a fearful point!
Shall I not then be stifled in the vault,
To whose foul mouth no healthsome air breathes in,
And there die strangled ere my Romeo comes?
Or, if I live, is it not very like
The horrible conceit of death and night,
Together with the terror of the place-
As in a vault, an ancient receptacle
Where for this many hundred years the bones
Of all my buried ancestors are pack'd;
Where bloody Tybalt, yet but green in earth,
Lies fest'ring in his shroud; where, as they say,
At some hours in the night spirits resort-
Alack, alack, is it not like that I,

So early waking- what with loathsome smells,
And shrieks like mandrakes torn out of the earth,
That living mortals, hearing them, run mad-
O, if I wake, shall I not be distraught,
Environed with all these hideous fears,
And madly play with my forefathers' joints,
And pluck the mangled Tybalt from his shroud.,
And, in this rage, with some great kinsman's bone
As with a club dash out my desp'rate brains?
O, look! methinks I see my cousin's ghost
Seeking out Romeo, that did spit his body
Upon a rapier's point. Stay, Tybalt, stay!
Romeo, I come! this do I drink to thee.
  She Drinks And Falls upon Her Bed Within the Curtains.

ACT IV. SCENE IV. Capulet's House.
Enter Lady of the House and Nurse.

LADY: Hold, take these keys and fetch more spices, nurse.

NURSE: They call for dates and quinces in the pastry.
  Enter Old Capulet.

CAPULET: Come, stir, stir, stir! The second cock hath crow'd,
The curfew bell hath rung, 'tis three o'clock.
Look to the bak'd meats, good Angelica;
Spare not for cost.

NURSE: Go, you cot-quean, go,
Get you to bed! Faith, you'll be sick to-morrow
For this night's watching.

CAPULET: No, not a whit. What, I have watch'd ere now
All night for lesser cause, and ne'er been sick.

LADY: Ay, you have been a mouse-hunt in your time;
But I will watch you from such watching now.

Exeunt Lady and Nurse.

CAPULET: A jealous hood, a jealous hood!
  Enter Three or Four Fellows, with Spits and Logs and Baskets.

What is there? Now, fellow,
Fellow. Things for the cook, sir; but I know not what.

CAPULET: Make haste, make haste.
  Exit Fellow.
Sirrah, fetch drier logs.
Call Peter; he will show thee where they are.
Fellow. I have a head, sir, that will find out logs
And never trouble Peter for the matter.

CAPULET: Mass, and well said; a merry whoreson, ha!
Thou shalt be loggerhead.
  Exit Fellow.
Good faith, 'tis day.
The County will be here with music straight,
For so he said he would. Play music.
I hear him near.
Nurse! Wife! What, ho! What, nurse, I say!
  Enter Nurse.

Go waken Juliet; go and trim her up.
I'll go and chat with Paris. Hie, make haste,
Make haste! The bridegroom he is come already:
Make haste, I say.
  Exeunt.

ACT IV. SCENE V. Juliet's Chamber.

Enter Nurse.

NURSE: Mistress! what, mistress! Juliet! Fast, I warrant her, she.
Why, lamb! why, lady! Fie, you slug-abed!
Why, love, I say! madam! sweetheart! Why, bride!
What, not a word? You take your pennyworths now!

Sleep for a week; for the next night, I warrant,
The County Paris hath set up his rest
That you shall rest but little. God forgive me!
Marry, and amen. How sound is she asleep!
I needs must wake her. Madam, madam, madam!
Ay, let the County take you in your bed!
He'll fright you up, i' faith. Will it not be?
   Draws Aside the Curtains.
What, dress'd, and in your clothes, and down again?
I must needs wake you. Lady! lady! lady!
Alas, alas! Help, help! My lady's dead!
O weraday that ever I was born!
Some aqua-vitae, ho! My lord! my lady!
   Enter Mother.

MOTHER: What noise is here?

NURSE: O lamentable day!

MOTHER: What is the matter?

NURSE: Look, look! O heavy day!

MOTHER: O me, O me! My child, my only life!
Revive, look up, or I will die with thee!
Help, help! Call help.
   Enter Father.

FATHER: For shame, bring Juliet forth; her lord is come.

NURSE: She's dead, deceas'd; she's dead! Alack the day!

MOTHER: Alack the day, she's dead, she's dead, she's dead!

CAPULET: Ha! let me see her. Out alas! she's cold,
Her blood is settled, and her joints are stiff;
Life and these lips have long been separated.

Death lies on her like an untimely frost
Upon the sweetest flower of all the field.

NURSE: O lamentable day!

MOTHER: O woful time!

CAPULET: Death, that hath ta'en her hence to make me wail,
Ties up my tongue and will not let me speak.
   Enter Friar Laurence and the County Paris, with Musicians.

FRIAR: Come, is the bride ready to go to church?

CAPULET: Ready to go, but never to return.
O son, the night before thy wedding day
Hath Death lain with thy wife. See, there she lies,
Flower as she was, deflowered by him.
Death is my son-in-law, Death is my heir;
My daughter he hath wedded. I will die
And leave him all. Life, living, all is Death's.

PARIS: Have I thought long to see this morning's face,
And doth it give me such a sight as this?

MOTHER: Accurs'd, unhappy, wretched, hateful day!
Most miserable hour that e'er time saw
In lasting labour of his pilgrimage!
But one, poor one, one poor and loving child,
But one thing to rejoice and solace in,
And cruel Death hath catch'd it from my sight!

NURSE: O woe? O woful, woful, woful day!
Most lamentable day, most woful day
That ever ever I did yet behold!
O day! O day! O day! O hateful day!
Never was seen so black a day as this.
O woful day! O woful day!

PARIS: Beguil'd, divorced, wronged, spited, slain!
Most detestable Death, by thee beguil'd,
By cruel cruel thee quite overthrown!
O love! O life! not life, but love in death

CAPULET: Despis'd, distressed, hated, martyr'd, kill'd!
Uncomfortable time, why cam'st thou now
To murther, murther our solemnity?
O child! O child! my soul, and not my child!
Dead art thou, dead! alack, my child is dead,
And with my child my joys are buried!

FRIAR: Peace, ho, for shame! Confusion's cure lives not
In these confusions. Heaven and yourself
Had part in this fair maid! now heaven hath all,
And all the better is it for the maid.
Your part in her you could not keep from death,
But heaven keeps his part in eternal life.
The most you sought was her promotion,
For 'twas your heaven she should be advanc'd;
And weep ye now, seeing she is advanc'd
Above the clouds, as high as heaven itself?
O, in this love, you love your child so ill
That you run mad, seeing that she is well.
She's not well married that lives married long,
But she's best married that dies married young.
Dry up your tears and stick your rosemary
On this fair corse, and, as the custom is,
In all her best array bear her to church;
For though fond nature bids us all lament,
Yet nature's tears are reason's merriment.

CAPULET: All things that we ordained festival
Turn from their office to black funeral-
Our instruments to melancholy bells,
Our wedding cheer to a sad burial feast;
Our solemn hymns to sullen dirges change;
Our bridal flowers serve for a buried corse;

And all things change them to the contrary.

FRIAR: Sir, go you in; and, madam, go with him;
And go, Sir Paris. Every one prepare
To follow this fair corse unto her grave.
The heavens do low'r upon you for some ill;
Move them no more by crossing their high will.
  Exeunt. Manent Musicians and Nurse.

FIRST MUSICIAN: Faith, we may put up our pipes and be gone.

NURSE: Honest good fellows, ah, put up, put up!
For well you know this is a pitiful case.
  Exit.

FIRST MUSICIAN: Ay, by my troth, the case may be amended.
  Enter Peter.

PETER: Musicians, O, musicians, 'Heart's ease,' 'Heart's ease'!
O, an you will have me live, play 'Heart's ease.'

FIRST MUSICIAN: Why 'Heart's ease'',

PETER: O, musicians, because my heart itself plays 'My heart is full of woe.' O, play me some merry dump to comfort me.

FIRST MUSICIAN: Not a dump we! 'Tis no time to play now.

PETER: You will not then?

FIRST MUSICIAN: No.

PETER: I will then give it you soundly.

FIRST MUSICIAN: What will you give us?

PETER: No money, on my faith, but the gleek.

I will give you the minstrel.

FIRST MUSICIAN: Then will I give you the serving-creature.

PETER: Then will I lay the serving-creature's dagger on your pate. I will carry no crotchets. I'll re you, I'll fa you. Do you note me?

FIRST MUSICIAN: An you re us and fa us, you note us.

SECOND MUSICIAN: Pray you put up your dagger, and put out your wit.

PETER: Then have at you with my wit! I will dry-beat you with an iron wit, and put up my iron dagger. Answer me like men.
    'When griping grief the heart doth wound,
      And doleful dumps the mind oppress,
    Then music with her silver sound'-
Why 'silver sound'? Why 'music with her silver sound'?
What say you, Simon Catling?

FIRST MUSICIAN: Marry, sir, because silver hath a sweet sound.

PETER: Pretty! What say You, Hugh Rebeck?

SECOND MUSICIAN: I say 'silver sound' because musicians sound for silver.

PETER: Pretty too! What say you, James Soundpost?

THIRD MUSICIAN: Faith, I know not what to say.

PETER: O, I cry you mercy! you are the singer. I will say for you. It is 'music with her silver sound' because musicians have no gold for sounding.
    'Then Music with Her Silver Sound
      With Speedy Help Doth Lend Redress.'
    Exit.

FIRST MUSICIAN: What a pestilent knave is this same?

SECOND MUSICIAN: Hang him, Jack! Come, we'll in here, tarry for the mourners, and stay dinner.
Exeunt.

ACT V. SCENE I. Mantua. A Street.

Enter Romeo.

ROMEO: If I may trust the flattering truth of sleep
My dreams presage some joyful news at hand.
My bosom's lord sits lightly in his throne,
And all this day an unaccustom'd spirit
Lifts me above the ground with cheerful thoughts.
I dreamt my lady came and found me dead
(Strange dream that gives a dead man leave to think!)
And breath'd such life with kisses in my lips
That I reviv'd and was an emperor.
Ah me! how sweet is love itself possess'd,
When but love's shadows are so rich in joy!
Enter Romeo's Man Balthasar, Booted.
News from Verona! How now, Balthasar?
Dost thou not bring me letters from the friar?
How doth my lady? Is my father well?
How fares my Juliet? That I ask again,
For nothing can be ill if she be well.

BALTHASAR: Then she is well, and nothing can be ill.
Her body sleeps in Capel's monument,
And her immortal part with angels lives.
I saw her laid low in her kindred's vault
And presently took post to tell it you.
O, pardon me for bringing these ill news,
Since you did leave it for my office, sir.

ROMEO: Is it e'en so? Then I defy you, stars!
Thou knowest my lodging. Get me ink and paper
And hire posthorses. I will hence to-night.

BALTHASAR: I do beseech you, sir, have patience.
Your looks are pale and wild and do import
Some misadventure.

ROMEO: Tush, thou art deceiv'd.
Leave me and do the thing I bid thee do.
Hast thou no letters to me from the friar?

BALTHASAR: No, my good lord.

ROMEO: No matter. Get thee gone
And hire those horses. I'll be with thee straight.
   Exit Balthasar.
Well, Juliet, I will lie with thee to-night.
Let's see for means. O mischief, thou art swift
To enter in the thoughts of desperate men!
I do remember an apothecary,
And hereabouts 'a dwells, which late I noted
In tatt'red weeds, with overwhelming brows,
Culling of simples. Meagre were his looks,
Sharp misery had worn him to the bones;
And in his needy shop a tortoise hung,
An alligator stuff'd, and other skins
Of ill-shaped fishes; and about his shelves
A beggarly account of empty boxes,
Green earthen pots, bladders, and musty seeds,
Remnants of packthread, and old cakes of roses
Were thinly scattered, to make up a show.
Noting this penury, to myself I said,
'An if a man did need a poison now
Whose sale is present death in Mantua,
Here lives a caitiff wretch would sell it him.'
O, this same thought did but forerun my need,
And this same needy man must sell it me.
As I remember, this should be the house.
Being holiday, the beggar's shop is shut. What, ho! apothecary!
   Enter Apothecary.

William Shakespeare

APOTHECARY: Who calls so loud?

ROMEO: Come hither, man. I see that thou art poor.
Hold, there is forty ducats. Let me have
A dram of poison, such soon-speeding gear
As will disperse itself through all the veins
That the life-weary taker mall fall dead,
And that the trunk may be discharg'd of breath
As violently as hasty powder fir'd
Doth hurry from the fatal cannon's womb.

APOTHECARY: Such mortal drugs I have; but Mantua's law
Is death to any he that utters them.

ROMEO: Art thou so bare and full of wretchedness
And fearest to die? Famine is in thy cheeks,
Need and oppression starveth in thine eyes,
Contempt and beggary hangs upon thy back:
The world is not thy friend, nor the world's law;
The world affords no law to make thee rich;
Then be not poor, but break it and take this.

APOTHECARY: My poverty but not my will consents.

ROMEO: I pay thy poverty and not thy will.

APOTHECARY: Put this in any liquid thing you will
And drink it off, and if you had the strength
Of twenty men, it would dispatch you straight.

ROMEO: There is thy gold- worse poison to men's souls,
Doing more murther in this loathsome world,
Than these poor compounds that thou mayst not sell.
I sell thee poison; thou hast sold me none.
Farewell. Buy food and get thyself in flesh.
Come, cordial and not poison, go with me
To Juliet's grave; for there must I use thee.

Exeunt.

ACT V. SCENE II. Verona. Friar Laurence's Cell.
Enter Friar John to Friar Laurence.

FRIAR JOHN: Holy Franciscan friar, brother, ho!
Enter Friar Laurence.

FRIAR LAURENCE: This same should be the voice of Friar John.
Welcome from Mantua. What says Romeo?
Or, if his mind be writ, give me his letter.

FRIAR JOHN: Going to find a barefoot brother out,
One of our order, to associate me
Here in this city visiting the sick,
And finding him, the searchers of the town,
Suspecting that we both were in a house
Where the infectious pestilence did reign,
Seal'd up the doors, and would not let us forth,
So that my speed to Mantua there was stay'd.

FRIAR LAURENCE Who bare my letter, then, to Romeo?

FRIAR JOHN: I could not send it- here it is again-
Nor get a messenger to bring it thee,
So fearful were they of infection.

FRIAR LAURENCE Unhappy fortune! By my brotherhood,
The letter was not nice, but full of charge,
Of dear import; and the neglecting it
May do much danger. Friar John, go hence,
Get me an iron crow and bring it straight
Unto my cell.

FRIAR JOHN: Brother, I'll go and bring it thee.
Exit.

FRIAR LAURENCE Now, must I to the monument alone.
Within this three hours will fair Juliet wake.
She will beshrew me much that Romeo
Hath had no notice of these accidents;
But I will write again to Mantua,
And keep her at my cell till Romeo come—
Poor living corse, clos'd in a dead man's tomb!
   Exit.

ACT V. SCENE III. Verona. A Churchyard; in it the Monument of the Capulets.

Enter Paris and His Page with Flowers and a Torch.

PARIS: Give me thy torch, boy. Hence, and stand aloof.
Yet put it out, for I would not be seen.
Under yond yew tree lay thee all along,
Holding thine ear close to the hollow ground.
So shall no foot upon the churchyard tread
(Being loose, unfirm, with digging up of graves)
But thou shalt hear it. Whistle then to me,
As signal that thou hear'st something approach.
Give me those flowers. Do as I bid thee, go.

PAGE: *Aside* I am almost afraid to stand alone
Here in the churchyard; yet I will adventure.
   Retires.

PARIS: Sweet flower, with flowers thy bridal bed I strew
(O woe! thy canopy is dust and stones)
Which with sweet water nightly I will dew;
Or, wanting that, with tears distill'd by moans.
The obsequies that I for thee will keep
Nightly shall be to strew, thy grave and weep.
   Whistle Boy.
The boy gives warning something doth approach.
What cursed foot wanders this way to-night
To cross my obsequies and true love's rite?
What, with a torch? Muffle me, night, awhile.

Retires.
Enter Romeo, and Balthasar with a Torch, a Mattock, and a Crow of Iron.

ROMEO: Give me that mattock and the wrenching iron.
Hold, take this letter. Early in the morning
See thou deliver it to my lord and father.
Give me the light. Upon thy life I charge thee,
Whate'er thou hearest or seest, stand all aloof
And do not interrupt me in my course.
Why I descend into this bed of death
Is partly to behold my lady's face,
But chiefly to take thence from her dead finger
A precious ring- a ring that I must use
In dear employment. Therefore hence, be gone.
But if thou, jealous, dost return to pry
In what I farther shall intend to do,
By heaven, I will tear thee joint by joint
And strew this hungry churchyard with thy limbs.
The time and my intents are savage-wild,
More fierce and more inexorable far
Than empty tigers or the roaring sea.

BALTHASAR: I will be gone, sir, and not trouble you.

ROMEO: So shalt thou show me friendship. Take thou that.
Live, and be prosperous; and farewell, good fellow.

BALTHASAR: *Aside* For all this same, I'll hide me hereabout.
His looks I fear, and his intents I doubt.
   Retires.

ROMEO: Thou detestable maw, thou womb of death,
Gorg'd with the dearest morsel of the earth,
Thus I enforce thy rotten jaws to open,
And in despite I'll cram thee with more food.
   Romeo Opens the Tomb.

PARIS: This is that banish'd haughty Montague

That murd'red my love's cousin- with which grief
It is supposed the fair creature died-
And here is come to do some villanous shame
To the dead bodies. I will apprehend him.
Stop thy unhallowed toil, vile Montague!
Can vengeance be pursu'd further than death?
Condemned villain, I do apprehend thee.
Obey, and go with me; for thou must die.

ROMEO: I must indeed; and therefore came I hither.
Good gentle youth, tempt not a desp'rate man.
Fly hence and leave me. Think upon these gone;
Let them affright thee. I beseech thee, youth,
But not another sin upon my head
By urging me to fury. O, be gone!
By heaven, I love thee better than myself,
For I come hither arm'd against myself.
Stay not, be gone. Live, and hereafter say
A madman's mercy bid thee run away.

PARIS: I do defy thy, conjuration
And apprehend thee for a felon here.

ROMEO: Wilt thou provoke me? Then have at thee, boy!
They Fight.

PAGE: O Lord, they fight! I will go call the watch.
Exit. Paris Falls.

PARIS: O, I am slain! If thou be merciful,
Open the tomb, lay me with Juliet.
Dies.

ROMEO: In faith, I will. Let me peruse this face.
Mercutio's kinsman, noble County Paris!
What said my man when my betossed soul
Did not attend him as we rode? I think
He told me Paris should have married Juliet.

Said he not so? or did I dream it so?
Or am I mad, hearing him talk of Juliet
To think it was so? O, give me thy hand,
One writ with me in sour misfortune's book!
I'll bury thee in a triumphant grave.
A grave? O, no, a lanthorn, slaught'red youth,
For here lies Juliet, and her beauty makes
This vault a feasting presence full of light.
Death, lie thou there, by a dead man interr'd.
   Lays Him in the Tomb.
How oft when men are at the point of death
Have they been merry! which their keepers call
A lightning before death. O, how may I
Call this a lightning? O my love! my wife!
Death, that hath suck'd the honey of thy breath,
Hath had no power yet upon thy beauty.
Thou art not conquer'd. Beauty's ensign yet
Is crimson in thy lips and in thy cheeks,
And death's pale flag is not advanced there.
Tybalt, liest thou there in thy bloody sheet?
O, what more favour can I do to thee
Than with that hand that cut thy youth in twain
To sunder his that was thine enemy?
Forgive me, cousin.' Ah, dear Juliet,
Why art thou yet so fair? Shall I believe
That unsubstantial Death is amorous,
And that the lean abhorred monster keeps
Thee here in dark to be his paramour?
For fear of that I still will stay with thee
And never from this palace of dim night
Depart again. Here, here will I remain
With worms that are thy chambermaids. O, here
Will I set up my everlasting rest
And shake the yoke of inauspicious stars
From this world-wearied flesh. Eyes, look your last!
Arms, take your last embrace! and, lips, O you
The doors of breath, seal with a righteous kiss
A dateless bargain to engrossing death!

Come, bitter conduct; come, unsavoury guide!
Thou desperate pilot, now at once run on
The dashing rocks thy seasick weary bark!
Here's to my love! *Drinks.* O true apothecary!
Thy drugs are quick. Thus with a kiss I die. Falls.
   Enter Friar Laurence, with Lanthorn, Crow, and Spade.

FRIAR: Saint Francis be my speed! how oft to-night
Have my old feet stumbled at graves! Who's there?

BALTHASAR: Here's one, a friend, and one that knows you well.

FRIAR: Bliss be upon you! Tell me, good my friend,
What torch is yond that vainly lends his light
To grubs and eyeless skulls? As I discern,
It burneth in the Capels' monument.

BALTHASAR: It doth so, holy sir; and there's my master,
One that you love.

FRIAR: Who is it?

BALTHASAR: Romeo.

FRIAR: How long hath he been there?

BALTHASAR: Full half an hour.

FRIAR: Go with me to the vault.

BALTHASAR: I dare not, sir.
My master knows not but I am gone hence,
And fearfully did menace me with death
If I did stay to look on his intents.

FRIAR: Stay then; I'll go alone. Fear comes upon me.
O, much I fear some ill unthrifty thing.

BALTHASAR: As I did sleep under this yew tree here,
I dreamt my master and another fought,
And that my master slew him.

FRIAR: Romeo!
Alack, alack, what blood is this which stains
The stony entrance of this sepulchre?
What mean these masterless and gory swords
To lie discolour'd by this place of peace?
   Enters the tomb.
Romeo! O, pale! Who else? What, Paris too?
And steep'd in blood? Ah, what an unkind hour
Is guilty of this lamentable chance! The lady stirs.
   Juliet Rises.

JULIET: O comfortable friar! where is my lord?
I do remember well where I should be,
And there I am. Where is my Romeo?

FRIAR: I hear some noise. Lady, come from that nest
Of death, contagion, and unnatural sleep.
A greater power than we can contradict
Hath thwarted our intents. Come, come away.
Thy husband in thy bosom there lies dead;
And Paris too. Come, I'll dispose of thee
Among a sisterhood of holy nuns.
Stay not to question, for the watch is coming.
Come, go, good Juliet. I dare no longer stay.

JULIET: Go, get thee hence, for I will not away.
   Exit Friar.
What's here? A cup, clos'd in my true love's hand?
Poison, I see, hath been his timeless end.
O churl! drunk all, and left no friendly drop
To help me after? I will kiss thy lips.
Haply some poison yet doth hang on them
To make me die with a restorative. *Kisses Him.*
Thy lips are warm!

Chief Watch. *Within* Lead, boy. Which way?
Yea, noise? Then I'll be brief. O happy dagger!
   Snatches Romeo's Dagger.
This is thy sheath; there rest, and let me die.
   She Stabs Herself and Falls on Romeo's Body.
   Enter Paris's Boy and Watch.

BOY: This is the place. There, where the torch doth burn.
Chief Watch. 'the ground is bloody. Search about the churchyard.
Go, some of you; whoe'er you find attach.
   Exeunt Some of the Watch.
Pitiful sight! here lies the County slain;
And Juliet bleeding, warm, and newly dead,
Who here hath lain this two days buried.
Go, tell the Prince; run to the Capulets;
Raise up the Montagues; some others search.
   Exeunt Others of the Watch.
We see the ground whereon these woes do lie,
But the true ground of all these piteous woes
We cannot without circumstance descry.
   Enter Some of the Watch, with Romeo's Man Balthasar.

SECOND WATCH: Here's Romeo's man.
We found him in the churchyard.

CHIEF WATCH: Hold him in safety till the Prince come hither.
   Enter Friar Laurence and another Watchman.

THIRD WATCH: Here is a friar that trembles, sighs, and weeps.
We took this mattock and this spade from him
As he was coming from this churchyard side.
Chief Watch. A great suspicion! Stay the friar too.
   Enter the Prince and Attendants.

PRINCE: What misadventure is so early up,
That calls our person from our morning rest?
   Enter Capulet and His Wife with Others.

CAPULET: What should it be, that they so shriek abroad?

WIFE: The people in the street cry 'Romeo,'
Some 'Juliet,' and some 'Paris'; and all run,
With open outcry, toward our monument.

PRINCE: What fear is this which startles in our ears?
Chief Watch. Sovereign, here lies the County Paris slain;
And Romeo dead; and Juliet, dead before,
Warm and new kill'd.

PRINCE: Search, seek, and know how this foul murder comes.

CHIEF WATCH: Here is a friar, and slaughter'd Romeo's man,
With instruments upon them fit to open
These dead men's tombs.

CAPULET: O heavens! O wife, look how our daughter bleeds!
This dagger hath mista'en, for, lo, his house
Is empty on the back of Montague,
And it missheathed in my daughter's bosom!

WIFE: O me! this sight of death is as a bell
That warns my old age to a sepulchre.
   Enter Montague and Others.

PRINCE: Come, Montague; for thou art early up
To see thy son and heir more early down.

MONTAGUE: Alas, my liege, my wife is dead to-night!
Grief of my son's exile hath stopp'd her breath.
What further woe conspires against mine age?

PRINCE: Look, and thou shalt see.

MONTAGUE: O thou untaught! what manners is in this,
To press before thy father to a grave?

PRINCE: Seal up the mouth of outrage for a while,
Till we can clear these ambiguities
And know their spring, their head, their true descent;
And then will I be general of your woes
And lead you even to death. Meantime forbear,
And let mischance be slave to patience.
Bring forth the parties of suspicion.

FRIAR: I am the greatest, able to do least,
Yet most suspected, as the time and place
Doth make against me, of this direful murther;
And here I stand, both to impeach and purge
Myself condemned and myself excus'd.

PRINCE: Then say it once what thou dost know in this.

FRIAR: I will be brief, for my short date of breath
Is not so long as is a tedious tale.
Romeo, there dead, was husband to that Juliet;
And she, there dead, that Romeo's faithful wife.
I married them; and their stol'n marriage day
Was Tybalt's doomsday, whose untimely death
Banish'd the new-made bridegroom from this city;
For whom, and not for Tybalt, Juliet pin'd.
You, to remove that siege of grief from her,
Betroth'd and would have married her perforce
To County Paris. Then comes she to me
And with wild looks bid me devise some mean
To rid her from this second marriage,
Or in my cell there would she kill herself.
Then gave I her (so tutored by my art)
A sleeping potion; which so took effect
As I intended, for it wrought on her
The form of death. Meantime I writ to Romeo
That he should hither come as this dire night
To help to take her from her borrowed grave,
Being the time the potion's force should cease.
But he which bore my letter, Friar John,

Was stay'd by accident, and yesternight
Return'd my letter back. Then all alone
At the prefixed hour of her waking
Came I to take her from her kindred's vault;
Meaning to keep her closely at my cell
Till I conveniently could send to Romeo.
But when I came, some minute ere the time
Of her awaking, here untimely lay
The noble Paris and true Romeo dead.
She wakes; and I entreated her come forth
And bear this work of heaven with patience;
But then a noise did scare me from the tomb,
And she, too desperate, would not go with me,
But, as it seems, did violence on herself.
All this I know, and to the marriage
Her nurse is privy; and if aught in this
Miscarried by my fault, let my old life
Be sacrific'd, some hour before his time,
Unto the rigour of severest law.

PRINCE: We still have known thee for a holy man.
Where's Romeo's man? What can he say in this?

BALTHASAR: I brought my master news of Juliet's death;
And then in post he came from Mantua
To this same place, to this same monument.
This letter he early bid me give his father,
And threat'ned me with death, going in the vault,
If I departed not and left him there.

PRINCE: Give me the letter. I will look on it.
Where is the County's page that rais'd the watch?
Sirrah, what made your master in this place?

BOY: He came with flowers to strew his lady's grave;
And bid me stand aloof, and so I did.
Anon comes one with light to ope the tomb;
And by-and-by my master drew on him;

And then I ran away to call the watch.

PRINCE: This letter doth make good the friar's words,
Their course of love, the tidings of her death;
And here he writes that he did buy a poison
Of a poor pothecary, and therewithal
Came to this vault to die, and lie with Juliet.
Where be these enemies? Capulet, Montage,
See what a scourge is laid upon your hate,
That heaven finds means to kill your joys with love!
And I, for winking at you, discords too,
Have lost a brace of kinsmen. All are punish'd.

CAPULET: O brother Montague, give me thy hand.
This is my daughter's jointure, for no more
Can I demand.

MONTAGUE: But I can give thee more;
For I will raise her Statue in pure gold,
That whiles Verona by that name is known,
There shall no figure at such rate be set
As that of true and faithful Juliet.

CAPULET: As rich shall Romeo's by his lady's lie-
Poor sacrifices of our enmity!

PRINCE: A glooming peace this morning with it brings.
The sun for sorrow will not show his head.
Go hence, to have more talk of these sad things;
Some shall be pardon'd, and some punished;
For never was a story of more woe
Than this of Juliet and her Romeo.
    Exeunt Omnes.

END

Hamlet

Dramatis Personae

CLAUDIUS, King of Denmark.
HAMLET, son to the former, and nephew to the present king.
POLONIUS, Lord Chamberlain.
HORATIO, friend to Hamlet.
LAERTES, son to Polonius.
VOLTEMAND, courtier.
CORNELIUS, courtier.
ROSENCRANTZ, courtier.
GUILDENSTERN, courtier.
OSRIC, courtier.
A GENTLEMAN, courtier.
A PRIEST.
MARCELLUS, officer.
BERNARDO, officer.
FRANCISCO, a soldier
REYNALDO, servant to Polonius.
PLAYERS.
LUCIANUS.
TWO CLOWNS
GRAVEDIGGERS.
FORTINBRAS, Prince of Norway.
A NORWEGIAN CAPTAIN.
ENGLISH AMBASSADORS.
GETRUDE, Queen of Denmark, mother to Hamlet.
OPHELIA, daughter to Polonius.
GHOST of Hamlet's Father.

Lords, ladies, Officers, Soldiers, Sailors, Messengers, Attendants.

SCENE.- Elsinore.

ACT I. SCENE I. Elsinore. A Platform Before the Castle.

Enter Two Sentinels-First, Francisco, Who Paces up and down at His Post; Then Bernardo, Who Approaches Him.

BERNARDO: Who's there.?

FRANCISCO: Nay, answer me. Stand and unfold yourself.

BERNARDO: Long live the King!

FRANCISCO: Bernardo?

BERNARDO: He.

FRANCISCO: You come most carefully upon your hour.

BERNARDO: 'Tis now struck twelve. Get thee to bed, Francisco.

FRANCISCO: For this relief much thanks. 'Tis bitter cold,
And I am sick at heart.

BERNARDO: Have you had quiet guard?

FRANCISCO: Not a mouse stirring.

BERNARDO: Well, good night.
If you do meet Horatio and Marcellus,
The rivals of my watch, bid them make haste.
  Enter Horatio and Marcellus.

FRANCISCO: I think I hear them. Stand, ho! Who is there?

HORATIO: Friends to this ground.

MARCELLUS: And liegemen to the Dane.

FRANCISCO: Give you good night.

MARCELLUS: O, farewell, honest soldier.
Who hath reliev'd you?

FRANCISCO: Bernardo hath my place.
Give you good night.
   Exit.

MARCELLUS: Holla, Bernardo!

BERNARDO: Say-
What, is Horatio there ?

HORATIO: A piece of him.

BERNARDO: Welcome, Horatio. Welcome, good Marcellus.

MARCELLUS: What, has this thing appear'd again to-night?

BERNARDO: I have seen nothing.

MARCELLUS: Horatio says 'tis but our fantasy,
And will not let belief take hold of him
Touching this dreaded sight, twice seen of us.
Therefore I have entreated him along,
With us to watch the minutes of this night,
That, if again this apparition come,
He may approve our eyes and speak to it.

HORATIO: Tush, tush, 'twill not appear.

BERNARDO: Sit down awhile,
And let us once again assail your ears,
That are so fortified against our story,
What we two nights have seen.

HORATIO: Well, sit we down,
And let us hear Bernardo speak of this.

BERNARDO: Last night of all,
When yond same star that's westward from the pole
Had made his course t' illume that part of heaven
Where now it burns, Marcellus and myself,
The bell then beating one-
  Enter Ghost.

MARCELLUS: Peace! break thee off! Look where it comes again!

BERNARDO: In the same figure, like the King that's dead.

MARCELLUS: Thou art a scholar; speak to it, Horatio.

BERNARDO: Looks it not like the King? Mark it, Horatio.

HORATIO: Most like. It harrows me with fear and wonder.

BERNARDO: It would be spoke to.

MARCELLUS: Question it, Horatio.

HORATIO: What art thou that usurp'st this time of night
Together with that fair and warlike form
In which the majesty of buried Denmark
Did sometimes march? By heaven I charge thee speak!

MARCELLUS: It is offended.

BERNARDO: See, it stalks away!

HORATIO: Stay! Speak, speak! I charge thee speak!
  Exit Ghost.

MARCELLUS: 'Tis gone and will not answer.

BERNARDO: How now, Horatio? You tremble and look pale.
Is not this something more than fantasy?
What think you on't?

HORATIO: Before my God, I might not this believe
Without the sensible and true avouch
Of mine own eyes.

MARCELLUS: Is it not like the King?

HORATIO: As thou art to thyself.
Such was the very armour he had on
When he th' ambitious Norway combated.
So frown'd he once when, in an angry parle,
He smote the sledded Polacks on the ice.
'Tis strange.

MARCELLUS: Thus twice before, and jump at this dead hour,
With martial stalk hath he gone by our watch.

HORATIO: In what particular thought to work I know not;
But, in the gross and scope of my opinion,
This bodes some strange eruption to our state.

MARCELLUS: Good now, sit down, and tell me he that knows,
Why this same strict and most observant watch
So nightly toils the subject of the land,
And why such daily cast of brazen cannon
And foreign mart for implements of war;
Why such impress of shipwrights, whose sore task
Does not divide the Sunday from the week.
What might be toward, that this sweaty haste
Doth make the night joint-labourer with the day?
Who is't that can inform me?

HORATIO: That can I.
At least, the whisper goes so. Our last king,

Whose image even but now appear'd to us,
Was, as you know, by Fortinbras of Norway,
Thereto prick'd on by a most emulate pride,
Dar'd to the combat; in which our valiant Hamlet
(For so this side of our known world esteem'd him)
Did slay this Fortinbras; who, by a seal'd compact,
Well ratified by law and heraldry,
Did forfeit, with his life, all those his lands
Which he stood seiz'd of, to the conqueror;
Against the which a moiety competent
Was gaged by our king; which had return'd
To the inheritance of Fortinbras,
Had he been vanquisher, as, by the same comart
And carriage of the article design'd,
His fell to Hamlet. Now, sir, young Fortinbras,
Of unimproved mettle hot and full,
Hath in the skirts of Norway, here and there,
Shark'd up a list of lawless resolutes,
For food and diet, to some enterprise
That hath a stomach in't; which is no other,
As it doth well appear unto our state,
But to recover of us, by strong hand
And terms compulsatory, those foresaid lands
So by his father lost; and this, I take it,
Is the main motive of our preparations,
The source of this our watch, and the chief head
Of this post-haste and romage in the land.

BERNARDO: I think it be no other but e'en so.
Well may it sort that this portentous figure
Comes armed through our watch, so like the King
That was and is the question of these wars.

HORATIO: A mote it is to trouble the mind's eye.
In the most high and palmy state of Rome,
A little ere the mightiest Julius fell,
The graves stood tenantless, and the sheeted dead
Did squeak and gibber in the Roman streets;

As stars with trains of fire, and dews of blood,
Disasters in the sun; and the moist star
Upon whose influence Neptune's empire stands
Was sick almost to doomsday with eclipse.
And even the like precurse of fierce events,
As harbingers preceding still the fates
And prologue to the omen coming on,
Have heaven and earth together demonstrated
Unto our climature and countrymen.
  Enter Ghost Again.
But soft! behold! Lo, where it comes again!
I'll cross it, though it blast me.- Stay illusion!
  Spreads His Arms.
If thou hast any sound, or use of voice,
Speak to me.
If there be any good thing to be done,
That may to thee do ease, and, race to me,
Speak to me.
If thou art privy to thy country's fate,
Which happily foreknowing may avoid,
O, speak!
Or if thou hast uphoarded in thy life
Extorted treasure in the womb of earth
(For which, they say, you spirits oft walk in death),
  The Cock Crows.
Speak of it! Stay, and speak!- Stop it, Marcellus!

MARCELLUS: Shall I strike at it with my partisan?

HORATIO: Do, if it will not stand.

BERNARDO: 'Tis here!

HORATIO: 'Tis here!

MARCELLUS: 'Tis gone!
  Exit Ghost.
We do it wrong, being so majestical,

To offer it the show of violence;
For it is as the air, invulnerable,
And our vain blows malicious mockery.

BERNARDO: It was about to speak, when the cock crew.

HORATIO: And then it started, like a guilty thing
Upon a fearful summons. I have heard
The cock, that is the trumpet to the morn,
Doth with his lofty and shrill-sounding throat
Awake the god of day; and at his warning,
Whether in sea or fire, in earth or air,
Th' extravagant and erring spirit hies
To his confine; and of the truth herein
This present object made probation.

MARCELLUS: It faded on the crowing of the cock.
Some say that ever, 'gainst that season comes
Wherein our Saviour's birth is celebrated,
The bird of dawning singeth all night long;
And then, they say, no spirit dare stir abroad,
The nights are wholesome, then no planets strike,
No fairy takes, nor witch hath power to charm,
So hallow'd and so gracious is the time.

HORATIO: So have I heard and do in part believe it.
But look, the morn, in russet mantle clad,
Walks o'er the dew of yon high eastward hill.
Break we our watch up; and by my advice
Let us impart what we have seen to-night
Unto young Hamlet; for, upon my life,
This spirit, dumb to us, will speak to him.
Do you consent we shall acquaint him with it,
As needful in our loves, fitting our duty?
Let's do't, I pray; and I this morning know
Where we shall find him most conveniently.
   Exeunt.

William Shakespeare

ACT II. SCENE II. Elsinore. A Room of State in the Castle.

Flourish. Enter Claudius, King of Denmark, Gertrude the Queen, Hamlet, Polonius, Laertes and His Sister Ophelia, Voltemand, Cornelius, Lords Attendant.

KING CLAUDIUS: Though yet of Hamlet our dear brother's death
The memory be green, and that it us befitted
To bear our hearts in grief, and our whole kingdom
To be contracted in one brow of woe,
Yet so far hath discretion fought with nature
That we with wisest sorrow think on him
Together with remembrance of ourselves.
Therefore our sometime sister, now our queen,
Th' imperial jointress to this warlike state,
Have we, as 'twere with a defeated joy,
With an auspicious, and a dropping eye,
With mirth in funeral, and with dirge in marriage,
In equal scale weighing delight and dole,
Taken to wife; nor have we herein barr'd
Your better wisdoms, which have freely gone
With this affair along. For all, our thanks.
Now follows, that you know, young Fortinbras,
Holding a weak supposal of our worth,
Or thinking by our late dear brother's death
Our state to be disjoint and out of frame,
Colleagued with this dream of his advantage,
He hath not fail'd to pester us with message
Importing the surrender of those lands
Lost by his father, with all bands of law,
To our most valiant brother. So much for him.
Now for ourself and for this time of meeting.
Thus much the business is: we have here writ
To Norway, uncle of young Fortinbras,
Who, impotent and bedrid, scarcely hears
Of this his nephew's purpose, to suppress
His further gait herein, in that the levies,
The lists, and full proportions are all made
Out of his subject; and we here dispatch
You, good Cornelius, and you, Voltemand,

For bearers of this greeting to old Norway,
Giving to you no further personal power
To business with the King, more than the scope
Of these dilated articles allow.
   Gives a Paper.
Farewell, and let your haste commend your duty.

CORNELIUS: Volt. In that, and all things, will we show our duty.

KING CLAUDIUS: We doubt it nothing. Heartily farewell.
   Exeunt Voltemand and Cornelius.
And now, Laertes, what's the news with you?
You told us of some suit. What is't, Laertes?
You cannot speak of reason to the Dane
And lose your voice. What wouldst thou beg, Laertes,
That shall not be my offer, not thy asking?
The head is not more native to the heart,
The hand more instrumental to the mouth,
Than is the throne of Denmark to thy father.
What wouldst thou have, Laertes?

LAERTES: My dread lord,
Your leave and favour to return to France;
From whence though willingly I came to Denmark
To show my duty in your coronation,
Yet now I must confess, that duty done,
My thoughts and wishes bend again toward France
And bow them to your gracious leave and pardon.

KING CLAUDIUS: Have you your father's leave? What says Polonius?

POLONIUS: He hath, my lord, wrung from me my slow leave
By laboursome petition, and at last
Upon his will I seal'd my hard consent.
I do beseech you give him leave to go.

KING CLAUDIUS: Take thy fair hour, Laertes. Time be thine,
And thy best graces spend it at thy will!

But now, my cousin Hamlet, and my son-

HAMLET: *Aside* A little more than kin, and less than kind!

KING CLAUDIUS: How is it that the clouds still hang on you?

HAMLET: Not so, my lord. I am too much i' th' sun.

QUEEN GETRUDE: Good Hamlet, cast thy nighted colour off,
And let thine eye look like a friend on Denmark.
Do not for ever with thy vailed lids
Seek for thy noble father in the dust.
Thou know'st 'tis common. All that lives must die,
Passing through nature to eternity.

HAMLET: Ay, madam, it is common.

QUEEN GETRUDE: If it be,
Why seems it so particular with thee?

HAMLET: Seems, madam, Nay, it is. I know not 'seems.'
'Tis not alone my inky cloak, good mother,
Nor customary suits of solemn black,
Nor windy suspiration of forc'd breath,
No, nor the fruitful river in the eye,
Nor the dejected havior of the visage,
Together with all forms, moods, shapes of grief,
'That can denote me truly. These indeed seem,
For they are actions that a man might play;
But I have that within which passeth show-
These but the trappings and the suits of woe.

KING CLAUDIUS: 'Tis sweet and commendable in your nature, Hamlet,
To give these mourning duties to your father;
But you must know, your father lost a father;
That father lost, lost his, and the survivor bound
In filial obligation for some term

To do obsequious sorrow. But to persever
In obstinate condolement is a course
Of impious stubbornness. 'Tis unmanly grief;
It shows a will most incorrect to heaven,
A heart unfortified, a mind impatient,
An understanding simple and unschool'd;
For what we know must be, and is as common
As any the most vulgar thing to sense,
Why should we in our peevish opposition
Take it to heart? Fie! 'tis a fault to heaven,
A fault against the dead, a fault to nature,
To reason most absurd, whose common theme
Is death of fathers, and who still hath cried,
From the first corse till he that died to-day,
'This must be so.' We pray you throw to earth
This unprevailing woe, and think of us
As of a father; for let the world take note
You are the most immediate to our throne,
And with no less nobility of love
Than that which dearest father bears his son
Do I impart toward you. For your intent
In going back to school in Wittenberg,
It is most retrograde to our desire;
And we beseech you, bend you to remain
Here in the cheer and comfort of our eye,
Our chiefest courtier, cousin, and our son.

QUEEN GETRUDE: Let not thy mother lose her prayers, Hamlet.
I pray thee stay with us, go not to Wittenberg.

HAMLET: I shall in all my best obey you, madam.

KING CLAUDIUS: Why, 'tis a loving and a fair reply.
Be as ourself in Denmark. Madam, come.
This gentle and unforc'd accord of Hamlet
Sits smiling to my heart; in grace whereof,
No jocund health that Denmark drinks to-day
But the great cannon to the clouds shall tell,

And the King's rouse the heaven shall bruit again,
Respeaking earthly thunder. Come away.
   Flourish. Exeunt all but Hamlet.

HAMLET: O that this too too solid flesh would melt,
Thaw, and resolve itself into a dew!
Or that the Everlasting had not fix'd
His canon 'gainst self-slaughter! O God! God!
How weary, stale, flat, and unprofitable
Seem to me all the uses of this world!
Fie on't! ah, fie! 'Tis an unweeded garden
That grows to seed; things rank and gross in nature
Possess it merely. That it should come to this!
But two months dead! Nay, not so much, not two.
So excellent a king, that was to this
Hyperion to a satyr; so loving to my mother
That he might not beteem the winds of heaven
Visit her face too roughly. Heaven and earth!
Must I remember? Why, she would hang on him
As if increase of appetite had grown
By what it fed on; and yet, within a month-
Let me not think on't! Frailty, thy name is woman!-
A little month, or ere those shoes were old
With which she followed my poor father's body
Like Niobe, all tears- why she, even she
(O God! a beast that wants discourse of reason
Would have mourn'd longer) married with my uncle;
My father's brother, but no more like my father
Than I to Hercules. Within a month,
Ere yet the salt of most unrighteous tears
Had left the flushing in her galled eyes,
She married. O, most wicked speed, to post
With such dexterity to incestuous sheets!
It is not, nor it cannot come to good.
But break my heart, for I must hold my tongue!
   Enter Horatio, Marcellus, and Bernardo.

HORATIO: Hail to your lordship!

HAMLET: I am glad to see you well.
Horatio!- or I do forget myself.

HORATIO: The same, my lord, and your poor servant ever.

HAMLET: Sir, my good friend- I'll change that name with you.
And what make you from Wittenberg, Horatio? Marcellus?

MARCELLUS: My good lord!

HAMLET: I am very glad to see you.- *To Bernardo* Good even, sir.-
But what, in faith, make you from Wittenberg?

HORATIO: A truant disposition, good my lord.

HAMLET: I would not hear your enemy say so,
Nor shall you do my ear that violence
To make it truster of your own report
Against yourself. I know you are no truant.
But what is your affair in Elsinore?
We'll teach you to drink deep ere you depart.

HORATIO: My lord, I came to see your father's funeral.

HAMLET: I prithee do not mock me, fellow student.
I think it was to see my mother's wedding.

HORATIO: Indeed, my lord, it followed hard upon.

HAMLET: Thrift, thrift, Horatio! The funeral bak'd meats
Did coldly furnish forth the marriage tables.
Would I had met my dearest foe in heaven
Or ever I had seen that day, Horatio!
My father- methinks I see my father.

HORATIO: O, where, my lord?

HAMLET: In my mind's eye, Horatio.

HORATIO: I saw him once. He was a goodly king.

HAMLET: He was a man, take him for all in all.
I shall not look upon his like again.

HORATIO: My lord, I think I saw him yesternight.

HAMLET: Saw? who?

HORATIO: My lord, the King your father.

HAMLET: The King my father?

HORATIO: Season your admiration for a while
With an attent ear, till I may deliver
Upon the witness of these gentlemen,
This marvel to you.

HAMLET: For God's love let me hear!

HORATIO: Two nights together had these gentlemen
(Marcellus and Bernardo) on their watch
In the dead vast and middle of the night
Been thus encount'red. A figure like your father,
Armed at point exactly, cap-a-pe,
Appears before them and with solemn march
Goes slow and stately by them. Thrice he walk'd
By their oppress'd and fear-surprised eyes,
Within his truncheon's length; whilst they distill'd
Almost to jelly with the act of fear,
Stand dumb and speak not to him. This to me
In dreadful secrecy impart they did,
And I with them the third night kept the watch;
Where, as they had deliver'd, both in time,
Form of the thing, each word made true and good,

The apparition comes. I knew your father.
These hands are not more like.

HAMLET: But where was this?

MARCELLUS: My lord, upon the platform where we watch'd.

HAMLET: Did you not speak to it?

HORATIO: My lord, I did;
But answer made it none. Yet once methought
It lifted up it head and did address
Itself to motion, like as it would speak;
But even then the morning cock crew loud,
And at the sound it shrunk in haste away
And vanish'd from our sight.

HAMLET: 'Tis very strange.

HORATIO: As I do live, my honour'd lord, 'tis true;
And we did think it writ down in our duty
To let you know of it.

HAMLET: Indeed, indeed, sirs. But this troubles me.
Hold you the watch to-night?

BOTH: *Marcellus and Bernardo* We do, my lord.

HAMLET: Arm'd, say you?

BOTH: Arm'd, my lord.

HAMLET: From top to toe?

BOTH: My lord, from head to foot.

HAMLET: Then saw you not his face?

HORATIO: O, yes, my lord! He wore his beaver up.

HAMLET: What, look'd he frowningly.

HORATIO: A countenance more in sorrow than in anger.

HAMLET: Pale or red?

HORATIO: Nay, very pale.

HAMLET: And fix'd his eyes upon you?

HORATIO: Most constantly.

HAMLET: I would I had been there.

HORATIO: It would have much amaz'd you.

HAMLET: Very like, very like. Stay'd it long?

HORATIO: While one with moderate haste might tell a hundred.

BOTH: Longer, longer.

HORATIO: Not when I saw't.

HAMLET: His beard was grizzled- no?

HORATIO: It was, as I have seen it in his life,
A sable silver'd.

HAMLET: I will watch to-night.
Perchance 'twill walk again.

HORATIO: I warr'nt it will.

HAMLET: If it assume my noble father's person,

I'll speak to it, though hell itself should gape
And bid me hold my peace. I pray you all,
If you have hitherto conceal'd this sight,
Let it be tenable in your silence still;
And whatsoever else shall hap to-night,
Give it an understanding but no tongue.
I will requite your loves. So, fare you well.
Upon the platform, 'twixt eleven and twelve,
I'll visit you.

ALL: Our duty to your honour.

HAMLET: Your loves, as mine to you. Farewell.
Exeunt All but Hamlet.
My father's spirit- in arms? All is not well.
I doubt some foul play. Would the night were come!
Till then sit still, my soul. Foul deeds will rise,
Though all the earth o'erwhelm them, to men's eyes.
Exit.

ACT II. SCENE III. Elsinore. A Room in the House of Polonius.
Enter Laertes and Ophelia.

LAERTES: My necessaries are embark'd. Farewell.
And, sister, as the winds give benefit
And convoy is assistant, do not sleep,
But let me hear from you.

OPHELIA: Do you doubt that?

LAERTES: For Hamlet, and the trifling of his favour,
Hold it a fashion, and a toy in blood;
A violet in the youth of primy nature,
Forward, not permanent- sweet, not lasting;
The perfume and suppliance of a minute;
No more.

William Shakespeare

OPHELIA: No more but so?

LAERTES: Think it no more.
For nature crescent does not grow alone
In thews and bulk; but as this temple waxes,
The inward service of the mind and soul
Grows wide withal. Perhaps he loves you now,
And now no soil nor cautel doth besmirch
The virtue of his will; but you must fear,
His greatness weigh'd, his will is not his own;
For he himself is subject to his birth.
He may not, as unvalued persons do,
Carve for himself, for on his choice depends
The safety and health of this whole state,
And therefore must his choice be circumscrib'd
Unto the voice and yielding of that body
Whereof he is the head. Then if he says he loves you,
It fits your wisdom so far to believe it
As he in his particular act and place
May give his saying deed; which is no further
Than the main voice of Denmark goes withal.
Then weigh what loss your honour may sustain
If with too credent ear you list his songs,
Or lose your heart, or your chaste treasure open
To his unmast'red importunity.
Fear it, Ophelia, fear it, my dear sister,
And keep you in the rear of your affection,
Out of the shot and danger of desire.
The chariest maid is prodigal enough
If she unmask her beauty to the moon.
Virtue itself scopes not calumnious strokes.
The canker galls the infants of the spring
Too oft before their buttons be disclos'd,
And in the morn and liquid dew of youth
Contagious blastments are most imminent.
Be wary then; best safety lies in fear.
Youth to itself rebels, though none else near.

OPHELIA: I shall th' effect of this good lesson keep
As watchman to my heart. But, good my brother,
Do not as some ungracious pastors do,
Show me the steep and thorny way to heaven,
Whiles, like a puff'd and reckless libertine,
Himself the primrose path of dalliance treads
And recks not his own rede.

LAERTES: O, fear me not!
  Enter Polonius.
I stay too long. But here my father comes.
A double blessing is a double grace;
Occasion smiles upon a second leave.

POLONIUS: Yet here, Laertes? Aboard, aboard, for shame!
The wind sits in the shoulder of your sail,
And you are stay'd for. There- my blessing with thee!
And these few precepts in thy memory
Look thou character. Give thy thoughts no tongue,
Nor any unproportion'd thought his act.
Be thou familiar, but by no means vulgar:
Those friends thou hast, and their adoption tried,
Grapple them unto thy soul with hoops of steel;
But do not dull thy palm with entertainment
Of each new-hatch'd, unfledg'd comrade. Beware
Of entrance to a quarrel; but being in,
Bear't that th' opposed may beware of thee.
Give every man thine ear, but few thy voice;
Take each man's censure, but reserve thy judgment.
Costly thy habit as thy purse can buy,
But not express'd in fancy; rich, not gaudy;
For the apparel oft proclaims the man,
And they in France of the best rank and station
Are most select and generous, chief in that.
Neither a borrower nor a lender be;
For loan oft loses both itself and friend,
And borrowing dulls the edge of husbandry.
This above all- to thine own self be true,

And it must follow, as the night the day,
Thou canst not then be false to any man.
Farewell. My blessing season this in thee!

LAERTES: Most humbly do I take my leave, my lord.

POLONIUS: The time invites you. Go, your servants tend.

LAERTES: Farewell, Ophelia, and remember well
What I have said to you.

OPHELIA: 'Tis in my memory lock'd,
And you yourself shall keep the key of it.

LAERTES: Farewell.
   Exit.

POLONIUS: What is't, Ophelia, he hath said to you?

OPHELIA: So please you, something touching the Lord Hamlet.

POLONIUS: Marry, well bethought!
'Tis told me he hath very oft of late
Given private time to you, and you yourself
Have of your audience been most free and bounteous.
If it be so- as so 'tis put on me,
And that in way of caution- I must tell you
You do not understand yourself so clearly
As it behooves my daughter and your honour.
What is between you? Give me up the truth.

OPHELIA: He hath, my lord, of late made many tenders
Of his affection to me.

POLONIUS: Affection? Pooh! You speak like a green girl,
Unsifted in such perilous circumstance.
Do you believe his tenders, as you call them?

OPHELIA: I do not know, my lord, what I should think,

POLONIUS: Marry, I will teach you! Think yourself a baby
That you have ta'en these tenders for true pay,
Which are not sterling. Tender yourself more dearly,
Or (not to crack the wind of the poor phrase,
Running it thus) you'll tender me a fool.

OPHELIA: My lord, he hath importun'd me with love
In honourable fashion.

POLONIUS: Ay, fashion you may call it. Go to, go to!

OPHELIA: And hath given countenance to his speech, my lord,
With almost all the holy vows of heaven.

POLONIUS: Ay, springes to catch woodcocks! I do know,
When the blood burns, how prodigal the soul
Lends the tongue vows. These blazes, daughter,
Giving more light than heat, extinct in both
Even in their promise, as it is a-making,
You must not take for fire. From this time
Be something scanter of your maiden presence.
Set your entreatments at a higher rate
Than a command to parley. For Lord Hamlet,
Believe so much in him, that he is young,
And with a larger tether may he walk
Than may be given you. In few, Ophelia,
Do not believe his vows; for they are brokers,
Not of that dye which their investments show,
But mere implorators of unholy suits,
Breathing like sanctified and pious bawds,
The better to beguile. This is for all:
I would not, in plain terms, from this time forth
Have you so slander any moment leisure
As to give words or talk with the Lord Hamlet.
Look to't, I charge you. Come your ways.

OPHELIA: I shall obey, my lord.
Exeunt.

ACT II. SCENE IV. Elsinore. The Platform Before the Castle.
Enter Hamlet, Horatio, and Marcellus.

HAMLET: The air bites shrewdly; it is very cold.

HORATIO: It is a nipping and an eager air.

HAMLET: What hour now?

HORATIO: I think it lacks of twelve.

MARCELLUS: No, it is struck.

HORATIO: Indeed? I heard it not. It then draws near the season
Wherein the spirit held his wont to walk.
   A Flourish of Trumpets, and Two Pieces Go Off.
What does this mean, my lord?

HAMLET: The King doth wake to-night and takes his rouse,
Keeps wassail, and the swagg'ring upspring reels,
And, as he drains his draughts of Rhenish down,
The kettledrum and trumpet thus bray out
The triumph of his pledge.

HORATIO: Is it a custom?

HAMLET: Ay, marry, is't;
But to my mind, though I am native here
And to the manner born, it is a custom
More honour'd in the breach than the observance.
This heavy-headed revel east and west
Makes us traduc'd and tax'd of other nations;
They clip us drunkards and with swinish phrase
Soil our addition; and indeed it takes

From our achievements, though perform'd at height,
The pith and marrow of our attribute.
So oft it chances in particular men
That, for some vicious mole of nature in them,
As in their birth,- wherein they are not guilty,
Since nature cannot choose his origin,-
By the o'ergrowth of some complexion,
Oft breaking down the pales and forts of reason,
Or by some habit that too much o'erleavens
The form of plausive manners, that these men
Carrying, I say, the stamp of one defect,
Being nature's livery, or fortune's star,
Their virtues else- be they as pure as grace,
As infinite as man may undergo-
Shall in the general censure take corruption
From that particular fault. The dram of e'il
Doth all the noble substance often dout To his own scandal.
   Enter Ghost.

HORATIO: Look, my lord, it comes!

HAMLET: Angels and ministers of grace defend us!
Be thou a spirit of health or goblin damn'd,
Bring with thee airs from heaven or blasts from hell,
Be thy intents wicked or charitable,
Thou com'st in such a questionable shape
That I will speak to thee. I'll call thee Hamlet,
King, father, royal Dane. O, answer me?
Let me not burst in ignorance, but tell
Why thy canoniz'd bones, hearsed in death,
Have burst their cerements; why the sepulchre
Wherein we saw thee quietly inurn'd,
Hath op'd his ponderous and marble jaws
To cast thee up again. What may this mean
That thou, dead corse, again in complete steel,
Revisits thus the glimpses of the moon,
Making night hideous, and we fools of nature
So horridly to shake our disposition

With thoughts beyond the reaches of our souls?
Say, why is this? wherefore? What should we do?
　Ghost Beckons Hamlet.

HORATIO: It beckons you to go away with it,
As if it some impartment did desire
To you alone.

MARCELLUS: Look with what courteous action
It waves you to a more removed ground.
But do not go with it!

HORATIO: No, by no means!

HAMLET: It will not speak. Then will I follow it.

HORATIO: Do not, my lord!

HAMLET: Why, what should be the fear?
I do not set my life at a pin's fee;
And for my soul, what can it do to that,
Being a thing immortal as itself?
It waves me forth again. I'll follow it.

HORATIO: What if it tempt you toward the flood, my lord,
Or to the dreadful summit of the cliff
That beetles o'er his base into the sea,
And there assume some other, horrible form
Which might deprive your sovereignty of reason
And draw you into madness? Think of it.
The very place puts toys of desperation,
Without more motive, into every brain
That looks so many fadoms to the sea
And hears it roar beneath.

HAMLET: It waves me still.
Go on. I'll follow thee.

MARCELLUS: You shall not go, my lord.

HAMLET: Hold off your hands!

HORATIO: Be rul'd. You shall not go.

HAMLET: My fate cries out
And makes each petty artire in this body
As hardy as the Nemean lion's nerve.
  Ghost Beckons.
Still am I call'd. Unhand me, gentlemen.
By heaven, I'll make a ghost of him that lets me!-
I say, away!- Go on. I'll follow thee.
  Exeunt Ghost and Hamlet.

HORATIO: He waxes desperate with imagination.

MARCELLUS: Let's follow. 'Tis not fit thus to obey him.

HORATIO: Have after. To what issue wail this come?

MARCELLUS: Something is rotten in the state of Denmark.

HORATIO: Heaven will direct it.

MARCELLUS: Nay, let's follow him.
  Exeunt.

ACT I. SCENE V. Elsinore. The Castle. Another Part of the Fortifications.

Enter Ghost and Hamlet.

HAMLET: Whither wilt thou lead me? Speak! I'll go no further.

GHOST: Mark me.

HAMLET: I will.

GHOST: My hour is almost come,
When I to sulph'rous and tormenting flames
Must render up myself.

HAMLET: Alas, poor ghost!

GHOST: Pity me not, but lend thy serious hearing
To what I shall unfold.

HAMLET: Speak. I am bound to hear.

GHOST: So art thou to revenge, when thou shalt hear.

HAMLET: What?

GHOST: I am thy father's spirit,
Doom'd for a certain term to walk the night,
And for the day confin'd to fast in fires,
Till the foul crimes done in my days of nature
Are burnt and purg'd away. But that I am forbid
To tell the secrets of my prison house,
I could a tale unfold whose lightest word
Would harrow up thy soul, freeze thy young blood,
Make thy two eyes, like stars, start from their spheres,
Thy knotted and combined locks to part,
And each particular hair to stand an end
Like quills upon the fretful porpentine.
But this eternal blazon must not be
To ears of flesh and blood. List, list, O, list!
If thou didst ever thy dear father love-

HAMLET: O God!

GHOST: Revenge his foul and most unnatural murther.

HAMLET: Murther?

GHOST: Murther most foul, as in the best it is;
But this most foul, strange, and unnatural.

HAMLET: Haste me to know't, that I, with wings as swift
As meditation or the thoughts of love,
May sweep to my revenge.

GHOST: I find thee apt;
And duller shouldst thou be than the fat weed
That rots itself in ease on Lethe wharf,
Wouldst thou not stir in this. Now, Hamlet, hear.
'Tis given out that, sleeping in my orchard,
A serpent stung me. So the whole ear of Denmark
Is by a forged process of my death
Rankly abus'd. But know, thou noble youth,
The serpent that did sting thy father's life
Now wears his crown.

HAMLET: O my prophetic soul! My uncle?

GHOST: Ay, that incestuous, that adulterate beast,
With witchcraft of his wit, with traitorous gifts-
O wicked wit and gifts, that have the power
So to seduce!- won to his shameful lust
The will of my most seeming-virtuous queen.
O Hamlet, what a falling-off was there,
From me, whose love was of that dignity
That it went hand in hand even with the vow
I made to her in marriage, and to decline
Upon a wretch whose natural gifts were poor
To those of mine!
But virtue, as it never will be mov'd,
Though lewdness court it in a shape of heaven,
So lust, though to a radiant angel link'd,
Will sate itself in a celestial bed
And prey on garbage.
But soft! methinks I scent the morning air.
Brief let me be. Sleeping within my orchard,

My custom always of the afternoon,
Upon my secure hour thy uncle stole,
With juice of cursed hebona in a vial,
And in the porches of my ears did pour
The leperous distilment; whose effect
Holds such an enmity with blood of man
That swift as quicksilverr it courses through
The natural gates and alleys of the body,
And with a sudden vigour it doth posset
And curd, like eager droppings into milk,
The thin and wholesome blood. So did it mine;
And a most instant tetter bark'd about,
Most lazar-like, with vile and loathsome crust
All my smooth body.
Thus was I, sleeping, by a brother's hand
Of life, of crown, of queen, at once dispatch'd;
Cut off even in the blossoms of my sin,
Unhous'led, disappointed, unanel'd,
No reckoning made, but sent to my account
With all my imperfections on my head.

HAMLET: O, horrible! O, horrible! most horrible!

GHOST: If thou hast nature in thee, bear it not.
Let not the royal bed of Denmark be
A couch for luxury and damned incest.
But, howsoever thou pursuest this act,
Taint not thy mind, nor let thy soul contrive
Against thy mother aught. Leave her to heaven,
And to those thorns that in her bosom lodge
To prick and sting her. Fare thee well at once.
The glowworm shows the matin to be near
And gins to pale his uneffectual fire.
Adieu, adieu, adieu! Remember me.
    Exit.

HAMLET: O all you host of heaven! O earth! What else?
And shall I couple hell? Hold, hold, my heart!

And you, my sinews, grow not instant old,
But bear me stiffly up. Remember thee?
Ay, thou poor ghost, while memory holds a seat
In this distracted globe. Remember thee?
Yea, from the table of my memory
I'll wipe away all trivial fond records,
All saws of books, all forms, all pressures past
That youth and observation copied there,
And thy commandment all alone shall live
Within the book and volume of my brain,
Unmix'd with baser matter. Yes, by heaven!
O most pernicious woman!
O villain, villain, smiling, damned villain!
My tables! Meet it is I set it down
That one may smile, and smile, and be a villain;
At least I am sure it may be so in Denmark.
   Writes.
So, uncle, there you are. Now to my word:
It is 'Adieu, adieu! Remember me.'
I have sworn't.

HORATIO: (within) My lord, my lord!
   Enter Horatio and Marcellus.

MARCELLUS: Lord Hamlet!

HORATIO: Heaven secure him!

HAMLET: So be it!

MARCELLUS: Illo, ho, ho, my lord!

HAMLET: Hillo, ho, ho, boy! Come, bird, come.

MARCELLUS: How is't, my noble lord?

HORATIO: What news, my lord?

MARCELLUS: O, wonderful!

HORATIO: Good my lord, tell it.

HAMLET: No, you will reveal it.

HORATIO: Not I, my lord, by heaven!

MARCELLUS: Nor I, my lord.

HAMLET: How say you then? Would heart of man once think it?
But you'll be secret?

BOTH: Ay, by heaven, my lord.

HAMLET: There's neer a villain dwelling in all Denmark
But he's an arrant knave.

HORATIO: There needs no ghost, my lord, come from the grave
To tell us this.

HAMLET: Why, right! You are in the right!
And so, without more circumstance at all,
I hold it fit that we shake hands and part;
You, as your business and desires shall point you,
For every man hath business and desire,
Such as it is; and for my own poor part,
Look you, I'll go pray.

HORATIO: These are but wild and whirling words, my lord.

HAMLET: I am sorry they offend you, heartily;
Yes, faith, heartily.

HORATIO: There's no offence, my lord.

HAMLET: Yes, by Saint Patrick, but there is, Horatio,

And much offence too. Touching this vision here,
It is an honest ghost, that let me tell you.
For your desire to know what is between us,
O'ermaster't as you may. And now, good friends,
As you are friends, scholars, and soldiers,
Give me one poor request.

HORATIO: What is't, my lord? We will.

HAMLET: Never make known what you have seen to-night.

BOTH: My lord, we will not.

HAMLET: Nay, but swear't.

HORATIO: In faith,
My lord, not I.

MARCELLUS: Nor I, my lord- in faith.

HAMLET: Upon my sword.

MARCELLUS: We have sworn, my lord, already.

HAMLET: Indeed, upon my sword, indeed.
  Ghost Cries under the Stage.

GHOST: Swear.

HAMLET: Aha boy, say'st thou so? Art thou there, truepenny?
Come on! You hear this fellow in the cellarage.
Consent to swear.

HORATIO: Propose the oath, my lord.

HAMLET: Never to speak of this that you have seen.
Swear by my sword.

GHOST: *Beneath* Swear.

HAMLET: Hic et ubique? Then we'll shift our ground.
Come hither, gentlemen,
And lay your hands again upon my sword.
Never to speak of this that you have heard:
Swear by my sword.

GHOST: *Beneath* Swear by his sword.

HAMLET: Well said, old mole! Canst work i' th' earth so fast?
A worthy pioner! Once more remove, good friends."

HORATIO: O day and night, but this is wondrous strange!

HAMLET: And therefore as a stranger give it welcome.
There are more things in heaven and earth, Horatio,
Than are dreamt of in your philosophy.
But come!
Here, as before, never, so help you mercy,
How strange or odd soe'er I bear myself
(As I perchance hereafter shall think meet
To put an antic disposition on),
That you, at such times seeing me, never shall,
With arms encumb'red thus, or this head-shake,
Or by pronouncing of some doubtful phrase,
As 'Well, well, we know,' or 'We could, an if we would,'
Or 'If we list to speak,' or 'There be, an if they might,'
Or such ambiguous giving out, to note
That you know aught of me- this is not to do,
So grace and mercy at your most need help you, Swear.

GHOST: *Beneath* Swear.
  They Swear.

HAMLET: Rest, rest, perturbed spirit! So, gentlemen,

With all my love I do commend me to you;
And what so poor a man as Hamlet is
May do t' express his love and friending to you,
God willing, shall not lack. Let us go in together;
And still your fingers on your lips, I pray.
The time is out of joint. O cursed spite
That ever I was born to set it right!
Nay, come, let's go together.
   Exeunt.

ACT II. SCENE I. Elsinore. A Room in the House of Polonius.
Enter Polonius and Reynaldo.

POLONIUS: Give him this money and these notes, Reynaldo.

REYNALDO: I will, my lord.

POLONIUS: You shall do marvell's wisely, good Reynaldo,
Before You visit him, to make inquire
Of his behaviour.

REYNALDO: My lord, I did intend it.

POLONIUS: Marry, well said, very well said. Look you, sir,
Enquire me first what Danskers are in Paris;
And how, and who, what means, and where they keep,
What company, at what expense; and finding
By this encompassment and drift of question
That they do know my son, come you more nearer
Than your particular demands will touch it.
Take you, as 'twere, some distant knowledge of him;
As thus, 'I know his father and his friends,
And in part him.' Do you mark this, Reynaldo?

REYNALDO: Ay, very well, my lord.

POLONIUS: 'And in part him, but,' you may say, 'not well.

But if't be he I mean, he's very wild
Addicted so and so'; and there put on him
What forgeries you please; marry, none so rank
As may dishonour him- take heed of that;
But, sir, such wanton, wild, and usual slips
As are companions noted and most known
To youth and liberty.

REYNALDO: As gaming, my lord.

POLONIUS: Ay, or drinking, fencing, swearing, quarrelling,
Drabbing. You may go so far.

REYNALDO: My lord, that would dishonour him.

POLONIUS: Faith, no, as you may season it in the charge.
You must not put another scandal on him,
That he is open to incontinency.
That's not my meaning. But breathe his faults so quaintly
That they may seem the taints of liberty,
The flash and outbreak of a fiery mind,
A savageness in unreclaimed blood,
Of general assault.

REYNALDO: But, my good lord-

POLONIUS: Wherefore should you do this?

REYNALDO: Ay, my lord,
I would know that.

POLONIUS: Marry, sir, here's my drift,
And I believe it is a fetch of warrant.
You laying these slight sullies on my son
As 'twere a thing a little soil'd i' th' working,
Mark you,
Your party in converse, him you would sound,

Having ever seen in the prenominate crimes
The youth you breathe of guilty, be assur'd
He closes with you in this consequence:
'Good sir,' or so, or 'friend,' or 'gentleman'-
According to the phrase or the addition
Of man and country-

REYNALDO: Very good, my lord.

POLONIUS: And then, sir, does 'a this- 'a does- What was I about to say? By the mass, I was about to say something! Where did I leave?

REYNALDO: At 'closes in the consequence,' at 'friend or so,' and

GENTLEMAN:'

POLONIUS: At 'closes in the consequence'- Ay, marry!
He closes thus: 'I know the gentleman.
I saw him yesterday, or t'other day,
Or then, or then, with such or such; and, as you say,
There was 'a gaming; there o'ertook in's rouse;
There falling out at tennis'; or perchance,
'I saw him enter such a house of sale,'
Videlicet, a brothel, or so forth.
See you now-
Your bait of falsehood takes this carp of truth;
And thus do we of wisdom and of reach,
With windlasses and with assays of bias,
By indirections find directions out.
So, by my former lecture and advice,
Shall you my son. You have me, have you not

REYNALDO: My lord, I have.

POLONIUS: God b' wi' ye, fare ye well!

REYNALDO: Good my lord!

Going.

POLONIUS: Observe his inclination in yourself.

REYNALDO: I shall, my lord.

POLONIUS: And let him ply his music.

REYNALDO: Well, my lord.

POLONIUS: Farewell!
  Exit Reynaldo.
  Enter Ophelia.
How now, Ophelia? What's the matter?

OPHELIA: O my lord, my lord, I have been so affrighted!

POLONIUS: With what, i' th' name of God I

OPHELIA: My lord, as I was sewing in my closet,
Lord Hamlet, with his doublet all unbrac'd,
No hat upon his head, his stockings foul'd,
Ungart'red, and down-gyved to his ankle;
Pale as his shirt, his knees knocking each other,
And with a look so piteous in purport
As if he had been loosed out of hell
To speak of horrors- he comes before me.

POLONIUS: Mad for thy love?

OPHELIA: My lord, I do not know,
But truly I do fear it.

POLONIUS: What said he?

OPHELIA: He took me by the wrist and held me hard;
Then goes he to the length of all his arm,

And, with his other hand thus o'er his brow,
He falls to such perusal of my face
As he would draw it. Long stay'd he so.
At last, a little shaking of mine arm,
And thrice his head thus waving up and down,
He rais'd a sigh so piteous and profound
As it did seem to shatter all his bulk
And end his being. That done, he lets me go,
And with his head over his shoulder turn'd
He seem'd to find his way without his eyes,
For out o' doors he went without their help
And to the last bended their light on me.

POLONIUS: Come, go with me. I will go seek the King.
This is the very ecstasy of love,
Whose violent property fordoes itself
And leads the will to desperate undertakings
As oft as any passion under heaven
That does afflict our natures. I am sorry.
What, have you given him any hard words of late?

OPHELIA: No, my good lord; but, as you did command,
I did repel his letters and denied
His access to me.

POLONIUS: That hath made him mad.
I am sorry that with better heed and judgment
I had not quoted him. I fear'd he did but trifle
And meant to wrack thee; but beshrew my jealousy!
By heaven, it is as proper to our age
To cast beyond ourselves in our opinions
As it is common for the younger sort
To lack discretion. Come, go we to the King.
This must be known; which, being kept close, might move
More grief to hide than hate to utter love.
Come.
   Exeunt.

William Shakespeare

ACT II. SCENE II. Elsinore. A Room in the Castle.

Flourish. Enter King and Queen, Rosencrantz and Guildenstern, cum Aliis.

KING CLAUDIUS: Welcome, dear Rosencrantz and Guildenstern.
Moreover that we much did long to see you,
The need we have to use you did provoke
Our hasty sending. Something have you heard
Of Hamlet's transformation. So I call it,
Sith nor th' exterior nor the inward man
Resembles that it was. What it should be,
More than his father's death, that thus hath put him
So much from th' understanding of himself,
I cannot dream of. I entreat you both
That, being of so young clays brought up with him,
And since so neighbour'd to his youth and haviour,
That you vouchsafe your rest here in our court
Some little time; so by your companies
To draw him on to pleasures, and to gather
So much as from occasion you may glean,
Whether aught to us unknown afflicts him thus
That, open'd, lies within our remedy.

QUEEN GETRUDE: Good gentlemen, he hath much talk'd of you,
And sure I am two men there are not living
To whom he more adheres. If it will please you
To show us so much gentry and good will
As to expend your time with us awhile
For the supply and profit of our hope,
Your visitation shall receive such thanks
As fits a king's remembrance.

ROSENCRANTZ: Both your Majesties
Might, by the sovereign power you have of us,
Put your dread pleasures more into command
Than to entreaty.

GUILDENSTERN: But we both obey,
And here give up ourselves, in the full bent,

To lay our service freely at your feet,
To be commanded.

KING CLAUDIUS: Thanks, Rosencrantz and gentle Guildenstern.

QUEEN GETRUDE: Thanks, Guildenstern and gentle Rosencrantz.
And I beseech you instantly to visit
My too much changed son.- Go, some of you,
And bring these gentlemen where Hamlet is.

GUILDENSTERN: Heavens make our presence and our practices
Pleasant and helpful to him!

QUEEN GETRUDE: Ay, amen!
  Exeunt Rosencrantz and Guildenstern, With Some Attendants.
  Enter Polonius.

POLONIUS: Th' ambassadors from Norway, my good lord,
Are joyfully return'd.

KING CLAUDIUS: Thou still hast been the father of good news.

POLONIUS: Have I, my lord? Assure you, my good liege,
I hold my duty as I hold my soul,
Both to my God and to my gracious king;
And I do think- or else this brain of mine
Hunts not the trail of policy so sure
As it hath us'd to do- that I have found
The very cause of Hamlet's lunacy.

KING CLAUDIUS: O, speak of that! That do I long to hear.

POLONIUS: Give first admittance to th' ambassadors.
My news shall be the fruit to that great feast.

KING CLAUDIUS: Thyself do grace to them, and bring them in.
  Exit Polonius.

William Shakespeare

He tells me, my dear Gertrude, he hath found
The head and source of all your son's distemper.

QUEEN GETRUDE: I doubt it is no other but the main,
His father's death and our o'erhasty marriage.

KING CLAUDIUS: Well, we shall sift him.
   Enter Polonius, Voltemand, and Cornelius.
Welcome, my good friends.
Say, Voltemand, what from our brother Norway?

VOLTEMAND: Most fair return of greetings and desires.
Upon our first, he sent out to suppress
His nephew's levies; which to him appear'd
To be a preparation 'gainst the Polack,
But better look'd into, he truly found
It was against your Highness; whereat griev'd,
That so his sickness, age, and impotence
Was falsely borne in hand, sends out arrests
On Fortinbras; which he, in brief, obeys,
Receives rebuke from Norway, and, in fine,
Makes vow before his uncle never more
To give th' assay of arms against your Majesty.
Whereon old Norway, overcome with joy,
Gives him three thousand crowns in annual fee
And his commission to employ those soldiers,
So levied as before, against the Polack;
With an entreaty, herein further shown,
   Gives a Paper.
That it might please you to give quiet pass
Through your dominions for this enterprise,
On such regards of safety and allowance
As therein are set down.

KING CLAUDIUS: It likes us well;
And at our more consider'd time we'll read,
Answer, and think upon this business.
Meantime we thank you for your well-took labour.

Go to your rest; at night we'll feast together.
Most welcome home!
   Exeunt Ambassadors.

POLONIUS: This business is well ended.
My liege, and madam, to expostulate
What majesty should be, what duty is,
Why day is day, night is night, and time is time.
Were nothing but to waste night, day, and time.
Therefore, since brevity is the soul of wit,
And tediousness the limbs and outward flourishes,
I will be brief. Your noble son is mad.
Mad call I it; for, to define true madness,
What is't but to be nothing else but mad?
But let that go.

QUEEN GETRUDE: More matter, with less art.

POLONIUS: Madam, I swear I use no art at all.
That he is mad, 'tis true: 'tis true 'tis pity;
And pity 'tis 'tis true. A foolish figure!
But farewell it, for I will use no art.
Mad let us grant him then. And now remains
That we find out the cause of this effect-
Or rather say, the cause of this defect,
For this effect defective comes by cause.
Thus it remains, and the remainder thus. Perpend.
I have a daughter (have while she is mine),
Who in her duty and obedience, mark,
Hath given me this. Now gather, and surmise.
   Reads the Letter.
'To the celestial, and my soul's idol, the most beautified
   Ophelia,'-
That's an ill phrase, a vile phrase; 'beautified' is a vile
   phrase.
But you shall hear. Thus:
   Reads.
'In her excellent white bosom, these, etc.'

QUEEN GETRUDE: Came this from Hamlet to her?

POLONIUS: Good madam, stay awhile. I will be faithful. *Reads.*
    'Doubt thou the stars are fire;
      Doubt that the sun doth move;
      Doubt truth to be a liar;
      But never doubt I love.
'O dear Ophelia, I am ill at these numbers; I have not art to reckon my groans; but that I love thee best, O most best, believe it. Adieu.
  'Thine evermore, most dear lady, whilst this machine is to him,
                           Hamlet.'

This, in obedience, hath my daughter shown me;
And more above, hath his solicitings,
As they fell out by time, by means, and place,
All given to mine ear.

KING CLAUDIUS: But how hath she
Receiv'd his love?

POLONIUS: What do you think of me?

KING CLAUDIUS: As of a man faithful and honourable.

POLONIUS: I would fain prove so. But what might you think,
When I had seen this hot love on the wing
(As I perceiv'd it, I must tell you that,
Before my daughter told me), what might you,
Or my dear Majesty your queen here, think,
If I had play'd the desk or table book,
Or given my heart a winking, mute and dumb,
Or look'd upon this love with idle sight?
What might you think? No, I went round to work
And my young mistress thus I did bespeak:
'Lord Hamlet is a prince, out of thy star.
This must not be.' And then I prescripts gave her,
That she should lock herself from his resort,

Admit no messengers, receive no tokens.
Which done, she took the fruits of my advice,
And he, repulsed, a short tale to make,
Fell into a sadness, then into a fast,
Thence to a watch, thence into a weakness,
Thence to a lightness, and, by this declension,
Into the madness wherein now he raves,
And all we mourn for.

KING CLAUDIUS: Do you think 'tis this?

QUEEN GETRUDE: it may be, very like.

POLONIUS: Hath there been such a time- I would fain know that-
That I have Positively said ''Tis so,'
When it prov'd otherwise.?

KING CLAUDIUS: Not that I know.

POLONIUS: *Points to His Head and Shoulder* Take this from this,
if this be otherwise.
If circumstances lead me, I will find
Where truth is hid, though it were hid indeed
Within the centre.

KING CLAUDIUS: How may we try it further?

POLONIUS: You know sometimes he walks four hours together
Here in the lobby.

QUEEN GETRUDE: So he does indeed.

POLONIUS: At such a time I'll loose my daughter to him.
Be you and I behind an arras then.
Mark the encounter. If he love her not,
And he not from his reason fall'n thereon
Let me be no assistant for a state,

But keep a farm and carters.

KING CLAUDIUS: We will try it.
Enter Hamlet, Reading on a Book.

QUEEN GETRUDE: But look where sadly the poor wretch comes reading.

POLONIUS: Away, I do beseech you, both away
I'll board him presently. O, give me leave.
Exeunt King and Queen, With Attendants.
How does my good Lord Hamlet?

HAMLET: Well, God-a-mercy.

POLONIUS: Do you know me, my lord?

HAMLET: Excellent well. You are a fishmonger.

POLONIUS: Not I, my lord.

HAMLET: Then I would you were so honest a man.

POLONIUS: Honest, my lord?

HAMLET: Ay, sir. To be honest, as this world goes, is to be one man pick'd out of ten thousand.

POLONIUS: That's very true, my lord.

HAMLET: For if the sun breed maggots in a dead dog, being a god kissing carrion- Have you a daughter?

POLONIUS: I have, my lord.

HAMLET: Let her not walk i' th' sun. Conception is a blessing, but not as your daughter may conceive. Friend, look to't.

POLONIUS: *Aside* How say you by that? Still harping on my daughter. Yet he knew me not at first. He said I was a fishmonger. He is far gone, far gone! And truly in my youth I suff'red much extremity for love- very near this. I'll speak to him again.- What do you read, my lord?

HAMLET: Words, words, words.

POLONIUS: What is the matter, my lord?

HAMLET: Between who?

POLONIUS: I mean, the matter that you read, my lord.

HAMLET: Slanders, sir; for the satirical rogue says here that old men have grey beards; that their faces are wrinkled; their eyes purging thick amber and plum-tree gum; and that they have a plentiful lack of wit, together with most weak hams. All which, sir, though I most powerfully and potently believe, yet I hold it not honesty to have it thus set down; for you yourself, sir, should be old as I am if, like a crab, you could go backward.

POLONIUS: *Aside* Though this be madness, yet there is a method in't.- Will You walk out of the air, my lord?

HAMLET: Into my grave?

POLONIUS: Indeed, that is out o' th' air. *Aside* How pregnant sometimes his replies are! a happiness that often madness hits on, which reason and sanity could not so prosperously be delivered of. I will leave him and suddenly contrive the means of meeting between him and my daughter.- My honourable lord, I will most humbly take my leave of you.

HAMLET: You cannot, sir, take from me anything that I will more willingly part withal- except my life, except my life, except my life.
   Enter Rosencrantz and Guildenstern.

POLONIUS: Fare you well, my lord.

HAMLET: These tedious old fools!

POLONIUS: You go to seek the Lord Hamlet. There he is.

ROSENCRANTZ: *To Polonius* God save you, sir!
Exit Polonius.

GUILDENSTERN: My honour'd lord!

ROSENCRANTZ: My most dear lord!

HAMLET: My excellent good friends! How dost thou, Guildenstern? Ah, Rosencrantz! Good lads, how do ye both?

ROSENCRANTZ: As the indifferent children of the earth.

GUILDENSTERN: Happy in that we are not over-happy. On Fortune's cap we are not the very button.

HAMLET: Nor the soles of her shoe?

ROSENCRANTZ: Neither, my lord.

HAMLET: Then you live about her waist, or in the middle of her favours?

GUILDENSTERN: Faith, her privates we.

HAMLET: In the secret parts of Fortune? O! most true! she is a strumpet. What news?

ROSENCRANTZ: None, my lord, but that the world's grown honest.

HAMLET: Then is doomsday near! But your news is not true. Let me question more in particular. What have you, my good friends, deserved at the hands of Fortune that she sends you to prison hither?

GUILDENSTERN: Prison, my lord?

HAMLET: Denmark's a prison.

ROSENCRANTZ: Then is the world one.

HAMLET: A goodly one; in which there are many confines, wards, and dungeons, Denmark being one o' th' worst.

ROSENCRANTZ: We think not so, my lord.

HAMLET: Why, then 'tis none to you; for there is nothing either good or bad but thinking makes it so. To me it is a prison.

ROSENCRANTZ: Why, then your ambition makes it one. 'Tis too narrow for your mind.

HAMLET: O God, I could be bounded in a nutshell and count myself a king of infinite space, were it not that I have bad dreams.

GUILDENSTERN: Which dreams indeed are ambition; for the very substance of the ambitious is merely the shadow of a dream.

HAMLET: A dream itself is but a shadow.

ROSENCRANTZ: Truly, and I hold ambition of so airy and light a quality that it is but a shadow's shadow.

HAMLET: Then are our beggars bodies, and our monarchs and outstretch'd heroes the beggars' shadows. Shall we to th' court? for, by my fay, I cannot reason.

BOTH: We'll wait upon you.

HAMLET: No such matter! I will not sort you with the rest of my servants; for, to speak to you like an honest man, I am most dreadfully attended. But in the beaten way of friendship, what make you at Elsinore?

ROSENCRANTZ: To visit you, my lord; no other occasion.

HAMLET: Beggar that I am, I am even poor in thanks; but I thank you; and sure, dear friends, my thanks are too dear a halfpenny. Were you not sent for? Is it your own inclining? Is it a free visitation? Come, deal justly with me. Come, come! Nay, speak.

GUILDENSTERN: What should we say, my lord?

HAMLET: Why, anything- but to th' purpose. You were sent for; and there is a kind of confession in your looks, which your modesties have not craft enough to colour. I know the good King and Queen have sent for you.

ROSENCRANTZ: To what end, my lord?

HAMLET: That you must teach me. But let me conjure you by the rights of our fellowship, by the consonancy of our youth, by the obligation of our ever-preserved love, and by what more dear a better proposer could charge you withal, be even and direct with me, whether you were sent for or no.

ROSENCRANTZ: *Aside to Guildenstern* What say you?

HAMLET: *Aside* Nay then, I have an eye of you.- If you love me, hold not off.

GUILDENSTERN: My lord, we were sent for.

HAMLET: I will tell you why. So shall my anticipation prevent your discovery, and your secrecy to the King and Queen moult no feather. I have of late- but wherefore I know not- lost all my mirth, forgone all custom of exercises; and indeed, it goes so heavily with my disposition that this goodly frame, the earth, seems to me a sterile promontory; this most excellent canopy, the air, look you, this brave o'erhanging firmament, this majestical roof fretted with golden fire- why, it appeareth no other thing to me than a foul and pestilent congregation of vapours. What a piece of work is a man! how noble in reason! how infinite in faculties! in form and moving how express and admirable! in action how like an angel! in apprehension how like a god! the beauty of the world, the paragon of animals! And yet to me what is this quintessence of dust? Man delights not me- no, nor woman neither, though by your smiling you seem to say so.

ROSENCRANTZ: My lord, there was no such stuff in my thoughts.

HAMLET: Why did you laugh then, when I said 'Man delights not me'?

ROSENCRANTZ: To think, my lord, if you delight not in man, what lenten entertainment the players shall receive from you. We coted them on the way, and hither are they coming to offer you service.

HAMLET: He that plays the king shall be welcome- his Majesty shall have tribute of me; the adventurous knight shall use his foil and target; the lover shall not sigh gratis; the humorous man shall end his part in peace; the clown shall make those laugh whose lungs are tickle o' th' sere; and the lady shall say her mind freely, or the blank verse shall halt fort. What players are they?

ROSENCRANTZ: Even those you were wont to take such delight in, the tragedians of the city.

HAMLET: How chances it they travel? Their residence, both in reputation and profit, was better both ways.

ROSENCRANTZ: I think their inhibition comes by the means of the late innovation.

HAMLET: Do they hold the same estimation they did when I was in the city? Are they so follow'd?

ROSENCRANTZ: No indeed are they not.

HAMLET: How comes it? Do they grow rusty?

ROSENCRANTZ: Nay, their endeavour keeps in the wonted pace; but there is, sir, an eyrie of children, little eyases, that cry out on the top of question and are most tyrannically clapp'd fort. These are now the fashion, and so berattle the common stages (so they call them) that many wearing rapiers are afraid of goosequills and dare scarce come thither.

HAMLET: What, are they children? Who maintains 'em? How are they escoted? Will they pursue the quality no longer than they can sing? Will they not say afterwards, if they should grow themselves to common players (as it is most like, if their means are no better), their writers do them wrong to make them exclaim against their own succession.

ROSENCRANTZ: Faith, there has been much to do on both sides; and the nation holds it no sin to tarre them to controversy. There was, for a while, no money bid for argument unless the poet and the player went to cuffs in the question.

HAMLET: Is't possible?

GUILDENSTERN: O, there has been much throwing about of brains.

HAMLET: Do the boys carry it away?

ROSENCRANTZ: Ay, that they do, my lord- Hercules and his load too.

HAMLET: It is not very strange; for my uncle is King of Denmark, and those that would make mows at him while my father lived give twenty, forty, fifty, a hundred ducats apiece for his picture in

little. 'Sblood, there is something in this more than natural, if philosophy could find it out.
Flourish for the Players.

GUILDENSTERN: There are the players.

HAMLET: Gentlemen, you are welcome to Elsinore. Your hands, come! Th' appurtenance of welcome is fashion and ceremony. Let me comply with you in this garb, lest my extent to the players (which I tell you must show fairly outwards) should more appear like entertainment than yours. You are welcome. But my uncle-father and aunt-mother are deceiv'd.

GUILDENSTERN: In what, my dear lord?

HAMLET: I am but mad north-north-west. When the wind is southerly I know a hawk from a handsaw.
Enter Polonius.

POLONIUS: Well be with you, gentlemen!

HAMLET: Hark you, Guildenstern- and you too- at each ear a hearer! That great baby you see there is not yet out of his swaddling clouts.

ROSENCRANTZ: Happily he's the second time come to them; for they say an old man is twice a child.

HAMLET: I will prophesy he comes to tell me of the players. Mark it.- You say right, sir; a Monday morning; twas so indeed.

POLONIUS: My lord, I have news to tell you.

HAMLET: My lord, I have news to tell you. When Roscius was an actor in Rome-

POLONIUS: The actors are come hither, my lord.

HAMLET: Buzz, buzz!

POLONIUS: Upon my honour–

HAMLET: Then came each actor on his ass–

POLONIUS: The best actors in the world, either for tragedy, comedy, history, pastoral, pastoral-comical, historical-pastoral, tragical-historical, tragical-comical-historical-pastoral; scene individable, or poem unlimited. Seneca cannot be too heavy, nor Plautus too light. For the law of writ and the liberty, these are the only men.

HAMLET: O Jephthah, judge of Israel, what a treasure hadst thou!

POLONIUS: What treasure had he, my lord?

HAMLET: Why,
    'One fair daughter, and no more,
      The which he loved passing well.'

POLONIUS: *Aside* Still on my daughter.

HAMLET: Am I not i' th' right, old Jephthah?

POLONIUS: If you call me Jephthah, my lord, I have a daughter that I love passing well.

HAMLET: Nay, that follows not.

POLONIUS: What follows then, my lord?

HAMLET: Why,
'As by lot, God wot,'
and then, you know,
'It came to pass, as most like it was.'
The first row of the pious chanson will show you more;

for look where my abridgment comes.
Enter Four or Five Players.
You are welcome, masters; welcome, all.- I am glad to see thee well.- Welcome, good friends.- O, my old friend? Why, thy face is valanc'd since I saw thee last. Com'st' thou to' beard me in Denmark?- What, my young lady and mistress? By'r Lady, your ladyship is nearer to heaven than when I saw you last by the altitude of a chopine. Pray God your voice, like a piece of uncurrent gold, be not crack'd within the ring.- Masters, you are all welcome. We'll e'en to't like French falconers, fly at anything we see. We'll have a speech straight. Come, give us a taste of your quality. Come, a passionate speech.

FIRST PLAYER: What speech, my good lord?

HAMLET: I heard thee speak me a speech once, but it was never acted; or if it was, not above once; for the play, I remember, pleas'd not the million, 'twas caviary to the general; but it was (as I receiv'd it, and others, whose judgments in such matters cried in the top of mine) an excellent play, well digested in the scenes, set down with as much modesty as cunning. I remember one said there were no sallets in the lines to make the matter savoury, nor no matter in the phrase that might indict the author of affectation; but call'd it an honest method, as wholesome as sweet, and by very much more handsome than fine. One speech in't I chiefly lov'd. 'Twas AEneas' tale to Dido, and thereabout of it especially where he speaks of Priam's slaughter. If it live in your memory, begin at this line- let me see, let me see:
'The rugged Pyrrhus, like th' Hyrcanian beast-'
'Tis not so; it begins with Pyrrhus:
    'The rugged Pyrrhus, he whose sable arms,
    Black as his purpose, did the night resemble
    When he lay couched in the ominous horse,
    Hath now this dread and black complexion smear'd
    With heraldry more dismal. Head to foot
    Now is be total gules, horridly trick'd
    With blood of fathers, mothers, daughters, sons,
    Bak'd and impasted with the parching streets,

           That lend a tyrannous and a damned light
           To their lord's murther. Roasted in wrath and fire,
           And thus o'ersized with coagulate gore,
           With eyes like carbuncles, the hellish Pyrrhus
           Old grandsire Priam seeks.'
So, proceed you.

POLONIUS: Fore God, my lord, well spoken, with good accent and good discretion.

FIRST PLAYER: 'Anon he finds him,
   Striking too short at Greeks. His antique sword,
   Rebellious to his arm, lies where it falls,
   Repugnant to command. Unequal match'd,
   Pyrrhus at Priam drives, in rage strikes wide;
   But with the whiff and wind of his fell sword
   Th' unnerved father falls. Then senseless Ilium,
   Seeming to feel this blow, with flaming top
   Stoops to his base, and with a hideous crash
   Takes prisoner Pyrrhus' ear. For lo! his sword,
   Which was declining on the milky head
   Of reverend Priam, seem'd i' th' air to stick.
   So, as a painted tyrant, Pyrrhus stood,
   And, like a neutral to his will and matter, did nothing.
   But, as we often see, against some storm,
   A silence in the heavens, the rack stand still,
   The bold winds speechless, and the orb below
   As hush as death- anon the dreadful thunder
   Doth rend the region; so, after Pyrrhus' pause,
   Aroused vengeance sets him new awork;
   And never did the Cyclops' hammers fall
   On Mars's armour, forg'd for proof eterne,
   With less remorse than Pyrrhus' bleeding sword
   Now falls on Priam.
   Out, out, thou strumpet Fortune! All you gods,
   In general synod take away her power;
   Break all the spokes and fellies from her wheel,
   And bowl the round nave down the hill of heaven,

As low as to the fiends!

POLONIUS: This is too long.

HAMLET: It shall to the barber's, with your beard.- Prithee say on. He's for a jig or a tale of bawdry, or he sleeps. Say on; come to Hecuba.

FIRST PLAYER: 'But who, O who, had seen the mobled queen-'

HAMLET: 'The mobled queen'?

POLONIUS: That's good! 'Mobled queen' is good.

FIRST PLAYER: 'Run barefoot up and down, threat'ning the flames
With bisson rheum; a clout upon that head
Where late the diadem stood, and for a robe,
About her lank and all o'erteemed loins,
A blanket, in the alarm of fear caught up-
Who this had seen, with tongue in venom steep'd
'Gainst Fortune's state would treason have pronounc'd.
But if the gods themselves did see her then,
When she saw Pyrrhus make malicious sport
In Mincing with his sword her husband's limbs,
The instant burst of clamour that she made
(Unless things mortal move them not at all)
Would have made milch the burning eyes of heaven
And passion in the gods.'

POLONIUS: Look, whe'r he has not turn'd his colour, and has tears in's eyes. Prithee no more!

HAMLET: 'Tis well. I'll have thee speak out the rest of this soon.- Good my lord, will you see the players well bestow'd? Do you hear? Let them be well us'd; for they are the abstract and brief chronicles of the time. After your death you were better have a bad epitaph than their ill report while you live.

POLONIUS: My lord, I will use them according to their desert.

HAMLET: God's bodykins, man, much better! Use every man after his desert, and who should scape whipping? Use them after your own honour and dignity. The less they deserve, the more merit is in your bounty. Take them in.

POLONIUS: Come, sirs.

HAMLET: Follow him, friends. We'll hear a play to-morrow.
   Exeunt Polonius and Players Except the First.
Dost thou hear me, old friend? Can you play 'The Murther of Gonzago'?

FIRST PLAYER: Ay, my lord.

HAMLET: We'll ha't to-morrow night. You could, for a need, study a speech of some dozen or sixteen lines which I would set down and insert in't, could you not?

FIRST PLAYER: Ay, my lord.

HAMLET: Very well. Follow that lord- and look you mock him not.
   Exit First Player.
My good friends, I'll leave you till night. You are welcome to Elsinore.

ROSENCRANTZ: Good my lord!

HAMLET: Ay, so, God b' wi' ye!
   Exeunt Rosencrantz and Guildenstern
Now I am alone.
O what a rogue and peasant slave am I!
Is it not monstrous that this player here,
But in a fiction, in a dream of passion,
Could force his soul so to his own conceit
That, from her working, all his visage wann'd,
Tears in his eyes, distraction in's aspect,
A broken voice, and his whole function suiting

With forms to his conceit? And all for nothing!
For Hecuba!
What's Hecuba to him, or he to Hecuba,
That he should weep for her? What would he do,
Had he the motive and the cue for passion
That I have? He would drown the stage with tears
And cleave the general ear with horrid speech;
Make mad the guilty and appal the free,
Confound the ignorant, and amaze indeed
The very faculties of eyes and ears.
Yet I, a dull and muddy-mettled rascal, peak
Like John-a-dreams, unpregnant of my cause,
And can say nothing! No, not for a king,
Upon whose property and most dear life
A damn'd defeat was made. Am I a coward?
Who calls me villain? breaks my pate across?
Plucks off my beard and blows it in my face?
Tweaks me by th' nose? gives me the lie i' th' throat
As deep as to the lungs? Who does me this, ha?
'Swounds, I should take it! for it cannot be
But I am pigeon-liver'd and lack gall
To make oppression bitter, or ere this
I should have fatted all the region kites
With this slave's offal. Bloody bawdy villain!
Remorseless, treacherous, lecherous, kindless villain!
O, vengeance! Why, what an ass am I! This is most brave,
That I, the son of a dear father murther'd,
Prompted to my revenge by heaven and hell,
Must (like a whore) unpack my heart with words
And fall a-cursing like a very drab, a scullion!
Fie upon't! foh! About, my brain! Hum, I have heard
That guilty creatures, sitting at a play,
Have by the very cunning of the scene
Been struck so to the soul that presently
They have proclaim'd their malefactions;
For murther, though it have no tongue, will speak
With most miraculous organ, I'll have these Players
Play something like the murther of my father

Before mine uncle. I'll observe his looks;
I'll tent him to the quick. If he but blench,
I know my course. The spirit that I have seen
May be a devil; and the devil hath power
T' assume a pleasing shape; yea, and perhaps
Out of my weakness and my melancholy,
As he is very potent with such spirits,
Abuses me to damn me. I'll have grounds
More relative than this. The play's the thing
Wherein I'll catch the conscience of the King.
   Exit.

ACT III. SCENE I. Elsinore. A Room in the Castle.
Enter King, Queen, Polonius, Ophelia, Rosencrantz, Guildenstern, and Lords.

KING CLAUDIUS: And can you by no drift of circumstance
Get from him why he puts on this confusion,
Grating so harshly all his days of quiet
With turbulent and dangerous lunacy?

ROSENCRANTZ: He does confess he feels himself distracted,
But from what cause he will by no means speak.

GUILDENSTERN: Nor do we find him forward to be sounded,
But with a crafty madness keeps aloof
When we would bring him on to some confession
Of his true state.

QUEEN GETRUDE: Did he receive you well?

ROSENCRANTZ: Most like a gentleman.

GUILDENSTERN: But with much forcing of his disposition.

ROSENCRANTZ: Niggard of question, but of our demands
Most free in his reply.

QUEEN GETRUDE: Did you assay him
To any pastime?

ROSENCRANTZ: Madam, it so fell out that certain players
We o'erraught on the way. Of these we told him,
And there did seem in him a kind of joy
To hear of it. They are here about the court,
And, as I think, they have already order
This night to play before him.

POLONIUS: 'Tis most true;
And he beseech'd me to entreat your Majesties
To hear and see the matter.

KING CLAUDIUS: With all my heart, and it doth much content me
To hear him so inclin'd.
Good gentlemen, give him a further edge
And drive his purpose on to these delights.

ROSENCRANTZ: We shall, my lord.
  Exeunt Rosencrantz and Guildenstern.

KING CLAUDIUS: Sweet Gertrude, leave us too;
For we have closely sent for Hamlet hither,
That he, as 'twere by accident, may here
Affront Ophelia.
Her father and myself (lawful espials)
Will so bestow ourselves that, seeing unseen,
We may of their encounter frankly judge
And gather by him, as he is behav'd,
If't be th' affliction of his love, or no,
That thus he suffers for.

QUEEN GETRUDE: I shall obey you;
And for your part, Ophelia, I do wish
That your good beauties be the happy cause
Of Hamlet's wildness. So shall I hope your virtues

Will bring him to his wonted way again,
To both your honours.

OPHELIA: Madam, I wish it may.
Exit Queen.

POLONIUS: Ophelia, walk you here.- Gracious, so please you,
We will bestow ourselves.- *To Ophelia* Read on this book,
That show of such an exercise may colour
Your loneliness.- We are oft to blame in this,
'Tis too much prov'd, that with devotion's visage
And pious action we do sugar o'er
The Devil himself.

KING CLAUDIUS: *Aside* O, 'tis too true!
How smart a lash that speech doth give my conscience!
The harlot's cheek, beautied with plast'ring art,
Is not more ugly to the thing that helps it
Than is my deed to my most painted word.
O heavy burthen!

POLONIUS: I hear him coming. Let's withdraw, my lord.
Exeunt King and Polonius.
Enter Hamlet.

HAMLET: To be, or not to be- that is the question:
Whether 'tis nobler in the mind to suffer
The slings and arrows of outrageous fortune
Or to take arms against a sea of troubles,
And by opposing end them. To die- to sleep-
No more; and by a sleep to say we end
The heartache, and the thousand natural shocks
That flesh is heir to. 'Tis a consummation
Devoutly to be wish'd. To die- to sleep.
To sleep- perchance to dream: ay, there's the rub!
For in that sleep of death what dreams may come
When we have shuffled off this mortal coil,
Must give us pause. There's the respect

That makes calamity of so long life.
For who would bear the whips and scorns of time,
Th' oppressor's wrong, the proud man's contumely,
The pangs of despis'd love, the law's delay,
The insolence of office, and the spurns
That patient merit of th' unworthy takes,
When he himself might his quietus make
With a bare bodkin? Who would these fardels bear,
To grunt and sweat under a weary life,
But that the dread of something after death-
The undiscover'd country, from whose bourn
No traveller returns- puzzles the will,
And makes us rather bear those ills we have
Than fly to others that we know not of?
Thus conscience does make cowards of us all,
And thus the native hue of resolution
Is sicklied o'er with the pale cast of thought,
And enterprises of great pith and moment
With this regard their currents turn awry
And lose the name of action.- Soft you now!
The fair Ophelia!- Nymph, in thy orisons
Be all my sins rememb'red.

OPHELIA: Good my lord,
How does your honour for this many a day?

HAMLET: I humbly thank you; well, well, well.

OPHELIA: My lord, I have remembrances of yours
That I have longed long to re-deliver.
I pray you, now receive them.

HAMLET: No, not I!
I never gave you aught.

OPHELIA: My honour'd lord, you know right well you did,
And with them words of so sweet breath compos'd
As made the things more rich. Their perfume lost,

Take these again; for to the noble mind
Rich gifts wax poor when givers prove unkind.
There, my lord.

HAMLET: Ha, ha! Are you honest?

OPHELIA: My lord?

HAMLET: Are you fair?

OPHELIA: What means your lordship?

HAMLET: That if you be honest and fair, your honesty should admit no discourse to your beauty.

OPHELIA: Could beauty, my lord, have better commerce than with honesty?

HAMLET: Ay, truly; for the power of beauty will sooner transform honesty from what it is to a bawd than the force of honesty can translate beauty into his likeness. This was sometime a paradox, but now the time gives it proof. I did love you once.

OPHELIA: Indeed, my lord, you made me believe so.

HAMLET: You should not have believ'd me; for virtue cannot so inoculate our old stock but we shall relish of it. I loved you not.

OPHELIA: I was the more deceived.

HAMLET: Get thee to a nunnery! Why wouldst thou be a breeder of sinners? I am myself indifferent honest, but yet I could accuse me of such things that it were better my mother had not borne me. I am very proud, revengeful, ambitious; with more offences at my beck than I have thoughts to put them in, imagination to give them shape, or time to act them in. What should such fellows as I do, crawling between earth and heaven? We are arrant knaves all;

believe none of us. Go thy ways to a nunnery. Where's your father?

OPHELIA: At home, my lord.

HAMLET: Let the doors be shut upon him, that he may play the fool nowhere but in's own house. Farewell.

OPHELIA: O, help him, you sweet heavens!

HAMLET: If thou dost marry, I'll give thee this plague for thy dowry: be thou as chaste as ice, as pure as snow, thou shalt not escape calumny. Get thee to a nunnery. Go, farewell. Or if thou wilt needs marry, marry a fool; for wise men know well enough what monsters you make of them. To a nunnery, go; and quickly too. Farewell.

OPHELIA: O heavenly powers, restore him!

HAMLET: I have heard of your paintings too, well enough. God hath given you one face, and you make yourselves another. You jig, you amble, and you lisp; you nickname God's creatures and make your wantonness your ignorance. Go to, I'll no more on't! it hath made me mad. I say, we will have no moe marriages. Those that are married already- all but one- shall live; the rest shall keep as they are. To a nunnery, go.
   Exit.

OPHELIA: O, what a noble mind is here o'erthrown!
The courtier's, scholar's, soldier's, eye, tongue, sword,
Th' expectancy and rose of the fair state,
The glass of fashion and the mould of form,
Th' observ'd of all observers- quite, quite down!
And I, of ladies most deject and wretched,
That suck'd the honey of his music vows,
Now see that noble and most sovereign reason,
Like sweet bells jangled, out of tune and harsh;

That unmatch'd form and feature of blown youth
Blasted with ecstasy. O, woe is me
T' have seen what I have seen, see what I see!
Enter King and Polonius.

KING CLAUDIUS: Love? his affections do not that way tend;
Nor what he spake, though it lack'd form a little,
Was not like madness. There's something in his soul
O'er which his melancholy sits on brood;
And I do doubt the hatch and the disclose
Will be some danger; which for to prevent,
I have in quick determination
Thus set it down: he shall with speed to England
For the demand of our neglected tribute.
Haply the seas, and countries different,
With variable objects, shall expel
This something-settled matter in his heart,
Whereon his brains still beating puts him thus
From fashion of himself. What think you on't?

POLONIUS: It shall do well. But yet do I believe
The origin and commencement of his grief
Sprung from neglected love.- How now, Ophelia?
You need not tell us what Lord Hamlet said.
We heard it all.- My lord, do as you please;
But if you hold it fit, after the play
Let his queen mother all alone entreat him
To show his grief. Let her be round with him;
And I'll be plac'd so please you, in the ear
Of all their conference. If she find him not,
To England send him; or confine him where
Your wisdom best shall think.

KING CLAUDIUS: It shall be so.
Madness in great ones must not unwatch'd go.
Exeunt.

ACT III. SCENE II. Elsinore. Hall in the Castle.

Enter Hamlet and Three of the Players.

HAMLET: Speak the speech, I pray you, as I pronounc'd it to you, trippingly on the tongue. But if you mouth it, as many of our players do, I had as live the town crier spoke my lines. Nor do not saw the air too much with your hand, thus, but use all gently; for in the very torrent, tempest, and (as I may say) whirlwind of your passion, you must acquire and beget a temperance that may give it smoothness. O, it offends me to the soul to hear a robustious periwig-pated fellow tear a passion to tatters, to very rags, to split the cars of the groundlings, who (for the most part) are capable of nothing but inexplicable dumb shows and noise. I would have such a fellow whipp'd for o'erdoing Termagant. It out-herods Herod. Pray you avoid it.

PLAYER: I warrant your honour.

HAMLET: Be not too tame neither; but let your own discretion be your tutor. Suit the action to the word, the word to the action; with this special observance, that you o'erstep not the modesty of nature: for anything so overdone is from the purpose of playing, whose end, both at the first and now, was and is, to hold, as 'twere, the mirror up to nature; to show Virtue her own feature, scorn her own image, and the very age and body of the time his form and pressure. Now this overdone, or come tardy off, though it make the unskilful laugh, cannot but make the judicious grieve; the censure of the which one must in your allowance o'erweigh a whole theatre of others. O, there be players that I have seen play, and heard others praise, and that highly (not to speak it profanely), that, neither having the accent of Christians, nor the gait of Christian, pagan, nor man, have so strutted and bellowed that I have thought some of Nature's journeymen had made men, and not made them well, they imitated humanity so abominably.

PLAYER: I hope we have reform'd that indifferently with us, sir.

HAMLET: O, reform it altogether! And let those that play your clowns

speak no more than is set down for them. For there be of them that will themselves laugh, to set on some quantity of barren spectators to laugh too, though in the mean time some necessary question of the play be then to be considered. That's villanous and shows a most pitiful ambition in the fool that uses it. Go make you ready.
Exeunt Players.
Enter Polonius, Rosencrantz, and Guildenstern.
How now, my lord? Will the King hear this piece of work?

POLONIUS: And the Queen too, and that presently.

HAMLET: Bid the players make haste,
Exit Polonius.
Will you two help to hasten them?

BOTH: We will, my lord.
Exeunt They Two.

HAMLET: What, ho, Horatio!
Enter Horatio.

HORATIO: Here, sweet lord, at your service.

HAMLET: Horatio, thou art e'en as just a man
As e'er my conversation cop'd withal.

HORATIO: O, my dear lord!

HAMLET: Nay, do not think I flatter;
For what advancement may I hope from thee,
That no revenue hast but thy good spirits
To feed and clothe thee? Why should the poor be flatter'd?
No, let the candied tongue lick absurd pomp,
And crook the pregnant hinges of the knee
Where thrift may follow fawning. Dost thou hear?
Since my dear soul was mistress of her choice

And could of men distinguish, her election
Hath scald thee for herself. For thou hast been
As one, in suff'ring all, that suffers nothing;
A man that Fortune's buffets and rewards
Hast ta'en with equal thanks; and blest are those
Whose blood and judgment are so well commingled
That they are not a pipe for Fortune's finger
To sound what stop she please. Give me that man
That is not passion's slave, and I will wear him
In my heart's core, ay, in my heart of heart,
As I do thee. Something too much of this I
There is a play to-night before the King.
One scene of it comes near the circumstance,
Which I have told thee, of my father's death.
I prithee, when thou seest that act afoot,
Even with the very comment of thy soul
Observe my uncle. If his occulted guilt
Do not itself unkennel in one speech,
It is a damned ghost that we have seen,
And my imaginations are as foul
As Vulcan's stithy. Give him heedful note;
For I mine eyes will rivet to his face,
And after we will both our judgments join
In censure of his seeming.

HORATIO: Well, my lord.
If he steal aught the whilst this play is playing,
And scape detecting, I will pay the theft.

Sound a Flourish. Enter Trumpets and Kettledrums. Danish March. Enter King, Queen, Polonius, Ophelia, Rosencrantz, Guildenstern, and Other Lords Attendant, with the Guard Carrying Torches.

HAMLET: They are coming to the play. I must be idle.
Get you a place.

KING CLAUDIUS: How fares our cousin Hamlet?

HAMLET: Excellent, i' faith; of the chameleon's dish. I eat the air, promise-cramm'd. You cannot feed capons so.

KING CLAUDIUS: I have nothing with this answer, Hamlet. These words are not mine.

HAMLET: No, nor mine now. *To Polonius* My lord, you play'd once i' th' university, you say?

POLONIUS: That did I, my lord, and was accounted a good actor.

HAMLET: What did you enact?

POLONIUS: I did enact Julius Caesar; I was kill'd i' th' Capitol; Brutus kill'd me.

HAMLET: It was a brute part of him to kill so capital a calf there. Be the players ready.

ROSENCRANTZ: Ay, my lord. They stay upon your patience.

QUEEN GETRUDE: Come hither, my dear Hamlet, sit by me.

HAMLET: No, good mother. Here's metal more attractive.

POLONIUS: *To the King* O, ho! do you mark that?

HAMLET: Lady, shall I lie in your lap?
Sits down at Ophelia's Feet.

OPHELIA: No, my lord.

HAMLET: I mean, my head upon your lap?

OPHELIA: Ay, my lord.

HAMLET: Do you think I meant country matters?

OPHELIA: I think nothing, my lord.

HAMLET: That's a fair thought to lie between maids' legs.

OPHELIA: What is, my lord?

HAMLET: Nothing.

OPHELIA: You are merry, my lord.

HAMLET: Who, I?

OPHELIA: Ay, my lord.

HAMLET: O God, your only jig-maker!
What should a man do but be merry?
For look you how cheerfully my mother looks, and my father died within 's two hours.

OPHELIA: Nay 'tis twice two months, my lord.

HAMLET: So long? Nay then, let the devil wear black, for I'll have a suit of sables. O heavens! die two months ago, and not forgotten yet? Then there's hope a great man's memory may outlive his life half a year. But, by'r Lady, he must build churches then; or else shall he suffer not thinking on, with the hobby-horse, whose epitaph is 'For O, for O, the hobby-horse is forgot!'
Hautboys play. The dumb show enters.
  Enter a King and a Queen very lovingly; the Queen embracing him and he her. She kneels, and makes show of protestation unto him. He takes her up, and declines his head upon her neck. He lays him down upon a bank of flowers. She, seeing him asleep, leaves him. Anon comes in a fellow, takes off his crown, kisses it, pours poison in the sleeper's ears, and leaves him. The Queen returns, finds the King dead, and makes passionate action. The Poisoner with some three or four Mutes, comes in again, seem to condole with her. The dead body is carried away. The Poisoner wooes the Queen with gifts; she seems harsh and unwilling awhile, but in the end accepts his love.

Exeunt.

OPHELIA: What means this, my lord?

HAMLET: Marry, this is miching malhecho; it means mischief.

OPHELIA: Belike this show imports the argument of the play.
Enter Prologue.

HAMLET: We shall know by this fellow. The players cannot keep counsel; they'll tell all.

OPHELIA: Will he tell us what this show meant?

HAMLET: Ay, or any show that you'll show him. Be not you asham'd to show, he'll not shame to tell you what it means.

OPHELIA: You are naught, you are naught! I'll mark the play.

PROLOGUE
For us, and for our tragedy,
Here stooping to your clemency,
We beg your hearing patiently.
Exit.

HAMLET: Is this a prologue, or the posy of a ring?

OPHELIA: 'Tis brief, my lord.

HAMLET: As woman's love.
Enter Two Players as King and Queen.

PLAYER KING: Full thirty times hath Phoebus' cart gone round
Neptune's salt wash and Tellus' orbed ground,
And thirty dozed moons with borrowed sheen
About the world have times twelve thirties been,
Since love our hearts, and Hymen did our hands,

Unite comutual in most sacred bands.

PLAYER QUEEN: So many journeys may the sun and moon
Make us again count o'er ere love be done!
But woe is me! you are so sick of late,
So far from cheer and from your former state.
That I distrust you. Yet, though I distrust,
Discomfort you, my lord, it nothing must;
For women's fear and love holds quantity,
In neither aught, or in extremity.
Now what my love is, proof hath made you know;
And as my love is siz'd, my fear is so.
Where love is great, the littlest doubts are fear;
Where little fears grow great, great love grows there.

PLAYER KING: Faith, I must leave thee, love, and shortly too;
My operant powers their functions leave to do.
And thou shalt live in this fair world behind,
Honour'd, belov'd, and haply one as kind
For husband shalt thou-

PLAYER QUEEN: O, confound the rest!
Such love must needs be treason in my breast.
When second husband let me be accurst!
None wed the second but who killed the first.

HAMLET: *Aside* Wormwood, wormwood!

PLAYER QUEEN: The instances that second marriage move
Are base respects of thrift, but none of love.
A second time I kill my husband dead
When second husband kisses me in bed.

PLAYER KING: I do believe you think what now you speak;
But what we do determine oft we break.
Purpose is but the slave to memory,
Of violent birth, but poor validity;
Which now, like fruit unripe, sticks on the tree,

But fill unshaken when they mellow be.
Most necessary 'tis that we forget
To pay ourselves what to ourselves is debt.
What to ourselves in passion we propose,
The passion ending, doth the purpose lose.
The violence of either grief or joy
Their own enactures with themselves destroy.
Where joy most revels, grief doth most lament;
Grief joys, joy grieves, on slender accident.
This world is not for aye, nor 'tis not strange
That even our loves should with our fortunes change;
For 'tis a question left us yet to prove,
Whether love lead fortune, or else fortune love.
The great man down, you mark his favourite flies,
The poor advanc'd makes friends of enemies;
And hitherto doth love on fortune tend,
For who not needs shall never lack a friend,
And who in want a hollow friend doth try,
Directly seasons him his enemy.
But, orderly to end where I begun,
Our wills and fates do so contrary run
That our devices still are overthrown;
Our thoughts are ours, their ends none of our own.
So think thou wilt no second husband wed;
But die thy thoughts when thy first lord is dead.

PLAYER QUEEN: Nor earth to me give food, nor heaven light,
Sport and repose lock from me day and night,
To desperation turn my trust and hope,
An anchor's cheer in prison be my scope,
Each opposite that blanks the face of joy
Meet what I would have well, and it destroy,
Both here and hence pursue me lasting strife,
If, once a widow, ever I be wife!

HAMLET: If she should break it now!

PLAYER KING: 'Tis deeply sworn. Sweet, leave me here awhile.

My spirits grow dull, and fain I would beguile
The tedious day with sleep.

PLAYER QUEEN: Sleep rock thy brain,
He sleeps.
And never come mischance between us twain!
Exit.

HAMLET: Madam, how like you this play?

QUEEN GETRUDE: The lady doth protest too much, methinks.

HAMLET: O, but she'll keep her word.

KING CLAUDIUS: Have you heard the argument? Is there no offence in't?

HAMLET: No, no! They do but jest, poison in jest; no offence i' th' world.

KING CLAUDIUS: What do you call the play?

HAMLET: 'The Mousetrap.' Marry, how? Tropically. This play is the image of a murther done in Vienna. Gonzago is the duke's name; his wife, Baptista. You shall see anon. 'Tis a knavish piece of work; but what o' that? Your Majesty, and we that have free souls, it touches us not. Let the gall'd jade winch; our withers are unwrung.
Enter Lucianus.
This is one Lucianus, nephew to the King.

OPHELIA: You are as good as a chorus, my lord.

HAMLET: I could interpret between you and your love, if I could see the puppets dallying.

OPHELIA: You are keen, my lord, you are keen.

HAMLET: It would cost you a groaning to take off my edge.

OPHELIA: Still better, and worse.

HAMLET: So you must take your husbands.- Begin, murtherer. Pox, leave thy damnable faces, and begin! Come, the croaking raven doth bellow for revenge.

LUCIANUS: Thoughts black, hands apt, drugs fit, and time agreeing;
Confederate season, else no creature seeing;
Thou mixture rank, of midnight weeds collected,
With Hecate's ban thrice blasted, thrice infected,
Thy natural magic and dire property
On wholesome life usurp immediately.
   Pours the Poison in His Ears.

HAMLET: He poisons him i' th' garden for's estate. His name's Gonzago. The story is extant, and written in very choice Italian. You shall see anon how the murtherer gets the love of Gonzago's wife.

OPHELIA: The King rises.

HAMLET: What, frighted with false fire?

QUEEN GETRUDE: How fares my lord?

POLONIUS: Give o'er the play.

KING CLAUDIUS: Give me some light! Away!

ALL: Lights, lights, lights!
   Exeunt All but Hamlet and Horatio.

HAMLET: Why, let the strucken deer go weep,
   The hart ungalled play;
   For some must watch, while some must sleep:
   Thus runs the world away.

Would not this, sir, and a forest of feathers- if the rest of my fortunes turn Turk with me-with two Provincial roses on my raz'd shoes, get me a fellowship in a cry of players, sir?

HORATIO: Half a share.

HAMLET: A whole one I!
    For thou dost know, O Damon dear,
      This realm dismantled was
    Of Jove himself; and now reigns here
      A very, very- pajock.

HORATIO: You might have rhym'd.

HAMLET: O good Horatio, I'll take the ghost's word for a thousand pound! Didst perceive?

HORATIO: Very well, my lord.

HAMLET: Upon the talk of the poisoning?

HORATIO: I did very well note him.

HAMLET: Aha! Come, some music! Come, the recorders!
    For if the King like not the comedy,
    Why then, belike he likes it not, perdy.
Come, some music!
    Enter Rosencrantz and Guildenstern.

GUILDENSTERN: Good my lord, vouchsafe me a word with you.

HAMLET: Sir, a whole history.

GUILDENSTERN: The King, sir-

HAMLET: Ay, sir, what of him?

GUILDENSTERN: Is in his retirement, marvellous distemper'd.

HAMLET: With drink, sir?

GUILDENSTERN: No, my lord; rather with choler.

HAMLET: Your wisdom should show itself more richer to signify this to the doctor; for me to put him to his purgation would perhaps plunge him into far more choler.

GUILDENSTERN: Good my lord, put your discourse into some frame, and start not so wildly from my affair.

HAMLET: I am tame, sir; pronounce.

GUILDENSTERN: The Queen, your mother, in most great affliction of spirit hath sent me to you.

HAMLET: You are welcome.

GUILDENSTERN: Nay, good my lord, this courtesy is not of the right breed. If it shall please you to make me a wholesome answer, I will do your mother's commandment; if not, your pardon and my return shall be the end of my business.

HAMLET: Sir, I cannot.

GUILDENSTERN: What, my lord?

HAMLET: Make you a wholesome answer; my wit's diseas'd. But, sir, such answer is I can make, you shall command; or rather, as you say, my mother. Therefore no more, but to the matter! My mother, you say-

ROSENCRANTZ: Then thus she says: your behaviour hath struck her into amazement and admiration.

HAMLET: O wonderful son, that can so stonish a mother! But is there no sequel at the heels of this mother's admiration? Impart.

ROSENCRANTZ: She desires to speak with you in her closet ere you go to bed.

HAMLET: We shall obey, were she ten times our mother. Have you any further trade with us?

ROSENCRANTZ: My lord, you once did love me.

HAMLET: And do still, by these pickers and stealers!

ROSENCRANTZ: Good my lord, what is your cause of distemper? You do surely bar the door upon your own liberty, if you deny your griefs to your friend.

HAMLET: Sir, I lack advancement.

ROSENCRANTZ: How can that be, when you have the voice of the King himself for your succession in Denmark?

HAMLET: Ay, sir, but 'while the grass grows'- the proverb is something musty.
  Enter the Players with Recorders.
O, the recorders! Let me see one. To withdraw with you- why do you go about to recover the wind of me, as if you would drive me into a toil?

GUILDENSTERN: O my lord, if my duty be too bold, my love is too unmannerly.

HAMLET: I do not well understand that. Will you play upon this pipe?

GUILDENSTERN: My lord, I cannot.

HAMLET: I pray you.

GUILDENSTERN: Believe me, I cannot.

HAMLET: I do beseech you.

GUILDENSTERN: I know, no touch of it, my lord.

HAMLET: It is as easy as lying. Govern these ventages with your fingers and thumbs, give it breath with your mouth, and it will discourse most eloquent music. Look you, these are the stops.

GUILDENSTERN: But these cannot I command to any utt'rance of harmony. I have not the skill.

HAMLET: Why, look you now, how unworthy a thing you make of me! You would play upon me; you would seem to know my stops; you would pluck out the heart of my mystery; you would sound me from my lowest note to the top of my compass; and there is much music, excellent voice, in this little organ, yet cannot you make it speak. 'Sblood, do you think I am easier to be play'd on than a pipe? Call me what instrument you will, though you can fret me, you cannot play upon me.
   Enter Polonius.
God bless you, sir!

POLONIUS: My lord, the Queen would speak with you, and presently.

HAMLET: Do you see yonder cloud that's almost in shape of a camel?

POLONIUS: By th' mass, and 'tis like a camel indeed.

HAMLET: Methinks it is like a weasel.

POLONIUS: It is back'd like a weasel.

HAMLET: Or like a whale.

POLONIUS: Very like a whale.

HAMLET: Then will I come to my mother by-and-by. They fool me to the top of my bent. I will come by-and-by.

POLONIUS: I will say so.
Exit.

HAMLET: 'By-and-by' is easily said.- Leave me, friends.
Exeunt All but Hamlet.
'Tis now the very witching time of night,
When churchyards yawn, and hell itself breathes out
Contagion to this world. Now could I drink hot blood
And do such bitter business as the day
Would quake to look on. Soft! now to my mother!
O heart, lose not thy nature; let not ever
The soul of Nero enter this firm bosom.
Let me be cruel, not unnatural;
I will speak daggers to her, but use none.
My tongue and soul in this be hypocrites-
How in my words somever she be shent,
To give them seals never, my soul, consent!
Exit.

ACT III. SCENE III. A Room in the Castle.
Enter King, Rosencrantz, and Guildenstern.

KING CLAUDIUS: I like him not, nor stands it safe with us
To let his madness range. Therefore prepare you;
I your commission will forthwith dispatch,
And he to England shall along with you.
The terms of our estate may not endure
Hazard so near us as doth hourly grow
Out of his lunacies.

GUILDENSTERN: We will ourselves provide.
Most holy and religious fear it is
To keep those many many bodies safe
That live and feed upon your Majesty.

ROSENCRANTZ: The single and peculiar life is bound
With all the strength and armour of the mind
To keep itself from noyance; but much more
That spirit upon whose weal depends and rests
The lives of many. The cesse of majesty
Dies not alone, but like a gulf doth draw
What's near it with it. It is a massy wheel,
Fix'd on the summit of the highest mount,
To whose huge spokes ten thousand lesser things
Are mortis'd and adjoin'd; which when it falls,
Each small annexment, petty consequence,
Attends the boist'rous ruin. Never alone
Did the king sigh, but with a general groan.

KING CLAUDIUS: Arm you, I pray you, to th', speedy voyage;
For we will fetters put upon this fear,
Which now goes too free-footed.

BOTH: We will haste us.
   Exeunt Gentlemen.
   Enter Polonius.

POLONIUS: My lord, he's going to his mother's closet.
Behind the arras I'll convey myself
To hear the process. I'll warrant she'll tax him home;
And, as you said, and wisely was it said,
'Tis meet that some more audience than a mother,
Since nature makes them partial, should o'erhear
The speech, of vantage. Fare you well, my liege.
I'll call upon you ere you go to bed
And tell you what I know.

KING CLAUDIUS: Thanks, dear my lord.
   Exit Polonius.
O, my offence is rank, it smells to heaven;
It hath the primal eldest curse upon't,
A brother's murther! Pray can I not,
Though inclination be as sharp as will.

My stronger guilt defeats my strong intent,
And, like a man to double business bound,
I stand in pause where I shall first begin,
And both neglect. What if this cursed hand
Were thicker than itself with brother's blood,
Is there not rain enough in the sweet heavens
To wash it white as snow? Whereto serves mercy
But to confront the visage of offence?
And what's in prayer but this twofold force,
To be forestalled ere we come to fall,
Or pardon'd being down? Then I'll look up;
My fault is past. But, O, what form of prayer
Can serve my turn? 'Forgive me my foul murther'?
That cannot be; since I am still possess'd
Of those effects for which I did the murther-
My crown, mine own ambition, and my queen.
May one be pardon'd and retain th' offence?
In the corrupted currents of this world
Offence's gilded hand may shove by justice,
And oft 'tis seen the wicked prize itself
Buys out the law; but 'tis not so above.
There is no shuffling; there the action lies
In his true nature, and we ourselves compell'd,
Even to the teeth and forehead of our faults,
To give in evidence. What then? What rests?
Try what repentance can. What can it not?
Yet what can it when one cannot repent?
O wretched state! O bosom black as death!
O limed soul, that, struggling to be free,
Art more engag'd! Help, angels! Make assay.
Bow, stubborn knees; and heart with strings of steel,
Be soft as sinews of the new-born babe!
All may be well. He kneels.
   Enter Hamlet.

HAMLET: Now might I do it pat, now he is praying;
And now I'll do't. And so he goes to heaven,
And so am I reveng'd. That would be scann'd.

A villain kills my father; and for that,
I, his sole son, do this same villain send
To heaven.
Why, this is hire and salary, not revenge!
He took my father grossly, full of bread,
With all his crimes broad blown, as flush as May;
And how his audit stands, who knows save heaven?
But in our circumstance and course of thought,
'Tis heavy with him; and am I then reveng'd,
To take him in the purging of his soul,
When he is fit and seasoned for his passage?
No. Up, sword, and know thou a more horrid hent.
When he is drunk asleep; or in his rage;
Or in th' incestuous pleasure of his bed;
At gaming, swearing, or about some act
That has no relish of salvation in't-
Then trip him, that his heels may kick at heaven,
And that his soul may be as damn'd and black
As hell, whereto it goes. My mother stays.
This physic but prolongs thy sickly days.
   Exit.

KING CLAUDIUS: *Rises* My words fly up, my thoughts remain below.
Words without thoughts never to heaven go. *Exit.*

ACT III. SCENE IV. The Queen's Closet.
Enter Queen and Polonius.

POLONIUS: He will come straight. Look you lay home to him.
Tell him his pranks have been too broad to bear with,
And that your Grace hath screen'd and stood between
Much heat and him. I'll silence me even here.
Pray you be round with him.

HAMLET: (*within*) Mother, mother, mother!

QUEEN GETRUDE: I'll warrant you; fear me not. Withdraw; I hear him coming.

Polonius Hides Behind the Arras.
Enter Hamlet.

HAMLET: Now, mother, what's the matter?

QUEEN GETRUDE: Hamlet, thou hast thy father much offended.

HAMLET: Mother, you have my father much offended.

QUEEN GETRUDE: Come, come, you answer with an idle tongue.

HAMLET: Go, go, you question with a wicked tongue.

QUEEN GETRUDE: Why, how now, Hamlet?

HAMLET: What's the matter now?

QUEEN GETRUDE: Have you forgot me?

HAMLET: No, by the rood, not so!
You are the Queen, your husband's brother's wife,
And (would it were not so!) you are my mother.

QUEEN GETRUDE: Nay, then I'll set those to you that can speak.

HAMLET: Come, come, and sit you down. You shall not budge I
You go not till I set you up a glass
Where you may see the inmost part of you.

QUEEN GETRUDE: What wilt thou do? Thou wilt not murther me?
Help, help, ho!

POLONIUS: *Behind* What, ho! help, help, help!

HAMLET: *Draws* How now? a rat? Dead for a ducat, dead!
  Makes a Pass Through the Arras And Kills Polonius.

William Shakespeare

POLONIUS: *Behind* O, I am slain!

QUEEN GETRUDE: O me, what hast thou done?

HAMLET: Nay, I know not. Is it the King?

QUEEN GETRUDE: O, what a rash and bloody deed is this!

HAMLET: A bloody deed- almost as bad, good mother,
As kill a king, and marry with his brother.

QUEEN GETRUDE: As kill a king?

HAMLET: Ay, lady, it was my word.
  Lifts up the Arras and Sees Polonius.
Thou wretched, rash, intruding fool, farewell!
I took thee for thy better. Take thy fortune.
Thou find'st to be too busy is some danger.
Leave wringing of your hinds. Peace! sit you down
And let me wring your heart; for so I shall
If it be made of penetrable stuff;
If damned custom have not braz'd it so
That it is proof and bulwark against sense.

QUEEN GETRUDE: What have I done that thou dar'st wag thy tongue
In noise so rude against me?

HAMLET: Such an act
That blurs the grace and blush of modesty;
Calls virtue hypocrite; takes off the rose
From the fair forehead of an innocent love,
And sets a blister there; makes marriage vows
As false as dicers' oaths. O, such a deed
As from the body of contraction plucks
The very soul, and sweet religion makes
A rhapsody of words! Heaven's face doth glow;
Yea, this solidity and compound mass,

With tristful visage, as against the doom,
Is thought-sick at the act.

QUEEN GETRUDE: Ay me, what act,
That roars so loud and thunders in the index?

HAMLET: Look here upon th's picture, and on this,
The counterfeit presentment of two brothers.
See what a grace was seated on this brow;
Hyperion's curls; the front of Jove himself;
An eye like Mars, to threaten and command;
A station like the herald Mercury
New lighted on a heaven-kissing hill:
A combination and a form indeed
Where every god did seem to set his seal
To give the world assurance of a man.
This was your husband. Look you now what follows.
Here is your husband, like a mildew'd ear
Blasting his wholesome brother. Have you eyes?
Could you on this fair mountain leave to feed,
And batten on this moor? Ha! have you eyes
You cannot call it love; for at your age
The heyday in the blood is tame, it's humble,
And waits upon the judgment; and what judgment
Would step from this to this? Sense sure you have,
Else could you not have motion; but sure that sense
Is apoplex'd; for madness would not err,
Nor sense to ecstacy was ne'er so thrall'd
But it reserv'd some quantity of choice
To serve in such a difference. What devil was't
That thus hath cozen'd you at hoodman-blind?
Eyes without feeling, feeling without sight,
Ears without hands or eyes, smelling sans all,
Or but a sickly part of one true sense
Could not so mope.
O shame! where is thy blush? Rebellious hell,
If thou canst mutine in a matron's bones,
To flaming youth let virtue be as wax

And melt in her own fire. Proclaim no shame
When the compulsive ardour gives the charge,
Since frost itself as actively doth burn,
And reason panders will.

QUEEN GETRUDE: O Hamlet, speak no more!
Thou turn'st mine eyes into my very soul,
And there I see such black and grained spots
As will not leave their tinct.

HAMLET: Nay, but to live
In the rank sweat of an enseamed bed,
Stew'd in corruption, honeying and making love
Over the nasty sty!

QUEEN GETRUDE: O, speak to me no more!
These words like daggers enter in mine ears.
No more, sweet Hamlet!

HAMLET: A murtherer and a villain!
A slave that is not twentieth part the tithe
Of your precedent lord; a vice of kings;
A cutpurse of the empire and the rule,
That from a shelf the precious diadem stole
And put it in his pocket!

QUEEN GETRUDE: No more!
   Enter the Ghost in His Nightgown.

HAMLET: A king of shreds and patches!-
Save me and hover o'er me with your wings,
You heavenly guards! What would your gracious figure?

QUEEN GETRUDE: Alas, he's mad!

HAMLET: Do you not come your tardy son to chide,
That, laps'd in time and passion, lets go by

Th' important acting of your dread command?
O, say!

GHOST: Do not forget. This visitation
Is but to whet thy almost blunted purpose.
But look, amazement on thy mother sits.
O, step between her and her fighting soul
Conceit in weakest bodies strongest works.
Speak to her, Hamlet.

HAMLET: How is it with you, lady?

QUEEN GETRUDE: Alas, how is't with you,
That you do bend your eye on vacancy,
And with th' encorporal air do hold discourse?
Forth at your eyes your spirits wildly peep;
And, as the sleeping soldiers in th' alarm,
Your bedded hairs, like life in excrements,
Start up and stand an end. O gentle son,
Upon the beat and flame of thy distemper
Sprinkle cool patience! Whereon do you look?

HAMLET: On him, on him! Look you how pale he glares!
His form and cause conjoin'd, preaching to stones,
Would make them capable.- Do not look upon me,
Lest with this piteous action you convert
My stern effects. Then what I have to do
Will want true colour- tears perchance for blood.

QUEEN GETRUDE: To whom do you speak this?

HAMLET: Do you see nothing there?

QUEEN GETRUDE: Nothing at all; yet all that is I see.

HAMLET: Nor did you nothing hear?

QUEEN GETRUDE: No, nothing but ourselves.

HAMLET: Why, look you there! Look how it steals away!
My father, in his habit as he liv'd!
Look where he goes even now out at the portal!
  Exit Ghost.

QUEEN GETRUDE: This is the very coinage of your brain.
This bodiless creation ecstasy
Is very cunning in.

HAMLET: Ecstasy?
My pulse as yours doth temperately keep time
And makes as healthful music. It is not madness
That I have utt'red. Bring me to the test,
And I the matter will reword; which madness
Would gambol from. Mother, for love of grace,
Lay not that flattering unction to your soul
That not your trespass but my madness speaks.
It will but skin and film the ulcerous place,
Whiles rank corruption, mining all within,
Infects unseen. Confess yourself to heaven;
Repent what's past; avoid what is to come;
And do not spread the compost on the weeds
To make them ranker. Forgive me this my virtue;
For in the fatness of these pursy times
Virtue itself of vice must pardon beg-
Yea, curb and woo for leave to do him good.

QUEEN GETRUDE: O Hamlet, thou hast cleft my heart in twain.

HAMLET: O, throw away the worser part of it,
And live the purer with the other half,
Good night- but go not to my uncle's bed.
Assume a virtue, if you have it not.
That monster, custom, who all sense doth eat
Of habits evil, is angel yet in this,
That to the use of actions fair and good

He likewise gives a frock or livery,
That aptly is put on. Refrain to-night,
And that shall lend a kind of easiness
To the next abstinence; the next more easy;
For use almost can change the stamp of nature,
And either Master the devil, or throw him out
With wondrous potency. Once more, good night;
And when you are desirous to be blest,
I'll blessing beg of you.- For this same lord,
I do repent; but heaven hath pleas'd it so,
To punish me with this, and this with me,
That I must be their scourge and minister.
I will bestow him, and will answer well
The death I gave him. So again, good night.
I must be cruel, only to be kind;
Thus bad begins, and worse remains behind.
One word more, good lady.

QUEEN GETRUDE: What shall I do?

HAMLET: Not this, by no means, that I bid you do:
Let the bloat King tempt you again to bed;
Pinch wanton on your cheek; call you his mouse;
And let him, for a pair of reechy kisses,
Or paddling in your neck with his damn'd fingers,
Make you to ravel all this matter out,
That I essentially am not in madness,
But mad in craft. 'Twere good you let him know;
For who that's but a queen, fair, sober, wise,
Would from a paddock, from a bat, a gib
Such dear concernings hide? Who would do so?
No, in despite of sense and secrecy,
Unpeg the basket on the house's top,
Let the birds fly, and like the famous ape,
To try conclusions, in the basket creep
And break your own neck down.

QUEEN GETRUDE: Be thou assur'd, if words be made of breath,

And breath of life, I have no life to breathe
What thou hast said to me.

HAMLET: I must to England; you know that?

QUEEN GETRUDE: Alack,
I had forgot! 'Tis so concluded on.

HAMLET: There's letters seal'd; and my two schoolfellows,
Whom I will trust as I will adders fang'd,
They bear the mandate; they must sweep my way
And marshal me to knavery. Let it work;
For 'tis the sport to have the enginer
Hoist with his own petar; and 't shall go hard
But I will delve one yard below their mines
And blow them at the moon. O, 'tis most sweet
When in one line two crafts directly meet.
This man shall set me packing.
I'll lug the guts into the neighbour room.-
Mother, good night.- Indeed, this counsellor
Is now most still, most secret, and most grave,
Who was in life a foolish peating knave.
Come, sir, to draw toward an end with you.
Good night, mother.
   Exit the Queen. Then Exit Hamlet, Tugging in Polonius.

ACT IV. SCENE I. Elsinore. A Room in the Castle.
Enter King and Queen, with Rosencrantz and Guildenstern.

KING CLAUDIUS: There's matter in these sighs. These profound heaves
You must translate; 'tis fit we understand them.
Where is your son?

QUEEN GETRUDE: Bestow this place on us a little while.
   Exeunt Rosencrantz and Guildenstern.
Ah, mine own lord, what have I seen to-night!

KING CLAUDIUS: What, Gertrude? How does Hamlet?

QUEEN GETRUDE: Mad as the sea and wind when both contend
Which is the mightier. In his lawless fit
Behind the arras hearing something stir,
Whips out his rapier, cries 'A rat, a rat!'
And in this brainish apprehension kills
The unseen good old man.

KING CLAUDIUS: O heavy deed!
It had been so with us, had we been there.
His liberty is full of threats to all-
To you yourself, to us, to every one.
Alas, how shall this bloody deed be answer'd?
It will be laid to us, whose providence
Should have kept short, restrain'd, and out of haunt
This mad young man. But so much was our love
We would not understand what was most fit,
But, like the owner of a foul disease,
To keep it from divulging, let it feed
Even on the pith of life. Where is he gone?

QUEEN GETRUDE: To draw apart the body he hath kill'd;
O'er whom his very madness, like some ore
Among a mineral of metals base,
Shows itself pure. He weeps for what is done.

KING CLAUDIUS: O Gertrude, come away!
The sun no sooner shall the mountains touch
But we will ship him hence; and this vile deed
We must with all our majesty and skill
Both countenance and excuse. Ho, Guildenstern!
  Enter Rosencrantz and Guildenstern.
Friends both, go join you with some further aid.
Hamlet in madness hath Polonius slain,
And from his mother's closet hath he dragg'd him.
Go seek him out; speak fair, and bring the body
Into the chapel. I pray you haste in this.

Exeunt Rosencrantz and Guildenstern.
Come, Gertrude, we'll call up our wisest friends
And let them know both what we mean to do
And what's untimely done. So Haply Slander-
Whose whisper o'er the world's diameter,
As level as the cannon to his blank,
Transports his poisoned shot- may miss our name
And hit the woundless air.- O, come away!
My soul is full of discord and dismay.
   Exeunt.

ACT IV. SCENE II. Elsinore. A Passage in the Castle.
Enter Hamlet.

HAMLET: Safely stow'd.

GENTLEMEN: (within) Hamlet! Lord Hamlet!

HAMLET: But soft! What noise? Who calls on Hamlet? O, here they come.
   Enter Rosencrantz and Guildenstern.

ROSENCRANTZ: What have you done, my lord, with the dead body?

HAMLET: Compounded it with dust, whereto 'tis kin.

ROSENCRANTZ: Tell us where 'tis, that we may take it thence
And bear it to the chapel.

HAMLET: Do not believe it.

ROSENCRANTZ: Believe what?

HAMLET: That I can keep your counsel, and not mine own. Besides, to be demanded of a sponge, what replication should be made by the son of a king?

ROSENCRANTZ: Take you me for a sponge, my lord?

HAMLET: Ay, sir; that soaks up the King's countenance, his rewards, his authorities. But such officers do the King best service in the end. He keeps them, like an ape, in the corner of his jaw; first mouth'd, to be last Swallowed. When he needs what you have glean'd, it is but squeezing you and, sponge, you shall be dry again.

ROSENCRANTZ: I understand you not, my lord.

HAMLET: I am glad of it. A knavish speech sleeps in a foolish ear.

ROSENCRANTZ: My lord, you must tell us where the body is and go with us to the King.

HAMLET: The body is with the King, but the King is not with the body. The King is a thing-

GUILDENSTERN: A thing, my lord?

HAMLET: Of nothing. Bring me to him. Hide fox, and all after.
Exeunt.

ACT IV. SCENE III. Elsinore. A Room in the Castle.
Enter King.

KING CLAUDIUS: I have sent to seek him and to find the body.
How dangerous is it that this man goes loose!
Yet must not we put the strong law on him.
He's lov'd of the distracted multitude,
Who like not in their judgment, but their eyes;
And where 'tis so, th' offender's scourge is weigh'd,
But never the offence. To bear all smooth and even,
This sudden sending him away must seem
Deliberate pause. Diseases desperate grown
By desperate appliance are reliev'd,
Or not at all.
Enter Rosencrantz.

How now O What hath befall'n?

ROSENCRANTZ: Where the dead body is bestow'd, my lord,
We cannot get from him.

KING CLAUDIUS: But where is he?

ROSENCRANTZ: Without, my lord; guarded, to know your pleasure.

KING CLAUDIUS: Bring him before us.

ROSENCRANTZ: Ho, Guildenstern! Bring in my lord.
Enter Hamlet and Guildenstern With Attendants.

KING CLAUDIUS: Now, Hamlet, where's Polonius?

HAMLET: At supper.

KING CLAUDIUS: At supper? Where?

HAMLET: Not where he eats, but where he is eaten. A certain convocation of politic worms are e'en at him. Your worm is your only emperor for diet. We fat all creatures else to fat us, and we fat ourselves for maggots. Your fat king and your lean beggar is but variable service- two dishes, but to one table. That's the end.

KING CLAUDIUS: Alas, alas!

HAMLET: A man may fish with the worm that hath eat of a king, and eat of the fish that hath fed of that worm.

KING CLAUDIUS: What dost thou mean by this?

HAMLET: Nothing but to show you how a king may go a progress through the guts of a beggar.

KING CLAUDIUS: Where is Polonius?

HAMLET: In heaven. Send thither to see. If your messenger find him not there, seek him i' th' other place yourself. But indeed, if you find him not within this month, you shall nose him as you go up the stair, into the lobby.

KING CLAUDIUS: Go seek him there.
  To Attendants.

HAMLET: He will stay till you come.
  Exeunt Attendants.

KING CLAUDIUS: Hamlet, this deed, for thine especial safety,-
Which we do tender as we dearly grieve
For that which thou hast done,- must send thee hence
With fiery quickness. Therefore prepare thyself.
The bark is ready and the wind at help,
Th' associates tend, and everything is bent
For England.

HAMLET: For England?

KING CLAUDIUS: Ay, Hamlet.

HAMLET: Good.

KING CLAUDIUS: So is it, if thou knew'st our purposes.

HAMLET: I see a cherub that sees them. But come, for England! Farewell, dear mother.

KING CLAUDIUS: Thy loving father, Hamlet.

HAMLET: My mother! Father and mother is man and wife; man and wife is one flesh; and so, my mother. Come, for England!
  Exit.

KING CLAUDIUS: Follow him at foot; tempt him with speed aboard.

Delay it not; I'll have him hence to-night.
Away! for everything is seal'd and done
That else leans on th' affair. Pray you make haste.
 Exeunt Rosencrantz and Guildenstern
And, England, if my love thou hold'st at aught,-
As my great power thereof may give thee sense,
Since yet thy cicatrice looks raw and red
After the Danish sword, and thy free awe
Pays homage to us,- thou mayst not coldly set
Our sovereign process, which imports at full,
By letters congruing to that effect,
The present death of Hamlet. Do it, England;
For like the hectic in my blood he rages,
And thou must cure me. Till I know 'tis done,
Howe'er my haps, my joys were ne'er begun.
 Exit.

ACT IV. SCENE IV. Near Elsinore.
Enter Fortinbras with His Army over the Stage.

FORTINBRAS: Go, Captain, from me greet the Danish king.
Tell him that by his license Fortinbras
Craves the conveyance of a promis'd march
Over his kingdom. You know the rendezvous.
if that his Majesty would aught with us,
We shall express our duty in his eye;
And let him know so.

CAPTAIN: I will do't, my lord.

FORTINBRAS: Go softly on.
 Exeunt All but the Captain.
 Enter Hamlet, Rosencrantz, Guildenstern, and Others.

HAMLET: Good sir, whose powers are these?

CAPTAIN: They are of Norway, sir.

HAMLET: How purpos'd, sir, I pray you?

CAPTAIN: Against some part of Poland.

HAMLET: Who commands them, sir?

CAPTAIN: The nephew to old Norway, Fortinbras.

HAMLET: Goes it against the main of Poland, sir,
Or for some frontier?

CAPTAIN: Truly to speak, and with no addition,
We go to gain a little patch of ground
That hath in it no profit but the name.
To pay five ducats, five, I would not farm it;
Nor will it yield to Norway or the Pole
A ranker rate, should it be sold in fee.

HAMLET: Why, then the Polack never will defend it.

CAPTAIN: Yes, it is already garrison'd.

HAMLET: Two thousand souls and twenty thousand ducats
Will not debate the question of this straw.
This is th' imposthume of much wealth and peace,
That inward breaks, and shows no cause without
Why the man dies.- I humbly thank you, sir.

CAPTAIN: God b' wi' you, sir.
  Exit.

ROSENCRANTZ: Will't please you go, my lord?

HAMLET: I'll be with you straight. Go a little before.
  Exeunt all but Hamlet.
How all occasions do inform against me
And spur my dull revenge! What is a man,

If his chief good and market of his time
Be but to sleep and feed? A beast, no more.
Sure he that made us with such large discourse,
Looking before and after, gave us not
That capability and godlike reason
To fust in us unus'd. Now, whether it be
Bestial oblivion, or some craven scruple
Of thinking too precisely on th' event,-
A thought which, quarter'd, hath but one part wisdom
And ever three parts coward,- I do not know
Why yet I live to say 'This thing's to do,'
Sith I have cause, and will, and strength, and means
To do't. Examples gross as earth exhort me.
Witness this army of such mass and charge,
Led by a delicate and tender prince,
Whose spirit, with divine ambition puff'd,
Makes mouths at the invisible event,
Exposing what is mortal and unsure
To all that fortune, death, and danger dare,
Even for an eggshell. Rightly to be great
Is not to stir without great argument,
But greatly to find quarrel in a straw
When honour's at the stake. How stand I then,
That have a father klll'd, a mother stain'd,
Excitements of my reason and my blood,
And let all sleep, while to my shame I see
The imminent death of twenty thousand men
That for a fantasy and trick of fame
Go to their graves like beds, fight for a plot
Whereon the numbers cannot try the cause,
Which is not tomb enough and continent
To hide the slain? O, from this time forth,
My thoughts be bloody, or be nothing worth!
   Exit.

ACT IV. SCENE V. Elsinore. A Room in the Castle.
Enter Horatio, Queen, and a Gentleman.

QUEEN GETRUDE: I will not speak with her.

GENTLEMEN: She is importunate, indeed distract.
Her mood will needs be pitied.

QUEEN GETRUDE: What would she have?

GENTLEMEN: She speaks much of her father; says she hears
There's tricks i' th' world, and hems, and beats her heart;
Spurns enviously at straws; speaks things in doubt,
That carry but half sense. Her speech is nothing,
Yet the unshaped use of it doth move
The hearers to collection; they aim at it,
And botch the words up fit to their own thoughts;
Which, as her winks and nods and gestures yield them,
Indeed would make one think there might be thought,
Though nothing sure, yet much unhappily.

HORATIO: 'Twere good she were spoken with; for she may strew
Dangerous conjectures in ill-breeding minds.

QUEEN GETRUDE: Let her come in.
  Exit Gentleman.
Aside To my sick soul (as sin's true nature is)
Each toy seems Prologue to some great amiss.
So full of artless jealousy is guilt
It spills itself in fearing to be spilt.
  Enter Ophelia Distracted.

OPHELIA: Where is the beauteous Majesty of Denmark?

QUEEN GETRUDE: How now, Ophelia?

OPHELIA: (sings)

How should I your true-love know
　From another one?
By his cockle bat and' staff
　And his sandal shoon.

QUEEN GETRUDE: Alas, sweet lady, what imports this song?

OPHELIA: Say you? Nay, pray You mark.
　(*Sings*) He is dead and gone, lady,
　　He is dead and gone;
　At his head a grass-green turf,
　　At his heels a stone.
O, ho!

QUEEN GETRUDE: Nay, but Ophelia-

OPHELIA: Pray you mark.
　Sings White his shroud as the mountain snow-
　Enter King.

QUEEN GETRUDE: Alas, look here, my lord!

OPHELIA: (Sings)
　　Larded all with sweet flowers;
　Which bewept to the grave did not go
　　With true-love showers.

KING CLAUDIUS: How do you, pretty lady?

OPHELIA: Well, God dild you! They say the owl was a baker's daughter. Lord, we know what we are, but know not what we may be. God be at your table!

KING CLAUDIUS: Conceit upon her father.

OPHELIA: Pray let's have no words of this; but when they ask, you what it means, say you this:

Sings To-morrow is Saint Valentine's day,
    All in the morning bedtime,
And I a maid at your window,
    To be your Valentine.

Then up he rose and donn'd his clo'es
    And dupp'd the chamber door,
Let in the maid, that out a maid
    Never departed more.

KING CLAUDIUS: Pretty Ophelia!

OPHELIA: Indeed, la, without an oath, I'll make an end on't!
Sings By Gis and by Saint Charity,
    Alack, and fie for shame!
Young men will do't if they come to't
    By Cock, they are to blame.

Quoth she, 'Before you tumbled me,
    You promis'd me to wed.'
He answers:
'So would I 'a' done, by yonder sun,
    An thou hadst not come to my bed.'

KING CLAUDIUS: How long hath she been thus?

OPHELIA: I hope all will be well. We must be patient; but I cannot choose but weep to think they would lay him i' th' cold ground. My brother shall know of it; and so I thank you for your good counsel. Come, my coach! Good night, ladies. Good night, sweet ladies. Good night, good night.
    Exit

KING CLAUDIUS: Follow her close; give her good watch, I pray you.
    Exit Horatio.
O, this is the poison of deep grief; it springs
All from her father's death. O Gertrude, Gertrude,
When sorrows come, they come not single spies.

William Shakespeare

But in battalions! First, her father slain;
Next, Your son gone, and he most violent author
Of his own just remove; the people muddied,
Thick and and unwholesome in their thoughts and whispers
For good Polonius' death, and we have done but greenly
In hugger-mugger to inter him; Poor Ophelia
Divided from herself and her fair-judgment,
Without the which we are Pictures or mere beasts;
Last, and as such containing as all these,
Her brother is in secret come from France;
And wants not buzzers to infect his ear
Feeds on his wonder, keep, himself in clouds,
With pestilent speeches of his father's death,
Wherein necessity, of matter beggar'd,
Will nothing stick Our person to arraign
In ear and ear. O my dear Gertrude, this,
Like to a murd'ring piece, in many places
Give, me superfluous death. A noise within.

QUEEN GETRUDE: Alack, what noise is this?

KING CLAUDIUS: Where are my Switzers? Let them guard the door.
   Enter a Messenger.
What is the matter?

MESSENGER: Save Yourself, my lord:
The ocean, overpeering of his list,
Eats not the flats with more impetuous haste
Than Young Laertes, in a riotous head,
O'erbears Your offices. The rabble call him lord;
And, as the world were now but to begin,
Antiquity forgot, custom not known,
The ratifiers and props of every word,
They cry 'Choose we! Laertes shall be king!'
Caps, hands, and tongues applaud it to the clouds,
'Laertes shall be king! Laertes king!'
   A Noise Within.

QUEEN GETRUDE: How cheerfully on the false trail they cry!
O, this is counter, you false Danish dogs!

KING CLAUDIUS: The doors are broke.
Enter Laertes with Others.

LAERTES: Where is this king?- Sirs, staid you all without.

ALL: No, let's come in!

LAERTES: I pray you give me leave.

ALL: We will, we will!

LAERTES: I thank you. Keep the door.
Exeunt his Followers.
O thou vile king,
Give me my father!

QUEEN GETRUDE: Calmly, good Laertes.

LAERTES: That drop of blood that's calm proclaims me bastard;
Cries cuckold to my father; brands the harlot
Even here between the chaste unsmirched brows
Of my true mother.

KING CLAUDIUS: What is the cause, Laertes,
That thy rebellion looks so giantlike?
Let him go, Gertrude. Do not fear our person.
There's such divinity doth hedge a king
That treason can but peep to what it would,
Acts little of his will. Tell me, Laertes,
Why thou art thus incens'd. Let him go, Gertrude.
Speak, man.

LAERTES: Where is my father?

KING CLAUDIUS: Dead.

QUEEN GETRUDE: But not by him!

KING CLAUDIUS: Let him demand his fill.

LAERTES: How came he dead? I'll not be juggled with:
To hell, allegiance! vows, to the blackest devil
Conscience and grace, to the profoundest pit!
I dare damnation. To this point I stand,
That both the world, I give to negligence,
Let come what comes; only I'll be reveng'd
Most throughly for my father.

KING CLAUDIUS: Who shall stay you?

LAERTES: My will, not all the world!
And for my means, I'll husband them so well
They shall go far with little.

KING CLAUDIUS: Good Laertes,
If you desire to know the certainty
Of your dear father's death, is't writ in Your revenge
That swoopstake you will draw both friend and foe,
Winner and loser?

LAERTES: None but his enemies.

KING CLAUDIUS: Will you know them then?

LAERTES: To his good friends thus wide I'll ope my arms
And, like the kind life-rend'ring pelican,
Repast them with my blood.

KING CLAUDIUS: Why, now You speak
Like a good child and a true gentleman.
That I am guiltless of your father's death,

And am most sensibly in grief for it,
It shall as level to your judgment pierce
As day does to your eye.
   A Noise Within:
'Let her come in.'

LAERTES: How now? What noise is that?
   Enter Ophelia.
O heat, dry up my brains! Tears seven times salt
Burn out the sense and virtue of mine eye!
By heaven, thy madness shall be paid by weight
Till our scale turn the beam. O rose of May!
Dear maid, kind sister, sweet Ophelia!
O heavens! is't possible a young maid's wits
Should be as mortal as an old man's life?
Nature is fine in love, and where 'tis fine,
It sends some precious instance of itself
After the thing it loves.

OPHELIA: (sings)
   They bore him barefac'd on the bier
      (Hey non nony, nony, hey nony)
   And in his grave rain'd many a tear.
Fare you well, my dove!

LAERTES: Hadst thou thy wits, and didst persuade revenge,
It could not move thus.

OPHELIA: You must sing 'A-down a-down, and you call him a-down-a.' O, how the wheel becomes it! It is the false steward, that stole his master's daughter.

LAERTES: This nothing's more than matter.

OPHELIA: There's rosemary, that's for remembrance. Pray you, love, remember. And there is pansies, that's for thoughts.

LAERTES: A document in madness! Thoughts and remembrance fitted.

OPHELIA: There's fennel for you, and columbines. There's rue for you, and here's some for me. We may call it herb of grace o' Sundays. O, you must wear your rue with a difference! There's a daisy. I would give you some violets, but they wither'd all when my father died. They say he made a good end.
   Sings For bonny sweet Robin is all my joy.

LAERTES: Thought and affliction, passion, hell itself,
She turns to favour and to prettiness.

OPHELIA: (*sings*)
   And will he not come again?
   And will he not come again?
     No, no, he is dead;
     Go to thy deathbed;
   He never will come again.

   His beard was as white as snow,
   All flaxen was his poll.
     He is gone, he is gone,
     And we cast away moan.
   God 'a'mercy on his soul!
And of all Christian souls, I pray God. God b' wi', you.
   Exit.

LAERTES: Do you see this, O God?

KING CLAUDIUS: Laertes, I must commune with your grief,
Or you deny me right. Go but apart,
Make choice of whom your wisest friends you will,
And they shall hear and judge 'twixt you and me.
If by direct or by collateral hand
They find us touch'd, we will our kingdom give,
Our crown, our life, and all that we call ours,
To you in satisfaction; but if not,

Be you content to lend your patience to us,
And we shall jointly labour with your soul
To give it due content.

LAERTES: Let this be so.
His means of death, his obscure funeral-
No trophy, sword, nor hatchment o'er his bones,
No noble rite nor formal ostentation,-
Cry to be heard, as 'twere from heaven to earth,
That I must call't in question.

KING CLAUDIUS: So you shall;
And where th' offence is let the great axe fall.
I pray you go with me.
    Exeunt

ACT IV. SCENE VI. Elsinore. Another Room in the Castle.
Enter Horatio with an Attendant.

HORATIO: What are they that would speak with me?

SERVANT: Seafaring men, sir. They say they have letters for you.

HORATIO: Let them come in.
    Exit Attendant.
I do not know from what part of the world
I should be greeted, if not from Lord Hamlet.
    Enter Sailors.

SAILOR: God bless you, sir.

HORATIO: Let him bless thee too.

SAILOR: 'A shall, sir, an't please him. There's a letter for you, sir,- it comes from th' ambassador that was bound for England- if your name be Horatio, as I am let to know it is.

HORATIO: (reads the letter) 'Horatio, when thou shalt have overlook'd this, give these fellows some means to the King. They have letters for him. Ere we were two days old at sea, a pirate of very warlike appointment gave us chase. Finding ourselves too slow of sail, we put on a compelled valour, and in the grapple I boarded them. On the instant they got clear of our ship; so I alone became their prisoner. They have dealt with me like thieves of mercy; but they knew what they did: I am to do a good turn for them. Let the King have the letters I have sent, and repair thou to me with as much speed as thou wouldst fly death. I have words to speak in thine ear will make thee dumb; yet are they much too light for the bore of the matter. These good fellows will bring thee where I am. Rosencrantz and Guildenstern hold their course for England. Of them I have much to tell thee. Farewell.
  'He that thou knowest thine, Hamlet.'
Come, I will give you way for these your letters,
And do't the speedier that you may direct me
To him from whom you brought them.
  Exeunt.

ACT IV. SCENE VII. Elsinore. Another Room in the Castle.
Enter King and Laertes.

KING CLAUDIUS: Now must your conscience my acquittance seal,
And You must put me in your heart for friend,
Sith you have heard, and with a knowing ear,
That he which hath your noble father slain
Pursued my life.

LAERTES: It well appears. But tell me
Why you proceeded not against these feats
So crimeful and so capital in nature,
As by your safety, wisdom, all things else,
You mainly were stirr'd up.

KING CLAUDIUS: O, for two special reasons,
Which may to you, perhaps, seein much unsinew'd,
But yet to me they are strong. The Queen his mother

Lives almost by his looks; and for myself,-
My virtue or my plague, be it either which,-
She's so conjunctive to my life and soul
That, as the star moves not but in his sphere,
I could not but by her. The other motive
Why to a public count I might not go
Is the great love the general gender bear him,
Who, dipping all his faults in their affection,
Would, like the spring that turneth wood to stone,
Convert his gives to graces; so that my arrows,
Too slightly timber'd for so loud a wind,
Would have reverted to my bow again,
And not where I had aim'd them.

LAERTES: And so have I a noble father lost;
A sister driven into desp'rate terms,
Whose worth, if praises may go back again,
Stood challenger on mount of all the age
For her perfections. But my revenge will come.

KING CLAUDIUS: Break not your sleeps for that. You must not think
That we are made of stuff so flat and dull
That we can let our beard be shook with danger,
And think it pastime. You shortly shall hear more.
I lov'd your father, and we love ourself,
And that, I hope, will teach you to imagine-
   Enter a Messenger with Letters.
How now? What news?

MESSENGER: Letters, my lord, from Hamlet:
This to your Majesty; this to the Queen.

KING CLAUDIUS: From Hamlet? Who brought them?

MESSENGER: Sailors, my lord, they say; I saw them not.
They were given me by Claudio; he receiv'd them
Of him that brought them.

KING CLAUDIUS: Laertes, you shall hear them.
Leave us.
  Exit Messenger.
Reads'High and Mighty,-You shall know I am set naked on your kingdom. To-morrow shall I beg leave to see your kingly eyes; when I shall (first asking your pardon thereunto) recount the occasion of my sudden and more strange return.
                              'Hamlet.'
What should this mean? Are all the rest come back?
Or is it some abuse, and no such thing?

LAERTES: Know you the hand?

KING CLAUDIUS: 'Tis Hamlet's character. 'Naked!'
And in a postscript here, he says 'alone.'
Can you advise me?

LAERTES: I am lost in it, my lord. But let him come!
It warms the very sickness in my heart
That I shall live and tell him to his teeth,
'Thus didest thou.'

KING CLAUDIUS: If it be so, Laertes
(As how should it be so? how otherwise?),
Will you be rul'd by me?

LAERTES: Ay my lord,
So you will not o'errule me to a peace.

KING CLAUDIUS: To thine own peace. If he be now return'd
As checking at his voyage, and that he means
No more to undertake it, I will work him
To exploit now ripe in my device,
Under the which he shall not choose but fall;
And for his death no wind
But even his mother shall uncharge the practice
And call it accident.

LAERTES: My lord, I will be rul'd;
The rather, if you could devise it so
That I might be the organ.

KING CLAUDIUS: It falls right.
You have been talk'd of since your travel much,
And that in Hamlet's hearing, for a quality
Wherein they say you shine, Your sun of parts
Did not together pluck such envy from him
As did that one; and that, in my regard,
Of the unworthiest siege.

LAERTES: What part is that, my lord?

KING CLAUDIUS: A very riband in the cap of youth-
Yet needfull too; for youth no less becomes
The light and careless livery that it wears
Thin settled age his sables and his weeds,
Importing health and graveness. Two months since
Here was a gentleman of Normandy.
I have seen myself, and serv'd against, the French,
And they can well on horseback; but this gallant
Had witchcraft in't. He grew unto his seat,
And to such wondrous doing brought his horse
As had he been incorps'd and demi-natur'd
With the brave beast. So far he topp'd my thought
That I, in forgery of shapes and tricks,
Come short of what he did.

LAERTES: A Norman was't?

KING CLAUDIUS: A Norman.

LAERTES: Upon my life, Lamound.

KING CLAUDIUS: The very same.

LAERTES: I know him well. He is the broach indeed
And gem of all the nation.

KING CLAUDIUS: He made confession of you;
And gave you such a masterly report
For art and exercise in your defence,
And for your rapier most especially,
That he cried out 'twould be a sight indeed
If one could match you. The scrimers of their nation
He swore had neither motion, guard, nor eye,
If you oppos'd them. Sir, this report of his
Did Hamlet so envenom with his envy
That he could nothing do but wish and beg
Your sudden coming o'er to play with you.
Now, out of this—

LAERTES: What out of this, my lord?

KING CLAUDIUS: Laertes, was your father dear to you?
Or are you like the painting of a sorrow,
A face without a heart,'

LAERTES: Why ask you this?

KING CLAUDIUS: Not that I think you did not love your father;
But that I know love is begun by time,
And that I see, in passages of proof,
Time qualifies the spark and fire of it.
There lives within the very flame of love
A kind of wick or snuff that will abate it;
And nothing is at a like goodness still;
For goodness, growing to a plurisy,
Dies in his own too-much. That we would do,
We should do when we would; for this 'would' changes,
And hath abatements and delays as many
As there are tongues, are hands, are accidents;
And then this 'should' is like a spendthrift sigh,
That hurts by easing. But to the quick o' th' ulcer!

Hamlet comes back. What would you undertake
To show yourself your father's son in deed
More than in words?

LAERTES: To cut his throat i' th' church!

KING CLAUDIUS: No place indeed should murther sanctuarize;
Revenge should have no bounds. But, good Laertes,
Will you do this? Keep close within your chamber.
Will return'd shall know you are come home.
We'll put on those shall praise your excellence
And set a double varnish on the fame
The Frenchman gave you; bring you in fine together
And wager on your heads. He, being remiss,
Most generous, and free from all contriving,
Will not peruse the foils; so that with ease,
Or with a little shuffling, you may choose
A sword unbated, and, in a pass of practice,
Requite him for your father.

LAERTES: I will do't!
And for that purpose I'll anoint my sword.
I bought an unction of a mountebank,
So mortal that, but dip a knife in it,
Where it draws blood no cataplasm so rare,
Collected from all simples that have virtue
Under the moon, can save the thing from death
This is but scratch'd withal. I'll touch my point
With this contagion, that, if I gall him slightly,
It may be death.

KING CLAUDIUS: Let's further think of this,
Weigh what convenience both of time and means
May fit us to our shape. If this should fall,
And that our drift look through our bad performance.
'Twere better not assay'd. Therefore this project
Should have a back or second, that might hold
If this did blast in proof. Soft! let me see.

We'll make a solemn wager on your cunnings-
I ha't! When in your motion you are hot and dry-
As make your bouts more violent to that end-
And that he calls for drink, I'll have prepar'd him
A chalice for the nonce; whereon but sipping,
If he by chance escape your venom'd stuck,
Our purpose may hold there.- But stay, what noise,
   Enter Queen.
How now, sweet queen?

QUEEN GETRUDE: One woe doth tread upon another's heel,
So fast they follow. Your sister's drown'd, Laertes.

LAERTES: Drown'd! O, where?

QUEEN GETRUDE: There is a willow grows aslant a brook,
That shows his hoar leaves in the glassy stream.
There with fantastic garlands did she come
Of crowflowers, nettles, daisies, and long purples,
That liberal shepherds give a grosser name,
But our cold maids do dead men's fingers call them.
There on the pendant boughs her coronet weeds
Clamb'ring to hang, an envious sliver broke,
When down her weedy trophies and herself
Fell in the weeping brook. Her clothes spread wide
And, mermaid-like, awhile they bore her up;
Which time she chaunted snatches of old tunes,
As one incapable of her own distress,
Or like a creature native and indued
Unto that element; but long it could not be
Till that her garments, heavy with their drink,
Pull'd the poor wretch from her melodious lay
To muddy death.

LAERTES: Alas, then she is drown'd?

QUEEN GETRUDE: Drown'd, drown'd.

LAERTES: Too much of water hast thou, poor Ophelia,
And therefore I forbid my tears; but yet
It is our trick; nature her custom holds,
Let shame say what it will. When these are gone,
The woman will be out. Adieu, my lord.
I have a speech of fire, that fain would blaze
But that this folly douts it.
   Exit.

KING CLAUDIUS: Let's follow, Gertrude.
How much I had to do to calm his rage I
Now fear I this will give it start again;
Therefore let's follow.
   Exeunt.

ACT V. SCENE I. Elsinore. A Churchyard.

Enter Two Clowns, With Spades and Pickaxes.

FIRST CLOWN: Is she to be buried in Christian burial when she wilfully seeks her own salvation?

SECOND CLOWN: I tell thee she is; therefore make her grave straight. The crowner hath sate on her, and finds it Christian burial.

FIRST CLOWN: How can that be, unless she drown'd herself in her own defence?

SECOND CLOWN: Why, 'tis found so.

FIRST CLOWN: It must be se offendendo; it cannot be else. For here lies the point: if I drown myself wittingly, it argues an act; and an act hath three branches-it is to act, to do, and to perform; argal, she drown'd herself wittingly.

SECOND CLOWN: Nay, but hear you, Goodman Delver!

FIRST CLOWN: Give me leave. Here lies the water; good. Here stands the man; good. If the man go to this water and drown himself, it is, will he nill he, he goes- mark you that. But if the water come to him and drown him, he drowns not himself. Argal, he that is not guilty of his own death shortens not his own life.

SECOND CLOWN: But is this law?

FIRST CLOWN: Ay, marry, is't- crowner's quest law.

SECOND CLOWN: Will you ha' the truth an't? If this had not been a gentlewoman, she should have been buried out o' Christian burial.

FIRST CLOWN: Why, there thou say'st! And the more pity that great folk should have count'nance in this world to drown or hang themselves more than their even-Christen. Come, my spade! There is no ancient gentlemen but gard'ners, ditchers, and grave-makers. They hold up Adam's profession.

SECOND CLOWN: Was he a gentleman?

FIRST CLOWN:: 'A was the first that ever bore arms.

SECOND CLOWN: Why, he had none.

FIRST CLOWN:: What, art a heathen? How dost thou understand the Scripture?
The Scripture says Adam digg'd. Could he dig without arms? I'll put another question to thee. If thou answerest me not to the purpose, confess thyself-

SECOND CLOWN: Go to!

FIRST CLOWN:: What is he that builds stronger than either the mason, the shipwright, or the carpenter?

SECOND CLOWN: The gallows-maker; for that frame outlives a thousand tenants.

FIRST CLOWN:: I like thy wit well, in good faith. The gallows does well. But how does it well? It does well to those that do ill. Now, thou dost ill to say the gallows is built stronger than the church. Argal, the gallows may do well to thee. To't again, come!

SECOND CLOWN: Who builds stronger than a mason, a shipwright, or a carpenter?

FIRST CLOWN:: Ay, tell me that, and unyoke.

SECOND CLOWN: Marry, now I can tell!

FIRST CLOWN:: To't.

SECOND CLOWN: Mass, I cannot tell.
  Enter Hamlet and Horatio Afar Off.

FIRST CLOWN:: Cudgel thy brains no more about it, for your dull ass will not mend his pace with beating; and when you are ask'd this question next, say 'a grave-maker.' The houses he makes lasts till doomsday. Go, get thee to Yaughan; fetch me a stoup of liquor.
  Exit Second Clown.
  Clown Digs And Sings.
  In youth when I did love, did love,
    Methought it was very sweet;
  To contract- O- the time for- a- my behove,
    O, methought there- a- was nothing- a- meet.

HAMLET: Has this fellow no feeling of his business, that he sings at grave-making?

HORATIO: Custom hath made it in him a Property of easiness.

HAMLET: 'Tis e'en so. The hand of little employment hath the daintier sense.

FIRST CLOWN:: (sings)
    But age with his stealing steps
        Hath clawed me in his clutch,
    And hath shipped me intil the land,
        As if I had never been such.
Throws up a Skull.

HAMLET: That skull had a tongue in it, and could sing once. How the knave jowls it to the ground, as if 'twere Cain's jawbone, that did the first murther! This might be the pate of a Politician, which this ass now o'erreaches; one that would circumvent God, might it not?

HORATIO: It might, my lord.

HAMLET: Or of a courtier, which could say 'Good morrow, sweet lord! How dost thou, good lord?' This might be my Lord Such-a-one, that prais'd my Lord Such-a-one's horse when he meant to beg it- might it not?

HORATIO: Ay, my lord.

HAMLET: Why, e'en so! and now my Lady Worm's, chapless, and knock'd about the mazzard with a sexton's spade. Here's fine revolution, and we had the trick to see't. Did these bones cost no more the breeding but to play at loggets with 'em? Mine ache to think on't.

FIRST CLOWN:: (Sings)
    A pickaxe and a spade, a spade,
        For and a shrouding sheet;
    O, a Pit of clay for to be made
        For such a guest is meet.
Throws up Another Skull.

HAMLET: There's another. Why may not that be the skull of a lawyer? Where be his quiddits now, his quillets, his cases, his tenures, and his tricks? Why does he suffer this rude knave now to knock him about the sconce with a dirty shovel, and will not tell him of his action of battery? Hum! This fellow might be in's time a great buyer of land, with his statutes, his recognizances, his fines, his double vouchers, his recoveries. Is this the fine of his fines, and the recovery of his recoveries, to have his fine pate full of fine dirt? Will his vouchers vouch him no more of his purchases, and double ones too, than the length and breadth of a pair of indentures? The very conveyances of his lands will scarcely lie in this box; and must th' inheritor himself have no more, ha?

HORATIO: Not a jot more, my lord.

HAMLET: Is not parchment made of sheepskins?

HORATIO: Ay, my lord, And of calveskins too.

HAMLET: They are sheep and calves which seek out assurance in that. I will speak to this fellow. Whose grave's this, sirrah?

FIRST CLOWN: Mine, sir.
   Sings O, a pit of clay for to be made
      For such a guest is meet.

HAMLET: I think it be thine indeed, for thou liest in't.

FIRST CLOWN: You lie out on't, sir, and therefore 'tis not yours. For my part, I do not lie in't, yet it is mine.

HAMLET: Thou dost lie in't, to be in't and say it is thine. 'Tis for the dead, not for the quick; therefore thou liest.

FIRST CLOWN: 'Tis a quick lie, sir; 'twill away again from me to you.

HAMLET: What man dost thou dig it for?

FIRST CLOWN: For no man, sir.

HAMLET: What woman then?

FIRST CLOWN: For none neither.

HAMLET: Who is to be buried in't?

FIRST CLOWN: One that was a woman, sir; but, rest her soul, she's dead.

HAMLET: How absolute the knave is! We must speak by the card, or equivocation will undo us. By the Lord, Horatio, this three years I have taken note of it, the age is grown so picked that the toe of the peasant comes so near the heel of the courtier he galls his kibe.- How long hast thou been a grave-maker?

FIRST CLOWN:: Of all the days i' th' year, I came to't that day that our last king Hamlet overcame Fortinbras.

HAMLET: How long is that since?

FIRST CLOWN: Cannot you tell that? Every fool can tell that. It was the very day that young Hamlet was born- he that is mad, and sent into England.

HAMLET: Ay, marry, why was be sent into England?

FIRST CLOWN:: Why, because 'a was mad. 'A shall recover his wits there; or, if 'a do not, 'tis no great matter there.

HAMLET: Why?

FIRST CLOWN: 'Twill not he seen in him there. There the men are as mad as he.

HAMLET: How came he mad?

FIRST CLOWN: Very strangely, they say.

HAMLET: How strangely?

FIRST CLOWN:: Faith, e'en with losing his wits.

HAMLET: Upon what ground?

FIRST CLOWN:: Why, here in Denmark. I have been sexton here, man and boy thirty years.

HAMLET: How long will a man lie i' th' earth ere he rot?

FIRST CLOWN:: Faith, if 'a be not rotten before 'a die (as we have many pocky corses now-a-days that will scarce hold the laying in, I will last you some eight year or nine year. A tanner will last you nine year.

HAMLET: Why he more than another?

FIRST CLOWN:: Why, sir, his hide is so tann'd with his trade that 'a will keep out water a great while; and your water is a sore decayer of your whoreson dead body. Here's a skull now. This skull hath lien you i' th' earth three-and-twenty years.

HAMLET: Whose was it?

FIRST CLOWN:: A whoreson, mad fellow's it was. Whose do you think it was?

HAMLET: Nay, I know not.

FIRST CLOWN: A pestilence on him for a mad rogue! 'A pour'd a flagon of
Rhenish on my head once. This same skull, sir, was Yorick's skull, the King's jester.

HAMLET: This?

FIRST CLOWN:: E'en that.

HAMLET: Let me see.
Takes the Skull.
Alas, poor Yorick! I knew him,
Horatio. A fellow of infinite jest, of most excellent fancy. He
hath borne me on his back a thousand tunes. And now how abhorred
in my imagination it is! My gorge rises at it. Here hung those
lips that I have kiss'd I know not how oft. Where be your gibes
now? your gambols? your songs? your flashes of merriment that
were wont to set the table on a roar? Not one now, to mock your
own grinning? Quite chap- fall'n? Now get you to my lady's
chamber, and tell her, let her paint an inch thick, to this
favour she must come. Make her laugh at that. Prithee, Horatio,
tell me one thing.

HORATIO: What's that, my lord?

HAMLET: Dost thou think Alexander look'd o' this fashion i' th' earth?

HORATIO: E'en so.

HAMLET: And smelt so? Pah!
Puts down the Skull.

HORATIO: E'en so, my lord.

HAMLET: To what base uses we may return, Horatio!
Why may not imagination trace the noble dust of
Alexander till he find it stopping a bunghole?

HORATIO: 'Twere to consider too curiously, to consider so.

HAMLET: No, faith, not a jot; but to follow him thither with modesty
enough, and likelihood to lead it; as thus: Alexander died,

Alexander was buried, Alexander returneth into dust; the dust is earth; of earth we make loam; and why of that loam (whereto he was converted) might they not stop a beer barrel?
Imperious Caesar, dead and turn'd to clay,
Might stop a hole to keep the wind away.
O, that that earth which kept the world in awe
Should patch a wall t' expel the winter's flaw!
But soft! but soft! aside! Here comes the King-

Enter priests with a coffin in funeral procession, King, Queen, Laertes, with Lords attendant.

The Queen, the courtiers. Who is this they follow?
And with such maimed rites? This doth betoken
The corse they follow did with desp'rate hand
Fordo it own life. 'Twas of some estate.
Couch we awhile, and mark.

Retires with Horatio.

LAERTES: What ceremony else?

HAMLET: That is Laertes,
A very noble youth. Mark.

LAERTES: What ceremony else?

PRIEST: Her obsequies have been as far enlarg'd
As we have warranty. Her death was doubtful;
And, but that great command o'ersways the order,
She should in ground unsanctified have lodg'd
Till the last trumpet. For charitable prayers,
Shards, flints, and pebbles should be thrown on her.
Yet here she is allow'd her virgin crants,
Her maiden strewments, and the bringing home
Of bell and burial.

LAERTES: Must there no more be done?

PRIEST: No more be done.
We should profane the service of the dead

To sing a requiem and such rest to her
As to peace-parted souls.

LAERTES: Lay her i' th' earth;
And from her fair and unpolluted flesh
May violets spring! I tell thee, churlish priest,
A minist'ring angel shall my sister be
When thou liest howling.

HAMLET: What, the fair Ophelia?

QUEEN GETRUDE: Sweets to the sweet! Farewell.
   Scatters Flowers.
I hop'd thou shouldst have been my Hamlet's wife;
I thought thy bride-bed to have deck'd, sweet maid,
And not have strew'd thy grave.

LAERTES: O, treble woe
Fall ten times treble on that cursed head
Whose wicked deed thy most ingenious sense
Depriv'd thee of! Hold off the earth awhile,
Till I have caught her once more in mine arms.
   Leaps in the Grave.
Now pile your dust upon the quick and dead
Till of this flat a mountain you have made
T' o'ertop old Pelion or the skyish head
Of blue Olympus.

HAMLET: *Comes Forward* What is he whose grief
Bears such an emphasis? whose phrase of sorrow
Conjures the wand'ring stars, and makes them stand
Like wonder-wounded hearers? This is I,
Hamlet the Dane.
   Leaps in after Laertes.

LAERTES: The devil take thy soul!
   Grapples with Him.

HAMLET: Thou pray'st not well.
I prithee take thy fingers from my throat;
For, though I am not splenitive and rash,
Yet have I in me something dangerous,
Which let thy wisdom fear. Hold off thy hand!

KING CLAUDIUS: Pluck thein asunder.

QUEEN GETRUDE: Hamlet, Hamlet!

ALL: Gentlemen!

HORATIO: Good my lord, be quiet.
 The Attendants Part Them, and They Come out of the Grave.

HAMLET: Why, I will fight with him upon this theme
Until my eyelids will no longer wag.

QUEEN GETRUDE: O my son, what theme?

HAMLET: I lov'd Ophelia. Forty thousand brothers
Could not (with all their quantity of love)
Make up my sum. What wilt thou do for her?

KING CLAUDIUS: O, he is mad, Laertes.

QUEEN GETRUDE: For love of God, forbear him!

HAMLET: 'Swounds, show me what thou't do.
Woo't weep? woo't fight? woo't fast? woo't tear thyself?
Woo't drink up esill? eat a crocodile?
I'll do't. Dost thou come here to whine?
To outface me with leaping in her grave?
Be buried quick with her, and so will I.
And if thou prate of mountains, let them throw
Millions of acres on us, till our ground,
Singeing his pate against the burning zone,

Make Ossa like a wart! Nay, an thou'lt mouth,
I'll rant as well as thou.

QUEEN GETRUDE: This is mere madness;
And thus a while the fit will work on him.
Anon, as patient as the female dove
When that her golden couplets are disclos'd,
His silence will sit drooping.

HAMLET: Hear you, sir!
What is the reason that you use me thus?
I lov'd you ever. But it is no matter.
Let Hercules himself do what he may,
The cat will mew, and dog will have his day.
   Exit.

KING CLAUDIUS: I pray thee, good Horatio, wait upon him.
   Exit Horatio.
   To Laertes Strengthen your patience in our last night's speech.
We'll put the matter to the present push.-
Good Gertrude, set some watch over your son.-
This grave shall have a living monument.
An hour of quiet shortly shall we see;
Till then in patience our proceeding be.
   Exeunt.

ACT V. SCENE II. Elsinore. A Hall in the Castle.
Enter Hamlet and Horatio.

HAMLET: So much for this, sir; now shall you see the other.
You do remember all the circumstance?

HORATIO: Remember it, my lord!

HAMLET: Sir, in my heart there was a kind of fighting
That would not let me sleep. Methought I lay
Worse than the mutinies in the bilboes. Rashly-

And prais'd be rashness for it; let us know,
Our indiscretion sometime serves us well
When our deep plots do pall; and that should learn us
There's a divinity that shapes our ends,
Rough-hew them how we will-

HORATIO: That is most certain.

HAMLET: Up from my cabin,
My sea-gown scarf'd about me, in the dark
Grop'd I to find out them; had my desire,
Finger'd their packet, and in fine withdrew
To mine own room again; making so bold
(My fears forgetting manners) to unseal
Their grand commission; where I found, Horatio
(O royal knavery!), an exact command,
Larded with many several sorts of reasons,
Importing Denmark's health, and England's too,
With, hoo! such bugs and goblins in my life-
That, on the supervise, no leisure bated,
No, not to stay the finding of the axe,
My head should be struck off.

HORATIO: Is't possible?

HAMLET: Here's the commission; read it at more leisure.
But wilt thou bear me how I did proceed?

HORATIO: I beseech you.

HAMLET: Being thus benetted round with villanies,
Or I could make a prologue to my brains,
They had begun the play. I sat me down;
Devis'd a new commission; wrote it fair.
I once did hold it, as our statists do,
A baseness to write fair, and labour'd much
How to forget that learning; but, sir, now
It did me yeoman's service. Wilt thou know

Th' effect of what I wrote?

HORATIO: Ay, good my lord.

HAMLET: An earnest conjuration from the King,
As England was his faithful tributary,
As love between them like the palm might flourish,
As peace should still her wheaten garland wear
And stand a comma 'tween their amities,
And many such-like as's of great charge,
That, on the view and knowing of these contents,
Without debatement further, more or less,
He should the bearers put to sudden death,
Not shriving time allow'd.

HORATIO: How was this seal'd?

HAMLET: Why, even in that was heaven ordinant.
I had my father's signet in my purse,
which was the model of that Danish seal;
Folded the writ up in the form of th' other,
Subscrib'd it, gave't th' impression, plac'd it safely,
The changeling never known. Now, the next day
Was our sea-fight; and what to this was sequent
Thou know'st already.

HORATIO: So Guildenstern and Rosencrantz go to't.

HAMLET: Why, man, they did make love to this employment!
They are not near my conscience; their defeat
Does by their own insinuation grow.
'Tis dangerous when the baser nature comes
Between the pass and fell incensed points
Of mighty opposites.

HORATIO: Why, what a king is this!

HAMLET: Does it not, thinks't thee, stand me now upon-
He that hath kill'd my king, and whor'd my mother;
Popp'd in between th' election and my hopes;
Thrown out his angle for my Proper life,
And with such coz'nage- is't not perfect conscience
To quit him with this arm? And is't not to be damn'd
To let this canker of our nature come
In further evil?

HORATIO: It must be shortly known to him from England
What is the issue of the business there.

HAMLET: It will be short; the interim is mine,
And a man's life is no more than to say 'one.'
But I am very sorry, good Horatio,
That to Laertes I forgot myself,
For by the image of my cause I see
The portraiture of his. I'll court his favours.
But sure the bravery of his grief did put me
Into a tow'ring passion.

HORATIO: Peace! Who comes here?
  Enter Young Osric, a Courtier.

OSRIC: Your lordship is right welcome back to Denmark.

HAMLET: I humbly thank you, sir. *Aside to Horatio* Dost know this waterfly?

HORATIO: *Aside to Hamlet* No, my good lord.

HAMLET: *Aside to Horatio* Thy state is the more gracious; for 'tis a vice to know him. He hath much land, and fertile. Let a beast be lord of beasts, and his crib shall stand at the king's messenger 'Tis a chough; but, as I say, spacious in the possession of dirt.

OSRIC: Sweet lord, if your lordship were at leisure, I should impart

William Shakespeare

a thing to you from his Majesty.

HAMLET: I will receive it, sir, with all diligence of spirit. Put your bonnet to his right use. 'Tis for the head.

OSRIC: I thank your lordship, it is very hot.

HAMLET: No, believe me, 'tis very cold; the wind is northerly.

OSRIC: It is indifferent cold, my lord, indeed.

HAMLET: But yet methinks it is very sultry and hot for my complexion.

OSRIC: Exceedingly, my lord; it is very sultry, as 'twere- I cannot tell how. But, my lord, his Majesty bade me signify to you that he has laid a great wager on your head. Sir, this is the matter-

HAMLET: I beseech you remember.
   Hamlet Moves Him to Put on His Hat.

OSRIC: Nay, good my lord; for mine ease, in good faith. Sir, here is newly come to court Laertes; believe me, an absolute gentleman, full of most excellent differences, of very soft society and great showing. Indeed, to speak feelingly of him, he is the card or calendar of gentry; for you shall find in him the continent of what part a gentleman would see.

HAMLET: Sir, his definement suffers no perdition in you; though, I know, to divide him inventorially would dozy th' arithmetic of memory, and yet but yaw neither in respect of his quick sail. But, in the verity of extolment, I take him to be a soul of great article, and his infusion of such dearth and rareness as, to make true diction of him, his semblable is his mirror, and who else would trace him, his umbrage, nothing more.

OSRIC: Your lordship speaks most infallibly of him.

HAMLET: The concernancy, sir? Why do we wrap the gentleman in our more rawer breath

OSRIC: Sir? *Aside to Hamlet* Is't not possible to understand in another tongue? You will do't, sir, really.

HAMLET: What imports the nomination of this gentleman

OSRIC: Of Laertes?

HORATIO: *Aside* His purse is empty already. All's golden words are spent.

HAMLET: Of him, sir.

OSRIC: I know you are not ignorant-

HAMLET: I would you did, sir; yet, in faith, if you did, it would not much approve me. Well, sir?

OSRIC: You are not ignorant of what excellence Laertes is-

HAMLET: I dare not confess that, lest I should compare with him in excellence; but to know a man well were to know himself.

OSRIC: I mean, sir, for his weapon; but in the imputation laid on him by them, in his meed he's unfellowed.

HAMLET: What's his weapon?

OSRIC: Rapier and dagger.

HAMLET: That's two of his weapons- but well.

OSRIC: The King, sir, hath wager'd with him six Barbary horses; against the which he has impon'd, as I take it, six French rapiers and poniards, with their assigns, as girdle, hangers, and

so. Three of the carriages, in faith, are very dear to fancy,
very responsive to the hilts, most delicate carriages, and of
very liberal conceit.

HAMLET: What call you the carriages?

HORATIO: *Aside to Hamlet* I knew you must be edified by the margent
ere you had done.

OSRIC: The carriages, sir, are the hangers.

HAMLET: The phrase would be more germane to the matter if we could
carry cannon by our sides. I would it might be hangers till then.
But on! Six Barbary horses against six French swords, their
assigns, and three liberal-conceited carriages: that's the French
bet against the Danish. Why is this all impon'd, as you call it?

OSRIC: The King, sir, hath laid that, in a dozen passes between
yourself and him, he shall not exceed you three hits; he hath
laid on twelve for nine, and it would come to immediate trial
if your lordship would vouchsafe the answer.

HAMLET: How if I answer no?

OSRIC: I mean, my lord, the opposition of your person in trial.

HAMLET: Sir, I will walk here in the hall. If it please his Majesty,
it is the breathing time of day with me. Let the foils be
brought, the gentleman willing, and the King hold his purpose,
I will win for him if I can; if not, I will gain nothing but my
shame and the odd hits.

OSRIC: Shall I redeliver you e'en so?

HAMLET: To this effect, sir, after what flourish your nature will.

OSRIC: I commend my duty to your lordship.

HAMLET: Yours, yours.
  Exit Osric.
He does well to commend it himself; there are no tongues else for's turn.

HORATIO: This lapwing runs away with the shell on his head.

HAMLET: He did comply with his dug before he suck'd it. Thus has he, and many more of the same bevy that I know the drossy age dotes on, only got the tune of the time and outward habit of encounter- a kind of yesty collection, which carries them through and through the most fann'd and winnowed opinions; and do but blow them to their trial-the bubbles are out,
  Enter a Lord.

LORD: My lord, his Majesty commended him to you by young Osric, who brings back to him, that you attend him in the hall. He sends to know if your pleasure hold to play with Laertes, or that you will take longer time.

HAMLET: I am constant to my purposes; they follow the King's pleasure. If his fitness speaks, mine is ready; now or whensoever, provided I be so able as now.

LORD: The King and Queen and all are coming down.

HAMLET: In happy time.

LORD: The Queen desires you to use some gentle entertainment to Laertes before you fall to play.

HAMLET: She well instructs me.
  Exit Lord.

HORATIO: You will lose this wager, my lord.

HAMLET: I do not think so. Since he went into France I have been in continual practice. I shall win at the odds. But thou wouldst not think how ill all's here about my heart. But it is no matter.

HORATIO: Nay, good my lord -

HAMLET: It is but foolery; but it is such a kind of gaingiving as would perhaps trouble a woman.

HORATIO: If your mind dislike anything, obey it. I will forestall their repair hither and say you are not fit.

HAMLET: Not a whit, we defy augury; there's a special providence in the fall of a sparrow. If it be now, 'tis not to come', if it be not to come, it will be now; if it be not now, yet it will come: the readiness is all. Since no man knows aught of what he leaves, what is't to leave betimes? Let be.
    Enter King, Queen, Laertes, Osric, and Lords, with other Attendants with foils and gauntlets. A table and flagons of wine on it.

KING CLAUDIUS: Come, Hamlet, come, and take this hand from me.
    The King Puts Laertes' Hand into Hamlet's.

HAMLET: Give me your pardon, sir. I have done you wrong;
But pardon't, as you are a gentleman.
This presence knows,
And you must needs have heard, how I am punish'd
With sore distraction. What I have done
That might your nature, honour, and exception
Roughly awake, I here proclaim was madness.
Was't Hamlet wrong'd Laertes? Never Hamlet.
If Hamlet from himself be taken away,
And when he's not himself does wrong Laertes,
Then Hamlet does it not, Hamlet denies it.
Who does it, then? His madness. If't be so,
Hamlet is of the faction that is wrong'd;
His madness is poor Hamlet's enemy.
Sir, in this audience,
Let my disclaiming from a purpos'd evil

Free me so far in your most generous thoughts
That I have shot my arrow o'er the house
And hurt my brother.

LAERTES: I am satisfied in nature,
Whose motive in this case should stir me most
To my revenge. But in my terms of honour
I stand aloof, and will no reconcilement
Till by some elder masters of known honour
I have a voice and precedent of peace
To keep my name ungor'd. But till that time
I do receive your offer'd love like love,
And will not wrong it.

HAMLET: I embrace it freely,
And will this brother's wager frankly play.
Give us the foils. Come on.

LAERTES: Come, one for me.

HAMLET: I'll be your foil, Laertes. In mine ignorance
Your skill shall, like a star i' th' darkest night,
Stick fiery off indeed.

LAERTES: You mock me, sir.

HAMLET: No, by this bad.

KING CLAUDIUS: Give them the foils, young Osric. Cousin Hamlet,
You know the wager?

HAMLET: Very well, my lord.
Your Grace has laid the odds o' th' weaker side.

KING CLAUDIUS: I do not fear it, I have seen you both;
But since he is better'd, we have therefore odds.

LAERTES: This is too heavy; let me see another.

HAMLET: This likes me well. These foils have all a length?
Prepare to Play.

OSRIC: Ay, my good lord.

KING CLAUDIUS: Set me the stoups of wine upon that table.
If Hamlet give the first or second hit,
Or quit in answer of the third exchange,
Let all the battlements their ordnance fire;
The King shall drink to Hamlet's better breath,
And in the cup an union shall he throw
Richer than that which four successive kings
In Denmark's crown have worn. Give me the cups;
And let the kettle to the trumpet speak,
The trumpet to the cannoneer without,
The cannons to the heavens, the heaven to earth,
'Now the King drinks to Hamlet.' Come, begin.
And you the judges, bear a wary eye.

HAMLET: Come on, sir.

LAERTES: Come, my lord. They play.

HAMLET: One.

LAERTES: No.

HAMLET: Judgment!

OSRIC: A hit, a very palpable hit.

LAERTES: Well, again!

KING CLAUDIUS: Stay, give me drink. Hamlet, this pearl is thine;
Here's to thy health.

Drum; Trumpets Sound; a Piece Goes off Within.
Give him the cup.

HAMLET: I'll play this bout first; set it by awhile.
Come. (They play.) Another hit. What say you?

LAERTES: A touch, a touch; I do confess't.

KING CLAUDIUS: Our son shall win.

QUEEN GETRUDE: He's fat, and scant of breath.
Here, Hamlet, take my napkin, rub thy brows.
The Queen carouses to thy fortune, Hamlet.

HAMLET: Good madam!

KING CLAUDIUS: Gertrude, do not drink.

QUEEN GETRUDE: I will, my lord; I pray you pardon me. Drinks.

KING CLAUDIUS: *Aside* It is the poison'd cup; it is too late.

HAMLET: I dare not drink yet, madam; by-and-by.

QUEEN GETRUDE: Come, let me wipe thy face.

LAERTES: My lord, I'll hit him now.

KING CLAUDIUS: I do not think't.

LAERTES: *Aside* And yet it is almost against my conscience.

HAMLET: Come for the third, Laertes! You but dally.
pray You Pass with your best violence;
I am afeard You make a wanton of me.

LAERTES: Say you so? Come on. Play.

William Shakespeare

OSRIC: Nothing neither way.

LAERTES: Have at you now!
Laertes Wounds Hamlet; Then in Scuffling, They Change Rapiers, And Hamlet Wounds Laertes.

KING CLAUDIUS: Part them! They are incens'd.

HAMLET: Nay come! again! The Queen falls.

OSRIC: Look to the Queen there, ho!

HORATIO: They bleed on both sides. How is it, my lord?

OSRIC: How is't, Laertes?

LAERTES: Why, as a woodcock to mine own springe, Osric.
I am justly kill'd with mine own treachery.

HAMLET: How does the Queen?

KING CLAUDIUS: She sounds to see them bleed.

QUEEN GETRUDE: No, no! the drink, the drink! O my dear Hamlet!
The drink, the drink! I am poison'd.
Dies.

HAMLET: O villany! Ho! let the door be lock'd.
Treachery! Seek it out.
Laertes Falls.

LAERTES: It is here, Hamlet. Hamlet, thou art slain;
No medicine in the world can do thee good.
In thee there is not half an hour of life.
The treacherous instrument is in thy hand,
Unbated and envenom'd. The foul practice
Hath turn'd itself on me. Lo, here I lie,

Never to rise again. Thy mother's poison'd.
I can no more. The King, the King's to blame.

HAMLET: The point envenom'd too?
Then, venom, to thy work. *Hurts the King.*

ALL: Treason! treason!

KING CLAUDIUS: O, yet defend me, friends! I am but hurt.

HAMLET: Here, thou incestuous, murd'rous, damned Dane,
Drink off this potion! Is thy union here?
Follow my mother. *King dies.*

LAERTES: He is justly serv'd.
It is a poison temper'd by himself.
Exchange forgiveness with me, noble Hamlet.
Mine and my father's death come not upon thee,
Nor thine on me! *Dies.*

HAMLET: Heaven make thee free of it! I follow thee.
I am dead, Horatio. Wretched queen, adieu!
You that look pale and tremble at this chance,
That are but mutes or audience to this act,
Had I but time (as this fell sergeant, Death,
Is strict in his arrest) O, I could tell you—
But let it be. Horatio, I am dead;
Thou liv'st; report me and my cause aright
To the unsatisfied.

HORATIO: Never believe it.
I am more an antique Roman than a Dane.
Here's yet some liquor left.

HAMLET: As th'art a man,
Give me the cup. Let go! By heaven, I'll ha't.
O good Horatio, what a wounded name

(Things standing thus unknown) shall live behind me!
If thou didst ever hold me in thy heart,
Absent thee from felicity awhile,
And in this harsh world draw thy breath in pain,
To tell my story.
  March Afar Off, and Shot Within.
What warlike noise is this?

OSRIC: Young Fortinbras, with conquest come from Poland,
To the ambassadors of England gives
This warlike volley.

HAMLET: O, I die, Horatio!
The potent poison quite o'ercrows my spirit.
I cannot live to hear the news from England,
But I do prophesy th' election lights
On Fortinbras. He has my dying voice.
So tell him, with th' occurrents, more and less,
Which have solicited- the rest is silence. Dies.

HORATIO: Now cracks a noble heart.
Good night, sweet prince,
And flights of angels sing thee to thy rest!
  March Within.
Why does the drum come hither?
  Enter Fortinbras and English Ambassadors, with Drum, Colours, and Attendants.

FORTINBRAS: Where is this sight?

HORATIO: What is it you will see?
If aught of woe or wonder, cease your search.

FORTINBRAS: This quarry cries on havoc. O proud Death,
What feast is toward in thine eternal cell
That thou so many princes at a shot
So bloodily hast struck.

AMBASSADOR: The sight is dismal;
And our affairs from England come too late.
The ears are senseless that should give us bearing
To tell him his commandment is fulfill'd
That Rosencrantz and Guildenstern are dead.
Where should We have our thanks?

HORATIO: Not from his mouth,
Had it th' ability of life to thank you.
He never gave commandment for their death.
But since, so jump upon this bloody question,
You from the Polack wars, and you from England,
Are here arriv'd, give order that these bodies
High on a stage be placed to the view;
And let me speak to the yet unknowing world
How these things came about. So shall You hear
Of carnal, bloody and unnatural acts;
Of accidental judgments, casual slaughters;
Of deaths put on by cunning and forc'd cause;
And, in this upshot, purposes mistook
Fall'n on th' inventors' heads. All this can I
Truly deliver.

FORTINBRAS: Let us haste to hear it,
And call the noblest to the audience.
For me, with sorrow I embrace my fortune.
I have some rights of memory in this kingdom
Which now, to claim my vantage doth invite me.

HORATIO: Of that I shall have also cause to speak,
And from his mouth whose voice will draw on more.
But let this same be presently perform'd,
Even while men's minds are wild, lest more mischance
On plots and errors happen.

FORTINBRAS: Let four captains
Bear Hamlet like a soldier to the stage;
For he was likely, had he been put on,

To have prov'd most royally; and for his passage
The soldiers' music and the rites of war
Speak loudly for him.
Take up the bodies. Such a sight as this
Becomes the field but here shows much amiss.
Go, bid the soldiers shoot.
   Exeunt Marching; after the Which a Peal of Ordnance Are Shot Off.

END

Macbeth

Dramatis Personae

DUNCAN, King of Scotland
MACBETH, Thane of Glamis and Cawdor, a general in the King's army
LADY MACBETH, his wife
MACDUFF, Thane of Fife, a nobleman of Scotland
LADY MACDUFF, his wife
MALCOLM, elder son of Duncan
DONALBAIN, younger son of Duncan
BANQUO, Thane of Lochaber, a general in the King's army
FLEANCE, his son
LENNOX, nobleman of Scotland
ROSS, nobleman of Scotland
MENTEITH nobleman of Scotland
ANGUS, nobleman of Scotland
CAITHNESS, nobleman of Scotland
SIWARD, Earl of Northumberland, general of the English forces
YOUNG SIWARD, his son
SEYTON, attendant to Macbeth
HECATE, Queen of the Witches
The Three Witches
Boy, Son of Macduff
Gentlewoman attending on Lady Macbeth
An English Doctor
A Scottish Doctor
A Sergeant
A Porter
An Old Man
The Ghost of Banquo and other Apparitions
Lords, Gentlemen, Officers, Soldiers, Murtherers, Attendants,
 and Messengers

SCENE: *Scotland and England*

ACT I. SCENE I. A Desert Place. Thunder and Lightning.
Enter Three Witches.

FIRST WITCH: When shall we three meet again?
In thunder, lightning, or in rain?

SECOND WITCH: When the hurlyburly's done,
When the battle's lost and won.

THIRD WITCH: That will be ere the set of sun.

FIRST WITCH: Where the place?

SECOND WITCH: Upon the heath.

THIRD WITCH: There to meet with Macbeth.

FIRST WITCH: I come, Graymalkin.

ALL: Paddock calls. Anon!
Fair is foul, and foul is fair.
Hover through the fog and filthy air.
   Exeunt.

ACT I. SCENE II. A Camp near Forres. Alarum Within.
Enter Duncan, Malcolm, Donalbain, Lennox, with Attendants, Meeting a Bleeding Sergeant.

DUNCAN: What bloody man is that? He can report,
As seemeth by his plight, of the revolt
The newest state.

MALCOLM: This is the sergeant
Who like a good and hardy soldier fought
'Gainst my captivity. Hail, brave friend!

Say to the King the knowledge of the broil
As thou didst leave it.

SERGEANT: Doubtful it stood,
As two spent swimmers that do cling together
And choke their art. The merciless Macdonwald-
Worthy to be a rebel, for to that
The multiplying villainies of nature
Do swarm upon him -from the Western Isles
Of kerns and gallowglasses is supplied;
And Fortune, on his damned quarrel smiling,
Show'd like a rebel's whore. But all's too weak;
For brave Macbeth -well he deserves that name-
Disdaining Fortune, with his brandish'd steel,
Which smoked with bloody execution,
Like Valor's minion carved out his passage
Till he faced the slave,
Which ne'er shook hands, nor bade farewell to him,
Till he unseam'd him from the nave to the chaps,
And fix'd his head upon our battlements.

DUNCAN: O valiant cousin! Worthy gentleman!

SERGEANT: As whence the sun 'gins his reflection
Shipwrecking storms and direful thunders break,
So from that spring whence comfort seem'd to come
Discomfort swells. Mark, King of Scotland, mark.
No sooner justice had, with valor arm'd,
Compell'd these skipping kerns to trust their heels,
But the Norweyan lord, surveying vantage,
With furbish'd arms and new supplies of men,
Began a fresh assault.

DUNCAN: Dismay'd not this
Our captains, Macbeth and Banquo.?

SERGEANT: Yes,
As sparrows eagles, or the hare the lion.

If I say sooth, I must report they were
As cannons overcharged with double cracks,
So they doubly redoubled strokes upon the foe.
Except they meant to bathe in reeking wounds,
Or memorize another Golgotha,
I cannot tell-
But I am faint; my gashes cry for help.

DUNCAN: So well thy words become thee as thy wounds;
They smack of honor both. Go get him surgeons.
   Exit Sergeant, Attended.
Who comes here?
   Enter Ross.

MALCOLM: The worthy Thane of Ross.

LENNOX: What a haste looks through his eyes! So should he look
That seems to speak things strange.

ROSS: God save the King!

DUNCAN: Whence camest thou, worthy Thane?

ROSS: From Fife, great King,
Where the Norweyan banners flout the sky
And fan our people cold.
Norway himself, with terrible numbers,
Assisted by that most disloyal traitor
The Thane of Cawdor, began a dismal conflict,
Till that Bellona's bridegroom, lapp'd in proof,
Confronted him with self-comparisons,
Point against point rebellious, arm 'gainst arm,
Curbing his lavish spirit; and, to conclude,
The victory fell on us.

DUNCAN: Great happiness!

ROSS: That now
Sweno, the Norways' king, craves composition;
Nor would we deign him burial of his men
Till he disbursed, at Saint Colme's Inch,
Ten thousand dollars to our general use.

DUNCAN: No more that Thane of Cawdor shall deceive
Our bosom interest. Go pronounce his present death,
And with his former title greet Macbeth.

ROSS: I'll see it done.

DUNCAN: What he hath lost, noble Macbeth hath won.
Exeunt.

ACT I. SCENE III. A Heath. Thunder.

Enter the Three Witches.

FIRST WITCH: Where hast thou been, sister?

SECOND WITCH: Killing swine.

THIRD WITCH: Sister, where thou?

FIRST WITCH: A sailor's wife had chestnuts in her lap,
And mounch'd, and mounch'd, and mounch'd. "Give me," quoth I.
"Aroint thee, witch!" the rump-fed ronyon cries.
Her husband's to Aleppo gone, master the Tiger;
But in a sieve I'll thither sail,
And, like a rat without a tail,
I'll do, I'll do, and I'll do.

SECOND WITCH: I'll give thee a wind.

FIRST WITCH: Thou'rt kind.

THIRD WITCH: And I another.

FIRST WITCH: I myself have all the other,
And the very ports they blow,
All the quarters that they know
I' the shipman's card.
I will drain him dry as hay:
Sleep shall neither night nor day
Hang upon his penthouse lid;
He shall live a man forbid.
Weary se'nnights nine times nine
Shall he dwindle, peak, and pine;
Though his bark cannot be lost,
Yet it shall be tempest-toss'd.
Look what I have.

SECOND WITCH: Show me, show me.

FIRST WITCH: Here I have a pilot's thumb,
Wreck'd as homeward he did come. Drum within.

THIRD WITCH: A drum, a drum!
Macbeth doth come.

ALL: The weird sisters, hand in hand,
Posters of the sea and land,
Thus do go about, about,
Thrice to thine, and thrice to mine,
And thrice again, to make up nine.
Peace! The charm's wound up.
  Enter Macbeth and Banquo.

MACBETH: So foul and fair a day I have not seen.

BANQUO: How far is't call'd to Forres? What are these
So wither'd and so wild in their attire,
That look not like the inhabitants o' the earth,
And yet are on't? Live you? or are you aught
That man may question? You seem to understand me,

By each at once her choppy finger laying
Upon her skinny lips. You should be women,
And yet your beards forbid me to interpret
That you are so.

MACBETH: Speak, if you can. What are you?

FIRST WITCH: All hail, Macbeth, hail to thee, Thane of Glamis!

SECOND WITCH: All hail, Macbeth, hail to thee, Thane of Cawdor!

THIRD WITCH: All hail, Macbeth, that shalt be King hereafter!

BANQUO: Good sir, why do you start, and seem to fear
Things that do sound so fair? I' the name of truth,
Are ye fantastical or that indeed
Which outwardly ye show? My noble partner
You greet with present grace and great prediction
Of noble having and of royal hope,
That he seems rapt withal. To me you speak not.
If you can look into the seeds of time,
And say which grain will grow and which will not,
Speak then to me, who neither beg nor fear
Your favors nor your hate.

FIRST WITCH: Hail!

SECOND WITCH: Hail!

THIRD WITCH: Hail!

FIRST WITCH: Lesser than Macbeth, and greater.

SECOND WITCH: Not so happy, yet much happier.

THIRD WITCH: Thou shalt get kings, though thou be none.
So all hail, Macbeth and Banquo!

FIRST WITCH: Banquo and Macbeth, all hail!

MACBETH: Stay, you imperfect speakers, tell me more.
By Sinel's death I know I am Thane of Glamis;
But how of Cawdor? The Thane of Cawdor lives,
A prosperous gentleman; and to be King
Stands not within the prospect of belief,
No more than to be Cawdor. Say from whence
You owe this strange intelligence, or why
Upon this blasted heath you stop our way
With such prophetic greeting? Speak, I charge you.
   Witches Vanish.

BANQUO: The earth hath bubbles as the water has,
And these are of them. Whither are they vanish'd?

MACBETH: Into the air, and what seem'd corporal melted
As breath into the wind. Would they had stay'd!

BANQUO: Were such things here as we do speak about?
Or have we eaten on the insane root
That takes the reason prisoner?

MACBETH: Your children shall be kings.

BANQUO: You shall be King.

MACBETH: And Thane of Cawdor too. Went it not so?

BANQUO: To the selfsame tune and words. Who's here?
   Enter Ross and Angus.

ROSS: The King hath happily received, Macbeth,
The news of thy success; and when he reads
Thy personal venture in the rebels' fight,
His wonders and his praises do contend
Which should be thine or his. Silenced with that,

In viewing o'er the rest o' the selfsame day,
He finds thee in the stout Norweyan ranks,
Nothing afeard of what thyself didst make,
Strange images of death. As thick as hail
Came post with post, and every one did bear
Thy praises in his kingdom's great defense,
And pour'd them down before him.

ANGUS: We are sent
To give thee, from our royal master, thanks;
Only to herald thee into his sight,
Not pay thee.

ROSS: And for an earnest of a greater honor,
He bade me, from him, call thee Thane of Cawdor.
In which addition, hail, most worthy Thane,
For it is thine.

BANQUO: What, can the devil speak true?

MACBETH: The Thane of Cawdor lives. Why do you dress me
In borrow'd robes?

ANGUS: Who was the Thane lives yet,
But under heavy judgement bears that life
Which he deserves to lose. Whether he was combined
With those of Norway, or did line the rebel
With hidden help and vantage, or that with both
He labor'd in his country's wreck, I know not;
But treasons capital, confess'd and proved,
Have overthrown him.

MACBETH: *Aside.* Glamis, and Thane of Cawdor!
The greatest is behind. *To Ross and Angus* Thanks for your pains.
Aside to Banquo Do you not hope your children shall be kings,
When those that gave the Thane of Cawdor to me
Promised no less to them?

BANQUO: *Aside to Macbeth.* That, trusted home,
Might yet enkindle you unto the crown,
Besides the Thane of Cawdor. But 'tis strange;
And oftentimes, to win us to our harm,
The instruments of darkness tell us truths,
Win us with honest trifles, to betray's
In deepest consequence-
Cousins, a word, I pray you.

MACBETH: *Aside.* Two truths are told,
As happy prologues to the swelling act
Of the imperial theme-I thank you, gentlemen.
Aside. This supernatural soliciting
Cannot be ill, cannot be good. If ill,
Why hath it given me earnest of success,
Commencing in a truth? I am Thane of Cawdor.
If good, why do I yield to that suggestion
Whose horrid image doth unfix my hair
And make my seated heart knock at my ribs,
Against the use of nature? Present fears
Are less than horrible imaginings:
My thought, whose murther yet is but fantastical,
Shakes so my single state of man that function
Is smother'd in surmise, and nothing is
But what is not.

BANQUO: Look, how our partner's rapt.

MACBETH: *Aside.* If chance will have me King, why, chance may crown me
Without my stir.

BANQUO: New honors come upon him,
Like our strange garments, cleave not to their mould
But with the aid of use.

MACBETH: *Aside.* Come what come may,
Time and the hour runs through the roughest day.

BANQUO: Worthy Macbeth, we stay upon your leisure.

MACBETH: Give me your favor; my dull brain was wrought
With things forgotten. Kind gentlemen, your pains
Are register'd where every day I turn
The leaf to read them. Let us toward the King.
Think upon what hath chanced, and at more time,
The interim having weigh'd it, let us speak
Our free hearts each to other.

BANQUO: Very gladly.

MACBETH: Till then, enough. Come, friends.
 Exeunt.

SCENE IV. Forres. The Palace.
Flourish. Enter Duncan, Malcolm, Donalbain, Lennox, and Attendants.

DUNCAN: Is execution done on Cawdor? Are not
Those in commission yet return'd?

MALCOLM: My liege,
They are not yet come back. But I have spoke
With one that saw him die, who did report
That very frankly he confess'd his treasons,
Implored your Highness' pardon, and set forth
A deep repentance. Nothing in his life
Became him like the leaving it; he died
As one that had been studied in his death,
To throw away the dearest thing he owed
As 'twere a careless trifle.

DUNCAN: There's no art
To find the mind's construction in the face:
He was a gentleman on whom I built
An absolute trust.
 Enter Macbeth, Banquo, Ross, and Angus.

O worthiest cousin!
The sin of my ingratitude even now
Was heavy on me. Thou art so far before,
That swiftest wing of recompense is slow
To overtake thee. Would thou hadst less deserved,
That the proportion both of thanks and payment
Might have been mine! Only I have left to say,
More is thy due than more than all can pay.

MACBETH: The service and the loyalty Iowe,
In doing it, pays itself. Your Highness' part
Is to receive our duties, and our duties
Are to your throne and state, children and servants,
Which do but what they should, by doing everything
Safe toward your love and honor.

DUNCAN: Welcome hither.
I have begun to plant thee, and will labor
To make thee full of growing. Noble Banquo,
That hast no less deserved, nor must be known
No less to have done so; let me infold thee
And hold thee to my heart.

BANQUO: There if I grow,
The harvest is your own.

DUNCAN: My plenteous joys,
Wanton in fullness, seek to hide themselves
In drops of sorrow. Sons, kinsmen, thanes,
And you whose places are the nearest, know
We will establish our estate upon
Our eldest, Malcolm, whom we name hereafter
The Prince of Cumberland; which honor must
Not unaccompanied invest him only,
But signs of nobleness, like stars, shall shine
On all deservers. From hence to Inverness,
And bind us further to you.

MACBETH: The rest is labor, which is not used for you.
I'll be myself the harbinger, and make joyful
The hearing of my wife with your approach;
So humbly take my leave.

DUNCAN: My worthy Cawdor!

MACBETH: *Aside.* The Prince of Cumberland! That is a step
On which I must fall down, or else o'erleap,
For in my way it lies. Stars, hide your fires;
Let not light see my black and deep desires.
The eye wink at the hand; yet let that be
Which the eye fears, when it is done, to see.
   Exit.

DUNCAN: True, worthy Banquo! He is full so valiant,
And in his commendations I am fed;
It is a banquet to me. Let's after him,
Whose care is gone before to bid us welcome.
It is a peerless kinsman. *Flourish.*
   Exeunt.

ACT I. SCENE V. Inverness. Macbeth's Castle.
Enter Lady Macbeth, Reading a Letter.

LADY MACBETH: "They met me in the day of success,
and I have learned by the perfectest report they have
more in them than mortal knowledge.
When I burned in desire to question them further,
they made themselves air, into which they vanished.
Whiles I stood rapt in the wonder of it, came missives from
the King, who all-hailed me 'Thane of Cawdor'; by
which title, before, these weird sisters saluted me and
referred me to the coming on of time with 'Hail,
King that shalt be!' This have I thought good
to deliver thee, my dearest partner of greatness,
that thou mightst not lose the dues of rejoicing,

by being ignorant of what greatness is promised
thee. Lay it to thy heart, and farewell."
Glamis thou art, and Cawdor, and shalt be
What thou art promised. Yet do I fear thy nature.
It is too full o' the milk of human kindness
To catch the nearest way. Thou wouldst be great;
Art not without ambition, but without
The illness should attend it. What thou wouldst highly,
That wouldst thou holily; wouldst not play false,
And yet wouldst wrongly win. Thou'ldst have, great Glamis,
That which cries, "Thus thou must do, if thou have it;
And that which rather thou dost fear to do
Than wishest should be undone." Hie thee hither,
That I may pour my spirits in thine ear,
And chastise with the valor of my tongue
All that impedes thee from the golden round,
Which fate and metaphysical aid doth seem
To have thee crown'd withal.
   Enter a Messenger.
What is your tidings?

MESSENGER: The King comes here tonight.

LADY MACBETH: Thou'rt mad to say it!
Is not thy master with him? who, were't so,
Would have inform'd for preparation.

MESSENGER: So please you, it is true; our Thane is coming.
One of my fellows had the speed of him,
Who, almost dead for breath, had scarcely more
Than would make up his message.

LADY MACBETH: Give him tending;
He brings great news.
   Exit Messenger.
The raven himself is hoarse
That croaks the fatal entrance of Duncan
Under my battlements. Come, you spirits

That tend on mortal thoughts, unsex me here
And fill me from the crown to the toe top-full
Of direst cruelty! Make thick my blood,
Stop up the access and passage to remorse,
That no compunctious visitings of nature
Shake my fell purpose nor keep peace between
The effect and it! Come to my woman's breasts,
And take my milk for gall, your murthering ministers,
Wherever in your sightless substances
You wait on nature's mischief! Come, thick night,
And pall thee in the dunnest smoke of hell
That my keen knife see not the wound it makes
Nor heaven peep through the blanket of the dark
To cry, "Hold, hold!"
   Enter Macbeth.
Great Glamis! Worthy Cawdor!
Greater than both, by the all-hail hereafter!
Thy letters have transported me beyond
This ignorant present, and I feel now
The future in the instant.

MACBETH: My dearest love,
Duncan comes here tonight.

LADY MACBETH: And when goes hence?

MACBETH: Tomorrow, as he purposes.

LADY MACBETH: O, never
Shall sun that morrow see!
Your face, my Thane, is as a book where men
May read strange matters. To beguile the time,
Look like the time; bear welcome in your eye,
Your hand, your tongue; look like the innocent flower,
But be the serpent under it. He that's coming
Must be provided for; and you shall put
This night's great business into my dispatch,
Which shall to all our nights and days to come

Give solely sovereign sway and masterdom.

MACBETH: We will speak further.

LADY MACBETH: Only look up clear;
To alter favor ever is to fear.
Leave all the rest to me.
   Exeunt.

ACT I. SCENE VI. Before Macbeth's Castle. Hautboys and Torches.
Enter Duncan, Malcolm, Donalbain, Banquo, Lennox, Macduff, Ross, Angus, and Attendants.

DUNCAN: This castle hath a pleasant seat; the air
Nimbly and sweetly recommends itself
Unto our gentle senses.

BANQUO: This guest of summer,
The temple-haunting martlet, does approve
By his loved mansionry that the heaven's breath
Smells wooingly here. No jutty, frieze,
Buttress, nor coign of vantage, but this bird
Hath made his pendant bed and procreant cradle;
Where they most breed and haunt, I have observed
The air is delicate.
   Enter Lady Macbeth.

DUNCAN: See, see, our honor'd hostess!
The love that follows us sometime is our trouble,
Which still we thank as love. Herein I teach you
How you shall bid God 'ield us for your pains,
And thank us for your trouble.

LADY MACBETH: All our service
In every point twice done, and then done double,
Were poor and single business to contend
Against those honors deep and broad wherewith

Your Majesty loads our house. For those of old,
And the late dignities heap'd up to them,
We rest your hermits.

DUNCAN: Where's the Thane of Cawdor?
We coursed him at the heels and had a purpose
To be his purveyor; but he rides well,
And his great love, sharp as his spur, hath holp him
To his home before us. Fair and noble hostess,
We are your guest tonight.

LADY MACBETH: Your servants ever
Have theirs, themselves, and what is theirs, in compt,
To make their audit at your Highness' pleasure,
Still to return your own.

DUNCAN: Give me your hand;
Conduct me to mine host. We love him highly,
And shall continue our graces towards him.
By your leave, hostess.
    Exeunt.

    ACT I. SCENE VII Macbeth's Castle. Hautboys and Torches.
Enter a Sewer and Divers Servants with Dishes and Service, Who Pass over the Stage. Then Enter Macbeth.

MACBETH: If it were done when 'tis done, then 'twere well
It were done quickly. If the assassination
Could trammel up the consequence, and catch,
With his surcease, success; that but this blow
Might be the be-all and the end-all -here,
But here, upon this bank and shoal of time,
We'ld jump the life to come. But in these cases
We still have judgement here, that we but teach
Bloody instructions, which being taught return
To plague the inventor. This even-handed justice
Commends the ingredients of our poison'd chalice
To our own lips. He's here in double trust:

First, as I am his kinsman and his subject,
Strong both against the deed; then, as his host,
Who should against his murtherer shut the door,
Not bear the knife myself. Besides, this Duncan
Hath borne his faculties so meek, hath been
So clear in his great office, that his virtues
Will plead like angels trumpet-tongued against
The deep damnation of his taking-off,
And pity, like a naked new-born babe
Striding the blast, or heaven's cherubin horsed
Upon the sightless couriers of the air,
Shall blow the horrid deed in every eye,
That tears shall drown the wind. I have no spur
To prick the sides of my intent, but only
Vaulting ambition, which o'erleaps itself
And falls on the other.
   Enter Lady Macbeth.
How now, what news?

LADY MACBETH: He has almost supp'd. Why have you left the chamber?

MACBETH: Hath he ask'd for me?

LADY MACBETH: Know you not he has?

MACBETH: We will proceed no further in this business:
He hath honor'd me of late, and I have bought
Golden opinions from all sorts of people,
Which would be worn now in their newest gloss,
Not cast aside so soon.

LADY MACBETH: Was the hope drunk
Wherein you dress'd yourself? Hath it slept since?
And wakes it now, to look so green and pale
At what it did so freely? From this time
Such I account thy love. Art thou afeard
To be the same in thine own act and valor
As thou art in desire? Wouldst thou have that

Which thou esteem'st the ornament of life
And live a coward in thine own esteem,
Letting "I dare not" wait upon "I would"
Like the poor cat i' the adage?

MACBETH: Prithee, peace!
I dare do all that may become a man;
Who dares do more is none.

LADY MACBETH: What beast wast then
That made you break this enterprise to me?
When you durst do it, then you were a man,
And, to be more than what you were, you would
Be so much more the man. Nor time nor place
Did then adhere, and yet you would make both.
They have made themselves, and that their fitness now
Does unmake you. I have given suck and know
How tender 'tis to love the babe that milks me-
I would, while it was smiling in my face,
Have pluck'd my nipple from his boneless gums
And dash'd the brains out had I so sworn as you
Have done to this.

MACBETH: If we should fail?

LADY MACBETH: We fail?
But screw your courage to the sticking-place
And we'll not fail. When Duncan is asleep-
Whereto the rather shall his day's hard journey
Soundly invite him- his two chamberlains
Will I with wine and wassail so convince
That memory, the warder of the brain,
Shall be a fume and the receipt of reason
A limbeck only. When in swinish sleep
Their drenched natures lie as in a death,
What cannot you and I perform upon
The unguarded Duncan? What not put upon
His spongy officers, who shall bear the guilt

Of our great quell?

MACBETH: Bring forth men-children only,
For thy undaunted mettle should compose
Nothing but males. Will it not be received,
When we have mark'd with blood those sleepy two
Of his own chamber and used their very daggers,
That they have done't?

LADY MACBETH: Who dares receive it other,
As we shall make our griefs and clamor roar
Upon his death?

MACBETH: I am settled and bend up
Each corporal agent to this terrible feat.
Away, and mock the time with fairest show:
False face must hide what the false heart doth know.
   Exeunt.

ACT II. SCENE I. Inverness. Court of Macbeth's Castle.
Enter Banquo and Fleance, Bearing a Torch Before Him.

BANQUO: How goes the night, boy?

FLEANCE: The moon is down; I have not heard the clock.

BANQUO: And she goes down at twelve.

FLEANCE: I take't 'tis later, sir.

BANQUO: Hold, take my sword. There's husbandry in heaven,
Their candles are all out. Take thee that too.
A heavy summons lies like lead upon me,
And yet I would not sleep. Merciful powers,
Restrain in me the cursed thoughts that nature
Gives way to in repose!
   Enter Macbeth and a Servant with a Torch.

Give me my sword.
Who's there?

MACBETH: A friend.

BANQUO: What, sir, not yet at rest? The King's abed.
He hath been in unusual pleasure and
Sent forth great largess to your offices.
This diamond he greets your wife withal,
By the name of most kind hostess, and shut up
In measureless content.

MACBETH: Being unprepared,
Our will became the servant to defect,
Which else should free have wrought.

BANQUO: All's well.
I dreamt last night of the three weird sisters:
To you they have show'd some truth.

MACBETH: I think not of them;
Yet, when we can entreat an hour to serve,
We would spend it in some words upon that business,
If you would grant the time.

BANQUO: At your kind'st leisure.

MACBETH: If you shall cleave to my consent, when 'tis,
It shall make honor for you.

BANQUO: So I lose none
In seeking to augment it, but still keep
My bosom franchised and allegiance clear,
I shall be counsel'd.

MACBETH: Good repose the while.

BANQUO: Thanks, sir, the like to you.
Exeunt Banquo. and Fleance.

MACBETH: Go bid thy mistress, when my drink is ready,
She strike upon the bell. Get thee to bed.
Exit Servant.
Is this a dagger which I see before me,
The handle toward my hand? Come, let me clutch thee.
I have thee not, and yet I see thee still.
Art thou not, fatal vision, sensible
To feeling as to sight? Or art thou but
A dagger of the mind, a false creation,
Proceeding from the heat-oppressed brain?
I see thee yet, in form as palpable
As this which now I draw.
Thou marshal'st me the way that I was going,
And such an instrument I was to use.
Mine eyes are made the fools o' the other senses,
Or else worth all the rest. I see thee still,
And on thy blade and dudgeon gouts of blood,
Which was not so before. There's no such thing:
It is the bloody business which informs
Thus to mine eyes. Now o'er the one half-world
Nature seems dead, and wicked dreams abuse
The curtain'd sleep; witchcraft celebrates
Pale Hecate's offerings; and wither'd Murther,
Alarum'd by his sentinel, the wolf,
Whose howl's his watch, thus with his stealthy pace,
With Tarquin's ravishing strides, towards his design
Moves like a ghost. Thou sure and firm-set earth,
Hear not my steps, which way they walk, for fear
Thy very stones prate of my whereabout,
And take the present horror from the time,
Which now suits with it. Whiles I threat, he lives;
Words to the heat of deeds too cold breath gives.
A Bell Rings.
I go, and it is done; the bell invites me.
Hear it not, Duncan, for it is a knell

That summons thee to heaven, or to hell. *Exit.*

ACT II. SCENE II. The Same.

Enter Lady Macbeth.

LADY MACBETH: That which hath made them drunk hath made me bold;
What hath quench'd them hath given me fire. Hark! Peace!
It was the owl that shriek'd, the fatal bellman,
Which gives the stern'st good night. He is about it:
The doors are open, and the surfeited grooms
Do mock their charge with snores. I have drugg'd their possets
That death and nature do contend about them,
Whether they live or die.

MACBETH: *Within.* Who's there' what, ho!

LADY MACBETH: Alack, I am afraid they have awaked
And 'tis not done. The attempt and not the deed
Confounds us. Hark! I laid their daggers ready;
He could not miss 'em. Had he not resembled
My father as he slept, I had done't.
 Enter Macbeth,
My husband!

MACBETH: I have done the deed. Didst thou not hear a noise?

LADY MACBETH: I heard the owl scream and the crickets cry.
Did not you speak?

MACBETH: When?

LADY MACBETH: Now.

MACBETH: As I descended?

LADY MACBETH: Ay.

MACBETH: Hark!
Who lies i' the second chamber?

LADY MACBETH: Donalbain.

MACBETH: This is a sorry sight.
  Looks on His Hands.

LADY MACBETH: A foolish thought, to say a sorry sight.

MACBETH: There's one did laugh in 's sleep, and one cried,
  "Murther!"
That they did wake each other. I stood and heard them,
But they did say their prayers and address'd them
Again to sleep.

LADY MACBETH: There are two lodged together.

MACBETH: One cried, "God bless us!" and "Amen" the other,
As they had seen me with these hangman's hands.
Listening their fear, I could not say "Amen,"
When they did say, "God bless us!"

LADY MACBETH: Consider it not so deeply.

MACBETH: But wherefore could not I pronounce "Amen"?
I had most need of blessing, and "Amen"
Stuck in my throat.

LADY MACBETH: These deeds must not be thought
After these ways; so, it will make us mad.

MACBETH: I heard a voice cry, "Sleep no more!
Macbeth does murther sleep" -the innocent sleep,
Sleep that knits up the ravel'd sleave of care,
The death of each day's life, sore labor's bath,
Balm of hurt minds, great nature's second course,

William Shakespeare

Chief nourisher in life's feast-

LADY MACBETH: What do you mean?

MACBETH: Still it cried, "Sleep no more!" to all the house;
"Glamis hath murther'd sleep, and therefore Cawdor
Shall sleep no more. Macbeth shall sleep no more."

LADY MACBETH: Who was it that thus cried? Why, worthy Thane,
You do unbend your noble strength, to think
So brainsickly of things. Go, get some water
And wash this filthy witness from your hand.
Why did you bring these daggers from the place?
They must lie there. Go carry them, and smear
The sleepy grooms with blood.

MACBETH: I'll go no more.
I am afraid to think what I have done;
Look on't again I dare not.

LADY MACBETH: Infirm of purpose!
Give me the daggers. The sleeping and the dead
Are but as pictures; 'tis the eye of childhood
That fears a painted devil. If he do bleed,
I'll gild the faces of the grooms withal,
For it must seem their guilt.
    Exit. Knocking Within.

MACBETH: Whence is that knocking?
How is't with me, when every noise appals me?
What hands are here? Ha, they pluck out mine eyes!
Will all great Neptune's ocean wash this blood
Clean from my hand? No, this my hand will rather
The multitudinous seas incarnadine,
Making the green one red.
    Re-enter Lady Macbeth.

LADY MACBETH: My hands are of your color, but I shame
To wear a heart so white. *Knocking Within.*
I hear knocking
At the south entry. Retire we to our chamber.
A little water clears us of this deed.
How easy is it then! Your constancy
Hath left you unattended. *Knocking Within.* Hark, more knocking.
Get on your nightgown, lest occasion call us
And show us to be watchers. Be not lost
So poorly in your thoughts.

MACBETH: To know my deed, 'twere best not know myself.
   Knocking Within.
Wake Duncan with thy knocking! I would thou couldst!
   Exeunt.

ACT II. SCENE III. The Same.
Enter a Porter. Knocking Within.

PORTER: Here's a knocking indeed! If a man were porter of Hell Gate, he should have old turning the key. *Knocking Within.* Knock, knock, knock! Who's there, i' the name of Belzebub? Here's a farmer that hanged himself on th' expectation of plenty. Come in time! Have napkins enow about you; here you'll sweat fort. *Knocking Within.* Knock, knock! Who's there, in th' other devil's name? Faith, here's an equivocator that could swear in both the scales against either scale, who committed treason enough for God's sake, yet could not equivocate to heaven. O, come in, equivocator. *Knocking Within.* Knock, knock, knock! Who's there? Faith, here's an English tailor come hither, for stealing out of a French hose. Come in, tailor; here you may roast your goose. *Knocking Within.* Knock, knock! Never at quiet! What are you? But this place is too cold for hell. I'll devil-porter it no further. I had thought to have let in some of all professions, that go the primrose way to the everlasting bonfire. *Knocking Within.* Anon, anon! I pray you, remember the Porter.
   Opens the Gate.
   Enter Macduff and Lennox.

MACDUFF: Was it so late, friend, ere you went to bed,
That you do lie so late?

PORTER: Faith, sir, we were carousing till the second cock; and drink, sir, is a great provoker of three things.

MACDUFF: What three things does drink especially provoke?

PORTER: Marry, sir, nose-painting, sleep, and urine. Lechery, sir, it provokes and unprovokes: it provokes the desire, but it takes away the performance. Therefore much drink may be said to be an equivocator with lechery: it makes him, and it mars him; it sets him on, and it takes him off; it persuades him and disheartens him; makes him stand to and not stand to; in conclusion, equivocates him in a sleep, and giving him the lie, leaves him.

MACDUFF: I believe drink gave thee the lie last night.

PORTER: That it did, sir, i' the very throat on me; but requited him for his lie, and, I think, being too strong for him, though he took up my legs sometime, yet I made shift to cast him.

MACDUFF: Is thy master stirring?
  Enter Macbeth.
Our knocking has awaked him; here he comes.

LENNOX: Good morrow, noble sir.

MACBETH: morrow, both.

MACDUFF: Is the King stirring, worthy Thane?

MACBETH: Not yet.

MACDUFF: He did command me to call timely on him;
I have almost slipp'd the hour.

MACBETH: I'll bring you to him.

MACDUFF: I know this is a joyful trouble to you,
But yet 'tis one.

MACBETH: The labor we delight in physics pain.
This is the door.

MACDUFF: I'll make so bold to call,
For 'tis my limited service.
　Exit.

LENNOX: Goes the King hence today?

MACBETH: He does; he did appoint so.

LENNOX: The night has been unruly. Where we lay,
Our chimneys were blown down, and, as they say,
Lamentings heard i' the air, strange screams of death,
And prophesying with accents terrible
Of dire combustion and confused events
New hatch'd to the woeful time. The obscure bird
Clamor'd the livelong night. Some say the earth
Was feverous and did shake.

MACBETH: 'Twas a rough fight.

LENNOX: My young remembrance cannot parallel
A fellow to it.
　Re-enter Macduff.

MACDUFF: O horror, horror, horror! Tongue nor heart
Cannot conceive nor name thee. Macbeth.

LENNOX: What's the matter?

MACDUFF: Confusion now hath made his masterpiece.

Most sacrilegious murther hath broke ope
The Lord's anointed temple and stole thence
The life o' the building.

MACBETH: What is't you say? the life?

LENNOX: Mean you his Majesty?

MACDUFF: Approach the chamber, and destroy your sight
With a new Gorgon. Do not bid me speak;
See, and then speak yourselves.
   Exeunt Macbeth and Lennox.
Awake, awake!
Ring the alarum bell. Murther and treason!
Banquo and Donalbain! Malcolm, awake!
Shake off this downy sleep, death's counterfeit,
And look on death itself! Up, up, and see
The great doom's image! Malcolm! Banquo!
As from your graves rise up, and walk like sprites
To countenance this horror! Ring the bell. *Bell rings.*
   Enter Lady Macbeth.

LADY MACBETH: What's the business,
That such a hideous trumpet calls to parley
The sleepers of the house? Speak, speak!

MACDUFF: O gentle lady,
'Tis not for you to hear what I can speak:
The repetition in a woman's ear
Would murther as it fell.
   Enter Banquo.
O Banquo, Banquo!
Our royal master's murther'd.

LADY MACBETH: Woe, alas!
What, in our house?

BANQUO: Too cruel anywhere.
Dear Duff, I prithee, contradict thyself,
And say it is not so.
   Re-enter Macbeth and Lennox, with Ross.

MACBETH: Had I but died an hour before this chance,
I had lived a blessed time, for from this instant
There's nothing serious in mortality.
All is but toys; renown and grace is dead,
The wine of life is drawn, and the mere lees
Is left this vault to brag of.
   Enter Malcolm and Donalbain.

DONALBAIN: What is amiss?

MACBETH: You are, and do not know't.
The spring, the head, the fountain of your blood
Is stopped, the very source of it is stopp'd.

MACDUFF: Your royal father's murther'd.

MALCOLM: O, by whom?

LENNOX: Those of his chamber, as it seem'd, had done't.
Their hands and faces were all badged with blood;
So were their daggers, which unwiped we found
Upon their pillows.
They stared, and were distracted; no man's life
Was to be trusted with them.

MACBETH: O, yet I do repent me of my fury,
That I did kill them.

MACDUFF: Wherefore did you so?

MACBETH: Who can be wise, amazed, temperate and furious,
Loyal and neutral, in a moment? No man.

The expedition of my violent love
Outrun the pauser reason. Here lay Duncan,
His silver skin laced with his golden blood,
And his gash'd stabs look'd like a breach in nature
For ruin's wasteful entrance; there, the murtherers,
Steep'd in the colors of their trade, their daggers
Unmannerly breech'd with gore. Who could refrain,
That had a heart to love, and in that heart
Courage to make 's love known?

LADY MACBETH: Help me hence, ho!

MACDUFF: Look to the lady.

MALCOLM: *Aside to Donalbain.* Why do we hold our tongues,
That most may claim this argument for ours?

DONALBAIN: *Aside to Malcolm.* What should be spoken here, where our fate,
Hid in an auger hole, may rush and seize us?
Let's away,
Our tears are not yet brew'd.

MALCOLM: *Aside to Donalbain.* Nor our strong sorrow
Upon the foot of motion.

BANQUO: Look to the lady.
   Lady Macbeth Is Carried Out.
And when we have our naked frailties hid,
That suffer in exposure, let us meet
And question this most bloody piece of work
To know it further. Fears and scruples shake us.
In the great hand of God I stand, and thence
Against the undivulged pretense I fight
Of treasonous malice.

MACDUFF: And so do I.

ALL: So all.

MACBETH: Let's briefly put on manly readiness
And meet i' the hall together.

ALL: Well contented.
   Exeunt All but Malcolm and Donalbain.

MALCOLM: What will you do? Let's not consort with them.
To show an unfelt sorrow is an office
Which the false man does easy. I'll to England.

DONALBAIN: To Ireland, I; our separated fortune
Shall keep us both the safer. Where we are
There's daggers in men's smiles; the near in blood,
The nearer bloody.

MALCOLM: This murtherous shaft that's shot
Hath not yet lighted, and our safest way
Is to avoid the aim. Therefore to horse;
And let us not be dainty of leave-taking,
But shift away. There's warrant in that theft
Which steals itself when there's no mercy left.
   Exeunt.

ACT II. SCENE IV. Outside Macbeth's Castle.
Enter Ross with an Old Man.

OLD MAN: Threescore and ten I can remember well,
Within the volume of which time I have seen
Hours dreadful and things strange, but this sore night
Hath trifled former knowings.

ROSS: Ah, good father,
Thou seest the heavens, as troubled with man's act,
Threaten his bloody stage. By the clock 'tis day,
And yet dark night strangles the traveling lamp.

Is't night's predominance, or the day's shame,
That darkness does the face of earth entomb,
When living light should kiss it?

OLD MAN: 'Tis unnatural,
Even like the deed that's done. On Tuesday last
A falcon towering in her pride of place
Was by a mousing owl hawk'd at and kill'd.

ROSS: And Duncan's horses-a thing most strange and certain-
Beauteous and swift, the minions of their race,
Turn'd wild in nature, broke their stalls, flung out,
Contending 'gainst obedience, as they would make
War with mankind.

OLD MAN: 'Tis said they eat each other.

ROSS: They did so, to the amazement of mine eyes
That look'd upon't.
 Enter Macduff.
Here comes the good Macduff.
How goes the world, sir, now?

MACDUFF: Why, see you not?

ROSS: Is't known who did this more than bloody deed?

MACDUFF: Those that Macbeth hath slain.

ROSS: Alas, the day!
What good could they pretend?

MACDUFF: They were suborn'd:
Malcolm and Donalbain, the King's two sons,
Are stol'n away and fled, which puts upon them
Suspicion of the deed.

ROSS: 'Gainst nature still!
Thriftless ambition, that wilt ravin up
Thine own life's means! Then 'tis most like
The sovereignty will fall upon Macbeth.

MACDUFF: He is already named, and gone to Scone
To be invested.

ROSS: Where is Duncan's body?

MACDUFF: Carried to Colmekill,
The sacred storehouse of his predecessors
And guardian of their bones.

ROSS: Will you to Scone?

MACDUFF: No, cousin, I'll to Fife.

ROSS: Well, I will thither.

MACDUFF: Well, may you see things well done there.
Adieu,
Lest our old robes sit easier than our new!

ROSS: Farewell, father.

OLD MAN: God's benison go with you and with those
That would make good of bad and friends of foes!
   Exeunt.

ACT III. SCENE I. Forres. The Palace.

Enter Banquo.

BANQUO: Thou hast it now: King, Cawdor, Glamis, all,
As the weird women promised, and I fear
Thou play'dst most foully for't; yet it was said
It should not stand in thy posterity,

But that myself should be the root and father
Of many kings. If there come truth from them
(As upon thee, Macbeth, their speeches shine)
Why, by the verities on thee made good,
May they not be my oracles as well
And set me up in hope? But hush, no more.
    Sennet Sounds. Enter Macbeth as King, Lady Macbeth as Queen, Lennox, Ross, Lords, Ladies, and Attendants.

MACBETH: Here's our chief guest.

LADY MACBETH: If he had been forgotten,
It had been as a gap in our great feast
And all thing unbecoming.

MACBETH: Tonight we hold a solemn supper, sir,
And I'll request your presence.

BANQUO: Let your Highness
Command upon me, to the which my duties
Are with a most indissoluble tie
Forever knit.

MACBETH: Ride you this afternoon?

BANQUO: Ay, my good lord.

MACBETH: We should have else desired your good advice,
Which still hath been both grave and prosperous
In this day's council; but we'll take tomorrow.
Is't far you ride'!

BANQUO: As far, my lord, as will fill up the time
'Twixt this and supper. Go not my horse the better,
I must become a borrower of the night
For a dark hour or twain.

MACBETH: Fail not our feast.

BANQUO: My lord, I will not.

MACBETH: We hear our bloody cousins are bestow'd
In England and in Ireland, not confessing
Their cruel parricide, filling their hearers
With strange invention. But of that tomorrow,
When therewithal we shall have cause of state
Craving us jointly. Hie you to horse; adieu,
Till you return at night. Goes Fleance with you?

BANQUO: Ay, my good lord. Our time does call upon 's.

MACBETH: I wish your horses swift and sure of foot,
And so I do commend you to their backs.
Farewell.
   Exit Banquo.
Let every man be master of his time
Till seven at night; to make society
The sweeter welcome, we will keep ourself
Till supper time alone. While then, God be with you!
   Exeunt all but Macbeth and an Attendant.
Sirrah, a word with you. Attend those men
Our pleasure?

ATTENDANT: They are, my lord, without the palace gate.

MACBETH: Bring them before us.
   Exit Attendant.
To be thus is nothing,
But to be safely thus. Our fears in Banquo.
Stick deep, and in his royalty of nature
Reigns that which would be fear'd. 'Tis much he dares,
And, to that dauntless temper of his mind,
He hath a wisdom that doth guide his valor
To act in safety. There is none but he

Whose being I do fear; and under him
My genius is rebuked, as it is said
Mark Antony's was by Caesar. He chid the sisters
When first they put the name of King upon me
And bade them speak to him; then prophet-like
They hail'd him father to a line of kings.
Upon my head they placed a fruitless crown
And put a barren sceptre in my gripe,
Thence to be wrench'd with an unlineal hand,
No son of mine succeeding. If't be so,
For Banquo's issue have I filed my mind,
For them the gracious Duncan have I murther'd,
Put rancors in the vessel of my peace
Only for them, and mine eternal jewel
Given to the common enemy of man,
To make them kings -the seed of Banquo kings!
Rather than so, come, Fate, into the list,
And champion me to the utterance! Who's there?
   Re-enter Attendant, with Two Murtherers.
Now go to the door, and stay there till we call.
   Exit Attendant.
Was it not yesterday we spoke together?

FIRST MURTHERER: It was, so please your Highness.

MACBETH: Well then, now
Have you consider'd of my speeches? Know
That it was he in the times past which held you
So under fortune, which you thought had been
Our innocent self? This I made good to you
In our last conference, pass'd in probation with you:
How you were borne in hand, how cross'd, the instruments,
Who wrought with them, and all things else that might
To half a soul and to a notion crazed
Say, "Thus did Banquo."

FIRST MURTHERER: You made it known to us.

MACBETH: I did so, and went further, which is now
Our point of second meeting. Do you find
Your patience so predominant in your nature,
That you can let this go? Are you so gospel'd,
To pray for this good man and for his issue,
Whose heavy hand hath bow'd you to the grave
And beggar'd yours forever?

FIRST MURTHERER: We are men, my liege.

MACBETH: Ay, in the catalogue ye go for men,
As hounds and greyhounds, mongrels, spaniels, curs,
Shoughs, waterrugs, and demi-wolves are clept
All by the name of dogs. The valued file
Distinguishes the swift, the slow, the subtle,
The housekeeper, the hunter, every one
According to the gift which bounteous nature
Hath in him closed, whereby he does receive
Particular addition, from the bill
That writes them all alike; and so of men.
Now if you have a station in the file,
Not i' the worst rank of manhood, say it,
And I will put that business in your bosoms
Whose execution takes your enemy off,
Grapples you to the heart and love of us,
Who wear our health but sickly in his life,
Which in his death were perfect.

SECOND MURTHERER: I am one, my liege,
Whom the vile blows and buffets of the world
Have so incensed that I am reckless what
I do to spite the world.

FIRST MURTHERER: And I another
So weary with disasters, tugg'd with fortune,
That I would set my life on any chance,
To mend it or be rid on't.

MACBETH: Both of you
Know Banquo was your enemy.

BOTH MURTHERERS: True, my lord.

MACBETH: So is he mine, and in such bloody distance
That every minute of his being thrusts
Against my near'st of life; and though I could
With barefaced power sweep him from my sight
And bid my will avouch it, yet I must not,
For certain friends that are both his and mine,
Whose loves I may not drop, but wail his fall
Who I myself struck down. And thence it is
That I to your assistance do make love,
Masking the business from the common eye
For sundry weighty reasons.

SECOND MURTHERER: We shall, my lord,
Perform what you command us.

FIRST MURTHERER: Though our lives-

MACBETH: Your spirits shine through you. Within this hour at most
I will advise you where to plant yourselves,
Acquaint you with the perfect spy o' the time,
The moment on't; fort must be done tonight
And something from the palace (always thought
That I require a clearness); and with him-
To leave no rubs nor botches in the work-
Fleance his son, that keeps him company,
Whose absence is no less material to me
Than is his father's, must embrace the fate
Of that dark hour. Resolve yourselves apart;
I'll come to you anon.

BOTH MURTHERERS: We are resolved, my lord.

MACBETH: I'll call upon you straight. Abide within.
Exeunt Murtherers.
It is concluded: Banquo, thy soul's flight,
If it find heaven, must find it out tonight. *Exit.*

ACT III. SCENE II. The Palace.

Enter Lady Macbeth and a Servant.

LADY MACBETH: Is Banquo gone from court?

SERVANT: Ay, madam, but returns again tonight.

LADY MACBETH: Say to the King I would attend his leisure
For a few words.

SERVANT: Madam, I will.
Exit.

LADY MACBETH: Nought's had, all's spent,
Where our desire is got without content.
'Tis safer to be that which we destroy
Than by destruction dwell in doubtful joy.
Enter Macbeth.
How now, my lord? Why do you keep alone,
Of sorriest fancies your companions making,
Using those thoughts which should indeed have died
With them they think on? Things without all remedy
Should be without regard. What's done is done.

MACBETH: We have scotch'd the snake, not kill'd it.
She'll close and be herself, whilst our poor malice
Remains in danger of her former tooth.
But let the frame of things disjoint, both the worlds suffer,
Ere we will eat our meal in fear and sleep
In the affliction of these terrible dreams
That shake us nightly. Better be with the dead,
Whom we, to gain our peace, have sent to peace,

Than on the torture of the mind to lie
In restless ecstasy. Duncan is in his grave;
After life's fitful fever he sleeps well.
Treason has done his worst; nor steel, nor poison,
Malice domestic, foreign levy, nothing,
Can touch him further.

LADY MACBETH: Come on,
Gentle my lord, sleek o'er your rugged looks;
Be bright and jovial among your guests tonight.

MACBETH: So shall I, love, and so, I pray, be you.
Let your remembrance apply to Banquo;
Present him eminence, both with eye and tongue:
Unsafe the while, that we
Must lave our honors in these flattering streams,
And make our faces vizards to our hearts,
Disguising what they are.

LADY MACBETH: You must leave this.

MACBETH: O, full of scorpions is my mind, dear wife!
Thou know'st that Banquo and his Fleance lives.

LADY MACBETH: But in them nature's copy's not eterne.

MACBETH: There's comfort yet; they are assailable.
Then be thou jocund. Ere the bat hath flown
His cloister'd flight, ere to black Hecate's summons
The shard-borne beetle with his drowsy hums
Hath rung night's yawning peal, there shall be done
A deed of dreadful note.

LADY MACBETH: What's to be done?

MACBETH: Be innocent of the knowledge, dearest chuck,
Till thou applaud the deed. Come, seeling night,

Scarf up the tender eye of pitiful day,
And with thy bloody and invisible hand
Cancel and tear to pieces that great bond
Which keeps me pale! Light thickens, and the crow
Makes wing to the rooky wood;
Good things of day begin to droop and drowse,
Whiles night's black agents to their preys do rouse.
Thou marvel'st at my words, but hold thee still:
Things bad begun make strong themselves by ill.
So, prithee, go with me.
   Exeunt.

ACT III. SCENE III. A Park near the Palace.
Enter three Murtherers.

FIRST MURTHERER: But who did bid thee join with us?

THIRD MURTHERER: Macbeth.

SECOND MURTHERER: He needs not our mistrust, since he delivers
Our offices and what we have to do
To the direction just.

FIRST MURTHERER: Then stand with us.
The west yet glimmers with some streaks of day;
Now spurs the lated traveler apace
To gain the timely inn, and near approaches
The subject of our watch.

THIRD MURTHERER: Hark! I hear horses.

BANQUO: *Within.* Give us a light there, ho!

SECOND MURTHERER: Then 'tis he; the rest
That are within the note of expectation
Already are i' the court.

FIRST MURTHERER: His horses go about.

THIRD MURTHERER: Almost a mile, but he does usually-
So all men do -from hence to the palace gate
Make it their walk.

SECOND MURTHERER: A light, a light!
Enter Banquo, and Fleance with a Torch.

THIRD MURTHERER: 'Tis he.

FIRST MURTHERER: Stand to't.

BANQUO: It will be rain tonight.

FIRST MURTHERER: Let it come down.
They Set upon Banquo.

BANQUO: O, treachery! Fly, good Fleance, fly, fly, fly!
Thou mayst revenge. O slave! Dies. Fleance escapes.

THIRD MURTHERER: Who did strike out the light?

FIRST MURTHERER: Wast not the way?

THIRD MURTHERER: There's but one down; the son is fled.

SECOND MURTHERER: We have lost
Best half of our affair.

FIRST MURTHERER: Well, let's away and say how much is done.
Exeunt.

ACT III. SCENE IV. A Hall in the Palace. A Banquet Prepared.
Enter Macbeth, Lady Macbeth, Ross, Lennox, Lords, and Attendants.

MACBETH: You know your own degrees; sit down. At first

And last the hearty welcome.

LORDS: Thanks to your Majesty.

MACBETH: Ourself will mingle with society
And play the humble host.
Our hostess keeps her state, but in best time
We will require her welcome.

LADY MACBETH: Pronounce it for me, sir, to all our friends,
For my heart speaks they are welcome.
 Enter first Murtherer to the door.

MACBETH: See, they encounter thee with their hearts' thanks.
Both sides are even; here I'll sit i' the midst.
Be large in mirth; anon we'll drink a measure
The table round. *Approaches the Door.* There's blood upon thy face.

MURTHERER: 'Tis Banquo's then.

MACBETH: 'Tis better thee without than he within.
Is he dispatch'd?

MURTHERER: My lord, his throat is cut; that I did for him.

MACBETH: Thou art the best o' the cut-throats! Yet he's good
That did the like for Fleance. If thou didst it,
Thou art the nonpareil.

MURTHERER: Most royal sir,
Fleance is 'scaped.

MACBETH: *Aside.* Then comes my fit again. I had else been perfect,
Whole as the marble, founded as the rock,
As broad and general as the casing air;
But now I am cabin'd, cribb'd, confin'd, bound in
To saucy doubts and fears -But Banquo's safe?

MURTHERER: Ay, my good lord. Safe in a ditch he bides,
With twenty trenched gashes on his head,
The least a death to nature.

MACBETH: Thanks for that.
There the grown serpent lies; the worm that's fled
Hath nature that in time will venom breed,
No teeth for the present. Get thee gone. Tomorrow
We'll hear ourselves again.
   Exit Murtherer.

LADY MACBETH: My royal lord,
You do not give the cheer. The feast is sold
That is not often vouch'd, while 'tis amaking,
'Tis given with welcome. To feed were best at home;
From thence the sauce to meat is ceremony;
Meeting were bare without it.

MACBETH: Sweet remembrancer!
Now good digestion wait on appetite,
And health on both!

LENNOX: May't please your Highness sit.
   The Ghost of Banquo Enters and Sits in Macbeth's Place.

MACBETH: Here had we now our country's honor roof'd,
Were the graced person of our Banquo present,
Who may I rather challenge for unkindness
Than pity for mischance!

ROSS: His absence, sir,
Lays blame upon his promise. Please't your Highness
To grace us with your royal company?

MACBETH: The table's full.

LENNOX: Here is a place reserved, sir.

MACBETH: Where?

LENNOX: Here, my good lord. What is't that moves your Highness?

MACBETH: Which of you have done this?

LORDS: What, my good lord?

MACBETH: Thou canst not say I did it; never shake
Thy gory locks at me.

ROSS: Gentlemen, rise; his Highness is well.

LADY MACBETH: Sit, worthy friends; my lord is often thus,
And hath been from his youth. Pray you, keep seat.
The fit is momentary; upon a thought
He will again be well. If much you note him,
You shall offend him and extend his passion.
Feed, and regard him not-Are you a man?

MACBETH: Ay, and a bold one, that dare look on that
Which might appal the devil.

LADY MACBETH: O proper stuff!
This is the very painting of your fear;
This is the air-drawn dagger which you said
Led you to Duncan. O, these flaws and starts,
Impostors to true fear, would well become
A woman's story at a winter's fire,
Authorized by her grandam. Shame itself!
Why do you make such faces? When all's done,
You look but on a stool.

MACBETH: Prithee, see there! Behold! Look! Lo! How say you?
Why, what care I? If thou canst nod, speak too.
If charnel houses and our graves must send
Those that we bury back, our monuments

Shall be the maws of kites.
Exit Ghost.

LADY MACBETH: What, quite unmann'd in folly?

MACBETH: If I stand here, I saw him.

LADY MACBETH: Fie, for shame!

MACBETH: Blood hath been shed ere now, i' the olden time,
Ere humane statute purged the gentle weal;
Ay, and since too, murthers have been perform'd
Too terrible for the ear. The time has been,
That, when the brains were out, the man would die,
And there an end; but now they rise again,
With twenty mortal murthers on their crowns,
And push us from our stools. This is more strange
Than such a murther is.

LADY MACBETH: My worthy lord,
Your noble friends do lack you.

MACBETH: I do forget.
Do not muse at me, my most worthy friends.
I have a strange infirmity, which is nothing
To those that know me. Come, love and health to all;
Then I'll sit down. Give me some wine, fill full.
I drink to the general joy o' the whole table,
And to our dear friend Banquo, whom we miss.
Would he were here! To all and him we thirst,
And all to all.

LORDS: Our duties and the pledge.
Re-enter Ghost.

MACBETH: Avaunt, and quit my sight! Let the earth hide thee!
Thy bones are marrowless, thy blood is cold;

Thou hast no speculation in those eyes
Which thou dost glare with.

LADY MACBETH: Think of this, good peers,
But as a thing of custom. 'Tis no other,
Only it spoils the pleasure of the time.

MACBETH: What man dare, I dare.
Approach thou like the rugged Russian bear,
The arm'd rhinoceros, or the Hyrcan tiger;
Take any shape but that, and my firm nerves
Shall never tremble. Or be alive again,
And dare me to the desert with thy sword.
If trembling I inhabit then, protest me
The baby of a girl. Hence, horrible shadow!
Unreal mockery, hence!
 Exit Ghost.
Why, so, being gone,
I am a man again. Pray you sit still.

LADY MACBETH: You have displaced the mirth, broke the good meeting,
With most admired disorder.

MACBETH: Can such things be,
And overcome us like a summer's cloud,
Without our special wonder? You make me strange
Even to the disposition that I owe
When now I think you can behold such sights
And keep the natural ruby of your cheeks
When mine is blanch'd with fear.

ROSS: What sights, my lord?

LADY MACBETH: I pray you, speak not; he grows worse and worse;
Question enrages him. At once, good night.
Stand not upon the order of your going,
But go at once.

LENNOX: Good night, and better health
Attend his Majesty!

LADY MACBETH: A kind good night to all!
Exeunt All but Macbeth and Lady Macbeth.

MACBETH: will have blood; they say blood will have blood.
Stones have been known to move and trees to speak;
Augures and understood relations have
By maggot pies and choughs and rooks brought forth
The secret'st man of blood. What is the night?

LADY MACBETH: Almost at odds with morning, which is which.

MACBETH: How say'st thou, that Macduff denies his person
At our great bidding?

LADY MACBETH: Did you send to him, sir?

MACBETH: I hear it by the way, but I will send.
There's not a one of them but in his house
I keep a servant feed. I will tomorrow,
And betimes I will, to the weird sisters.
More shall they speak; for now I am bent to know,
By the worst means, the worst. For mine own good
All causes shall give way. I am in blood
Stepp'd in so far that, should I wade no more,
Returning were as tedious as go o'er.
Strange things I have in head that will to hand,
Which must be acted ere they may be scann'd.

LADY MACBETH: You lack the season of all natures, sleep.

MACBETH: Come, we'll to sleep. My strange and self-abuse
Is the initiate fear that wants hard use.
We are yet but young in deed.
Exeunt.

ACT III. SCENE V. A Heath. Thunder.

Enter the Three Witches, Meeting Hecate.

FIRST WITCH: Why, how now, Hecate? You look angerly.

HECATE: Have I not reason, beldams as you are,
Saucy and overbold? How did you dare
To trade and traffic with Macbeth
In riddles and affairs of death,
And I, the mistress of your charms,
The close contriver of all harms,
Was never call'd to bear my part,
Or show the glory of our art?
And, which is worse, all you have done
Hath been but for a wayward son,
Spiteful and wrathful, who, as others do,
Loves for his own ends, not for you.
But make amends now. Get you gone,
And at the pit of Acheron
Meet me i' the morning. Thither he
Will come to know his destiny.
Your vessels and your spells provide,
Your charms and everything beside.
I am for the air; this night I'll spend
Unto a dismal and a fatal end.
Great business must be wrought ere noon:
Upon the corner of the moon
There hangs a vaporous drop profound;
I'll catch it ere it come to ground.
And that distill'd by magic sleights
Shall raise such artificial sprites
As by the strength of their illusion
Shall draw him on to his confusion.
He shall spurn fate, scorn death, and bear
His hopes 'bove wisdom, grace, and fear.
And you all know security
Is mortals' chiefest enemy.
  Music and a Song Within,

"Come Away, Come Away."
Hark! I am call'd; my little spirit, see,
Sits in a foggy cloud and stays for me. *Exit.*

FIRST WITCH: Come, let's make haste; she'll soon be back again.
Exeunt.

ACT III. SCENE VI. Forres. The Palace.
Enter Lennox and Another Lord.

LENNOX: My former speeches have but hit your thoughts,
Which can interpret farther; only I say
Thing's have been strangely borne. The gracious Duncan
Was pitied of Macbeth; marry, he was dead.
And the right valiant Banquo walk'd too late,
Whom, you may say, if't please you, Fleance kill'd,
For Fleance fled. Men must not walk too late.
Who cannot want the thought, how monstrous
It was for Malcolm and for Donalbain
To kill their gracious father? Damned fact!
How it did grieve Macbeth! Did he not straight,
In pious rage, the two delinquents tear
That were the slaves of drink and thralls of sleep?
Was not that nobly done? Ay, and wisely too,
For 'twould have anger'd any heart alive
To hear the men deny't. So that, I say,
He has borne all things well; and I do think
That, had he Duncan's sons under his key-
As, an't please heaven, he shall not -they should find
What 'twere to kill a father; so should Fleance.
But, peace! For from broad words, and 'cause he fail'd
His presence at the tyrant's feast, I hear,
Macduff lives in disgrace. Sir, can you tell
Where he bestows himself?

LORD: The son of Duncan,
From whom this tyrant holds the due of birth,
Lives in the English court and is received

Of the most pious Edward with such grace
That the malevolence of fortune nothing
Takes from his high respect. Thither Macduff
Is gone to pray the holy King, upon his aid
To wake Northumberland and warlike Siward;
That by the help of these, with Him above
To ratify the work, we may again
Give to our tables meat, sleep to our nights,
Free from our feasts and banquets bloody knives,
Do faithful homage, and receive free honors-
All which we pine for now. And this report
Hath so exasperate the King that he
Prepares for some attempt of war.

LENNOX: Sent he to Macduff?

LORD: He did, and with an absolute "Sir, not I,"
The cloudy messenger turns me his back,
And hums, as who should say, "You'll rue the time
That clogs me with this answer."

LENNOX: And that well might
Advise him to a caution, to hold what distance
His wisdom can provide. Some holy angel
Fly to the court of England and unfold
His message ere he come, that a swift blessing
May soon return to this our suffering country
Under a hand accursed!

LORD: I'll send my prayers with him.
Exeunt.

ACT IV. SCENE I. A Cavern. In the Middle, a Boiling Cauldron.
Thunder.

Enter the Three Witches.

FIRST WITCH: Thrice the brinded cat hath mew'd.

SECOND WITCH: Thrice and once the hedge-pig whined.

THIRD WITCH: Harpier cries, "'Tis time, 'tis time."

FIRST WITCH: Round about the cauldron go;
In the poison'd entrails throw.
Toad, that under cold stone
Days and nights has thirty-one
Swelter'd venom sleeping got,
Boil thou first i' the charmed pot.

ALL: Double, double, toil and trouble;
Fire burn and cauldron bubble.

SECOND WITCH: Fillet of a fenny snake,
In the cauldron boil and bake;
Eye of newt and toe of frog,
Wool of bat and tongue of dog,
Adder's fork and blind-worm's sting,
Lizard's leg and howlet's wing,
For a charm of powerful trouble,
Like a hell-broth boil and bubble.

ALL: Double, double, toil and trouble;
Fire burn and cauldron bubble.

THIRD WITCH: Scale of dragon, tooth of wolf,
Witch's mummy, maw and gulf
Of the ravin'd salt-sea shark,
Root of hemlock digg'd i' the dark,
Liver of blaspheming Jew,
Gall of goat and slips of yew
Sliver'd in the moon's eclipse,
Nose of Turk and Tartar's lips,
Finger of birth-strangled babe
Ditch-deliver'd by a drab,
Make the gruel thick and slab.

Add thereto a tiger's chawdron,
For the ingredients of our cawdron.

ALL: Double, double, toil and trouble;
Fire burn and cauldron bubble.

SECOND WITCH: Cool it with a baboon's blood,
Then the charm is firm and good.
   Enter Hecate to the Other Three Witches.

HECATE: O, well done! I commend your pains,
And everyone shall share i' the gains.
And now about the cauldron sing,
Like elves and fairies in a ring,
Enchanting all that you put in.
   Music and a Song, "Black Spirits."
   Hecate Retires.

SECOND WITCH: By the pricking of my thumbs,
Something wicked this way comes.
Open, locks,
Whoever knocks!
   Enter Macbeth.

MACBETH: How now, you secret, black, and midnight hags?
What is't you do?

ALL: A deed without a name.

MACBETH: I conjure you, by that which you profess
(Howeer you come to know it) answer me:
Though you untie the winds and let them fight
Against the churches, though the yesty waves
Confound and swallow navigation up,
Though bladed corn be lodged and trees blown down,
Though castles topple on their warders' heads,
Though palaces and pyramids do slope

Their heads to their foundations, though the treasure
Of nature's germaines tumble all together
Even till destruction sicken, answer me
To what I ask you.

FIRST WITCH: Speak.

SECOND WITCH: Demand.

THIRD WITCH: We'll answer.

FIRST WITCH: Say, if thou'dst rather hear it from our mouths,
Or from our masters'?

MACBETH: Call 'em, let me see 'em.

FIRST WITCH: Pour in sow's blood that hath eaten
Her nine farrow; grease that's sweaten
From the murtherer's gibbet throw
Into the flame.

ALL: Come, high or low;
Thyself and office deftly show!
  Thunder. First Apparition: an armed Head.

MACBETH: Tell me, thou unknown power—

FIRST WITCH: He knows thy thought:
Hear his speech, but say thou nought.

FIRST APPARITION: Macbeth! Macbeth! Macbeth! Beware Macduff,
Beware the Thane of Fife. Dismiss me. Enough.
  Descends.

MACBETH: Whate'er thou art, for thy good caution, thanks;
Thou hast harp'd my fear aright. But one word more—

FIRST WITCH: He will not be commanded. Here's another, More potent than the first.

Thunder. Second Apparition: a bloody Child.

SECOND APPARITION: Macbeth! Macbeth! Macbeth!

MACBETH: Had I three ears, I'd hear thee.

SECOND APPARITION: Be bloody, bold, and resolute: laugh to scorn
The power of man, for none of woman born
Shall harm Macbeth. *Descends.*

MACBETH: Then live, Macduff. What need I fear of thee?
But yet I'll make assurance double sure,
And take a bond of fate: thou shalt not live,
That I may tell pale-hearted fear it lies,
And sleep in spite of thunder.

Thunder. Third Apparition: a Child Crowned, with a Tree in His Hand.

What is this,
That rises like the issue of a king,
And wears upon his baby brow the round
And top of sovereignty?

ALL: Listen, but speak not to't.

THIRD APPARITION: Be lion-mettled, proud, and take no care
Who chafes, who frets, or where conspirers are.
Macbeth shall never vanquish'd be until
Great Birnam Wood to high Dunsinane Hill
Shall come against him. *Descends.*

MACBETH: That will never be.
Who can impress the forest, bid the tree
Unfix his earth-bound root? Sweet bodements, good!
Rebellion's head, rise never till the Wood
Of Birnam rise, and our high-placed Macbeth
Shall live the lease of nature, pay his breath

To time and mortal custom. Yet my heart
Throbs to know one thing: tell me, if your art
Can tell so much, shall Banquo's issue ever
Reign in this kingdom?

ALL: Seek to know no more.

MACBETH: I will be satisfied! Deny me this,
And an eternal curse fall on you! Let me know.
Why sinks that cauldron, and what noise is this?
Hautboys.

FIRST WITCH: Show!

SECOND WITCH: Show!

THIRD WITCH: Show!

ALL: Show his eyes, and grieve his heart;
Come like shadows, so depart!
A show of eight Kings, the last with a glass in his hand;
  Banquo's Ghost Following.

MACBETH: Thou are too like the spirit of Banquo Down!
Thy crown does sear mine eyeballs. And thy hair,
Thou other gold-bound brow, is like the first.
A third is like the former. Filthy hags!
Why do you show me this? A fourth! Start, eyes!
What, will the line stretch out to the crack of doom?
Another yet! A seventh! I'll see no more!
And yet the eighth appears, who bears a glass
Which shows me many more; and some I see
That twofold balls and treble sceptres carry.
Horrible sight! Now I see 'tis true;
For the blood-bolter'd Banquo smiles upon me,
And points at them for his. What, is this so?

FIRST WITCH: Ay, sir, all this is so. But why
Stands Macbeth thus amazedly?
Come, sisters, cheer we up his sprites,
And show the best of our delights.
I'll charm the air to give a sound,
While you perform your antic round,
That this great King may kindly say
Our duties did his welcome pay.
   Music. The Witches Dance and Then Vanish with Hecate.

MACBETH: are they? Gone? Let this pernicious hour
Stand ay accursed in the calendar!
Come in, without there!
   Enter Lennox.

LENNOX: What's your Grace's will?

MACBETH: Saw you the weird sisters?

LENNOX: No, my lord.

MACBETH: Came they not by you?

LENNOX: No indeed, my lord.

MACBETH: Infected be the 'air whereon they ride,
And damn'd all those that trust them! I did hear
The galloping of horse. Who wast came by?

LENNOX: 'Tis two or three, my lord, that bring you word
Macduff is fled to England.

MACBETH: Fled to England?

LENNOX: Ay, my good lord.

MACBETH: *Aside.* Time, thou anticipatest my dread exploits.

The flighty purpose never is o'ertook
Unless the deed go with it. From this moment
The very firstlings of my heart shall be
The firstlings of my hand. And even now,
To crown my thoughts with acts, be it thought and done:
The castle of Macduff I will surprise,
Seize upon Fife, give to the edge o' the sword
His wife, his babes, and all unfortunate souls
That trace him in his line. No boasting like a fool;
This deed I'll do before this purpose cool.
But no more sights! -Where are these gentlemen?
Come, bring me where they are.
    Exeunt.

ACT IV. SCENE II. Fife. Macduff's Castle.
Enter Lady Macduff, her Son, and Ross.

LADY MACDUFF: What had he done, to make him fly the land?

ROSS: You must have patience, madam.

LADY MACDUFF: He had none;
His flight was madness. When our actions do not,
Our fears do make us traitors.

ROSS: You know not
Whether it was his wisdom or his fear.

LADY MACDUFF: Wisdom? To leave his wife, to leave his babes,
His mansion, and his titles, in a place
From whence himself does fly? He loves us not;
He wants the natural touch; for the poor wren,
The most diminutive of birds, will fight,
Her young ones in her nest, against the owl.
All is the fear and nothing is the love;
As little is the wisdom, where the flight
So runs against all reason.

ROSS: My dearest coz,
I pray you, school yourself. But for your husband,
He is noble, wise, Judicious, and best knows
The fits o' the season. I dare not speak much further;
But cruel are the times when we are traitors
And do not know ourselves; when we hold rumor
From what we fear, yet know not what we fear,
But float upon a wild and violent sea
Each way and move. I take my leave of you;
Shall not be long but I'll be here again.
Things at the worst will cease or else climb upward
To what they were before. My pretty cousin,
Blessing upon you!

LADY MACDUFF: Father'd he is, and yet he's fatherless.

ROSS: I am so much a fool, should I stay longer,
It would be my disgrace and your discomfort.
I take my leave at once.
   Exit.

LADY MACDUFF: Sirrah, your father's dead.
And what will you do now? How will you live?

SON: As birds do, Mother.

LADY MACDUFF: What, with worms and flies?

SON: With what I get, I mean; and so do they.

LADY MACDUFF: Poor bird! Thou'ldst never fear the net nor lime,
The pitfall nor the gin.

SON: Why should I, Mother? Poor birds they are not set for.
My father is not dead, for all your saying.

LADY MACDUFF: Yes, he is dead. How wilt thou do for father?

SON: Nay, how will you do for a husband?

LADY MACDUFF: Why, I can buy me twenty at any market.

SON: Then you'll buy 'em to sell again.

LADY MACDUFF: Thou speak'st with all thy wit, and yet, i' faith, With wit enough for thee.

SON: Was my father a traitor, Mother?

LADY MACDUFF: Ay, that he was.

SON: What is a traitor?

LADY MACDUFF: Why one that swears and lies.

SON: And be all traitors that do so?

LADY MACDUFF: Everyone that does so is a traitor and must be hanged.

SON: And must they all be hanged that swear and lie?

LADY MACDUFF: Everyone.

SON: Who must hang them?

LADY MACDUFF: Why, the honest men.

SON: Then the liars and swearers are fools, for there are liars and swearers enow to beat the honest men and hang up them.

LADY MACDUFF: Now, God help thee, poor monkey! But how wilt thou do for a father?

SON: If he were dead, you'ld weep for him; if you would not, it were a good sign that I should quickly have a new father.

LADY MACDUFF: Poor prattler, how thou talk'st!
Enter a Messenger.

MESSENGER: Bless you, fair dame! I am not to you known,
Though in your state of honor I am perfect.
I doubt some danger does approach you nearly.
If you will take a homely man's advice,
Be not found here; hence, with your little ones.
To fright you thus, methinks I am too savage;
To do worse to you were fell cruelty,
Which is too nigh your person. Heaven preserve you!
I dare abide no longer.
  Exit.

LADY MACDUFF: Whither should I fly?
I have done no harm. But I remember now
I am in this earthly world, where to do harm
Is often laudable, to do good sometime
Accounted dangerous folly. Why then, alas,
Do I put up that womanly defense,
To say I have done no harm -What are these faces?
  Enter Murtherers.

FIRST MURTHERER: Where is your husband?

LADY MACDUFF: I hope, in no place so unsanctified
Where such as thou mayst find him.

FIRST MURTHERER: He's a traitor.

SON: Thou liest, thou shag-ear'd villain!

FIRST MURTHERER: What, you egg!
  Stabs him.
Young fry of treachery!

SON: He has kill'd me, Mother.
Run away, I pray you! Dies.
  Exit Lady Macduff, Crying "Murther!"
  Exeunt Murtherers, Following Her.

ACT IV. SCENE III. England. Before the King's Palace.
Enter Malcolm and Macduff.

MALCOLM: Let us seek out some desolate shade and there
Weep our sad bosoms empty.

MACDUFF: Let us rather
Hold fast the mortal sword, and like good men
Bestride our downfall'n birthdom. Each new morn
New widows howl, new orphans cry, new sorrows
Strike heaven on the face, that it resounds
As if it felt with Scotland and yell'd out
Like syllable of dolor.

MALCOLM: What I believe, I'll wail;
What know, believe; and what I can redress,
As I shall find the time to friend, I will.
What you have spoke, it may be so perchance.
This tyrant, whose sole name blisters our tongues,
Was once thought honest. You have loved him well;
He hath not touch'd you yet. I am young, but something
You may deserve of him through me, and wisdom
To offer up a weak, poor, innocent lamb
To appease an angry god.

MACDUFF: I am not treacherous.

MALCOLM: But Macbeth is.
A good and virtuous nature may recoil
In an imperial charge. But I shall crave your pardon;
That which you are, my thoughts cannot transpose.
Angels are bright still, though the brightest fell.

Though all things foul would wear the brows of grace,
Yet grace must still look so.

MACDUFF: I have lost my hopes.

MALCOLM: Perchance even there where I did find my doubts.
Why in that rawness left you wife and child,
Those precious motives, those strong knots of love,
Without leave-taking? I pray you,
Let not my jealousies be your dishonors,
But mine own safeties. You may be rightly just,
Whatever I shall think.

MACDUFF: Bleed, bleed, poor country!
Great tyranny, lay thou thy basis sure,
For goodness dare not check thee. Wear thou thy wrongs;
The title is affeer'd. Fare thee well, lord.
I would not be the villain that thou think'st
For the whole space that's in the tyrant's grasp
And the rich East to boot.

MALCOLM: Be not offended;
I speak not as in absolute fear of you.
I think our country sinks beneath the yoke;
It weeps, it bleeds, and each new day a gash
Is added to her wounds. I think withal
There would be hands uplifted in my right;
And here from gracious England have I offer
Of goodly thousands. But for all this,
When I shall tread upon the tyrant's head,
Or wear it on my sword, yet my poor country
Shall have more vices than it had before,
More suffer and more sundry ways than ever,
By him that shall succeed.

MACDUFF: What should he be?

MALCOLM: It is myself I mean, in whom I know

All the particulars of vice so grafted
That, when they shall be open'd, black Macbeth
Will seem as pure as snow, and the poor state
Esteem him as a lamb, being compared
With my confineless harms.

MACDUFF: Not in the legions
Of horrid hell can come a devil more damn'd
In evils to top Macbeth.

MALCOLM: I grant him bloody,
Luxurious, avaricious, false, deceitful,
Sudden, malicious, smacking of every sin
That has a name. But there's no bottom, none,
In my voluptuousness. Your wives, your daughters,
Your matrons, and your maids could not fill up
The cestern of my lust, and my desire
All continent impediments would o'erbear
That did oppose my will. Better Macbeth
Than such an one to reign.

MACDUFF: Boundless intemperance
In nature is a tyranny; it hath been
The untimely emptying of the happy throne,
And fall of many kings. But fear not yet
To take upon you what is yours. You may
Convey your pleasures in a spacious plenty
And yet seem cold, the time you may so hoodwink.
We have willing dames enough; there cannot be
That vulture in you to devour so many
As will to greatness dedicate themselves,
Finding it so inclined.

MALCOLM: With this there grows
In my most ill-composed affection such
A stanchless avarice that, were I King,
I should cut off the nobles for their lands,
Desire his jewels and this other's house,

And my more-having would be as a sauce
To make me hunger more, that I should forge
Quarrels unjust against the good and loyal,
Destroying them for wealth.

MACDUFF: This avarice
Sticks deeper, grows with more pernicious root
Than summer-seeming lust, and it hath been
The sword of our slain kings. Yet do not fear;
Scotland hath foisons to fill up your will
Of your mere own. All these are portable,
With other graces weigh'd.

MALCOLM: But I have none. The king-becoming graces,
As justice, verity, temperance, stableness,
Bounty, perseverance, mercy, lowliness,
Devotion, patience, courage, fortitude,
I have no relish of them, but abound
In the division of each several crime,
Acting it many ways. Nay, had I power, I should
Pour the sweet milk of concord into hell,
Uproar the universal peace, confound
All unity on earth.

MACDUFF: O Scotland, Scotland!

MALCOLM: If such a one be fit to govern, speak.
I am as I have spoken.

MACDUFF: Fit to govern?
No, not to live. O nation miserable!
With an untitled tyrant bloody-scepter'd,
When shalt thou see thy wholesome days again,
Since that the truest issue of thy throne
By his own interdiction stands accursed
And does blaspheme his breed? Thy royal father
Was a most sainted king; the queen that bore thee,
Oftener upon her knees than on her feet,

Died every day she lived. Fare thee well!
These evils thou repeat'st upon thyself
Have banish'd me from Scotland. O my breast,
Thy hope ends here!

MALCOLM: Macduff, this noble passion,
Child of integrity, hath from my soul
Wiped the black scruples, reconciled my thoughts
To thy good truth and honor. Devilish Macbeth
By many of these trains hath sought to win me
Into his power, and modest wisdom plucks me
From over-credulous haste. But God above
Deal between thee and me! For even now
I put myself to thy direction and
Unspeak mine own detraction; here abjure
The taints and blames I laid upon myself,
For strangers to my nature. I am yet
Unknown to woman, never was forsworn,
Scarcely have coveted what was mine own,
At no time broke my faith, would not betray
The devil to his fellow, and delight
No less in truth than life. My first false speaking
Was this upon myself. What I am truly
Is thine and my poor country's to command.
Whither indeed, before thy here-approach,
Old Siward, with ten thousand warlike men
Already at a point, was setting forth.
Now we'll together, and the chance of goodness
Be like our warranted quarrel! Why are you silent?

MACDUFF: Such welcome and unwelcome things at once
'Tis hard to reconcile.
   Enter a Doctor.

MALCOLM: Well, more anon. Comes the King forth, I pray you?

DOCTOR: Ay, sir, there are a crew of wretched souls
That stay his cure. Their malady convinces

The great assay of art, but at his touch,
Such sanctity hath heaven given his hand,
They presently amend.

MALCOLM: I thank you, Doctor.
Exit Doctor.

MACDUFF: What's the disease he means?

MALCOLM: 'Tis call'd the evil:
A most miraculous work in this good King,
Which often, since my here-remain in England,
I have seen him do. How he solicits heaven,
Himself best knows; but strangely-visited people,
All swol'n and ulcerous, pitiful to the eye,
The mere despair of surgery, he cures,
Hanging a golden stamp about their necks
Put on with holy prayers; and 'tis spoken,
To the succeeding royalty he leaves
The healing benediction. With this strange virtue
He hath a heavenly gift of prophecy,
And sundry blessings hang about his throne
That speak him full of grace.
Enter Ross.

MACDUFF: See, who comes here?

MALCOLM: My countryman, but yet I know him not.

MACDUFF: My ever gentle cousin, welcome hither.

MALCOLM: I know him now. Good God, betimes remove
The means that makes us strangers!

ROSS: Sir, amen.

MACDUFF: Stands Scotland where it did?

ROSS: Alas, poor country,
Almost afraid to know itself! It cannot
Be call'd our mother, but our grave. Where nothing,
But who knows nothing, is once seen to smile;
Where sighs and groans and shrieks that rend the air,
Are made, not mark'd; where violent sorrow seems
A modern ecstasy. The dead man's knell
Is there scarce ask'd for who, and good men's lives
Expire before the flowers in their caps,
Dying or ere they sicken.

MACDUFF: O, relation too nice, and yet too true!

MALCOLM: What's the newest grief?

ROSS: That of an hour's age doth hiss the speaker;
Each minute teems a new one.

MACDUFF: How does my wife?

ROSS: Why, well.

MACDUFF: And all my children?

ROSS: Well too.

MACDUFF: The tyrant has not batter'd at their peace?

ROSS: No, they were well at peace when I did leave 'em.

MACDUFF: Be not a niggard of your speech. How goest?

ROSS: When I came hither to transport the tidings,
Which I have heavily borne, there ran a rumor
Of many worthy fellows that were out,
Which was to my belief witness'd the rather,
For that I saw the tyrant's power afoot.

Now is the time of help; your eye in Scotland
Would create soldiers, make our women fight,
To doff their dire distresses.

MALCOLM: Be't their comfort
We are coming thither. Gracious England hath
Lent us good Siward and ten thousand men;
An older and a better soldier none
That Christendom gives out.

ROSS: Would I could answer
This comfort with the like! But I have words
That would be howl'd out in the desert air,
Where hearing should not latch them.

MACDUFF: What concern they?
The general cause? Or is it a fee-grief
Due to some single breast?

ROSS: No mind that's honest
But in it shares some woe, though the main part
Pertains to you alone.

MACDUFF: If it be mine,
Keep it not from me, quickly let me have it.

ROSS: Let not your ears despise my tongue forever,
Which shall possess them with the heaviest sound
That ever yet they heard.

MACDUFF: Humh! I guess at it.

ROSS: Your castle is surprised; your wife and babes
Savagely slaughter'd. To relate the manner
Were, on the quarry of these murther'd deer,
To add the death of you.

William Shakespeare

MALCOLM: Merciful heaven!
What, man! Neer pull your hat upon your brows;
Give sorrow words. The grief that does not speak
Whispers the o'erfraught heart, and bids it break.

MACDUFF: My children too?

ROSS: Wife, children, servants, all
That could be found.

MACDUFF: And I must be from thence!
My wife kill'd too?

ROSS: I have said.

MALCOLM: Be comforted.
Let's make us medicines of our great revenge,
To cure this deadly grief.

MACDUFF: He has no children. All my pretty ones?
Did you say all? O hell-kite! All?
What, all my pretty chickens and their dam
At one fell swoop?

MALCOLM: Dispute it like a man.

MACDUFF: I shall do so,
But I must also feel it as a man.
I cannot but remember such things were
That were most precious to me. Did heaven look on,
And would not take their part? Sinful Macduff,
They were all struck for thee! Naught that I am,
Not for their own demerits, but for mine,
Fell slaughter on their souls. Heaven rest them now!

MALCOLM: Be this the whetstone of your sword. Let grief
Convert to anger; blunt not the heart, enrage it.

MACDUFF: O, I could play the woman with mine eyes
And braggart with my tongue! But, gentle heavens,
Cut short all intermission; front to front
Bring thou this fiend of Scotland and myself;
Within my sword's length set him; if he 'scape,
Heaven forgive him too!

MALCOLM: This tune goes manly.
Come, go we to the King; our power is ready,
Our lack is nothing but our leave. Macbeth
Is ripe for shaking, and the powers above
Put on their instruments. Receive what cheer you may,
The night is long that never finds the day.
   Exeunt.

ACT V. SCENE I. Dunsinane. Anteroom in the Castle.
Enter a Doctor of Physic and a Waiting Gentlewoman.

DOCTOR: I have two nights watched with you, but can perceive no truth in your report. When was it she last walked?

GENTLEWOMAN: Since his Majesty went into the field, have seen her rise from her bed, throw her nightgown upon her, unlock her closet, take forth paper, fold it, write upon't, read it, afterwards seal it, and again return to bed; yet all this while in a most fast sleep.

DOCTOR: A great perturbation in nature, to receive at once the benefit of sleep and do the effects of watching! In this slumbery agitation, besides her walking and other actual performances, what, at any time, have you heard her say?

GENTLEWOMAN: That, sir, which I will not report after her.

DOCTOR: You may to me, and 'tis most meet you should.

GENTLEWOMAN: Neither to you nor anyone, having no witness to confirm my speech.

Enter Lady Macbeth with a Taper.

Lo you, here she comes! This is her very guise, and, upon my life, fast asleep. Observe her; stand close.

DOCTOR: How came she by that light?

GENTLEWOMAN: Why, it stood by her. She has light by her continually; 'tis her command.

DOCTOR: You see, her eyes are open.

GENTLEWOMAN: Ay, but their sense is shut.

DOCTOR: What is it she does now? Look how she rubs her hands.

GENTLEWOMAN: It is an accustomed action with her, to seem thus washing her hands. I have known her continue in this a quarter of an hour.

LADY MACBETH: Yet here's a spot.

DOCTOR: Hark, she speaks! I will set down what comes from her, to satisfy my remembrance the more strongly.

LADY MACBETH: Out, damned spot! Out, I say! One- two -why then 'tis time to do't. Hell is murky. Fie, my lord, fie! A soldier, and afeard? What need we fear who knows it, when none can call our power to account? Yet who would have thought the old man to have had so much blood in him?

DOCTOR: Do you mark that?

LADY MACBETH: The Thane of Fife had a wife; where is she now? What, will these hands neer be clean? No more o' that, my lord, no more o' that. You mar all with this starting.

DOCTOR: Go to, go to; you have known what you should not.

GENTLEWOMAN: She has spoke what she should not, I am sure of that. Heaven knows what she has known.

LADY MACBETH: Here's the smell of the blood still. All the perfumes of Arabia will not sweeten this little hand. Oh, oh, oh!

DOCTOR: What a sigh is there! The heart is sorely charged.

GENTLEWOMAN: I would not have such a heart in my bosom for the dignity of the whole body.

DOCTOR: Well, well, well-

GENTLEWOMAN: Pray God it be, sir.

DOCTOR: This disease is beyond my practice. Yet I have known those which have walked in their sleep who have died holily in their beds.

LADY MACBETH: Wash your hands, put on your nightgown, look not so pale. I tell you yet again, Banquo's buried; he cannot come out on's grave.

DOCTOR: Even so?

LADY MACBETH: To bed, to bed; there's knocking at the gate. Come, come, come, come, give me your hand. What's done cannot be undone. To bed, to bed, to bed.
  Exit.

DOCTOR: Will she go now to bed?

GENTLEWOMAN: Directly.

DOCTOR: Foul whisperings are abroad. Unnatural deeds
Do breed unnatural troubles; infected minds
To their deaf pillows will discharge their secrets.
More needs she the divine than the physician.
God, God, forgive us all! Look after her;

Remove from her the means of all annoyance,
And still keep eyes upon her. So good night.
My mind she has mated and amazed my sight.
I think, but dare not speak.

GENTLEWOMAN: Good night, good doctor.
Exeunt.

ACT V. SCENE II. The Country near Dunsinane. Drum and Colors.
Enter Menteith, Caithness, Angus, Lennox, and Soldiers.

MENTEITH: The English power is near, led on by Malcolm,
His uncle Siward, and the good Macduff.
Revenges burn in them, for their dear causes
Would to the bleeding and the grim alarm
Excite the mortified man.

ANGUS: Near Birnam Wood
Shall we well meet them; that way are they coming.

CAITHNESS: Who knows if Donalbain be with his brother?

LENNOX: For certain, sir, he is not; I have a file
Of all the gentry. There is Seward's son
And many unrough youths that even now
Protest their first of manhood.

MENTEITH: What does the tyrant?

CAITHNESS: Great Dunsinane he strongly fortifies.
Some say he's mad; others, that lesser hate him,
Do call it valiant fury; but, for certain,
He cannot buckle his distemper'd cause
Within the belt of rule.

ANGUS: Now does he feel
His secret murthers sticking on his hands,

Now minutely revolts upbraid his faith-breach;
Those he commands move only in command,
Nothing in love. Now does he feel his title
Hang loose about him, like a giant's robe
Upon a dwarfish thief.

MENTEITH: Who then shall blame
His pester'd senses to recoil and start,
When all that is within him does condemn
Itself for being there?

CAITHNESS: Well, march we on
To give obedience where 'tis truly owed.
Meet we the medicine of the sickly weal,
And with him pour we, in our country's purge,
Each drop of us.

LENNOX: Or so much as it needs
To dew the sovereign flower and drown the weeds.
Make we our march towards Birnam.
Exeunt Marching.

ACT V. SCENE III. Dunsinane. A Room in the Castle.
Enter Macbeth, Doctor, and Attendants.

MACBETH: Bring me no more reports; let them fly all!
Till Birnam Wood remove to Dunsinane
I cannot taint with fear. What's the boy Malcolm?
Was he not born of woman? The spirits that know
All mortal consequences have pronounced me thus:
"Fear not, Macbeth; no man that's born of woman
Shall e'er have power upon thee." Then fly, false Thanes,
And mingle with the English epicures!
The mind I sway by and the heart I bear
Shall never sag with doubt nor shake with fear.
Enter a Servant.
The devil damn thee black, thou cream-faced loon!
Where got'st thou that goose look?

SERVANT: There is ten thousand—

MACBETH: Geese, villain?

SERVANT: Soldiers, sir.

MACBETH: Go prick thy face and over-red thy fear,
Thou lily-liver'd boy. What soldiers, patch?
Death of thy soul! Those linen cheeks of thine
Are counselors to fear. What soldiers, whey-face?

SERVANT: The English force, so please you.

MACBETH: Take thy face hence.
  Exit Servant.
Seyton—I am sick at heart,
When I behold— Seyton, I say!— This push
Will cheer me ever or disseat me now.
I have lived long enough. My way of life
Is fall'n into the sear, the yellow leaf,
And that which should accompany old age,
As honor, love, obedience, troops of friends,
I must not look to have; but in their stead,
Curses, not loud but deep, mouth-honor, breath,
Which the poor heart would fain deny and dare not.
Seyton!
  Enter Seyton.

SEYTON: What's your gracious pleasure?

MACBETH: What news more?

SEYTON: All is confirm'd, my lord, which was reported.

MACBETH: I'll fight, 'til from my bones my flesh be hack'd.
Give me my armor.

SEYTON: 'Tis not needed yet.

MACBETH: I'll put it on.
Send out more horses, skirr the country round,
Hang those that talk of fear. Give me mine armor.
How does your patient, doctor?

DOCTOR: Not so sick, my lord,
As she is troubled with thick-coming fancies,
That keep her from her rest.

MACBETH: Cure her of that.
Canst thou not minister to a mind diseased,
Pluck from the memory a rooted sorrow,
Raze out the written troubles of the brain,
And with some sweet oblivious antidote
Cleanse the stuff'd bosom of that perilous stuff
Which weighs upon the heart?

DOCTOR: Therein the patient
Must minister to himself.

MACBETH: Throw physic to the dogs, I'll none of it.
Come, put mine armor on; give me my staff.
Seyton, send out. Doctor, the Thanes fly from me.
Come, sir, dispatch. If thou couldst, doctor, cast
The water of my land, find her disease
And purge it to a sound and pristine health,
I would applaud thee to the very echo,
That should applaud again. Pull't off, I say.
What rhubarb, cyme, or what purgative drug
Would scour these English hence? Hearst thou of them?

DOCTOR: Ay, my good lord, your royal preparation
Makes us hear something.

MACBETH: Bring it after me.

I will not be afraid of death and bane
Till Birnam Forest come to Dunsinane.

DOCTOR: *Aside.* Were I from Dunsinane away and clear,
Profit again should hardly draw me here. *Exeunt.*

ACT V. SCENE IV. Country near Birnam Wood. Drum and Colors.
Enter Malcolm, Old Seward and His Son, Macduff, Menteith, Caithness, Angus, Lennox, Ross, and Soldiers, Marching.

MALCOLM: Cousins, I hope the days are near at hand
That chambers will be safe.

MENTEITH: We doubt it nothing.

SIWARD: What wood is this before us?

MENTEITH: The Wood of Birnam.

MALCOLM: Let every soldier hew him down a bough,
And bear't before him; thereby shall we shadow
The numbers of our host, and make discovery
Err in report of us.

SOLDIERS: It shall be done.

SIWARD: We learn no other but the confident tyrant
Keeps still in Dunsinane and will endure
Our setting down before't.

MALCOLM: 'Tis his main hope;
For where there is advantage to be given,
Both more and less have given him the revolt,
And none serve with him but constrained things
Whose hearts are absent too.

MACDUFF: Let our just censures

Attend the true event, and put we on
Industrious soldiership.

SIWARD: The time approaches
That will with due decision make us know
What we shall say we have and what we owe.
Thoughts speculative their unsure hopes relate,
But certain issue strokes must arbitrate.
Towards which advance the war.
  Exeunt Marching.

ACT V. SCENE V. Dunsinane. Within the Castle.
Enter Macbeth, Seyton, and Soldiers, with Drum and Colors.

MACBETH: Hang out our banners on the outward walls;
The cry is still, "They come!" Our castle's strength
Will laugh a siege to scorn. Here let them lie
Till famine and the ague eat them up.
Were they not forced with those that should be ours,
We might have met them dareful, beard to beard,
And beat them backward home.
  A Cry of Women Within.
What is that noise?

SEYTON: It is the cry of women, my good lord.
  Exit.

MACBETH: I have almost forgot the taste of fears:
The time has been, my senses would have cool'd
To hear a night-shriek, and my fell of hair
Would at a dismal treatise rouse and stir
As life were in't. I have supp'd full with horrors;
Direness, familiar to my slaughterous thoughts,
Cannot once start me.
  Re-enter Seyton.
Wherefore was that cry?

SEYTON: The Queen, my lord, is dead.

MACBETH: She should have died hereafter;
There would have been a time for such a word.
Tomorrow, and tomorrow, and tomorrow
Creeps in this petty pace from day to day
To the last syllable of recorded time;
And all our yesterdays have lighted fools
The way to dusty death. Out, out, brief candle!
Life's but a walking shadow, a poor player
That struts and frets his hour upon the stage
And then is heard no more. It is a tale
Told by an idiot, full of sound and fury,
Signifying nothing.
   Enter a Messenger.
Thou comest to use thy tongue; thy story quickly.

MESSENGER: Gracious my lord,
I should report that which I say I saw,
But know not how to do it.

MACBETH: Well, say, sir.

MESSENGER: As I did stand my watch upon the hill,
I look'd toward Birnam, and anon, methought,
The Wood began to move.

MACBETH: Liar and slave!

MESSENGER: Let me endure your wrath, if't be not so.
Within this three mile may you see it coming;
I say, a moving grove.

MACBETH: If thou speak'st false,
Upon the next tree shalt thou hang alive,
Till famine cling thee; if thy speech be sooth,
I care not if thou dost for me as much.

I pull in resolution and begin
To doubt the equivocation of the fiend
That lies like truth. "Fear not, till Birnam Wood
Do come to Dunsinane," and now a wood
Comes toward Dunsinane. Arm, arm, and out!
If this which he avouches does appear,
There is nor flying hence nor tarrying here.
I 'gin to be aweary of the sun
And wish the estate o' the world were now undone.
Ring the alarum bell! Blow, wind! Come, wrack!
At least we'll die with harness on our back.
   Exeunt.

ACT V. SCENE VI. Dunsinane. Before the Castle.

Enter Malcolm, Old Siward, Macduff, and Their Army, with Boughs. Drum and Colors.

MALCOLM: Now near enough; your leavy screens throw down,
And show like those you are. You, worthy uncle,
Shall with my cousin, your right noble son,
Lead our first battle. Worthy Macduff and we
Shall take upon 's what else remains to do, According to our order.

SIWARD: Fare you well.
Do we but find the tyrant's power tonight,
Let us be beaten if we cannot fight.

MACDUFF: Make all our trumpets speak, give them all breath,
Those clamorous harbingers of blood and death.
   Exeunt.

ACT V. SCENE VII. Dunsinane. Before the Castle. Alarums.
Enter Macbeth.

MACBETH: They have tied me to a stake; I cannot fly,
But bear-like I must fight the course. What's he
That was not born of woman? Such a one
Am I to fear, or none.

Enter Young Siward.

YOUNG SIWARD: What is thy name?

MACBETH: Thou'lt be afraid to hear it.

YOUNG SIWARD: No, though thou call'st thyself a hotter name
Than any is in hell.

MACBETH: My name's Macbeth.

YOUNG SIWARD: The devil himself could not pronounce a title
More hateful to mine ear.

MACBETH: No, nor more fearful.

YOUNG SIWARD: O Thou liest, abhorred tyrant; with my sword
I'll prove the lie thou speak'st.
   They Fight, and Young Seward Is Slain.

MACBETH: Thou wast born of woman.
But swords I smile at, weapons laugh to scorn,
Brandish'd by man that's of a woman born. *Exit.*
   Alarums. Enter Macduff.

MACDUFF: That way the noise is. Tyrant, show thy face!
If thou best slain and with no stroke of mine,
My wife and children's ghosts will haunt me still.
I cannot strike at wretched kerns, whose arms
Are hired to bear their staves. Either thou, Macbeth,
Or else my sword, with an unbatter'd edge,
I sheathe again undeeded. There thou shouldst be;
By this great clatter, one of greatest note
Seems bruited. Let me find him, Fortune!
And more I beg not.
   Exit. Alarums.
   Enter Malcolm and Old Siward.

SIWARD: This way, my lord; the castle's gently render'd.
The tyrant's people on both sides do fight,
The noble Thanes do bravely in the war,
The day almost itself professes yours,
And little is to do.

MALCOLM: We have met with foes
That strike beside us.

SIWARD: Enter, sir, the castle.
Exeunt. Alarum.

ACT V. SCENE VIII. Another Part of the Field.
Enter Macbeth.

MACBETH: Why should I play the Roman fool and die
On mine own sword? Whiles I see lives, the gashes
Do better upon them.
Enter Macduff.

MACDUFF: Turn, hell hound, turn!

MACBETH: Of all men else I have avoided thee.
But get thee back, my soul is too much charged
With blood of thine already.

MACDUFF: I have no words.
My voice is in my sword, thou bloodier villain
Than terms can give thee out! *They fight.*

MACBETH: Thou losest labor.
As easy mayst thou the intrenchant air
With thy keen sword impress as make me bleed.
Let fall thy blade on vulnerable crests;
I bear a charmed life, which must not yield
To one of woman born.

MACDUFF: Despair thy charm,
And let the angel whom thou still hast served
Tell thee, Macduff was from his mother's womb untimely ripp'd.

MACBETH: Accursed be that tongue that tells me so,
For it hath cow'd my better part of man!
And be these juggling fiends no more believed
That patter with us in a double sense,
That keep the word of promise to our ear
And break it to our hope. I'll not fight with thee.

MACDUFF: Then yield thee, coward,
And live to be the show and gaze o' the time.
We'll have thee, as our rarer monsters are,
Painted upon a pole, and underwrit,
"Here may you see the tyrant."

MACBETH: I will not yield,
To kiss the ground before young Malcolm's feet,
And to be baited with the rabble's curse.
Though Birnam Wood be come to Dunsinane,
And thou opposed, being of no woman born,
Yet I will try the last. Before my body
I throw my warlike shield! Lay on, Macduff,
And damn'd be him that first cries, "Hold, enough!"
Exeunt Fighting. Alarums.

ACT V. SCENE IX.

Retreat. Flourish. Enter, with Drum and Colors, Malcolm, Old Siward, Ross, the Other Thanes, and Soldiers.

MALCOLM: I would the friends we miss were safe arrived.

SIWARD: Some must go off, and yet, by these I see,
So great a day as this is cheaply bought.

MALCOLM: Macduff is missing, and your noble son.

ROSS: Your son, my lord, has paid a soldier's debt.
He only lived but till he was a man,
The which no sooner had his prowess confirm'd
In the unshrinking station where he fought,
But like a man he died.

SIWARD: Then he is dead?

ROSS: Ay, and brought off the field. Your cause of sorrow
Must not be measured by his worth, for then it hath no end.

SIWARD: Had he his hurts before?

ROSS: Ay, on the front.

SIWARD: Why then, God's soldier be he!
Had I as many sons as I have hairs,
I would not wish them to a fairer death.
And so his knell is knoll'd.

MALCOLM: He's worth more sorrow,
And that I'll spend for him.

SIWARD: He's worth no more:
They say he parted well and paid his score,
And so God be with him! Here comes newer comfort.
   Re-enter Macduff, with Macbeth's Head.

MACDUFF: Hail, King, for so thou art. Behold where stands
The usurper's cursed head. The time is free.
I see thee compass'd with thy kingdom's pearl
That speak my salutation in their minds,
Whose voices I desire aloud with mine- Hail, King of Scotland!

ALL: Hail, King of Scotland! Flourish.

MALCOLM: We shall not spend a large expense of time

Before we reckon with your several loves
And make us even with you. My Thanes and kinsmen,
Henceforth be Earls, the first that ever Scotland
In such an honor named. What's more to do,
Which would be planted newly with the time,
As calling home our exiled friends abroad
That fled the snares of watchful tyranny,
Producing forth the cruel ministers
Of this dead butcher and his fiend-like queen,
Who, as 'tis thought, by self and violent hands
Took off her life; this, and what needful else
That calls upon us, by the grace of Grace
We will perform in measure, time, and place.
So thanks to all at once and to each one,
Whom we invite to see us crown'd at Scone.
   Flourish. Exeunt.

END

Othello

Dramatis Personae

OTHELLO, the Moor, general of the Venetian forces
DESDEMONA, his wife
IAGO, ensign to Othello
EMILIA, his wife, lady-in-waiting to Desdemona
CASSIO, lieutenant to Othello
THE DUKE OF VENICE
BRABANTIO, Venetian Senator, father of Desdemona
GRATIANO, nobleman of Venice, brother of Brabantio
LODOVICO, nobleman of Venice, kinsman of Brabantio
RODERIGO, rejected suitor of Desdemona
BIANCA, mistress of Cassio
MONTANO, a Cypriot official
A Clown in service to Othello
Senators, Sailors, Messengers, Officers, Gentlemen, Musicians, and Attendants

SCENE: *Venice and Cyprus*

ACT I. SCENE I. Venice. A Street.

Enter Roderigo and Iago.

RODERIGO: Tush, never tell me! I take it much unkindly
That thou, Iago, who hast had my purse
As if the strings were thine, shouldst know of this.

IAGO: 'Sblood, but you will not hear me.
If ever I did dream of such a matter,
Abhor me.

RODERIGO: Thou told'st me thou didst hold him in thy hate.

IAGO: Despise me, if I do not. Three great ones of the city,
In personal suit to make me his lieutenant,
Off-capp'd to him; and, by the faith of man,
I know my price, I am worth no worse a place.
But he, as loving his own pride and purposes,
Evades them, with a bumbast circumstance
Horribly stuff'd with epithets of war,
And, in conclusion,
Nonsuits my mediators; for, "Certes," says he,
"I have already chose my officer."
And what was he?
Forsooth, a great arithmetician,
One Michael Cassio, a Florentine
(A fellow almost damn'd in a fair wife)
That never set a squadron in the field,
Nor the division of a battle knows
More than a spinster; unless the bookish theoric,
Wherein the toged consuls can propose
As masterly as he. Mere prattle without practice
Is all his soldiership. But he, sir, had the election;
And I, of whom his eyes had seen the proof
At Rhodes, at Cyprus, and on other grounds
Christian and heathen, must be belee'd and calm'd

William Shakespeare

By debitor and creditor. This counter-caster,
He, in good time, must his lieutenant be,
And I- God bless the mark!- his Moorship's ancient.

RODERIGO: By heaven, I rather would have been his hangman.

IAGO: Why, there's no remedy. 'Tis the curse of service,
Preferment goes by letter and affection,
And not by old gradation, where each second
Stood heir to the first. Now, sir, be judge yourself
Whether I in any just term am affined
To love the Moor.

RODERIGO: I would not follow him then.

IAGO: O, sir, content you.
I follow him to serve my turn upon him:
We cannot all be masters, nor all masters
Cannot be truly follow'd. You shall mark
Many a duteous and knee-crooking knave,
That doting on his own obsequious bondage
Wears out his time, much like his master's ass,
For nought but provender, and when he's old, cashier'd.
Whip me such honest knaves. Others there are
Who, trimm'd in forms and visages of duty,
Keep yet their hearts attending on themselves,
And throwing but shows of service on their lords
Do well thrive by them; and when they have lined their coats
Do themselves homage. These fellows have some soul,
And such a one do I profess myself.
For, sir, it is as sure as you are Roderigo,
Were I the Moor, I would not be Iago.
In following him, I follow but myself;
Heaven is my judge, not I for love and duty,
But seeming so, for my peculiar end.
For when my outward action doth demonstrate
The native act and figure of my heart
In complement extern, 'tis not long after

But I will wear my heart upon my sleeve
For daws to peck at: I am not what I am.

RODERIGO: What a full fortune does the thick-lips owe,
If he can carry't thus!

IAGO: Call up her father,
Rouse him, make after him, poison his delight,
Proclaim him in the streets, incense her kinsmen,
And, though he in a fertile climate dwell,
Plague him with flies. Though that his joy be joy,
Yet throw such changes of vexation on't
As it may lose some color.

RODERIGO: Here is her father's house; I'll call aloud.

IAGO: Do, with like timorous accent and dire yell
As when, by night and negligence, the fire
Is spied in populous cities.

RODERIGO: What, ho, Brabantio! Signior Brabantio, ho!

IAGO: Awake! What, ho, Brabantio! Thieves! Thieves! Thieves!
Look to your house, your daughter, and your bags!
Thieves! Thieves!
   Brabantio appears above, at a window.

BRABANTIO: What is the reason of this terrible summons?
What is the matter there?

RODERIGO: Signior, is all your family within?

IAGO: Are your doors lock'd?

BRABANTIO: Why? Wherefore ask you this?

IAGO: 'Zounds, sir, you're robb'd! For shame, put on your gown;

Your heart is burst, you have lost half your soul;
Even now, now, very now, an old black ram
Is tupping your white ewe. Arise, arise!
Awake the snorting citizens with the bell,
Or else the devil will make a grandsire of you.
Arise, I say!

BRABANTIO: What, have you lost your wits?

RODERIGO: Most reverend signior, do you know my voice?

BRABANTIO: Not I. What are you?

RODERIGO: My name is Roderigo.

BRABANTIO: The worser welcome.
I have charged thee not to haunt about my doors.
In honest plainness thou hast heard me say
My daughter is not for thee; and now, in madness,
Being full of supper and distempering draughts,
Upon malicious bravery, dost thou come
To start my quiet.

RODERIGO: Sir, sir, sir-

BRABANTIO: But thou must needs be sure
My spirit and my place have in them power
To make this bitter to thee.

RODERIGO: Patience, good sir.

BRABANTIO: What tell'st thou me of robbing? This is Venice;
My house is not a grange.

RODERIGO: Most grave Brabantio,
In simple and pure soul I come to you.

IAGO: 'Zounds, sir, you are one of those that will not serve God, if the devil bid you. Because we come to do you service and you think we are ruffians, you'll have your daughter covered with a Barbary horse; you'll have your nephews neigh to you; you'll have coursers for cousins, and gennets for germans.

BRABANTIO: What profane wretch art thou?

IAGO: I am one, sir, that comes to tell you your daughter and the Moor are now making the beast with two backs.

BRABANTIO: Thou are a villain.

IAGO: You are- a senator.

BRABANTIO: This thou shalt answer; I know thee, Roderigo.

RODERIGO: Sir, I will answer anything. But, I beseech you,
If't be your pleasure and most wise consent,
As partly I find it is, that your fair daughter,
At this odd-even and dull watch o' the night,
Transported with no worse nor better guard
But with a knave of common hire, a gondolier,
To the gross clasps of a lascivious Moor-
If this be known to you, and your allowance,
We then have done you bold and saucy wrongs;
But if you know not this, my manners tell me
We have your wrong rebuke. Do not believe
That, from the sense of all civility,
I thus would play and trifle with your reverence.
Your daughter, if you have not given her leave,
I say again, hath made a gross revolt,
Tying her duty, beauty, wit, and fortunes
In an extravagant and wheeling stranger
Of here and everywhere. Straight satisfy yourself:
If she be in her chamber or your house,
Let loose on me the justice of the state

For thus deluding you.

BRABANTIO: Strike on the tinder, ho!
Give me a taper! Call up all my people!
This accident is not unlike my dream;
Belief of it oppresses me already.
Light, I say, light!
   Exit above.

IAGO: Farewell, for I must leave you.
It seems not meet, nor wholesome to my place,
To be produced- as, if I stay, I shall-
Against the Moor; for I do know, the state,
However this may gall him with some check,
Cannot with safety cast him, for he's embark'd
With such loud reason to the Cyprus wars,
Which even now stands in act, that, for their souls,
Another of his fathom they have none
To lead their business; in which regard,
Though I do hate him as I do hell pains,
Yet for necessity of present life,
I must show out a flag and sign of love,
Which is indeed but sign. That you shall surely find him,
Lead to the Sagittary the raised search,
And there will I be with him. So farewell.
   Exit.
   Enter, Below, Brabantio, in His Nightgown, and Servants with Torches.

BRABANTIO: It is too true an evil: gone she is,
And what's to come of my despised time
Is nought but bitterness. Now, Roderigo,
Where didst thou see her? O unhappy girl!
With the Moor, say'st thou? Who would be a father!
How didst thou know 'twas she? O, she deceives me
Past thought! What said she to you? Get more tapers.
Raise all my kindred. Are they married, think you?

RODERIGO: Truly, I think they are.

BRABANTIO: O heaven! How got she out? O treason of the blood!
Fathers, from hence trust not your daughters' minds
By what you see them act. Is there not charms
By which the property of youth and maidhood
May be abused? Have you not read, Roderigo,
Of some such thing?

RODERIGO: Yes, sir, I have indeed.

BRABANTIO: Call up my brother. O, would you had had her!
Some one way, some another. Do you know
Where we may apprehend her and the Moor?

RODERIGO: I think I can discover him, if you please
To get good guard and go along with me.

BRABANTIO: Pray you, lead on. At every house I'll call;
I may command at most. Get weapons, ho!
And raise some special officers of night.
On, good Roderigo, I'll deserve your pains.
   Exeunt.

ACT I. SCENE II. Another Street.
Enter Othello, Iago, and Attendants with Torches.

IAGO: Though in the trade of war I have slain men,
Yet do I hold it very stuff o' the conscience
To do no contrived murther. I lack iniquity
Sometimes to do me service. Nine or ten times
I had thought to have yerk'd him here under the ribs.

OTHELLO: 'Tis better as it is.

IAGO: Nay, but he prated
And spoke such scurvy and provoking terms
Against your honor
That, with the little godliness I have,

I did full hard forbear him. But I pray you, sir,
Are you fast married? Be assured of this,
That the magnifico is much beloved,
And hath in his effect a voice potential
As double as the Duke's. He will divorce you,
Or put upon you what restraint and grievance
The law, with all his might to enforce it on,
Will give him cable.

OTHELLO: Let him do his spite.
My services, which I have done the signiory,
Shall out-tongue his complaints. 'Tis yet to know-
Which, when I know that boasting is an honor,
I shall promulgate- I fetch my life and being
From men of royal siege, and my demerits
May speak unbonneted to as proud a fortune
As this that I have reach'd. For know, Iago,
But that I love the gentle Desdemona,
I would not my unhoused free condition
Put into circumscription and confine
For the sea's worth. But, look! What lights come yond?

IAGO: Those are the raised father and his friends.
You were best go in.

OTHELLO: Not I; I must be found.
My parts, my title, and my perfect soul
Shall manifest me rightly. Is it they?

IAGO: By Janus, I think no.
   Enter Cassio and Certain Officers with Torches.

OTHELLO: The servants of the Duke? And my lieutenant?
The goodness of the night upon you, friends!
What is the news?

CASSIO: The Duke does greet you, general,

And he requires your haste-post-haste appearance,
Even on the instant.

OTHELLO: What is the matter, think you?

CASSIO: Something from Cyprus, as I may divine;
It is a business of some heat. The galleys
Have sent a dozen sequent messengers
This very night at one another's heels;
And many of the consuls, raised and met,
Are at the Duke's already. You have been hotly call'd for,
When, being not at your lodging to be found,
The Senate hath sent about three several quests
To search you out.

OTHELLO: 'Tis well I am found by you.
I will but spend a word here in the house
And go with you.
   Exit.

CASSIO: Ancient, what makes he here?

IAGO: Faith, he tonight hath boarded a land carack;
If it prove lawful prize, he's made forever.

CASSIO: I do not understand.

IAGO: He's married.

CASSIO: To who?
   Re-enter Othello.

IAGO: Marry, to- Come, captain, will you go?

OTHELLO: Have with you.

CASSIO: Here comes another troop to seek for you.

IAGO: It is Brabantio. General, be advised,
He comes to bad intent.
  Enter Brabantio, Roderigo, and Officers with Torches and Weapons.

OTHELLO: Holla! Stand there!

RODERIGO: Signior, it is the Moor.

BRABANTIO: Down with him, thief!
  They Draw on Both Sides.

IAGO: You, Roderigo! Come, sir, I am for you.

OTHELLO: Keep up your bright swords, for the dew will rust them.
Good signior, you shall more command with years
Than with your weapons.

BRABANTIO: O thou foul thief, where hast thou stow'd my daughter?
Damn'd as thou art, thou hast enchanted her,
For I'll refer me to all things of sense,
If she in chains of magic were not bound,
Whether a maid so tender, fair, and happy,
So opposite to marriage that she shunn'd
The wealthy, curled darlings of our nation,
Would ever have, to incur a general mock,
Run from her guardage to the sooty bosom
Of such a thing as thou- to fear, not to delight.
Judge me the world, if 'tis not gross in sense
That thou hast practiced on her with foul charms,
Abused her delicate youth with drugs or minerals
That weaken motion. I'll have't disputed on;
'Tis probable, and palpable to thinking.
I therefore apprehend and do attach thee
For an abuser of the world, a practicer
Of arts inhibited and out of warrant.
Lay hold upon him. If he do resist,
Subdue him at his peril.

OTHELLO: Hold your hands,
Both you of my inclining and the rest.
Were it my cue to fight, I should have known it
Without a prompter. Where will you that I go
To answer this your charge?

BRABANTIO: To prison, till fit time
Of law and course of direct session
Call thee to answer.

OTHELLO: What if I do obey?
How may the Duke be therewith satisfied,
Whose messengers are here about my side,
Upon some present business of the state
To bring me to him?

FIRST OFFICER: 'Tis true, most worthy signior;
The Duke's in council, and your noble self,
I am sure, is sent for.

BRABANTIO: How? The Duke in council?
In this time of the night? Bring him away;
Mine's not an idle cause. The Duke himself,
Or any of my brothers of the state,
Cannot but feel this wrong as 'twere their own;
For if such actions may have passage free,
Bond slaves and pagans shall our statesmen be.
  Exeunt.

ACT I. SCENE III. A Council Chamber.
The Duke and Senators Sitting at a Table; Officers Attending.

DUKE: There is no composition in these news
That gives them credit.

FIRST SENATOR: Indeed they are disproportion'd;
My letters say a hundred and seven galleys.

DUKE: And mine, a hundred and forty.

SECOND SENATOR: And mine, two hundred.
But though they jump not on a just account-
As in these cases, where the aim reports,
'Tis oft with difference- yet do they all confirm
A Turkish fleet, and bearing up to Cyprus.

DUKE: Nay, it is possible enough to judgement.
I do not so secure me in the error,
But the main article I do approve
In fearful sense.

SAILOR: *Within.* What, ho! What, ho! What, ho!

FIRST OFFICER: A messenger from the galleys.
   Enter Sailor.

DUKE: Now, what's the business?

SAILOR: The Turkish preparation makes for Rhodes,
So was I bid report here to the state
By Signior Angelo.

DUKE: How say you by this change?

FIRST SENATOR: This cannot be,
By no assay of reason; 'tis a pageant
To keep us in false gaze. When we consider
The importancy of Cyprus to the Turk,
And let ourselves again but understand
That as it more concerns the Turk than Rhodes,
So may he with more facile question bear it,
For that it stands not in such warlike brace,
But altogether lacks the abilities
That Rhodes is dress'd in. If we make thought of this,
We must not think the Turk is so unskillful

To leave that latest which concerns him first,
Neglecting an attempt of ease and gain,
To wake and wage a danger profitless.

DUKE: Nay, in all confidence, he's not for Rhodes.

FIRST OFFICER: Here is more news.
 Enter a Messenger.

MESSENGER: The Ottomites, reverend and gracious,
Steering with due course toward the isle of Rhodes,
Have there injointed them with an after fleet.

FIRST SENATOR: Ay, so I thought. How many, as you guess?

MESSENGER: Of thirty sail; and now they do re-stem
Their backward course, bearing with frank appearance
Their purposes toward Cyprus. Signior Montano,
Your trusty and most valiant servitor,
With his free duty recommends you thus,
And prays you to believe him.

DUKE: 'Tis certain then for Cyprus.
Marcus Luccicos, is not he in town?

FIRST SENATOR: He's now in Florence.

DUKE: Write from us to him, post-post-haste dispatch.

FIRST SENATOR: Here comes Brabantio and the valiant Moor.
 Enter Brabantio, Othello, Iago, Roderigo, and Officers.

DUKE: Valiant Othello, we must straight employ you
Against the general enemy Ottoman.
To Brabantio. I did not see you; welcome, gentle signior;
We lack'd your counsel and your help tonight.

BRABANTIO: So did I yours. Good your Grace, pardon me:
Neither my place nor aught I heard of business
Hath raised me from my bed, nor doth the general care
Take hold on me; for my particular grief
Is of so flood-gate and o'erbearing nature
That it engluts and swallows other sorrows,
And it is still itself.

DUKE: Why, what's the matter?

BRABANTIO: My daughter! O, my daughter!

ALL: Dead?

BRABANTIO: Ay, to me.
She is abused, stol'n from me and corrupted
By spells and medicines bought of mountebanks;
For nature so preposterously to err,
Being not deficient, blind, or lame of sense,
Sans witchcraft could not.

DUKE: Whoe'er he be that in this foul proceeding
Hath thus beguiled your daughter of herself
And you of her, the bloody book of law
You shall yourself read in the bitter letter
After your own sense, yea, though our proper son
Stood in your action.

BRABANTIO: Humbly I thank your Grace.
Here is the man, this Moor, whom now, it seems,
Your special mandate for the state affairs
Hath hither brought.

ALL: We are very sorry for't.

DUKE: *To Othello.* What in your own part can you say to this?

BRABANTIO: Nothing, but this is so.

OTHELLO: Most potent, grave, and reverend signiors,
My very noble and approved good masters,
That I have ta'en away this old man's daughter,
It is most true; true, I have married her;
The very head and front of my offending
Hath this extent, no more. Rude am I in my speech,
And little blest with the soft phrase of peace;
For since these arms of mine had seven years' pith,
Till now some nine moons wasted, they have used
Their dearest action in the tented field,
And little of this great world can I speak,
More than pertains to feats of broil and battle;
And therefore little shall I grace my cause
In speaking for myself. Yet, by your gracious patience,
I will a round unvarnish'd tale deliver
Of my whole course of love: what drugs, what charms,
What conjuration, and what mighty magic-
For such proceeding I am charged withal-
I won his daughter.

BRABANTIO: A maiden never bold,
Of spirit so still and quiet that her motion
Blush'd at herself; and she- in spite of nature,
Of years, of country, credit, everything-
To fall in love with what she fear'd to look on!
It is judgement maim'd and most imperfect,
That will confess perfection so could err
Against all rules of nature, and must be driven
To find out practices of cunning hell
Why this should be. I therefore vouch again
That with some mixtures powerful o'er the blood,
Or with some dram conjured to this effect,
He wrought upon her.

DUKE: To vouch this is no proof,
Without more certain and more overt test

Than these thin habits and poor likelihoods
Of modern seeming do prefer against him.

FIRST SENATOR: But, Othello, speak.
Did you by indirect and forced courses
Subdue and poison this young maid's affections?
Or came it by request, and such fair question
As soul to soul affordeth?

OTHELLO: I do beseech you,
Send for the lady to the Sagittary,
And let her speak of me before her father.
If you do find me foul in her report,
The trust, the office I do hold of you,
Not only take away, but let your sentence
Even fall upon my life.

DUKE: Fetch Desdemona hither.

OTHELLO: Ancient, conduct them; you best know the place.
  Exeunt Iago and Attendants.
And till she come, as truly as to heaven
I do confess the vices of my blood,
So justly to your grave ears I'll present
How I did thrive in this fair lady's love
And she in mine.

DUKE: Say it, Othello.

OTHELLO: Her father loved me, oft invited me,
Still question'd me the story of my life
From year to year, the battles, sieges, fortunes,
That I have pass'd.
I ran it through, even from my boyish days
To the very moment that he bade me tell it:
Wherein I spake of most disastrous chances,
Of moving accidents by flood and field,
Of hair-breadth 'scapes i' the imminent deadly breach,

Of being taken by the insolent foe
And sold to slavery, of my redemption thence
And portance in my travels' history;
Wherein of antres vast and deserts idle,
Rough quarries, rocks, and hills whose heads touch heaven,
It was my hint to speak- such was the process-
And of the Cannibals that each other eat,
The Anthropophagi, and men whose heads
Do grow beneath their shoulders. This to hear
Would Desdemona seriously incline;
But still the house affairs would draw her thence,
Which ever as she could with haste dispatch,
She'ld come again, and with a greedy ear
Devour up my discourse; which I observing,
Took once a pliant hour, and found good means
To draw from her a prayer of earnest heart
That I would all my pilgrimage dilate,
Whereof by parcels she had something heard,
But not intentively. I did consent,
And often did beguile her of her tears
When I did speak of some distressful stroke
That my youth suffer'd. My story being done,
She gave me for my pains a world of sighs;
She swore, in faith, 'twas strange, 'twas passing strange;
'Twas pitiful, 'twas wondrous pitiful.
She wish'd she had not heard it, yet she wish'd
That heaven had made her such a man; she thank'd me,
And bade me, if I had a friend that loved her,
I should but teach him how to tell my story,
And that would woo her. Upon this hint I spake:
She loved me for the dangers I had pass'd,
And I loved her that she did pity them.
This only is the witchcraft I have used.
Here comes the lady; let her witness it.
   Enter Desdemona, Iago, and Attendants.

DUKE: I think this tale would win my daughter too.
Good Brabantio,

Take up this mangled matter at the best:
Men do their broken weapons rather use
Than their bare hands.

BRABANTIO: I pray you, hear her speak.
If she confess that she was half the wooer,
Destruction on my head, if my bad blame
Light on the man! Come hither, gentle mistress.
Do you perceive in all this noble company
Where most you owe obedience?

DESDEMONA: My noble father,
I do perceive here a divided duty.
To you I am bound for life and education;
My life and education both do learn me
How to respect you; you are the lord of duty,
I am hitherto your daughter. But here's my husband,
And so much duty as my mother show'd
To you, preferring you before her father,
So much I challenge that I may profess
Due to the Moor, my lord.

BRABANTIO: God be with you! I have done.
Please it your Grace, on to the state affairs;
I had rather to adopt a child than get it.
Come hither, Moor.
I here do give thee that with all my heart
Which, but thou hast already, with all my heart
I would keep from thee. For your sake, jewel,
I am glad at soul I have no other child;
For thy escape would teach me tyranny,
To hang clogs on them. I have done, my lord.

DUKE: Let me speak like yourself, and lay a sentence
Which, as a grise or step, may help these lovers
Into your favor.
When remedies are past, the griefs are ended
By seeing the worst, which late on hopes depended.

To mourn a mischief that is past and gone
Is the next way to draw new mischief on.
What cannot be preserved when Fortune takes,
Patience her injury a mockery makes.
The robb'd that smiles steals something from the thief;
He robs himself that spends a bootless grief.

BRABANTIO: So let the Turk of Cyprus us beguile;
We lose it not so long as we can smile.
He bears the sentence well, that nothing bears
But the free comfort which from thence he hears;
But he bears both the sentence and the sorrow
That, to pay grief, must of poor patience borrow.
These sentences, to sugar or to gall,
Being strong on both sides, are equivocal.
But words are words; I never yet did hear
That the bruised heart was pierced through the ear.
I humbly beseech you, proceed to the affairs of state.

DUKE: The Turk with a most mighty preparation makes for Cyprus.
Othello, the fortitude of the place is best known to you; and
though we have there a substitute of most allowed sufficiency,
yet opinion, a sovereign mistress of effects, throws a more safer
voice on you. You must therefore be content to slubber the gloss
of your new fortunes with this more stubborn and boisterous
expedition.

OTHELLO: The tyrant custom, most grave senators,
Hath made the flinty and steel couch of war
My thrice-driven bed of down. I do agnize
A natural and prompt alacrity
I find in hardness and do undertake
These present wars against the Ottomites.
Most humbly therefore bending to your state,
I crave fit disposition for my wife,
Due reference of place and exhibition,
With such accommodation and besort
As levels with her breeding.

DUKE: If you please,
Be't at her father's.

BRABANTIO: I'll not have it so.

OTHELLO: Nor I.

DESDEMONA: Nor I. I would not there reside
To put my father in impatient thoughts
By being in his eye. Most gracious Duke,
To my unfolding lend your prosperous ear,
And let me find a charter in your voice
To assist my simpleness.

DUKE: What would you, Desdemona?

DESDEMONA: That I did love the Moor to live with him,
My downright violence and storm of fortunes
May trumpet to the world. My heart's subdued
Even to the very quality of my lord.
I saw Othello's visage in his mind,
And to his honors and his valiant parts
Did I my soul and fortunes consecrate.
So that, dear lords, if I be left behind,
A moth of peace, and he go to the war,
The rites for which I love him are bereft me,
And I a heavy interim shall support
By his dear absence. Let me go with him.

OTHELLO: Let her have your voices.
Vouch with me, heaven, I therefore beg it not
To please the palate of my appetite,
Nor to comply with heat- the young affects
In me defunct- and proper satisfaction;
But to be free and bounteous to her mind.
And heaven defend your good souls, that you think
I will your serious and great business scant

For she is with me. No, when light-wing'd toys
Of feather'd Cupid seel with wanton dullness
My speculative and officed instruments,
That my disports corrupt and taint my business,
Let housewives make a skillet of my helm,
And all indign and base adversities
Make head against my estimation!

DUKE: Be it as you shall privately determine,
Either for her stay or going. The affair cries haste,
And speed must answer't: you must hence tonight.

DESDEMONA: Tonight, my lord?

DUKE: This night.

OTHELLO: With all my heart.

DUKE: At nine i' the morning here we'll meet again.
Othello, leave some officer behind,
And he shall our commission bring to you,
With such things else of quality and respect
As doth import you.

OTHELLO: So please your Grace, my ancient;
A man he is of honesty and trust.
To his conveyance I assign my wife,
With what else needful your good Grace shall think
To be sent after me.

DUKE: Let it be so.
Good night to everyone. *To Brabantio.* And, noble signior,
If virtue no delighted beauty lack,
Your son-in-law is far more fair than black.

FIRST SENATOR: Adieu, brave Moor, use Desdemona well.

BRABANTIO: Look to her, Moor, if thou hast eyes to see;
She has deceived her father, and may thee.
  Exeunt Duke, Senators, and Officers.

OTHELLO: My life upon her faith! Honest Iago,
My Desdemona must I leave to thee.
I prithee, let thy wife attend on her,
And bring them after in the best advantage.
Come, Desdemona, I have but an hour
Of love, of worldly matters and direction,
To spend with thee. We must obey the time.
  Exeunt Othello and Desdemona.

RODERIGO: Iago!

IAGO: What say'st thou, noble heart?

RODERIGO: What will I do, thinkest thou?

IAGO: Why, go to bed and sleep.

RODERIGO: I will incontinently drown myself.

IAGO: If thou dost, I shall never love thee after.
Why, thou silly gentleman!

RODERIGO: It is silliness to live when to live is torment, and then have we a prescription to die when death is our physician.

IAGO: O villainous! I have looked upon the world for four times seven years, and since I could distinguish betwixt a benefit and an injury, I never found man that knew how to love himself. Ere I would say I would drown myself for the love of a guinea hen, I would change my humanity with a baboon.

RODERIGO: What should I do? I confess it is my shame to be so fond, but it is not in my virtue to amend it.

IAGO: Virtue? a fig! 'Tis in ourselves that we are thus or thus. Our bodies are gardens, to the which our wills are gardeners; so that if we will plant nettles or sow lettuce, set hyssop and weed up thyme, supply it with one gender of herbs or distract it with many, either to have it sterile with idleness or manured with industry, why, the power and corrigible authority of this lies in our wills. If the balance of our lives had not one scale of reason to poise another of sensuality, the blood and baseness of our natures would conduct us to most preposterous conclusions. But we have reason to cool our raging motions, our carnal stings, our unbitted lusts; whereof I take this, that you call love, to be a sect or scion.

RODERIGO: It cannot be.

IAGO: It is merely a lust of the blood and a permission of the will. Come, be a man! Drown thyself? Drown cats and blind puppies. I have professed me thy friend, and I confess me knit to thy deserving with cables of perdurable toughness; I could never better stead thee than now. Put money in thy purse; follow thou the wars; defeat thy favor with an usurped beard. I say, put money in thy purse. It cannot be that Desdemona should long continue her love to the Moor- put money in thy purse- nor he his to her. It was a violent commencement, and thou shalt see an answerable sequestration- put but money in thy purse. These Moors are changeable in their wills- fill thy purse with money. The food that to him now is as luscious as locusts, shall be to him shortly as acerb as the coloquintida. She must change for youth; when she is sated with his body, she will find the error of her choice. She must have change, she must; therefore put money in thy purse. If thou wilt needs damn thyself, do it a more delicate way than drowning. Make all the money thou canst. If sanctimony and a frail vow betwixt an erring barbarian and a supersubtle Venetian be not too hard for my wits and all the tribe of hell, thou shalt enjoy her- therefore make money. A pox of drowning thyself! It is clean out of the way. Seek thou rather to be hanged in compassing thy joy than to be drowned and go without her.

RODERIGO: Wilt thou be fast to my hopes, if I depend on the issue?

IAGO: Thou art sure of me- go, make money. I have told thee often, and I retell thee again and again, I hate the Moor. My cause is hearted; thine hath no less reason. Let us be conjunctive in our revenge against him. If thou canst cuckold him, thou dost thyself a pleasure, me a sport. There are many events in the womb of time which will be delivered. Traverse, go, provide thy money. We will have more of this tomorrow. Adieu.

RODERIGO: Where shall we meet i' the morning?

IAGO: At my lodging.

RODERIGO: I'll be with thee betimes.

IAGO: Go to, farewell. Do you hear, Roderigo?

RODERIGO: What say you?

IAGO: No more of drowning, do you hear?

RODERIGO: I am changed; I'll go sell all my land.
   Exit.

IAGO: Thus do I ever make my fool my purse;
For I mine own gain'd knowledge should profane
If I would time expend with such a snipe
But for my sport and profit. I hate the Moor,
And it is thought abroad that 'twixt my sheets
He has done my office. I know not if't be true,
But I for mere suspicion in that kind
Will do as if for surety. He holds me well,
The better shall my purpose work on him.
Cassio's a proper man. Let me see now-
To get his place, and to plume up my will
In double knavery- How, how?- Let's see-

After some time, to abuse Othello's ear
That he is too familiar with his wife.
He hath a person and a smooth dispose
To be suspected- framed to make women false.
The Moor is of a free and open nature,
That thinks men honest that but seem to be so,
And will as tenderly be led by the nose
As asses are.
I have't. It is engender'd. Hell and night
Must bring this monstrous birth to the world's light.
   Exit.

ACT II. SCENE I. A Seaport in Cyprus. An Open Place near the Quay.
   Enter Montano and Two Gentlemen.

MONTANO: What from the cape can you discern at sea?

FIRST GENTLEMAN: Nothing at all. It is a high-wrought flood;
I cannot, 'twixt the heaven and the main, descry a sail.

MONTANO: Methinks the wind hath spoke aloud at land;
A fuller blast ne'er shook our battlements.
If it hath ruffian'd so upon the sea,
What ribs of oak, when mountains melt on them,
Can hold the mortise? What shall we hear of this?

SECOND GENTLEMAN: A segregation of the Turkish fleet.
For do but stand upon the foaming shore,
The chidden billow seems to pelt the clouds;
The wind-shaked surge, with high and monstrous mane,
Seems to cast water on the burning bear,
And quench the guards of the ever-fixed pole.
I never did like molestation view
On the enchafed flood.

MONTANO: If that the Turkish fleet
Be not enshelter'd and embay'd, they are drown'd;
It is impossible to bear it out.

Enter a Third Gentleman.

THIRD GENTLEMAN: News, lads! Our wars are done.
The desperate tempest hath so bang'd the Turks,
That their designment halts. A noble ship of Venice
Hath seen a grievous wreck and sufferance
On most part of their fleet.

MONTANO: How? Is this true?

THIRD GENTLEMAN: The ship is here put in,
A Veronesa. Michael Cassio,
Lieutenant to the warlike Moor, Othello,
Is come on shore; the Moor himself at sea,
And is in full commission here for Cyprus.

MONTANO: I am glad on't; 'tis a worthy governor.

THIRD GENTLEMAN: But this same Cassio, though he speak of comfort
Touching the Turkish loss, yet he looks sadly
And prays the Moor be safe; for they were parted
With foul and violent tempest.

MONTANO: Pray heavens he be,
For I have served him, and the man commands
Like a full soldier. Let's to the seaside, ho!
As well to see the vessel that's come in
As to throw out our eyes for brave Othello,
Even till we make the main and the aerial blue
An indistinct regard.

THIRD GENTLEMAN: Come, let's do so,
For every minute is expectancy
Of more arrivance.
 Enter Cassio.

CASSIO: Thanks, you the valiant of this warlike isle,

That so approve the Moor! O, let the heavens
Give him defense against the elements,
For I have lost him on a dangerous sea.

MONTANO: Is she well shipp'd?

CASSIO: His bark is stoutly timber'd, and his pilot
Of very expert and approved allowance;
Therefore my hopes, not surfeited to death,
Stand in bold cure.
   A Cry Within, "A Sail, a Sail, a Sail!"
   Enter a Fourth Gentleman.
What noise?

FOURTH GENTLEMAN: The town is empty; on the brow o' the sea
Stand ranks of people, and they cry, "A sail!"

CASSIO: My hopes do shape him for the governor.
   Guns Heard.

SECOND GENTLEMAN: They do discharge their shot of courtesy-
Our friends at least.

CASSIO: I pray you, sir, go forth,
And give us truth who 'tis that is arrived.

SECOND GENTLEMAN: I shall.
   Exit.

MONTANO: But, good lieutenant, is your general wived?

CASSIO: Most fortunately: he hath achieved a maid
That paragons description and wild fame,
One that excels the quirks of blazoning pens,
And in the essential vesture of creation
Does tire the ingener.
   Re-enter second Gentleman.

How now! who has put in?

SECOND GENTLEMAN: 'Tis one Iago, ancient to the general.

CASSIO: He has had most favorable and happy speed:
Tempests themselves, high seas, and howling winds,
The gutter'd rocks, and congregated sands,
Traitors ensteep'd to clog the guiltless keel,
As having sense of beauty, do omit
Their mortal natures, letting go safely by
The divine Desdemona.

MONTANO: What is she?

CASSIO: She that I spake of, our great captain's captain,
Left in the conduct of the bold Iago,
Whose footing here anticipates our thoughts
A se'nnight's speed. Great Jove, Othello guard,
And swell his sail with thine own powerful breath,
That he may bless this bay with his tall ship,
Make love's quick pants in Desdemona's arms,
Give renew'd fire to our extincted spirits,
And bring all Cyprus comfort.
   Enter Desdemona, Emilia Iago, Roderigo, and Attendants.
O, behold, the riches of the ship is come on shore!
Ye men of Cyprus, let her have your knees.
Hall to thee, lady! And the grace of heaven,
Before, behind thee, and on every hand,
Enwheel thee round!

DESDEMONA: I thank you, valiant Cassio.
What tidings can you tell me of my lord?

CASSIO: He is not yet arrived, nor know I aught
But that he's well and will be shortly here.

DESDEMONA: O, but I fear- How lost you company?

CASSIO: The great contention of the sea and skies
Parted our fellowship- But, hark! a sail.
   A Cry Within, "A Sail, a Sail!" Guns Heard.

SECOND GENTLEMAN: They give their greeting to the citadel;
This likewise is a friend.

CASSIO: See for the news.
   Exit Gentleman.
Good ancient, you are welcome. *To Emilia.* Welcome, mistress.
Let it not gall your patience, good Iago,
That I extend my manners; 'tis my breeding
That gives me this bold show of courtesy. *Kisses her.*

IAGO: Sir, would she give you so much of her lips
As of her tongue she oft bestows on me,
You'ld have enough.

DESDEMONA: Alas, she has no speech.

IAGO: In faith, too much;
I find it still when I have list to sleep.
Marry, before your ladyship I grant,
She puts her tongue a little in her heart
And chides with thinking.

EMILIA: You have little cause to say so.

IAGO: Come on, come on. You are pictures out of doors,
Bells in your parlors, wildcats in your kitchens,
Saints in your injuries, devils being offended,
Players in your housewifery, and housewives in your beds.

DESDEMONA: O, fie upon thee, slanderer!

IAGO: Nay, it is true, or else I am a Turk:
You rise to play, and go to bed to work.

EMILIA: You shall not write my praise.

IAGO: No, let me not.

DESDEMONA: What wouldst thou write of me, if thou shouldst praise me?

IAGO: O gentle lady, do not put me to't,
For I am nothing if not critical.

DESDEMONA: Come on, assay- There's one gone to the harbor?

IAGO: Ay, madam.

DESDEMONA: I am not merry, but I do beguile
The thing I am by seeming otherwise.
Come, how wouldst thou praise me?

IAGO: I am about it, but indeed my invention
Comes from my pate as birdlime does from frieze;
It plucks out brains and all. But my Muse labors,
And thus she is deliver'd.
If she be fair and wise, fairness and wit,
The one's for use, the other useth it.

DESDEMONA: Well praised! How if she be black and witty?

IAGO: If she be black, and thereto have a wit,
She'll find a white that shall her blackness fit.

DESDEMONA: Worse and worse.

EMILIA: How if fair and foolish?

IAGO: She never yet was foolish that was fair,
For even her folly help'd her to an heir.

DESDEMONA: These are old fond paradoxes to make fools laugh i' the alehouse. What miserable praise hast thou for her that's foul and foolish?

IAGO: There's none so foul and foolish thereunto,
But does foul pranks which fair and wise ones do.

DESDEMONA: O heavy ignorance! Thou praisest the worst best. But what praise couldst thou bestow on a deserving woman indeed, one that in the authority of her merit did justly put on the vouch of very malice itself?

IAGO: She that was ever fair and never proud,
Had tongue at will and yet was never loud,
Never lack'd gold and yet went never gay,
Fled from her wish and yet said, "Now I may";
She that, being anger'd, her revenge being nigh,
Bade her wrong stay and her displeasure fly;
She that in wisdom never was so frail
To change the cod's head for the salmon's tail;
She that could think and ne'er disclose her mind,
See suitors following and not look behind;
She was a wight, if ever such wight were-

DESDEMONA: To do what?

IAGO: To suckle fools and chronicle small beer.

DESDEMONA: O most lame and impotent conclusion! Do not learn of him, Emilia, though he be thy husband. How say you, Cassio? Is he not a most profane and liberal counselor?

CASSIO: He speaks home, madam. You may relish him more in the soldier than in the scholar.

IAGO: *Aside.* He takes her by the palm; ay, well said, whisper. With as little a web as this will I ensnare as great a fly as

Cassio. Ay, smile upon her, do; I will gyve thee in thine own courtship. You say true; 'tis so, indeed. If such tricks as these strip you out of your lieutenantry, it had been better you had not kissed your three fingers so oft, which now again you are most apt to play the sir in. Very good. Well kissed! an excellent courtesy! 'tis so, indeed. Yet again your fingers to your lips? Would they were clyster-pipes for your sake! *Trumpet Within.* The Moor! I know his trumpet.

CASSIO: 'Tis truly so.

DESDEMONA: Let's meet him and receive him.

CASSIO: Lo, where he comes!
  Enter Othello and Attendants.

OTHELLO: O my fair warrior!

DESDEMONA: My dear Othello!

OTHELLO: It gives me wonder great as my content
To see you here before me. O my soul's joy!
If after every tempest come such calms,
May the winds blow till they have waken'd death!
And let the laboring bark climb hills of seas
Olympus-high, and duck again as low
As hell's from heaven! If it were now to die,
'Twere now to be most happy; for I fear
My soul hath her content so absolute
That not another comfort like to this
Succeeds in unknown fate.

DESDEMONA: The heavens forbid
But that our loves and comforts should increase,
Even as our days do grow!

OTHELLO: Amen to that, sweet powers!

I cannot speak enough of this content;
It stops me here; it is too much of joy.
And this, and this, the greatest discords be *Kisses her.*
That e'er our hearts shall make!

IAGO: *Aside.* O, you are well tuned now!
But I'll set down the pegs that make this music,
As honest as I am.

OTHELLO: Come, let us to the castle.
News, friends: our wars are done, the Turks are drown'd.
How does my old acquaintance of this isle?
Honey, you shall be well desired in Cyprus;
I have found great love amongst them. O my sweet,
I prattle out of fashion, and I dote
In mine own comforts. I prithee, good Iago,
Go to the bay and disembark my coffers.
Bring thou the master to the citadel;
He is a good one, and his worthiness
Does challenge much respect. Come, Desdemona,
Once more well met at Cyprus.
   Exeunt All but Iago and Roderigo.

IAGO: Do thou meet me presently at the harbor. Come hither. If thou be'st valiant- as they say base men being in love have then a nobility in their natures more than is native to them- list me. The lieutenant tonight watches on the court of guard. First, I must tell thee this: Desdemona is directly in love with him.

RODERIGO: With him? Why, 'tis not possible.

IAGO: Lay thy finger thus, and let thy soul be instructed. Mark me with what violence she first loved the Moor, but for bragging and telling her fantastical lies. And will she love him still for prating? Let not thy discreet heart think it. Her eye must be fed; and what delight shall she have to look on the devil? When the blood is made dull with the act of sport, there should be, again to inflame it and to give satiety a fresh appetite,

loveliness in favor, sympathy in years, manners, and beauties-
all which the Moor is defective in. Now, for want of these
required conveniences, her delicate tenderness will find itself
abused, begin to heave the gorge, disrelish and abhor the Moor;
very nature will instruct her in it and compel her to some second
choice. Now sir, this granted- as it is a most pregnant and
unforced position- who stands so eminently in the degree of this
fortune as Cassio does? A knave very voluble; no further
conscionable than in putting on the mere form of civil and humane
seeming, for the better compass of his salt and most hidden loose
affection? Why, none, why, none- a slipper and subtle knave, a
finder out of occasions, that has an eye can stamp and
counterfeit advantages, though true advantage never present
itself- a devilish knave! Besides, the knave is handsome, young,
and hath all those requisites in him that folly and green minds
look after- a pestilent complete knave, and the woman hath found
him already.

RODERIGO: I cannot believe that in her; she's full of most blest
condition.

IAGO: Blest fig's-end! The wine she drinks is made of grapes. If
she had been blest, she would never have loved the Moor. Blest
pudding! Didst thou not see her paddle with the palm of his hand?
Didst not mark that?

RODERIGO: Yes, that I did; but that was but courtesy.

IAGO: Lechery, by this hand; an index and obscure prologue to the
history of lust and foul thoughts. They met so near with their
lips that their breaths embraced together. Villainous thoughts,
Roderigo! When these mutualities so marshal the way, hard at hand
comes the master and main exercise, the incorporate conclusion.
Pish! But, sir, be you ruled by me. I have brought you from
Venice. Watch you tonight; for the command, I'll lay't upon you.
Cassio knows you not. I'll not be far from you. Do you find some
occasion to anger Cassio, either by speaking too loud, or
tainting his discipline, or from what other course you please,

which the time shall more favorably minister.

RODERIGO: Well.

IAGO: Sir, he is rash and very sudden in choler, and haply may strike at you. Provoke him, that he may; for even out of that will I cause these of Cyprus to mutiny, whose qualification shall come into no true taste again but by the displanting of Cassio. So shall you have a shorter journey to your desires by the means I shall then have to prefer them, and the impediment most profitably removed, without the which there were no expectation of our prosperity.
RODERIGO: I will do this, if I can bring it to any opportunity.

IAGO: I warrant thee. Meet me by and by at the citadel. I must fetch his necessaries ashore. Farewell.

RODERIGO: Adieu.
  Exit.

IAGO: That Cassio loves her, I do well believe it;
That she loves him, 'tis apt and of great credit.
The Moor, howbeit that I endure him not,
Is of a constant, loving, noble nature,
And I dare think he'll prove to Desdemona
A most dear husband. Now, I do love her too,
Not out of absolute lust, though peradventure
I stand accountant for as great a sin,
But partly led to diet my revenge,
For that I do suspect the lusty Moor
Hath leap'd into my seat; the thought whereof
Doth like a poisonous mineral gnaw my inwards,
And nothing can or shall content my soul
Till I am even'd with him, wife for wife.
Or failing so, yet that I put the Moor
At least into a jealousy so strong
That judgement cannot cure. Which thing to do,
If this poor trash of Venice, whom I trace

For his quick hunting, stand the putting on,
I'll have our Michael Cassio on the hip,
Abuse him to the Moor in the rank garb
(For I fear Cassio with my nightcap too),
Make the Moor thank me, love me, and reward me
For making him egregiously an ass
And practicing upon his peace and quiet
Even to madness. 'Tis here, but yet confused:
Knavery's plain face is never seen till used.
Exit.

ACT II. SCENE II. A Street.

Enter a Herald with a Proclamation; People Following.

HERALD: It is Othello's pleasure, our noble and valiant general, that upon certain tidings now arrived, importing the mere perdition of the Turkish fleet, every man put himself into triumph; some to dance, some to make bonfires, each man to what sport and revels his addiction leads him; for besides these beneficial news, it is the celebration of his nuptial. So much was his pleasure should be proclaimed. All offices are open, and there is full liberty of feasting from this present hour of five till the bell have told eleven. Heaven bless the isle of Cyprus and our noble general Othello!
Exeunt.

ACT II. SCENE III. A Hall in the Castle.

Enter Othello, Desdemona, Cassio, and Attendants.

OTHELLO: Good Michael, look you to the guard tonight.
Let's teach ourselves that honorable stop,
Not to outsport discretion.

CASSIO: Iago hath direction what to do;
But notwithstanding with my personal eye
Will I look to't.

OTHELLO: Iago is most honest.
Michael, good night. Tomorrow with your earliest
Let me have speech with you. Come, my dear love,
The purchase made, the fruits are to ensue;
That profit's yet to come 'tween me and you.
Good night.
  Exeunt Othello, Desdemona, and Attendants.
  Enter Iago.

CASSIO: Welcome, Iago; we must to the watch.

IAGO: Not this hour, lieutenant; 'tis not yet ten o' the clock. Our general cast us thus early for the love of his Desdemona; who let us not therefore blame. He hath not yet made wanton the night with her, and she is sport for Jove.

CASSIO: She's a most exquisite lady.

IAGO: And, I'll warrant her, full of game.

CASSIO: Indeed she's a most fresh and delicate creature.

IAGO: What an eye she has! Methinks it sounds a parley to provocation.

CASSIO: An inviting eye; and yet methinks right modest.

IAGO: And when she speaks, is it not an alarum to love?

CASSIO: She is indeed perfection.

IAGO: Well, happiness to their sheets! Come, lieutenant, I have a stope of wine, and here without are a brace of Cyprus gallants that would fain have a measure to the health of black Othello.

CASSIO: Not tonight, good Iago. I have very poor and unhappy brains for drinking. I could well wish courtesy would invent some other custom of entertainment.

IAGO: O, they are our friends! But one cup; I'll drink for you.

CASSIO: I have drunk but one cup tonight, and that was craftily qualified too, and behold what innovation it makes here. I am unfortunate in the infirmity, and dare not task my weakness with any more.

IAGO: What, man! 'Tis a night of revels, the gallants desire it.

CASSIO: Where are they?

IAGO: Here at the door; I pray you, call them in.

CASSIO: I'll do't, but it dislikes me.
  Exit.

IAGO: If I can fasten but one cup upon him,
With that which he hath drunk tonight already,
He'll be as full of quarrel and offense
As my young mistress' dog. Now my sick fool Roderigo,
Whom love hath turn'd almost the wrong side out,
To Desdemona hath tonight caroused
Potations pottle-deep; and he's to watch.
Three lads of Cyprus, noble swelling spirits,
That hold their honors in a wary distance,
The very elements of this warlike isle,
Have I tonight fluster'd with flowing cups,
And they watch too. Now, 'mongst this flock of drunkards,
Am I to put our Cassio in some action
That may offend the isle. But here they come.
If consequence do but approve my dream,
My boat sails freely, both with wind and stream.
  Re-enter Cassio; with Him Montano and Gentlemen; Servants Following with Wine.

CASSIO: 'Fore God, they have given me a rouse already.

MONTANO: Good faith, a little one; not past a pint, as I am a

SOLDIER:

IAGO: Some wine, ho!
Sings. "And let me the canakin clink, clink;
    And let me the canakin clink.
      A soldier's a man;
      O, man's life's but a span;
    Why then let a soldier drink."
Some wine, boys!

CASSIO: 'Fore God, an excellent song.

IAGO: I learned it in England, where indeed they are most potent in potting. Your Dane, your German, and your swag-bellied Hollander- Drink, ho!- are nothing to your English.

CASSIO: Is your Englishman so expert in his drinking?

IAGO: Why, he drinks you with facility your Dane dead drunk; he sweats not to overthrow your Almain; he gives your Hollander a vomit ere the next pottle can be filled.

CASSIO: To the health of our general!

MONTANO: I am for it, lieutenant, and I'll do you justice.

IAGO: O sweet England!
Sings. "King Stephen was and-a worthy peer,
    His breeches cost him but a crown;
    He held them sixpence all too dear,
      With that he call'd the tailor lown.

    "He was a wight of high renown,

>   And thou art but of low degree.
> 'Tis pride that pulls the country down;
>   Then take thine auld cloak about thee."

Some wine, ho!

CASSIO: Why, this is a more exquisite song than the other.

IAGO: Will you hear't again?

CASSIO: No, for I hold him to be unworthy of his place that does those things. Well, God's above all, and there be souls must be saved, and there be souls must not be saved.

IAGO: It's true, good lieutenant.

CASSIO: For mine own part- no offense to the general, nor any man of quality- I hope to be saved.

IAGO: And so do I too, lieutenant.

CASSIO: Ay, but, by your leave, not before me; the lieutenant is to be saved before the ancient. Let's have no more of this; let's to our affairs. God forgive us our sins! Gentlemen, let's look to our business. Do not think, gentlemen, I am drunk: this is my ancient, this is my right hand, and this is my left. I am not drunk now; I can stand well enough, and I speak well enough.

ALL: Excellent well.

CASSIO: Why, very well then; you must not think then that I am drunk.
   Exit.

MONTANO: To the platform, masters; come, let's set the watch.

IAGO: You see this fellow that is gone before;
He is a soldier fit to stand by Caesar

And give direction. And do but see his vice;
'Tis to his virtue a just equinox,
The one as long as the other. 'Tis pity of him.
I fear the trust Othello puts him in
On some odd time of his infirmity
Will shake this island.

MONTANO: But is he often thus?

IAGO: 'Tis evermore the prologue to his sleep.
He'll watch the horologe a double set,
If drink rock not his cradle.

MONTANO: It were well
The general were put in mind of it.
Perhaps he sees it not, or his good nature
Prizes the virtue that appears in Cassio
And looks not on his evils. Is not this true?
Enter Roderigo.

IAGO: *Aside to Him.* How now, Roderigo!
I pray you, after the lieutenant; go.
Exit Roderigo.

MONTANO: And 'tis great pity that the noble Moor
Should hazard such a place as his own second
With one of an ingraft infirmity.
It were an honest action to say
So to the Moor.

IAGO: Not I, for this fair island.
I do love Cassio well, and would do much
To cure him of this evil- But, hark! What noise?
A Cry Within, "Help, Help!"
Re-enter Cassio, Driving in Roderigo.

CASSIO: 'Zounds! You rogue! You rascal!

MONTANO: What's the matter, lieutenant?

CASSIO: A knave teach me my duty! But I'll beat the knave into a twiggen bottle.

RODERIGO: Beat me!

CASSIO: Dost thou prate, rogue? Strikes Roderigo.

MONTANO: Nay, good lieutenant; I pray you, sir, hold your hand.

CASSIO: Let me go, sir, or I'll knock you o'er the mazzard.

MONTANO: Come, come, you're drunk.

CASSIO: Drunk? They fight.

IAGO: *Aside to Roderigo.* Away, I say; go out and cry a mutiny.
   Exit Roderigo.
Nay, good lieutenant! God's will, gentlemen!
Help, ho!- Lieutenant- sir- Montano- sir-
Help, masters!- Here's a goodly watch indeed!
   A bell rings.
Who's that that rings the bell?- Diablo, ho!
The town will rise. God's will, lieutenant, hold!
You will be shamed forever.
   Re-enter Othello and Attendants.

OTHELLO: What is the matter here?

MONTANO: 'Zounds, I bleed still; I am hurt to the death.
   Faints.

OTHELLO: Hold, for your lives!

IAGO: Hold, ho! Lieutenant- sir- Montano- gentlemen-
Have you forgot all place of sense and duty?

Hold! the general speaks to you! Hold, hold, for shame!

OTHELLO: Why, how now, ho! from whence ariseth this?
Are we turn'd Turks, and to ourselves do that
Which heaven hath forbid the Ottomites?
For Christian shame, put by this barbarous brawl.
He that stirs next to carve for his own rage
Holds his soul light; he dies upon his motion.
Silence that dreadful bell; it frights the isle
From her propriety. What is the matter, masters?
Honest Iago, that look'st dead with grieving,
Speak: who began this? On thy love, I charge thee.

IAGO: I do not know. Friends all but now, even now,
In quarter, and in terms like bride and groom
Devesting them for bed; and then, but now
(As if some planet had unwitted men),
Swords out, and tilting one at other's breast,
In opposition bloody. I cannot speak
Any beginning to this peevish odds;
And would in action glorious I had lost
Those legs that brought me to a part of it!

OTHELLO: How comes it, Michael, you are thus forgot?

CASSIO: I pray you, pardon me; I cannot speak.

OTHELLO: Worthy Montano, you were wont be civil;
The gravity and stillness of your youth
The world hath noted, and your name is great
In mouths of wisest censure. What's the matter,
That you unlace your reputation thus,
And spend your rich opinion for the name
Of a night-brawler? Give me answer to it.

MONTANO: Worthy Othello, I am hurt to danger.
Your officer, Iago, can inform you—
While I spare speech, which something now offends me—

Of all that I do know. Nor know I aught
By me that's said or done amiss this night,
Unless self-charity be sometimes a vice,
And to defend ourselves it be a sin
When violence assails us.

OTHELLO: Now, by heaven,
My blood begins my safer guides to rule,
And passion, having my best judgement collied,
Assays to lead the way. If I once stir,
Or do but lift this arm, the best of you
Shall sink in my rebuke. Give me to know
How this foul rout began, who set it on,
And he that is approved in this offense,
Though he had twinn'd with me, both at a birth,
Shall lose me. What! in a town of war,
Yet wild, the people's hearts brimful of fear,
To manage private and domestic quarrel,
In night, and on the court and guard of safety!
'Tis monstrous. Iago, who began't?

MONTANO: If partially affined, or leagued in office,
Thou dost deliver more or less than truth,
Thou art no soldier.

IAGO: Touch me not so near:
I had rather have this tongue cut from my mouth
Than it should do offense to Michael Cassio;
Yet, I persuade myself, to speak the truth
Shall nothing wrong him. Thus it is, general.
Montano and myself being in speech,
There comes a fellow crying out for help,
And Cassio following him with determined sword,
To execute upon him. Sir, this gentleman
Steps in to Cassio and entreats his pause.
Myself the crying fellow did pursue,
Lest by his clamor- as it so fell out-
The town might fall in fright. He, swift of foot,

Outran my purpose; and I return'd the rather
For that I heard the clink and fall of swords,
And Cassio high in oath, which till tonight
I ne'er might say before. When I came back-
For this was brief- I found them close together,
At blow and thrust, even as again they were
When you yourself did part them.
More of this matter cannot I report.
But men are men; the best sometimes forget.
Though Cassio did some little wrong to him,
As men in rage strike those that wish them best,
Yet surely Cassio, I believe, received
From him that fled some strange indignity,
Which patience could not pass.

OTHELLO: I know, Iago,
Thy honesty and love doth mince this matter,
Making it light to Cassio. Cassio, I love thee,
But never more be officer of mine.
   Re-enter Desdemona, Attended.
Look, if my gentle love be not raised up!
I'll make thee an example.

DESDEMONA: What's the matter?

OTHELLO: All's well now, sweeting; come away to bed.
Sir, for your hurts, myself will be your surgeon.
Lead him off.
   Exit Montano, attended.
Iago, look with care about the town,
And silence those whom this vile brawl distracted.
Come, Desdemona, 'tis the soldiers' life.
To have their balmy slumbers waked with strife.
   Exeunt All but Iago and Cassio.

IAGO: What, are you hurt, lieutenant?

CASSIO: Ay, past all surgery.

IAGO: Marry, heaven forbid!

CASSIO: Reputation, reputation, reputation! O, I have lost my reputation! I have lost the immortal part of myself, and what remains is bestial. My reputation, Iago, my reputation!

IAGO: As I am an honest man, I thought you had received some bodily wound; there is more sense in that than in reputation. Reputation is an idle and most false imposition; oft got without merit and lost without deserving. You have lost no reputation at all, unless you repute yourself such a loser. What, man! there are ways to recover the general again. You are but now cast in his mood, a punishment more in policy than in malice; even so as one would beat his offenseless dog to affright an imperious lion. Sue to him again, and he's yours.

CASSIO: I will rather sue to be despised than to deceive so good a commander with so slight, so drunken, and so indiscreet an Officer. Drunk? and speak parrot? and squabble? swagger? swear? and discourse fustian with one's own shadow? O thou invisible spirit of wine, if thou hast no name to be known by, let us call thee devil!

IAGO: What was he that you followed with your sword? What had he done to you?

CASSIO: I know not.

IAGO: Is't possible?

CASSIO: I remember a mass of things, but nothing distinctly; a quarrel, but nothing wherefore. O God, that men should put an enemy in their mouths to steal away their brains! that we should, with joy, pleasance, revel, and applause, transform ourselves into beasts!

IAGO: Why, but you are now well enough. How came you thus

recovered?

CASSIO: It hath pleased the devil drunkenness to give place to the devil wrath: one unperfectness shows me another, to make me frankly despise myself.

IAGO: Come, you are too severe a moraler. As the time, the place, and the condition of this country stands, I could heartily wish this had not befallen; but since it is as it is, mend it for your own good.

CASSIO: I will ask him for my place again; he shall tell me I am a drunkard! Had I as many mouths as Hydra, such an answer would stop them all. To be now a sensible man, by and by a fool, and presently a beast! O strange! Every inordinate cup is unblest, and the ingredient is a devil.

IAGO: Come, come, good wine is a good familiar creature, if it be well used. Exclaim no more against it. And, good lieutenant, I think you think I love you.

CASSIO: I have well approved it, sir. I drunk!

IAGO: You or any man living may be drunk at some time, man. I'll tell you what you shall do. Our general's wife is now the general. I may say so in this respect, for that he hath devoted and given up himself to the contemplation, mark, and denotement of her parts and graces. Confess yourself freely to her; importune her help to put you in your place again. She is of so free, so kind, so apt, so blessed a disposition, she holds it a vice in her goodness not to do more than she is requested. This broken joint between you and her husband entreat her to splinter; and, my fortunes against any lay worth naming, this crack of your love shall grow stronger than it was before.

CASSIO: You advise me well.

IAGO: I protest, in the sincerity of love and honest kindness.

CASSIO: I think it freely; and betimes in the morning I will beseech the virtuous Desdemona to undertake for me. I am desperate of my fortunes if they check me here.

IAGO: You are in the right. Good night, lieutenant, I must to the Third Serving-Watch.

CASSIO: Good night, honest Iago.
   Exit.

IAGO: And what's he then that says I play the villain?
When this advice is free I give and honest,
Probal to thinking, and indeed the course
To win the Moor again? For 'tis most easy
The inclining Desdemona to subdue
In any honest suit. She's framed as fruitful
As the free elements. And then for her
To win the Moor, were't to renounce his baptism,
All seals and symbols of redeemed sin,
His soul is so enfetter'd to her love,
That she may make, unmake, do what she list,
Even as her appetite shall play the god
With his weak function. How am I then a villain
To counsel Cassio to this parallel course,
Directly to his good? Divinity of hell!
When devils will the blackest sins put on,
They do suggest at first with heavenly shows,
As I do now. For whiles this honest fool
Plies Desdemona to repair his fortune,
And she for him pleads strongly to the Moor,
I'll pour this pestilence into his ear,
That she repeals him for her body's lust;
And by how much she strives to do him good,
She shall undo her credit with the Moor.
So will I turn her virtue into pitch,
And out of her own goodness make the net

That shall enmesh them all.
Enter Roderigo.
How now, Roderigo!

RODERIGO: I do follow here in the chase, not like a hound that hunts, but one that fills up the cry. My money is almost spent; I have been tonight exceedingly well cudgeled; and I think the issue will be, I shall have so much experience for my pains; and so, with no money at all and a little more wit, return again to Venice.

IAGO: How poor are they that have not patience!
What wound did ever heal but by degrees?
Thou know'st we work by wit and not by witchcraft,
And wit depends on dilatory time.
Does't not go well? Cassio hath beaten thee,
And thou by that small hurt hast cashier'd Cassio.
Though other things grow fair against the sun,
Yet fruits that blossom first will first be ripe.
Content thyself awhile. By the mass, 'tis morning;
Pleasure and action make the hours seem short.
Retire thee; go where thou art billeted.
Away, I say. Thou shalt know more hereafter.
Nay, get thee gone.
  Exit Roderigo.
Two things are to be done:
My wife must move for Cassio to her mistress-
I'll set her on; myself the while to draw the Moor apart,
And bring him jump when he may Cassio find
Soliciting his wife. Ay, that's the way;
Dull not device by coldness and delay.
  Exit.

ACT III. SCENE I. Before the Castle.

Enter Cassio and Some Musicians.

CASSIO: Masters, play here, I will content your pains; Something that's brief; and bid "Good morrow, general." Music.

Enter Clown.

CLOWN: Why, masters, have your instruments been in Naples, that they speak i' the nose thus?

FIRST MUSICIAN: How, sir, how?

CLOWN: Are these, I pray you, wind instruments?

FIRST MUSICIAN: Ay, marry, are they, sir.

CLOWN: O, thereby hangs a tail.

FIRST MUSICIAN: Whereby hangs a tale, sir?

CLOWN: Marry, sir, by many a wind instrument that I know. But, masters, here's money for you; and the general so likes your music, that he desires you, for love's sake, to make no more noise with it.

FIRST MUSICIAN: Well, sir, we will not.

CLOWN: If you have any music that may not be heard, to't again; but, as they say, to hear music the general does not greatly care.

FIRST MUSICIAN: We have none such, sir.

CLOWN: Then put up your pipes in your bag, for I'll away. Go, vanish into air, away!
  Exeunt Musicians.

CASSIO: Dost thou hear, my honest friend?

CLOWN: No, I hear not your honest friend; I hear you.

CASSIO: Prithee, keep up thy quillets. There's a poor piece of gold

for thee. If the gentlewoman that attends the general's wife be
stirring, tell her there's one Cassio entreats her a little favor
of speech. Wilt thou do this?

CLOWN: She is stirring, sir. If she will stir hither, I shall seem
to notify unto her.

CASSIO: Do, good my friend.
  Exit Clown.
  Enter Iago.
In happy time, Iago.

IAGO: You have not been abed, then?

CASSIO: Why, no; the day had broke
Before we parted. I have made bold, Iago,
To send in to your wife. My suit to her
Is that she will to virtuous Desdemona
Procure me some access.

IAGO: I'll send her to you presently;
And I'll devise a mean to draw the Moor
Out of the way, that your converse and business
May be more free.

CASSIO: I humbly thank you for't.
  Exit Iago.
I never knew a Florentine more kind and honest.
  Enter Emilia.

EMILIA: Good morrow, good lieutenant. I am sorry
For your displeasure, but all will sure be well.
The general and his wife are talking of it,
And she speaks for you stoutly. The Moor replies
That he you hurt is of great fame in Cyprus
And great affinity and that in wholesome wisdom
He might not but refuse you; but he protests he loves you

And needs no other suitor but his likings
To take the safest occasion by the front
To bring you in again.

CASSIO: Yet, I beseech you,
If you think fit, or that it may be done,
Give me advantage of some brief discourse
With Desdemona alone.

EMILIA: Pray you, come in.
I will bestow you where you shall have time
To speak your bosom freely.

CASSIO: I am much bound to you.
Exeunt.

ACT III. SCENE II. A Room in the Castle.
Enter Othello, Iago, and Gentlemen.

OTHELLO: These letters give, Iago, to the pilot,
And by him do my duties to the Senate.
That done, I will be walking on the works;
Repair there to me.

IAGO: Well, my good lord, I'll do't.

OTHELLO: This fortification, gentlemen, shall we see't?

GENTLEMEN: We'll wait upon your lordship.
Exeunt.

ACT III. SCENE III. The Garden of the Castle.
Enter Desdemona, Cassio, and Emilia.

DESDEMONA: Be thou assured, good Cassio, I will do
All my abilities in thy behalf.

EMILIA: Good madam, do. I warrant it grieves my husband
As if the cause were his.

DESDEMONA: O, that's an honest fellow. Do not doubt, Cassio,
But I will have my lord and you again
As friendly as you were.

CASSIO: Bounteous madam,
Whatever shall become of Michael Cassio,
He's never anything but your true servant.

DESDEMONA: I know't: I thank you. You do love my lord:
You have known him long; and be you well assured
He shall in strangeness stand no farther off
Than in a politic distance.

CASSIO: Ay, but, lady,
That policy may either last so long,
Or feed upon such nice and waterish diet,
Or breed itself so out of circumstances,
That I being absent and my place supplied,
My general will forget my love and service.

DESDEMONA: Do not doubt that. Before Emilia here
I give thee warrant of thy place, assure thee,
If I do vow a friendship, I'll perform it
To the last article. My lord shall never rest;
I'll watch him tame and talk him out of patience;
His bed shall seem a school, his board a shrift;
I'll intermingle everything he does
With Cassio's suit. Therefore be merry, Cassio,
For thy solicitor shall rather die
Than give thy cause away.
    Enter Othello and Iago, at a Distance.

EMILIA: Madam, here comes my lord.

CASSIO: Madam, I'll take my leave.

DESDEMONA: Nay, stay and hear me speak.

CASSIO: Madam, not now. I am very ill at ease,
Unfit for mine own purposes.

DESDEMONA: Well, do your discretion.
  Exit Cassio.

IAGO: Ha! I like not that.

OTHELLO: What dost thou say?

IAGO: Nothing, my lord; or if- I know not what.

OTHELLO: Was not that Cassio parted from my wife?

IAGO: Cassio, my lord! No, sure, I cannot think it,
That he would steal away so guilty-like,
Seeing you coming.

OTHELLO: I do believe 'twas he.

DESDEMONA: How now, my lord!
I have been talking with a suitor here,
A man that languishes in your displeasure.

OTHELLO: Who is't you mean?

DESDEMONA: Why, your lieutenant, Cassio. Good my lord,
If I have any grace or power to move you,
His present reconciliation take;
For if he be not one that truly loves you,
That errs in ignorance and not in cunning,
I have no judgement in an honest face.
I prithee, call him back.

OTHELLO: Went he hence now?

DESDEMONA: Ay, sooth; so humbled
That he hath left part of his grief with me
To suffer with him. Good love, call him back.

OTHELLO: Not now, sweet Desdemona; some other time.

DESDEMONA: But shall't be shortly?

OTHELLO: The sooner, sweet, for you.

DESDEMONA: Shall't be tonight at supper?

OTHELLO: No, not tonight.

DESDEMONA: Tomorrow dinner then?

OTHELLO: I shall not dine at home;
I meet the captains at the citadel.

DESDEMONA: Why then tomorrow night, or Tuesday morn,
On Tuesday noon, or night, on Wednesday morn.
I prithee, name the time, but let it not
Exceed three days. In faith, he's penitent;
And yet his trespass, in our common reason-
Save that, they say, the wars must make example
Out of their best- is not almost a fault
To incur a private check. When shall he come?
Tell me, Othello. I wonder in my soul,
What you would ask me, that I should deny,
Or stand so mammering on. What? Michael Cassio,
That came awooing with you, and so many a time
When I have spoke of you dispraisingly
Hath ta'en your part- to have so much to do
To bring him in! Trust me, I could do much-

OTHELLO: Prithee, no more. Let him come when he will;
I will deny thee nothing.

DESDEMONA: Why, this is not a boon;
'Tis as I should entreat you wear your gloves,
Or feed on nourishing dishes, or keep you warm,
Or sue to you to do a peculiar profit
To your own person. Nay, when I have a suit
Wherein I mean to touch your love indeed,
It shall be full of poise and difficult weight,
And fearful to be granted.

OTHELLO: I will deny thee nothing,
Whereon, I do beseech thee, grant me this,
To leave me but a little to myself.

DESDEMONA: Shall I deny you? No. Farewell, my lord.

OTHELLO: Farewell, my Desdemona; I'll come to thee straight.

DESDEMONA: Emilia, come. Be as your fancies teach you;
Whate'er you be, I am obedient.
   Exeunt Desdemona and Emilia.

OTHELLO: Excellent wretch! Perdition catch my soul,
But I do love thee! and when I love thee not,
Chaos is come again.

IAGO: My noble lord-

OTHELLO: What dost thou say, Iago?

IAGO: Did Michael Cassio, when you woo'd my lady,
Know of your love?

OTHELLO: He did, from first to last. Why dost thou ask?

IAGO: But for a satisfaction of my thought;
No further harm.

OTHELLO: Why of thy thought, Iago?

IAGO: I did not think he had been acquainted with her.

OTHELLO: O, yes, and went between us very oft.

IAGO: Indeed!

OTHELLO: Indeed? ay, indeed. Discern'st thou aught in that?
Is he not honest?

IAGO: Honest, my lord?

OTHELLO: Honest? Ay, honest.

IAGO: My lord, for aught I know.

OTHELLO: What dost thou think?

IAGO: Think, my lord?

OTHELLO: Think, my lord? By heaven, he echoes me,
As if there were some monster in his thought
Too hideous to be shown. Thou dost mean something.
I heard thee say even now, thou like'st not that,
When Cassio left my wife. What didst not like?
And when I told thee he was of my counsel
In my whole course of wooing, thou criedst, "Indeed!"
And didst contract and purse thy brow together,
As if thou then hadst shut up in thy brain
Some horrible conceit. If thou dost love me,
Show me thy thought.

IAGO: My lord, you know I love you.

OTHELLO: I think thou dost;
And for I know thou'rt full of love and honesty
And weigh'st thy words before thou givest them breath,
Therefore these stops of thine fright me the more;
For such things in a false disloyal knave
Are tricks of custom; but in a man that's just
They're close dilations, working from the heart,
That passion cannot rule.

IAGO: For Michael Cassio,
I dare be sworn I think that he is honest.

OTHELLO: I think so too.

IAGO: Men should be what they seem;
Or those that be not, would they might seem none!

OTHELLO: Certain, men should be what they seem.

IAGO: Why then I think Cassio's an honest man.

OTHELLO: Nay, yet there's more in this.
I prithee, speak to me as to thy thinkings,
As thou dost ruminate, and give thy worst of thoughts
The worst of words.

IAGO: Good my lord, pardon me;
Though I am bound to every act of duty,
I am not bound to that all slaves are free to.
Utter my thoughts? Why, say they are vile and false;
As where's that palace whereinto foul things
Sometimes intrude not? Who has a breast so pure,
But some uncleanly apprehensions
Keep leets and law-days, and in session sit
With meditations lawful?

OTHELLO: Thou dost conspire against thy friend, Iago,

If thou but think'st him wrong'd and makest his ear
A stranger to thy thoughts.

IAGO: I do beseech you—
Though I perchance am vicious in my guess,
As, I confess, it is my nature's plague
To spy into abuses, and oft my jealousy
Shapes faults that are not—that your wisdom yet,
From one that so imperfectly conceits,
Would take no notice, nor build yourself a trouble
Out of his scattering and unsure observance.
It were not for your quiet nor your good,
Nor for my manhood, honesty, or wisdom,
To let you know my thoughts.

OTHELLO: What dost thou mean?

IAGO: Good name in man and woman, dear my lord,
Is the immediate jewel of their souls.
Who steals my purse steals trash; 'tis something, nothing;
'Twas mine, 'tis his, and has been slave to thousands;
But he that filches from me my good name
Robs me of that which not enriches him
And makes me poor indeed.

OTHELLO: By heaven, I'll know thy thoughts.

IAGO: You cannot, if my heart were in your hand;
Nor shall not, whilst 'tis in my custody.

OTHELLO: Ha!

IAGO: O, beware, my lord, of jealousy!
It is the green-eyed monster, which doth mock
The meat it feeds on. That cuckold lives in bliss
Who, certain of his fate, loves not his wronger;
But O, what damned minutes tells he o'er

Who dotes, yet doubts, suspects, yet strongly loves!

OTHELLO: O misery!

IAGO: Poor and content is rich, and rich enough;
But riches fineless is as poor as winter
To him that ever fears he shall be poor.
Good heaven, the souls of all my tribe defend
From jealousy!

OTHELLO: Why, why is this?
Think'st thou I'ld make a life of jealousy,
To follow still the changes of the moon
With fresh suspicions? No! To be once in doubt
Is once to be resolved. Exchange me for a goat
When I shall turn the business of my soul
To such exsufflicate and blown surmises,
Matching thy inference. 'Tis not to make me jealous
To say my wife is fair, feeds well, loves company,
Is free of speech, sings, plays, and dances well;
Where virtue is, these are more virtuous.
Nor from mine own weak merits will I draw
The smallest fear or doubt of her revolt;
For she had eyes and chose me. No, Iago,
I'll see before I doubt; when I doubt, prove;
And on the proof, there is no more but this-
Away at once with love or jealousy!

IAGO: I am glad of it, for now I shall have reason
To show the love and duty that I bear you
With franker spirit. Therefore, as I am bound,
Receive it from me. I speak not yet of proof.
Look to your wife; observe her well with Cassio;
Wear your eye thus, not jealous nor secure.
I would not have your free and noble nature
Out of self-bounty be abused. Look to't.
I know our country disposition well;
In Venice they do let heaven see the pranks

They dare not show their husbands; their best conscience
Is not to leave't undone, but keep't unknown.

OTHELLO: Dost thou say so?

IAGO: She did deceive her father, marrying you;
And when she seem'd to shake and fear your looks,
She loved them most.

OTHELLO: And so she did.

IAGO: Why, go to then.
She that so young could give out such a seeming,
To seel her father's eyes up close as oak-
He thought 'twas witchcraft- but I am much to blame;
I humbly do beseech you of your pardon
For too much loving you.

OTHELLO: I am bound to thee forever.

IAGO: I see this hath a little dash'd your spirits.

OTHELLO: Not a jot, not a jot.

IAGO: I'faith, I fear it has.
I hope you will consider what is spoke
Comes from my love. But I do see you're moved;
I am to pray you not to strain my speech
To grosser issues nor to larger reach
Than to suspicion.

OTHELLO: I will not.

IAGO: Should you do so, my lord,
My speech should fall into such vile success
Which my thoughts aim not at. Cassio's my worthy friend-
My lord, I see you're moved.

OTHELLO: No, not much moved.
I do not think but Desdemona's honest.

IAGO: Long live she so! and long live you to think so!

OTHELLO: And yet, how nature erring from itself—

IAGO: Ay, there's the point, as— to be bold with you—
Not to affect many proposed matches
Of her own clime, complexion, and degree,
Whereto we see in all things nature tends—
Foh, one may smell in such a will most rank,
Foul disproportion, thoughts unnatural.
But pardon me. I do not in position
Distinctly speak of her; though I may fear,
Her will, recoiling to her better judgement,
May fall to match you with her country forms,
And happily repent.

OTHELLO: Farewell, farewell.
If more thou dost perceive, let me know more;
Set on thy wife to observe. Leave me, Iago.

IAGO: *Going.* My lord, I take my leave.

OTHELLO: Why did I marry? This honest creature doubtless
Sees and knows more, much more, than he unfolds.

IAGO: *Returning.* My lord, I would I might entreat your honor
To scan this thing no further; leave it to time.
Though it be fit that Cassio have his place,
For sure he fills it up with great ability,
Yet, if you please to hold him off awhile,
You shall by that perceive him and his means.
Note if your lady strain his entertainment
With any strong or vehement importunity;
Much will be seen in that. In the meantime,

Let me be thought too busy in my fears-
As worthy cause I have to fear I am-
And hold her free, I do beseech your honor.

OTHELLO: Fear not my government.

IAGO: I once more take my leave.
   Exit.

OTHELLO: This fellow's of exceeding honesty,
And knows all qualities, with a learned spirit,
Of human dealings. If I do prove her haggard,
Though that her jesses were my dear heartstrings,
I'ld whistle her off and let her down the wind
To prey at fortune. Haply, for I am black
And have not those soft parts of conversation
That chamberers have, or for I am declined
Into the vale of years- yet that's not much-
She's gone. I am abused, and my relief
Must be to loathe her. O curse of marriage,
That we can call these delicate creatures ours,
And not their appetites! I had rather be a toad,
And live upon the vapor of a dungeon,
Than keep a corner in the thing I love
For others' uses. Yet, 'tis the plague of great ones:
Prerogatived are they less than the base;
'Tis destiny unshunnable, like death.
Even then this forked plague is fated to us
When we do quicken. Desdemona comes:
   Re-enter Desdemona and Emilia.
If she be false, O, then heaven mocks itself!
I'll not believe't.

DESDEMONA: How now, my dear Othello!
Your dinner, and the generous islanders
By you invited, do attend your presence.

OTHELLO: I am to blame.

DESDEMONA: Why do you speak so faintly?
Are you not well?

OTHELLO: I have a pain upon my forehead here.

DESDEMONA: Faith, that's with watching; 'twill away again.
Let me but bind it hard, within this hour
It will be well.

OTHELLO: Your napkin is too little;
He Puts the Handkerchief from Him, and She Drops It.
Let it alone. Come, I'll go in with you.

DESDEMONA: I am very sorry that you are not well.
Exeunt Othello and Desdemona.

EMILIA: I am glad I have found this napkin;
This was her first remembrance from the Moor.
My wayward husband hath a hundred times
Woo'd me to steal it; but she so loves the token,
For he conjured her she should ever keep it,
That she reserves it evermore about her
To kiss and talk to. I'll have the work ta'en out,
And give't Iago. What he will do with it
Heaven knows, not I;
I nothing but to please his fantasy.
Re-enter Iago.

IAGO: How now, what do you here alone?

EMILIA: Do not you chide; I have a thing for you.

IAGO: A thing for me? It is a common thing-

EMILIA: Ha!

IAGO: To have a foolish wife.

EMILIA: O, is that all? What will you give me now
For that same handkerchief?

IAGO: What handkerchief?

EMILIA: What handkerchief?
Why, that the Moor first gave to Desdemona,
That which so often you did bid me steal.

IAGO: Hast stol'n it from her?

EMILIA: No, faith; she let it drop by negligence,
And, to the advantage, I being here took't up.
Look, here it is.

IAGO: A good wench; give it me.

EMILIA: What will you do with't, that you have been so earnest
To have me filch it?

IAGO: *Snatching it.* Why, what is that to you?

EMILIA: If't be not for some purpose of import,
Give't me again. Poor lady, she'll run mad
When she shall lack it.

IAGO: Be not acknown on't; I have use for it.
Go, leave me.
   Exit Emilia.
I will in Cassio's lodging lose this napkin,
And let him find it. Trifles light as air
Are to the jealous confirmations strong
As proofs of holy writ; this may do something.
The Moor already changes with my poison:
Dangerous conceits are in their natures poisons,
Which at the first are scarce found to distaste,
But with a little act upon the blood

Burn like the mines of sulphur. I did say so.
Look, where he comes!
   Re-enter Othello.
Not poppy, nor mandragora,
Nor all the drowsy syrups of the world,
Shall ever medicine thee to that sweet sleep
Which thou owedst yesterday.

OTHELLO: Ha, ha, false to me?

IAGO: Why, how now, general! No more of that.

OTHELLO: Avaunt! be gone! Thou hast set me on the rack.
I swear 'tis better to be much abused
Than but to know't a little.

IAGO: How now, my lord?

OTHELLO: What sense had I of her stol'n hours of lust?
I saw't not, thought it not, it harm'd not me;
I slept the next night well, was free and merry;
I found not Cassio's kisses on her lips.
He that is robb'd, not wanting what is stol'n,
Let him not know't and he's not robb'd at all.

IAGO: I am sorry to hear this.

OTHELLO: I had been happy if the general camp,
Pioners and all, had tasted her sweet body,
So I had nothing known. O, now forever
Farewell the tranquil mind! Farewell content!
Farewell the plumed troop and the big wars
That make ambition virtue! O, farewell,
Farewell the neighing steed and the shrill trump,
The spirit-stirring drum, the ear-piercing fife,
The royal banner, and all quality,
Pride, pomp, and circumstance of glorious war!

And O you mortal engines, whose rude throats
The immortal Jove's dread clamors counterfeit,
Farewell! Othello's occupation's gone!

IAGO: Is't possible, my lord?

OTHELLO: Villain, be sure thou prove my love a whore;
Be sure of it. Give me the ocular proof;
Or, by the worth of man's eternal soul,
Thou hadst been better have been born a dog
Than answer my waked wrath!

IAGO: Is't come to this?

OTHELLO: Make me to see't; or at the least so prove it,
That the probation bear no hinge nor loop
To hang a doubt on; or woe upon thy life!

IAGO: My noble lord—

OTHELLO: If thou dost slander her and torture me,
Never pray more; abandon all remorse;
On horror's head horrors accumulate;
Do deeds to make heaven weep, all earth amazed;
For nothing canst thou to damnation add
Greater than that.

IAGO: O grace! O heaven defend me!
Are you a man? have you a soul or sense?
God be wi' you; take mine office. O wretched fool,
That livest to make thine honesty a vice!
O monstrous world! Take note, take note, O world,
To be direct and honest is not safe.
I thank you for this profit, and from hence
I'll love no friend sith love breeds such offense.

OTHELLO: Nay, stay; thou shouldst be honest.

IAGO: I should be wise; for honesty's a fool,
And loses that it works for.

OTHELLO: By the world,
I think my wife be honest, and think she is not;
I think that thou art just, and think thou art not.
I'll have some proof. Her name, that was as fresh
As Dian's visage, is now begrimed and black
As mine own face. If there be cords or knives,
Poison or fire, or suffocating streams,
I'll not endure it. Would I were satisfied!

IAGO: I see, sir, you are eaten up with passion;
I do repent me that I put it to you.
You would be satisfied?

OTHELLO: Would? Nay, I will.

IAGO: And may. But, how? how satisfied, my lord?
Would you, the supervisor, grossly gape on?
Behold her topp'd?

OTHELLO: Death and damnation! O!

IAGO: It were a tedious difficulty, I think,
To bring them to that prospect. Damn them then,
If ever mortal eyes do see them bolster
More than their own! What then? how then?
What shall I say? Where's satisfaction?
It is impossible you should see this
Were they as prime as goats, as hot as monkeys,
As salt as wolves in pride, and fools as gross
As ignorance made drunk. But yet, I say,
If imputation and strong circumstances,
Which lead directly to the door of truth,
Will give you satisfaction, you may have't.

OTHELLO: Give me a living reason she's disloyal.

IAGO: I do not like the office;
But sith I am enter'd in this cause so far,
Prick'd to't by foolish honesty and love,
I will go on. I lay with Cassio lately
And, being troubled with a raging tooth,
I could not sleep.
There are a kind of men so loose of soul,
That in their sleeps will mutter their affairs;
One of this kind is Cassio.
In sleep I heard him say, "Sweet Desdemona,
Let us be wary, let us hide our loves";
And then, sir, would he gripe and wring my hand,
Cry, "O sweet creature!" and then kiss me hard,
As if he pluck'd up kisses by the roots,
That grew upon my lips; then laid his leg
Over my thigh, and sigh'd and kiss'd; and then
Cried, "Cursed fate that gave thee to the Moor!"

OTHELLO: O monstrous! monstrous!

IAGO: Nay, this was but his dream.

OTHELLO: But this denoted a foregone conclusion.
'Tis a shrewd doubt, though it be but a dream.

IAGO: And this may help to thicken other proofs
That do demonstrate thinly.

OTHELLO: I'll tear her all to pieces.

IAGO: Nay, but be wise; yet we see nothing done;
She may be honest yet. Tell me but this;
Have you not sometimes seen a handkerchief
Spotted with strawberries in your wife's hand?

OTHELLO: I gave her such a one; 'twas my first gift.

IAGO: I know not that; but such a handkerchief-
I am sure it was your wife's- did I today
See Cassio wipe his beard with.

OTHELLO: If it be that-

IAGO: If it be that, or any that was hers,
It speaks against her with the other proofs.

OTHELLO: O, that the slave had forty thousand lives!
One is too poor, too weak for my revenge.
Now do I see 'tis true. Look here, Iago,
All my fond love thus do I blow to heaven.
'Tis gone.
Arise, black vengeance, from thy hollow hell!
Yield up, O love, thy crown and hearted throne
To tyrannous hate! Swell, bosom, with thy fraught,
For 'tis of aspics' tongues!

IAGO: Yet be content.

OTHELLO: O, blood, blood, blood!

IAGO: Patience, I say; your mind perhaps may change.

OTHELLO: Never, Iago. Like to the Pontic Sea,
Whose icy current and compulsive course
Ne'er feels retiring ebb, but keeps due on
To the Propontic and the Hellespont,
Even so my bloody thoughts, with violent pace,
Shall ne'er look back, ne'er ebb to humble love,
Till that a capable and wide revenge
Swallow them up. Now, by yond marble heaven,
In the due reverence of a sacred vow Kneels.
I here engage my words.

IAGO: Do not rise yet. *Kneels.*
Witness, you ever-burning lights above,
You elements that clip us round about,
Witness that here Iago doth give up
The execution of his wit, hands, heart,
To wrong'd Othello's service! Let him command,
And to obey shall be in me remorse,
What bloody business ever. *They rise.*

OTHELLO: I greet thy love,
Not with vain thanks, but with acceptance bounteous,
And will upon the instant put thee to't:
Within these three days let me hear thee say
That Cassio's not alive.

IAGO: My friend is dead, 'tis done at your request;
But let her live.

OTHELLO: Damn her, lewd minx! O, damn her!
Come, go with me apart; I will withdraw,
To furnish me with some swift means of death
For the fair devil. Now art thou my lieutenant.

IAGO: I am your own forever.
Exeunt.

ACT III. SCENE IV. Before the Castle.
Enter Desdemona, Emilia, and Clown.

DESDEMONA: Do you know, sirrah, where Lieutenant Cassio lies?

CLOWN: I dare not say he lies anywhere.

DESDEMONA: Why, man?

CLOWN: He's a soldier; and for one to say a soldier lies, is stabbing.

DESDEMONA: Go to! Where lodges he?

CLOWN: To tell you where he lodges, is to tell you where I lie.

DESDEMONA: Can anything be made of this?

CLOWN: I know not where he lodges, and for me to devise a lodging, and say he lies here or he lies there, were to lie in mine own throat.

DESDEMONA: Can you inquire him out and be edified by report?

CLOWN: I will catechize the world for him; that is, make questions and by them answer.

DESDEMONA: Seek him, bid him come hither. Tell him I have moved my lord on his behalf and hope all will be well.

CLOWN: To do this is within the compass of man's wit, and therefore I will attempt the doing it.
    Exit.

DESDEMONA: Where should I lose that handkerchief, Emilia?

EMILIA: I know not, madam.

DESDEMONA: Believe me, I had rather have lost my purse
Full of crusadoes; and, but my noble Moor
Is true of mind and made of no such baseness
As jealous creatures are, it were enough
To put him to ill thinking.

EMILIA: Is he not jealous?

DESDEMONA: Who, he? I think the sun where he was born
Drew all such humors from him.

EMILIA: Look, where he comes.

DESDEMONA: I will not leave him now till Cassio
Be call'd to him.
  Enter Othello.
How is't with you, my lord?

OTHELLO: Well, my good lady. *Aside.* O, hardness to dissemble!
How do you, Desdemona?

DESDEMONA: Well, my good lord.

OTHELLO: Give me your hand. This hand is moist, my lady.

DESDEMONA: It yet has felt no age nor known no sorrow.

OTHELLO: This argues fruitfulness and liberal heart;
Hot, hot, and moist. This hand of yours requires
A sequester from liberty, fasting, and prayer,
Much castigation, exercise devout,
For here's a young and sweating devil here
That commonly rebels. 'Tis a good hand,
A frank one.

DESDEMONA: You may, indeed, say so;
For 'twas that hand that gave away my heart.

OTHELLO: A liberal hand. The hearts of old gave hands;
But our new heraldry is hands, not hearts.

DESDEMONA: I cannot speak of this. Come now, your promise.

OTHELLO: What promise, chuck?

DESDEMONA: I have sent to bid Cassio come speak with you.

OTHELLO: I have a salt and sorry rheum offends me;
Lend me thy handkerchief.

DESDEMONA: Here, my lord.

OTHELLO: That which I gave you.

DESDEMONA: I have it not about me.

OTHELLO: Not?

DESDEMONA: No, faith, my lord.

OTHELLO: That's a fault. That handkerchief
Did an Egyptian to my mother give;
She was a charmer, and could almost read
The thoughts of people. She told her, while she kept it,
'Twould make her amiable and subdue my father
Entirely to her love, but if she lost it
Or made a gift of it, my father's eye
Should hold her loathed and his spirits should hunt
After new fancies. She dying gave it me,
And bid me, when my fate would have me wive,
To give it her. I did so, and take heed on't;
Make it a darling like your precious eye;
To lose't or give't away were such perdition
As nothing else could match.

DESDEMONA: Is't possible?

OTHELLO: 'Tis true; there's magic in the web of it.
A sibyl, that had number'd in the world
The sun to course two hundred compasses,
In her prophetic fury sew'd the work;
The worms were hallow'd that did breed the silk,
And it was dyed in mummy which the skillful
Conserved of maiden's hearts.

DESDEMONA: Indeed! is't true?

OTHELLO: Most veritable; therefore look to't well.

DESDEMONA: Then would to God that I had never seen't!

OTHELLO: Ha! wherefore?

DESDEMONA: Why do you speak so startingly and rash?

OTHELLO: Is't lost? is't gone? speak, is it out o' the way?

DESDEMONA: Heaven bless us!

OTHELLO: Say you?

DESDEMONA: It is not lost; but what an if it were?

OTHELLO: How?

DESDEMONA: I say, it is not lost.

OTHELLO: Fetch't, let me see it.

DESDEMONA: Why, so I can, sir, but I will not now.
This is a trick to put me from my suit.
Pray you, let Cassio be received again.
OTHELLO: Fetch me the handkerchief, my mind misgives.

DESDEMONA: Come, come,
You'll never meet a more sufficient man.

OTHELLO: The handkerchief!

DESDEMONA: I pray, talk me of Cassio.

OTHELLO: The handkerchief!

DESDEMONA: A man that all his time

Hath founded his good fortunes on your love,
Shared dangers with you—

OTHELLO: The handkerchief!

DESDEMONA: In sooth, you are to blame.

OTHELLO: Away!
Exit.

EMILIA: Is not this man jealous?

DESDEMONA: I ne'er saw this before.
Sure there's some wonder in this handkerchief;
I am most unhappy in the loss of it.

EMILIA: 'Tis not a year or two shows us a man.
They are all but stomachs and we all but food;
They eat us hungerly, and when they are full
They belch us. Look you! Cassio and my husband.
Enter Cassio and Iago.

IAGO: There is no other way; 'tis she must do't.
And, lo, the happiness! Go and importune her.

DESDEMONA: How now, good Cassio! What's the news with you?

CASSIO: Madam, my former suit: I do beseech you
That by your virtuous means I may again
Exist and be a member of his love
Whom I with all the office of my heart
Entirely honor. I would not be delay'd.
If my offense be of such mortal kind
That nor my service past nor present sorrows
Nor purposed merit in futurity
Can ransom me into his love again,
But to know so must be my benefit;

So shall I clothe me in a forced content
And shut myself up in some other course
To Fortune's alms.

DESDEMONA: Alas, thrice-gentle Cassio!
My advocation is not now in tune;
My lord is not my lord, nor should I know him
Were he in favor as in humor alter'd.
So help me every spirit sanctified,
As I have spoken for you all my best
And stood within the blank of his displeasure
For my free speech! You must awhile be patient.
What I can do I will; and more I will
Than for myself I dare. Let that suffice you.

IAGO: Is my lord angry?

EMILIA: He went hence but now,
And certainly in strange unquietness.

IAGO: Can he be angry? I have seen the cannon,
When it hath blown his ranks into the air
And, like the devil, from his very arm
Puff'd his own brother. And can he be angry?
Something of moment then. I will go meet him.
There's matter in't indeed if he be angry.

DESDEMONA: I prithee, do so.
  Exit Iago.
Something sure of state,
Either from Venice or some unhatch'd practice
Made demonstrable here in Cyprus to him,
Hath puddled his clear spirit; and in such cases
Men's natures wrangle with inferior things,
Though great ones are their object. 'Tis even so;
For let our finger ache, and it indues
Our other healthful members even to that sense
Of pain. Nay, we must think men are not gods,

Nor of them look for such observancy
As fits the bridal. Beshrew me much, Emilia,
I was, unhandsome warrior as I am,
Arraigning his unkindness with my soul;
But now I find I had suborn'd the witness,
And he's indicted falsely.

EMILIA: Pray heaven it be state matters, as you think,
And no conception nor no jealous toy
Concerning you.

DESDEMONA: Alas the day, I never gave him cause!

EMILIA: But jealous souls will not be answer'd so;
They are not ever jealous for the cause,
But jealous for they are jealous. 'Tis a monster
Begot upon itself, born on itself.

DESDEMONA: Heaven keep that monster from Othello's mind!

EMILIA: Lady, amen.

DESDEMONA: I will go seek him. Cassio, walk hereabout.
If I do find him fit, I'll move your suit,
And seek to effect it to my uttermost.

CASSIO: I humbly thank your ladyship.
  Exeunt Desdemona and Emilia.
  Enter Bianca.
BIANCA: Save you, friend Cassio!

CASSIO: What make you from home?
How is it with you, my most fair Bianca?
I'faith, sweet love, I was coming to your house.

BIANCA: And I was going to your lodging, Cassio.
What, keep a week away? seven days and nights?

Eight score eight hours? and lovers' absent hours,
More tedious than the dial eight score times?
O weary reckoning!

CASSIO: Pardon me, Bianca.
I have this while with leaden thoughts been press'd;
But I shall in a more continuate time
Strike off this score of absence. Sweet Bianca,
    Gives Her Desdemona's Handkerchief.
Take me this work out.

BIANCA: O Cassio, whence came this?
This is some token from a newer friend.
To the felt absence now I feel a cause.
Is't come to this? Well, well.

CASSIO: Go to, woman!
Throw your vile guesses in the devil's teeth,
From whence you have them. You are jealous now
That this is from some mistress, some remembrance.
No, by my faith, Bianca.

BIANCA: Why, whose is it?

CASSIO: I know not, sweet. I found it in my chamber.
I like the work well. Ere it be demanded-
As like enough it will- I'ld have it copied.
Take it, and do't; and leave me for this time.

BIANCA: Leave you! wherefore?

CASSIO: I do attend here on the general;
And think it no addition, nor my wish,
To have him see me woman'd.

BIANCA: Why, I pray you?

CASSIO: Not that I love you not.

BIANCA: But that you do not love me.
I pray you, bring me on the way a little,
And say if I shall see you soon at night.

CASSIO: 'Tis but a little way that I can bring you,
For I attend here, but I'll see you soon.

BIANCA: 'Tis very good; I must be circumstanced.
Exeunt.

ACT IV. SCENE I. Cyprus. Before the Castle.

Enter Othello and Iago.

IAGO: Will you think so?

OTHELLO: Think so, Iago?

IAGO: What,
To kiss in private?

OTHELLO: An unauthorized kiss.

IAGO: Or to be naked with her friend in bed
An hour or more, not meaning any harm?

OTHELLO: Naked in bed, Iago, and not mean harm!
It is hypocrisy against the devil.
They that mean virtuously and yet do so,
The devil their virtue tempts and they tempt heaven.

IAGO: So they do nothing, 'tis a venial slip.
But if I give my wife a handkerchief-

OTHELLO: What then?

IAGO: Why, then, 'tis hers, my lord, and being hers,
She may, I think, bestow't on any man.

OTHELLO: She is protectress of her honor too.
May she give that?

IAGO: Her honor is an essence that's not seen;
They have it very oft that have it not.
But for the handkerchief-

OTHELLO: By heaven, I would most gladly have forgot it.
Thou said'st- O, it comes o'er my memory,
As doth the raven o'er the infected house,
Boding to all- he had my handkerchief.

IAGO: Ay, what of that?

OTHELLO: That's not so good now.

IAGO: What,
If I had said I had seen him do you wrong?
Or heard him say- as knaves be such abroad,
Who having, by their own importunate suit,
Or voluntary dotage of some mistress,
Convinced or supplied them, cannot choose
But they must blab-

OTHELLO: Hath he said anything?

IAGO: He hath, my lord; but be you well assured,
No more than he'll unswear.

OTHELLO: What hath he said?

IAGO: Faith, that he did- I know not what he did.

OTHELLO: What? what?

IAGO: Lie—

OTHELLO: With her?

IAGO: With her, on her, what you will.

OTHELLO: Lie with her! lie on her! We say lie on her, when they belie her. Lie with her! 'Zounds, that's fulsome! Handkerchief— confessions— handkerchief! To confess and be hanged for his labor— first, to be hanged, and then to confess. I tremble at it. Nature would not invest herself in such shadowing passion without some instruction. It is not words that shakes me thus. Pish! Noses, ears, and lips. Is't possible? Confess? Handkerchief? O devil!
Falls in a Trance.

IAGO: Work on,
My medicine, work! Thus credulous fools are caught,
And many worthy and chaste dames even thus,
All guiltless, meet reproach. What, ho! My lord!
My lord, I say! Othello!
Enter Cassio.
How now, Cassio!

CASSIO: What's the matter?

IAGO: My lord is fall'n into an epilepsy.
This is his second fit; he had one yesterday.

CASSIO: Rub him about the temples.

IAGO: No, forbear;
The lethargy must have his quiet course.
If not, he foams at mouth, and by and by
Breaks out to savage madness. Look, he stirs.
Do you withdraw yourself a little while,
He will recover straight. When he is gone,
I would on great occasion speak with you.

Exit Cassio.
How is it, general? Have you not hurt your head?

OTHELLO: Dost thou mock me?

IAGO: I mock you? No, by heaven.
Would you would bear your fortune like a man!

OTHELLO: A horned man's a monster and a beast.

IAGO: There's many a beast then in a populous city,
And many a civil monster.

OTHELLO: Did he confess it?

IAGO: Good sir, be a man;
Think every bearded fellow that's but yoked
May draw with you. There's millions now alive
That nightly lie in those unproper beds
Which they dare swear peculiar. Your case is better.
O, 'tis the spite of hell, the fiend's arch-mock,
To lip a wanton in a secure couch,
And to suppose her chaste! No, let me know,
And knowing what I am, I know what she shall be.

OTHELLO: O, thou art wise; 'tis certain.

IAGO: Stand you awhile apart,
Confine yourself but in a patient list.
Whilst you were here o'erwhelmed with your grief—
A passion most unsuiting such a man—
Cassio came hither. I shifted him away,
And laid good 'scuse upon your ecstasy;
Bade him anon return and here speak with me
The which he promised. Do but encave yourself
And mark the fleers, the gibes, and notable scorns,
That dwell in every region of his face;

For I will make him tell the tale anew,
Where, how, how oft, how long ago, and when
He hath and is again to cope your wife.
I say, but mark his gesture. Marry, patience,
Or I shall say you are all in all in spleen,
And nothing of a man.

OTHELLO: Dost thou hear, Iago?
I will be found most cunning in my patience;
But (dost thou hear?) most bloody.

IAGO: That's not amiss;
But yet keep time in all. Will you withdraw?
   Othello retires.
Now will I question Cassio of Bianca,
A housewife that by selling her desires
Buys herself bread and clothes. It is a creature
That dotes on Cassio, as 'tis the strumpet's plague
To beguile many and be beguiled by one.
He, when he hears of her, cannot refrain
From the excess of laughter. Here he comes.
   Re-enter Cassio.
As he shall smile, Othello shall go mad;
And his unbookish jealousy must construe
Poor Cassio's smiles, gestures, and light behavior
Quite in the wrong. How do you now, lieutenant?

CASSIO: The worser that you give me the addition
Whose want even kills me.

IAGO: Ply Desdemona well, and you are sure on't.
Now, if this suit lay in Bianco's power,
How quickly should you speed!

CASSIO: Alas, poor caitiff!

OTHELLO: Look, how he laughs already!

IAGO: I never knew a woman love man so.

CASSIO: Alas, poor rogue! I think, i'faith, she loves me.

OTHELLO: Now he denies it faintly and laughs it out.

IAGO: Do you hear, Cassio?

OTHELLO: Now he importunes him
To tell it o'er. Go to; well said, well said.

IAGO: She gives it out that you shall marry her.
Do you intend it?

CASSIO: Ha, ha, ha!

OTHELLO: Do you triumph, Roman? Do you triumph?

CASSIO: I marry her! What? A customer! I prithee, bear some charity to my wit; do not think it so unwholesome. Ha, ha, ha!

OTHELLO: So, so, so, so. They laugh that win.

IAGO: Faith, the cry goes that you shall marry her.

CASSIO: Prithee, say true.

IAGO: I am a very villain else.

OTHELLO: Have you scored me? Well.

CASSIO: This is the monkey's own giving out. She is persuaded I will marry her, out of her own love and flattery, not out of my promise.

OTHELLO: Iago beckons me; now he begins the story.

CASSIO: She was here even now; she haunts me in every place. I was

the other day talking on the sea bank with certain Venetians, and
thither comes the bauble, and, by this hand, she falls me thus
about my neck-

OTHELLO: Crying, "O dear Cassio!" as it were; his gesture imports it.

CASSIO: So hangs and lolls and weeps upon me; so hales and pulls
me. Ha, ha, ha!

OTHELLO: Now he tells how she plucked him to my chamber. O, I see
that nose of yours, but not that dog I shall throw it to.

CASSIO: Well, I must leave her company.

IAGO: Before me! look where she comes.

CASSIO: 'Tis such another fitchew! marry, a perfumed one.
   Enter Bianca.
What do you mean by this haunting of me?

BIANCA: Let the devil and his dam haunt you! What did you mean by
that same handkerchief you gave me even now? I was a fine fool to
take it. I must take out the work? A likely piece of work that
you should find it in your chamber and not know who left it
there! This is some minx's token, and I must take out the work?
There, give it your hobbyhorse. Wheresoever you had it, I'll take
out no work on't.

CASSIO: How now, my sweet Bianca! how now! how now!

OTHELLO: By heaven, that should be my handkerchief!

BIANCA: An you'll come to supper tonight, you may; an you will not,
come when you are next prepared for.
   Exit.

IAGO: After her, after her.

CASSIO: Faith, I must; she'll rail i' the street else.

IAGO: Will you sup there?

CASSIO: Faith, I intend so.

IAGO: Well, I may chance to see you, for I would very fain speak with you.

CASSIO: Prithee, come; will you?

IAGO: Go to; say no more.
   Exit Cassio.

OTHELLO: *Advancing.* How shall I murther him, Iago?

IAGO: Did you perceive how he laughed at his vice?

OTHELLO: O Iago!

IAGO: And did you see the handkerchief?

OTHELLO: Was that mine?

IAGO: Yours, by this hand. And to see how he prizes the foolish woman your wife! She gave it him, and he hath given it his whore.

OTHELLO: I would have him nine years akilling. A fine woman! a fair woman! a sweet woman!

IAGO: Nay, you must forget that.

OTHELLO: Ay, let her rot, and perish, and be damned tonight, for she shall not live. No, my heart is turned to stone; I strike it, and it hurts my hand. O, the world hath not a sweeter creature. She might lie by an emperor's side, and command him tasks.

IAGO: Nay, that's not your way.

OTHELLO: Hang her! I do but say what she is. So delicate with her needle, an admirable musician. O, she will sing the savageness out of a bear. Of so high and plenteous wit and invention-

IAGO: She's the worse for all this.

OTHELLO: O, a thousand, a thousand times. And then, of so gentle a condition!

IAGO: Ay, too gentle.

OTHELLO: Nay, that's certain. But yet the pity of it, Iago! O Iago, the pity of it, Iago!

IAGO: If you are so fond over her iniquity, give her patent to offend, for, if it touch not you, it comes near nobody.

OTHELLO: I will chop her into messes. Cuckold me!

IAGO: O, 'tis foul in her.

OTHELLO: With mine officer!

IAGO: That's fouler.

OTHELLO: Get me some poison, Iago, this night. I'll not expostulate with her, lest her body and beauty unprovide my mind again. This night, Iago.

IAGO: Do it not with poison, strangle her in her bed, even the bed she hath contaminated.

OTHELLO: Good, good, the justice of it pleases, very good.

IAGO: And for Cassio, let me be his undertaker. You shall hear more by midnight.

OTHELLO: Excellent good. *A Trumpet Within.* What trumpet is that same?

IAGO: Something from Venice, sure. 'Tis Lodovico
Come from the Duke. And, see your wife is with him.
   Enter Lodovico, Desdemona, and Attendants.

LODOVICO: God save the worthy general!

OTHELLO: With all my heart, sir.

LODOVICO: The Duke and Senators of Venice greet you.
   Gives Him a Letter.

OTHELLO: I kiss the instrument of their pleasures.
   Opens the Letter, and Reads.

DESDEMONA: And what's the news, good cousin Lodovico?

IAGO: I am very glad to see you, signior;
Welcome to Cyprus.

LODOVICO: I thank you. How does Lieutenant Cassio?

IAGO: Lives, sir.

DESDEMONA: Cousin, there's fall'n between him and my lord
An unkind breech; but you shall make all well.

OTHELLO: Are you sure of that?

DESDEMONA: My lord?

OTHELLO: *Reads.* "This fail you not to do, as you will-"

LODOVICO: He did not call; he's busy in the paper.
Is there division 'twixt my lord and Cassio?

DESDEMONA: A most unhappy one. I would do much
To atone them, for the love I bear to Cassio.

OTHELLO: Fire and brimstone!

DESDEMONA: My lord?

OTHELLO: Are you wise?

DESDEMONA: What, is he angry?

LODOVICO: May be the letter moved him;
For, as I think, they do command him home,
Deputing Cassio in his government.

DESDEMONA: By my troth, I am glad on't.

OTHELLO: Indeed!

DESDEMONA: My lord?

OTHELLO: I am glad to see you mad.

DESDEMONA: Why, sweet Othello?

OTHELLO: Devil! Strikes her.

DESDEMONA: I have not deserved this.

LODOVICO: My lord, this would not be believed in Venice,
Though I should swear I saw't. 'Tis very much.
Make her amends; she weeps.

OTHELLO: O devil, devil!

If that the earth could teem with woman's tears,
Each drop she falls would prove a crocodile.
Out of my sight!

DESDEMONA: *Going.* I will not stay to offend you.

LODOVICO: Truly, an obedient lady.
I do beseech your lordship, call her back.

OTHELLO: Mistress!

DESDEMONA: My lord?

OTHELLO: What would you with her, sir?

LODOVICO: Who, I, my lord?

OTHELLO: Ay, you did wish that I would make her turn.
Sir, she can turn and turn, and yet go on,
And turn again; and she can weep, sir, weep;
And she's obedient, as you say, obedient,
Very obedient. Proceed you in your tears.
Concerning this, sir- O well-painted passion!-
I am commanded home. Get you away;
I'll send for you anon. Sir, I obey the mandate,
And will return to Venice. Hence, avaunt!
   Exit Desdemona.
Cassio shall have my place. And, sir, tonight,
I do entreat that we may sup together.
You are welcome, sir, to Cyprus. Goats and monkeys!
   Exit.

LODOVICO: Is this the noble Moor whom our full Senate
Call all in all sufficient? This the nature
Whom passion could not shake? whose solid virtue
The shot of accident nor dart of chance
Could neither graze nor pierce?

IAGO: He is much changed.

LODOVICO: Are his wits safe? Is he not light of brain?

IAGO: He's that he is. I may not breathe my censure
What he might be: if what he might he is not,
I would to heaven he were!

LODOVICO: What, strike his wife!

IAGO: Faith, that was not so well; yet would I knew
That stroke would prove the worst!

LODOVICO: Is it his use?
Or did the letters work upon his blood,
And new create this fault?

IAGO: Alas, alas!
It is not honesty in me to speak
What I have seen and known. You shall observe him,
And his own courses will denote him so
That I may save my speech. Do but go after,
And mark how he continues.

LODOVICO: I am sorry that I am deceived in him.
Exeunt.

ACT IV. SCENE II. A Room in the Castle.
Enter Othello and Emilia.

OTHELLO: You have seen nothing, then?

EMILIA: Nor ever heard, nor ever did suspect.

OTHELLO: Yes, you have seen Cassio and she together.

EMILIA: But then I saw no harm, and then I heard

Each syllable that breath made up between them.

OTHELLO: What, did they never whisper?

EMILIA: Never, my lord.

OTHELLO: Nor send you out o' the way?

EMILIA: Never.

OTHELLO: To fetch her fan, her gloves, her mask, nor nothing?

EMILIA: Never, my lord.

OTHELLO: That's strange.

EMILIA: I durst, my lord, to wager she is honest,
Lay down my soul at stake. If you think other,
Remove your thought; it doth abuse your bosom.
If any wretch have put this in your head,
Let heaven requite it with the serpent's curse!
For if she be not honest, chaste, and true,
There's no man happy; the purest of their wives
Is foul as slander.

OTHELLO: Bid her come hither; go.
   Exit Emilia.
She says enough; yet she's a simple bawd
That cannot say as much. This is a subtle whore,
A closet lock and key of villainous secrets.
And yet she'll kneel and pray; I have seen her do't.
   Enter Desdemona with Emilia.

DESDEMONA: My lord, what is your will?

OTHELLO: Pray, chuck, come hither.

DESDEMONA: What is your pleasure?

OTHELLO: Let me see your eyes;
Look in my face.

DESDEMONA: What horrible fancy's this?

OTHELLO: *To Emilia.* Some of your function, mistress,
Leave procreants alone and shut the door;
Cough, or cry "hem," if anybody come.
Your mystery, your mystery; nay, dispatch.
   Exit Emilia.

DESDEMONA: Upon my knees, what doth your speech import?
I understand a fury in your words,
But not the words.

OTHELLO: Why, what art thou?

DESDEMONA: Your wife, my lord, your true and loyal wife.

OTHELLO: Come, swear it, damn thyself;
Lest, being like one of heaven, the devils themselves
Should fear to seize thee. Therefore be double-damn'd;
Swear thou art honest.

DESDEMONA: Heaven doth truly know it.

OTHELLO: Heaven truly knows that thou art false as hell.

DESDEMONA: To whom, my lord? with whom? how am I false?

OTHELLO: O Desdemona! Away! away! away!

DESDEMONA: Alas the heavy day! Why do you weep?
Am I the motive of these tears, my lord?
If haply you my father do suspect

An instrument of this your calling back,
Lay not your blame on me. If you have lost him,
Why, I have lost him too.

OTHELLO: Had it pleased heaven
To try me with affliction, had they rain'd
All kinds of sores and shames on my bare head,
Steep'd me in poverty to the very lips,
Given to captivity me and my utmost hopes,
I should have found in some place of my soul
A drop of patience; but, alas, to make me
A fixed figure for the time of scorn
To point his slow unmoving finger at!
Yet could I bear that too, well, very well;
But there, where I have garner'd up my heart,
Where either I must live or bear no life;
The fountain from the which my current runs,
Or else dries up; to be discarded thence!
Or keep it as a cistern for foul toads
To knot and gender in! Turn thy complexion there,
Patience, thou young and rose-lipp'd cherubin,
Ay, there, look grim as hell!

DESDEMONA: I hope my noble lord esteems me honest.

OTHELLO: O, ay, as summer flies are in the shambles,
That quicken even with blowing. O thou weed,
Who art so lovely fair and smell'st so sweet
That the sense aches at thee, would thou hadst ne'er been born!

DESDEMONA: Alas, what ignorant sin have I committed?

OTHELLO: Was this fair paper, this most goodly book,
Made to write "whore" upon? What committed?
Committed? O thou public commoner!
I should make very forges of my cheeks,
That would to cinders burn up modesty,
Did I but speak thy deeds. What committed!

Heaven stops the nose at it, and the moon winks;
The bawdy wind, that kisses all it meets,
Is hush'd within the hollow mine of earth,
And will not hear it. What committed?
Impudent strumpet!

DESDEMONA: By heaven, you do me wrong.

OTHELLO: Are not you a strumpet?

DESDEMONA: No, as I am a Christian.
If to preserve this vessel for my lord
From any other foul unlawful touch
Be not to be a strumpet, I am none.

OTHELLO: What, not a whore?

DESDEMONA: No, as I shall be saved.

OTHELLO: Is't possible?

DESDEMONA: O, heaven forgive us!

OTHELLO: I cry you mercy then;
I took you for that cunning whore of Venice
That married with Othello. *Raises His Voice.* You, mistress,
That have the office opposite to Saint Peter,
And keep the gate of hell!
   Re-enter Emilia.
You, you, ay, you!
We have done our course; there's money for your pains.
I pray you, turn the key, and keep our counsel. *Exit.*

EMILIA: Alas, what does this gentleman conceive?
How do you, madam? How do you, my good lady?

DESDEMONA: Faith, half asleep.

EMILIA: Good madam, what's the matter with my lord?

DESDEMONA: With who?

EMILIA: Why, with my lord, madam.

DESDEMONA: Who is thy lord?

EMILIA: He that is yours, sweet lady.

DESDEMONA: I have none. Do not talk to me, Emilia;
I cannot weep, nor answer have I none
But what should go by water. Prithee, tonight
Lay on my bed my wedding sheets. Remember,
And call thy husband hither.

EMILIA: Here's a change indeed!
 Exit.

DESDEMONA: 'Tis meet I should be used so, very meet.
How have I been behaved, that he might stick
The small'st opinion on my least misuse?
 Re-enter Emilia with Iago.

IAGO: What is your pleasure, madam? How is't with you?

DESDEMONA: I cannot tell. Those that do teach young babes
Do it with gentle means and easy tasks.
He might have chid me so, for in good faith,
I am a child to chiding.

IAGO: What's the matter, lady?

EMILIA: Alas, Iago, my lord hath so bewhored her,
Thrown such despite and heavy terms upon her,
As true hearts cannot bear.

DESDEMONA: Am I that name, Iago?

IAGO: What name, fair lady?

DESDEMONA: Such as she says my lord did say I was.

EMILIA: He call'd her whore; a beggar in his drink
Could not have laid such terms upon his callet.

IAGO: Why did he so?

DESDEMONA: I do not know; I am sure I am none such.

IAGO: Do not weep, do not weep. Alas the day!

EMILIA: Hath she forsook so many noble matches,
Her father and her country and her friends,
To be call'd whore? Would it not make one weep?

DESDEMONA: It is my wretched fortune.

IAGO: Beshrew him for't!
How comes this trick upon him?

DESDEMONA: Nay, heaven doth know.

EMILIA: I will be hang'd, if some eternal villain,
Some busy and insinuating rogue,
Some cogging, cozening slave, to get some office,
Have not devised this slander; I'll be hang'd else.

IAGO: Fie, there is no such man; it is impossible.

DESDEMONA: If any such there be, heaven pardon him!

EMILIA: A halter pardon him! And hell gnaw his bones!
Why should he call her whore? Who keeps her company?

What place? What time? What form? What likelihood?
The Moor's abused by some most villainous knave,
Some base notorious knave, some scurvy fellow.
O heaven, that such companions thou'ldst unfold,
And put in every honest hand a whip
To lash the rascals naked through the world
Even from the east to the west!

IAGO: Speak within door.

EMILIA: O, fie upon them! Some such squire he was
That turn'd your wit the seamy side without,
And made you to suspect me with the Moor.

IAGO: You are a fool; go to.

DESDEMONA: O good Iago,
What shall I do to win my lord again?
Good friend, go to him, for by this light of heaven,
I know not how I lost him. Here I kneel:
If e'er my will did trespass 'gainst his love
Either in discourse of thought or actual deed,
Or that mine eyes, mine ears, or any sense,
Delighted them in any other form,
Or that I do not yet, and ever did,
And ever will, though he do shake me off
To beggarly divorcement, love him dearly,
Comfort forswear me! Unkindness may do much,
And his unkindness may defeat my life,
But never taint my love. I cannot say "whore."
It doth abhor me now I speak the word;
To do the act that might the addition earn
Not the world's mass of vanity could make me.

IAGO: I pray you, be content; 'tis but his humor:
The business of the state does him offense,
And he does chide with you.

DESDEMONA: If 'twere no other-

IAGO: 'Tis but so, I warrant. Trumpets within.
Hark, how these instruments summon to supper!
The messengers of Venice stay the meat.
Go in, and weep not; all things shall be well.
   Exeunt Desdemona and Emilia.
   Enter Roderigo.
How now, Roderigo!

RODERIGO: I do not find that thou dealest justly with me.

IAGO: What in the contrary?

RODERIGO: Every day thou daffest me with some device, Iago; and rather, as it seems to me now, keepest from me all conveniency than suppliest me with the least advantage of hope. I will indeed no longer endure it; nor am I yet persuaded to put up in peace what already I have foolishly suffered.

IAGO: Will you hear me, Roderigo?

RODERIGO: Faith, I have heard too much, for your words and performances are no kin together.

IAGO: You charge me most unjustly.

RODERIGO: With nought but truth. I have wasted myself out of my means. The jewels you have had from me to deliver to Desdemona would half have corrupted a votarist. You have told me she hath received them and returned me expectations and comforts of sudden respect and acquaintance; but I find none.

IAGO: Well, go to, very well.

RODERIGO: Very well! go to! I cannot go to, man; nor 'tis not very well. By this hand, I say 'tis very scurvy, and begin to find myself fopped in it.

IAGO: Very well.

RODERIGO: I tell you 'tis not very well. I will make myself known to Desdemona. If she will return me my jewels, I will give over my suit and repent my unlawful solicitation; if not, assure yourself I will seek satisfaction of you.

IAGO: You have said now.

RODERIGO: Ay, and said nothing but what I protest intendment of doing.

IAGO: Why, now I see there's mettle in thee; and even from this instant do build on thee a better opinion than ever before. Give me thy hand, Roderigo. Thou hast taken against me a most just exception; but yet, I protest, have dealt most directly in thy affair.

RODERIGO: It hath not appeared.

IAGO: I grant indeed it hath not appeared, and your suspicion is not without wit and judgement. But, Roderigo, if thou hast that in thee indeed, which I have greater reason to believe now than ever, I mean purpose, courage, and valor, this night show it; if thou the next night following enjoy not Desdemona, take me from this world with treachery and devise engines for my life.

RODERIGO: Well, what is it? Is it within reason and compass?

IAGO: Sir, there is especial commission come from Venice to depute Cassio in Othello's place.

RODERIGO: Is that true? Why then Othello and Desdemona return again to Venice.

IAGO: O, no; he goes into Mauritania, and takes away with him the fair Desdemona, unless his abode be lingered here by some accident; wherein none can be so determinate as the removing of Cassio.

RODERIGO: How do you mean, removing of him?

IAGO: Why, by making him uncapable of Othello's place; knocking out his brains.

RODERIGO: And that you would have me to do?

IAGO: Ay, if you dare do yourself a profit and a right. He sups tonight with a harlotry, and thither will I go to him. He knows not yet of his honorable fortune. If you will watch his going thence, which his will fashion to fall out between twelve and one, you may take him at your pleasure; I will be near to second your attempt, and he shall fall between us. Come, stand not amazed at it, but go along with me; I will show you such a necessity in his death that you shall think yourself bound to put it on him. It is now high supper-time, and the night grows to waste. About it.

RODERIGO: I will hear further reason for this.

IAGO: And you shall be satisfied.
Exeunt.

ACT IV. SCENE III. Another Room in the Castle.
Enter Othello, Lodovico, Desdemona, Emilia, and Attendants.

LODOVICO: I do beseech you, sir, trouble yourself no further.

OTHELLO: O, pardon me; 'twill do me good to walk.

LODOVICO: Madam, good night; I humbly thank your ladyship.

DESDEMONA: Your honor is most welcome.

OTHELLO: Will you walk, sir? O- Desdemona-

DESDEMONA: My lord?

OTHELLO: Get you to bed on the instant; I will be returned forthwith. Dismiss your attendant there; look it be done.

DESDEMONA: I will, my lord.
Exeunt Othello, Lodovico, and Attendants.

EMILIA: How goes it now? He looks gentler than he did.

DESDEMONA: He says he will return incontinent.
He hath commanded me to go to bed,
And bade me to dismiss you.

EMILIA: Dismiss me?

DESDEMONA: It was his bidding; therefore, good Emilia,
Give me my nightly wearing, and adieu.
We must not now displease him.

EMILIA: I would you had never seen him!

DESDEMONA: So would not I. My love doth so approve him,
That even his stubbornness, his checks, his frowns-
Prithee, unpin me- have grace and favor in them.

EMILIA: I have laid those sheets you bade me on the bed.

DESDEMONA: All's one. Good faith, how foolish are our minds!
If I do die before thee, prithee shroud me
In one of those same sheets.

EMILIA: Come, come, you talk.

DESDEMONA: My mother had a maid call'd Barbary;

She was in love, and he she loved proved mad
And did forsake her. She had a song of "willow";
An old thing 'twas, but it express'd her fortune,
And she died singing it. That song tonight
Will not go from my mind; I have much to do
But to go hang my head all at one side
And sing it like poor Barbary. Prithee, dispatch.

EMILIA: Shall I go fetch your nightgown?

DESDEMONA: No, unpin me here.
This Lodovico is a proper man.

EMILIA: A very handsome man.

DESDEMONA: He speaks well.

EMILIA: I know a lady in Venice would have walked barefoot to Palestine for a touch of his nether lip.

DESDEMONA: *Sings.*
　"The poor soul sat sighing by a sycamore tree,
　　Sing all a green willow;
　Her hand on her bosom, her head on her knee,
　　Sing willow, willow, willow.
　The fresh streams ran by her, and murmur'd her moans,
　　Sing willow, willow, willow;
　Her salt tears fell from her, and soften'd the stones-"
Lay be these-
Sings. "Sing willow, willow, willow-"
Prithee, hie thee; he'll come anon-
Sings. "Sing all a green willow must be my garland.
Let nobody blame him; his scorn I approve-"
Nay, that's not next. Hark, who is't that knocks?

EMILIA: It's the wind.

DESDEMONA: *Sings.*
"I call'd my love false love; but what said he then?
  Sing willow, willow, willow.
If I court moe women, you'll couch with moe men-"
So get thee gone; good night. Mine eyes do itch;
Doth that bode weeping?

EMILIA: 'Tis neither here nor there.

DESDEMONA: I have heard it said so. O, these men, these men!
Dost thou in conscience think- tell me, Emilia-
That there be women do abuse their husbands
In such gross kind?

EMILIA: There be some such, no question.

DESDEMONA: Wouldst thou do such a deed for all the world?

EMILIA: Why, would not you?

DESDEMONA: No, by this heavenly light!

EMILIA: Nor I neither by this heavenly light; I might do't as well i' the dark.

DESDEMONA: Wouldst thou do such a deed for all the world?

EMILIA: The world's a huge thing; it is a great price
For a small vice.

DESDEMONA: In troth, I think thou wouldst not.

EMILIA: In troth, I think I should, and undo't when I had done. Marry, I would not do such a thing for a joint-ring, nor for measures of lawn, nor for gowns, petticoats, nor caps, nor any petty exhibition; but, for the whole world- why, who would not make her husband a cuckold to make him a monarch? I should venture purgatory for't.

DESDEMONA: Beshrew me, if I would do such a wrong
For the whole world.

EMILIA: Why, the wrong is but a wrong i' the world; and having the
world for your labor, 'tis a wrong in your own world, and you
might quickly make it right.

DESDEMONA: I do not think there is any such woman.

EMILIA: Yes, a dozen, and as many to the vantage as would store the
  world they played for.
But I do think it is their husbands' faults
If wives do fall; say that they slack their duties
And pour our treasures into foreign laps,
Or else break out in peevish jealousies,
Throwing restraint upon us, or say they strike us,
Or scant our former having in despite,
Why, we have galls, and though we have some grace,
Yet have we some revenge. Let husbands know
Their wives have sense like them; they see and smell
And have their palates both for sweet and sour,
As husbands have. What is it that they do
When they change us for others? Is it sport?
I think it is. And doth affection breed it?
I think it doth. Is't frailty that thus errs?
It is so too. And have not we affections,
Desires for sport, and frailty, as men have?
Then let them use us well; else let them know,
The ills we do, their ills instruct us so.

DESDEMONA: Good night, good night. Heaven me such uses send,
Not to pick bad from bad, but by bad mend!
   Exeunt.

ACT V. SCENE I. Cyprus. A Street.

Enter Iago and Roderigo:

IAGO: Here, stand behind this bulk; straight will he come.
Wear thy good rapier bare, and put it home.
Quick, quick; fear nothing; I'll be at thy elbow.
It makes us, or it mars us; think on that,
And fix most firm thy resolution.

RODERIGO: Be near at hand; I may miscarry in't.

IAGO: Here, at thy hand, be bold, and take thy stand.
  Retires.

RODERIGO: I have no great devotion to the deed;
And yet he hath given me satisfying reasons.
'Tis but a man gone. Forth, my sword; he dies.

IAGO: I have rubb'd this young quat almost to the sense,
And he grows angry. Now, whether he kill Cassio,
Or Cassio him, or each do kill the other,
Every way makes my gain. Live Roderigo,
He calls me to a restitution large
Of gold and jewels that I bobb'd from him,
As gifts to Desdemona;
It must not be. If Cassio do remain,
He hath a daily beauty in his life
That makes me ugly; and besides, the Moor
May unfold me to him; there stand I in much peril.
No, he must die. Be't so. I hear him coming.
  Enter Cassio.

RODERIGO: I know his gait; 'tis he. Villain, thou diest!
  Makes a pass at Cassio.

CASSIO: That thrust had been mine enemy indeed,
But that my coat is better than thou know'st;

I will make proof of thine. *Draws, and wounds Roderigo.*

RODERIGO: O, I am slain!
Iago from Behind Wounds Cassio in the Leg, and Exit.

CASSIO: I am maim'd forever. Help, ho! Murther! Murther!
Falls.
Enter Othello.

OTHELLO: The voice of Cassio; Iago keeps his word.

RODERIGO: O, villain that I am!

OTHELLO: It is even so.

CASSIO: O, help, ho! Light! A surgeon!

OTHELLO: 'Tis he. O brave Iago, honest and just,
That hast such noble sense of thy friend's wrong!
Thou teachest me. Minion, your dear lies dead,
And your unblest fate hies. Strumpet, I come!
Forth of my heart those charms, thine eyes, are blotted;
Thy bed lust-stain'd shall with lust's blood be spotted.
Exit.
Enter Lodovico and Gratiano.

CASSIO: What, ho! No watch? No passage? Murther! Murther!

GRATIANO: 'Tis some mischance; the cry is very direful.

CASSIO: O, help!

LODOVICO: Hark!

RODERIGO: O wretched villain!

LODOVICO: Two or three groan; it is a heavy night.

These may be counterfeits; let's think't unsafe
To come in to the cry without more help.

RODERIGO: Nobody come? Then shall I bleed to death.

LODOVICO: Hark!
Re-enter Iago, with a Light.

GRATIANO: Here's one comes in his shirt, with light and weapons.

IAGO: Who's there? Whose noise is this that cries on murther?

LODOVICO: We do not know.

IAGO: Did not you hear a cry?

CASSIO: Here, here! for heaven's sake, help me!

IAGO: What's the matter?

GRATIANO: This is Othello's ancient, as I take it.

LODOVICO: The same indeed; a very valiant fellow.

IAGO: What are you here that cry so grievously?

CASSIO: Iago? O, I am spoil'd, undone by villains!
Give me some help.

IAGO: O me, lieutenant! What villains have done this?

CASSIO: I think that one of them is hereabout,
And cannot make away.

IAGO: O treacherous villains!
To Lodovico and Gratiano. What are you there?
Come in and give some help.

RODERIGO: O, help me here!

CASSIO: That's one of them.

IAGO: O murtherous slave! O villain!
   Stabs Roderigo.

RODERIGO: O damn'd Iago! O inhuman dog!

IAGO: Kill men i' the dark! Where be these bloody thieves?
How silent is this town! Ho! Murther! Murther!
What may you be? Are you of good or evil?

LODOVICO: As you shall prove us, praise us.

IAGO: Signior Lodovico?

LODOVICO: He, sir.

IAGO: I cry you mercy. Here's Cassio hurt by villains.

GRATIANO: Cassio?

IAGO: How is't, brother?

CASSIO: My leg is cut in two.

IAGO: Marry, heaven forbid!
Light, gentlemen; I'll bind it with my shirt.
   Enter Bianca.

BIANCA: What is the matter, ho? Who is't that cried?

IAGO: Who is't that cried?

BIANCA: O my dear Cassio, my sweet Cassio! O Cassio, Cassio, Cassio!

IAGO: O notable strumpet! Cassio, may you suspect
Who they should be that have thus mangled you?

CASSIO: No.

GRATIANO: I am sorry to find you thus; I have been to seek you.

IAGO: Lend me a garter. So. O, for a chair,
To bear him easily hence!

BIANCA: Alas, he faints! O Cassio, Cassio, Cassio!

IAGO: Gentlemen all, I do suspect this trash
To be a party in this injury.
Patience awhile, good Cassio. Come, come;
Lend me a light. Know we this face or no?
Alas, my friend and my dear countryman
Roderigo? No- yes, sure. O heaven! Roderigo.

GRATIANO: What, of Venice?

IAGO: Even he, sir. Did you know him?

GRATIANO: Know him! ay.

IAGO: Signior Gratiano? I cry you gentle pardon;
These bloody accidents must excuse my manners,
That so neglected you.

GRATIANO: I am glad to see you.

IAGO: How do you, Cassio? O, a chair, a chair!

GRATIANO: Roderigo!

IAGO: He, he, 'tis he. *A Chair Brought in.* O, that's well said: the chair.
Some good man bear him carefully from hence;

I'll fetch the general's surgeon. *To Bianca.* For you, mistress,
Save you your labor. He that lies slain here, Cassio,
Was my dear friend; what malice was between you?

CASSIO: None in the world; nor do I know the man.

IAGO: *To Bianca.* What, look you pale? O, bear him out o' the air.
  Cassio and Roderigo are borne off.
Stay you, good gentlemen. Look you pale, mistress?
Do you perceive the gastness of her eye?
Nay, if you stare, we shall hear more anon.
Behold her well; I pray you, look upon her.
Do you see, gentlemen? Nay, guiltiness will speak,
Though tongues were out of use.
  Enter Emilia.

EMILIA: 'Las, what's the matter? What's the matter, husband?

IAGO: Cassio hath here been set on in the dark
By Roderigo, and fellows that are 'scaped;
He's almost slain, and Roderigo dead.

EMILIA: Alas, good gentleman! alas, good Cassio!

IAGO: This is the fruit of whoring. Prithee, Emilia,
Go know of Cassio where he supp'd tonight.
What, do you shake at that?

BIANCA: He supp'd at my house; but I therefore shake not.

IAGO: O, did he so? I charge you, go with me.

EMILIA: Fie, fie upon thee, strumpet!

BIANCA: I am no strumpet, but of life as honest
As you that thus abuse me.

EMILIA: As I! foh! fie upon thee!

IAGO: Kind gentlemen, let's go see poor Cassio dress'd.
Come, mistress, you must tell's another tale.
Emilia, run you to the citadel,
And tell my lord and lady what hath happ'd!
Will you go on? *Aside.* This is the night
That either makes me or fordoes me quite. *Exeunt.*

ACT V. SCENE II. A Bedchamber in the Castle. Desdemona in Bed Asleep; a Light Burning.

Enter Othello.

OTHELLO: It is the cause, it is the cause, my soul.
Let me not name it to you, you chaste stars!
It is the cause. Yet I'll not shed her blood,
Nor scar that whiter skin of hers than snow
And smooth as monumental alabaster.
Yet she must die, else she'll betray more men.
Put out the light, and then put out the light.
If I quench thee, thou flaming minister,
I can again thy former light restore,
Should I repent me; but once put out thy light,
Thou cunning'st pattern of excelling nature,
I know not where is that Promethean heat
That can thy light relume. When I have pluck'd the rose,
I cannot give it vital growth again,
It must needs wither; I'll smell it on the tree. *Kisses her.*
O, balmy breath, that dost almost persuade
Justice to break her sword! One more, one more;
Be thus when thou art dead, and I will kill thee,
And love thee after. One more, and this the last;
So sweet was ne'er so fatal. I must weep,
But they are cruel tears; this sorrow's heavenly,
It strikes where it doth love. She wakes.

DESDEMONA: Who's there? Othello?

OTHELLO: Ay, Desdemona.

DESDEMONA: Will you come to bed, my lord?

OTHELLO: Have you pray'd tonight, Desdemona?

DESDEMONA: Ay, my lord.

OTHELLO: If you bethink yourself of any crime
Unreconciled as yet to heaven and grace,
Solicit for it straight.

DESDEMONA: Alas, my lord, what may you mean by that?

OTHELLO: Well, do it, and be brief; I will walk by.
I would not kill thy unprepared spirit.
No, heaven forfend! I would not kill thy soul.

DESDEMONA: Talk you of killing?

OTHELLO: Ay, I do.

DESDEMONA: Then heaven have mercy on me!

OTHELLO: Amen, with all my heart!

DESDEMONA: If you say so, I hope you will not kill me.

OTHELLO: Hum!

DESDEMONA: And yet I fear you, for you are fatal then
When your eyes roll so. Why I should fear I know not,
Since guiltiness I know not; but yet I feel I fear.

OTHELLO: Think on thy sins.

DESDEMONA: They are loves I bear to you.

OTHELLO: Ay, and for that thou diest.

DESDEMONA: That death's unnatural that kills for loving.
Alas, why gnaw you so your nether lip?
Some bloody passion shakes your very frame.
These are portents; but yet I hope, I hope,
They do not point on me.

OTHELLO: Peace, and be still!

DESDEMONA: I will so. What's the matter?

OTHELLO: That handkerchief which I so loved and gave thee
Thou gavest to Cassio.

DESDEMONA: No, by my life and soul!
Send for the man, and ask him.

OTHELLO: Sweet soul, take heed,
Take heed of perjury; thou are on thy deathbed.

DESDEMONA: Ay, but not yet to die.

OTHELLO: Yes, presently:
Therefore confess thee freely of thy sin,
For to deny each article with oath
Cannot remove nor choke the strong conception
That I do groan withal. Thou art to die.

DESDEMONA: Then Lord have mercy on me!

OTHELLO: I say, amen.

DESDEMONA: And have you mercy too! I never did
Offend you in my life; never loved Cassio
But with such general warranty of heaven
As I might love. I never gave him token.

OTHELLO: By heaven, I saw my handkerchief in 's hand.
O perjured woman! Thou dost stone my heart,
And makest me call what I intend to do
A murther, which I thought a sacrifice.
I saw the handkerchief.

DESDEMONA: He found it then;
I never gave it him. Send for him hither;
Let him confess a truth.

OTHELLO: He hath confess'd.

DESDEMONA: What, my lord?

OTHELLO: That he hath used thee.

DESDEMONA: How? unlawfully?

OTHELLO: Ay.

DESDEMONA: He will not say so.

OTHELLO: No, his mouth is stopp'd;
Honest Iago hath ta'en order for't.

DESDEMONA: O, my fear interprets! What, is he dead?

OTHELLO: Had all his hairs been lives, my great revenge
Had stomach for them all.

DESDEMONA: Alas, he is betray'd, and I undone!

OTHELLO: Out, strumpet! Weep'st thou for him to my face?

DESDEMONA: O, banish me, my lord, but kill me not!

OTHELLO: Down, strumpet!

DESDEMONA: Kill me tomorrow; let me live tonight!

OTHELLO: Nay, if you strive—

DESDEMONA: But half an hour!

OTHELLO: Being done, there is no pause.

DESDEMONA: But while I say one prayer!

OTHELLO: It is too late. *He stifles her.*

EMILIA: *Within.* My lord, my lord! What, ho! my lord, my lord!

OTHELLO: What noise is this? Not dead? not yet quite dead?
I that am cruel am yet merciful;
I would not have thee linger in thy pain.
So, so.

EMILIA: *Within.* What, ho! my lord, my lord!

OTHELLO: Who's there?

EMILIA: *Within.* O, good my lord, I would speak a word with you!

OTHELLO: Yes, 'tis Emilia. By and by. She's dead.
'Tis like she comes to speak of Cassio's death.
The noise was here. Ha! no more moving?
Still as the grave. Shall she come in? were't good?
I think she stirs again. No. What's best to do?
If she come in, she'll sure speak to my wife.
My wife! My wife! What wife? I have no wife.
O, insupportable! O heavy hour!
Methinks it should be now a huge eclipse
Of sun and moon, and that the affrighted globe
Should yawn at alteration.

EMILIA: *Within.* I do beseech you
That I may speak with you, O, good my lord!

OTHELLO: I had forgot thee. O, come in, Emilia.
Soft, by and by. Let me the curtains draw.
Where art thou? Unlocks the door.
   Enter Emilia.
What's the matter with thee now?

EMILIA: O, my good lord, yonder's foul murthers done!

OTHELLO: What, now?

EMILIA: But now, my lord.

OTHELLO: It is the very error of the moon;
She comes more nearer earth than she was wont
And makes men mad.

EMILIA: Cassio, my lord, hath kill'd a young Venetian
Call'd Roderigo.

OTHELLO: Roderigo kill'd?
And Cassio kill'd?

EMILIA: No, Cassio is not kill'd.

OTHELLO: Not Cassio kill'd! Then murther's out of tune,
And sweet revenge grows harsh.

DESDEMONA: O, falsely, falsely murther'd!

EMILIA: Alas, what cry is that?

OTHELLO: That? what?

EMILIA: Out, and alas! That was my lady's voice.

Help! help, ho! help! O lady, speak again!
Sweet Desdemona! O sweet mistress, speak!

DESDEMONA: A guiltless death I die.

EMILIA: O, who hath done this deed?

DESDEMONA: Nobody; I myself. Farewell;
Commend me to my kind lord. O, farewell! Dies.

OTHELLO: Why, how should she be murther'd?

EMILIA: Alas, who knows?

OTHELLO: You heard her say herself, it was not I.

EMILIA: She said so; I must needs report the truth.

OTHELLO: She's like a liar gone to burning hell;
'Twas I that kill'd her.

EMILIA: O, the more angel she,
And you the blacker devil!

OTHELLO: She turn'd to folly, and she was a whore.

EMILIA: Thou dost belie her, and thou art a devil.

OTHELLO: She was false as water.

EMILIA: Thou art rash as fire, to say
That she was false. O, she was heavenly true!

OTHELLO: Cassio did top her; ask thy husband else.
O, I were damn'd beneath all depth in hell,
But that I did proceed upon just grounds
To this extremity. Thy husband knew it all.

EMILIA: My husband?

OTHELLO: Thy husband.

EMILIA: That she was false to wedlock?

OTHELLO: Ay, with Cassio. Nay, had she been true,
If heaven would make me such another world
Of one entire and perfect chrysolite,
I'ld not have sold her for it.

EMILIA: My husband?

OTHELLO: Ay, 'twas he that told me first.
An honest man he is, and hates the slime
That sticks on filthy deeds.

EMILIA: My husband?

OTHELLO: What needs this iteration, woman? I say thy husband.

EMILIA: O mistress, villainy hath made mocks with love!
My husband say that she was false!

OTHELLO: He, woman;
I say thy husband. Dost understand the word?
My friend, thy husband, honest, honest Iago.

EMILIA: If he say so, may his pernicious soul
Rot half a grain a day! He lies to the heart.
She was too fond of her most filthy bargain.

OTHELLO: Ha!

EMILIA: Do thy worst;
This deed of thine is no more worthy heaven
Than thou wast worthy her.

OTHELLO: Peace, you were best.

EMILIA: Thou hast not half that power to do me harm
As I have to be hurt. O gull! O dolt!
As ignorant as dirt! Thou hast done a deed-
I care not for thy sword; I'll make thee known,
Though I lost twenty lives. Help! help, ho! help!
The Moor hath kill'd my mistress! Murther, murther!
   Enter Montano, Gratiano, Iago, and Others.

MONTANO: What is the matter? How now, general?

EMILIA: O, are you come, Iago? You have done well,
That men must lay their murthers on your neck.

GRATIANO: What is the matter?

EMILIA: Disprove this villain, if thou be'st a man.
He says thou told'st him that his wife was false;
I know thou didst not, thou'rt not such a villain.
Speak, for my heart is full.

IAGO: I told him what I thought, and told no more
Than what he found himself was apt and true.

EMILIA: But did you ever tell him she was false?

IAGO: I did.

EMILIA: You told a lie, an odious, damned lie;
Upon my soul, a lie, a wicked lie!
She false with Cassio? Did you say with Cassio?

IAGO: With Cassio, mistress. Go to, charm your tongue.

EMILIA: I will not charm my tongue; I am bound to speak.
My mistress here lies murther'd in her bed-

ALL: O heavens forfend!

EMILIA: And your reports have set the murther on.

OTHELLO: Nay, stare not, masters; it is true indeed.

GRATIANO: 'Tis a strange truth.

MONTANO: O monstrous act!

EMILIA: Villainy, villainy, villainy!
I think upon't, I think, I smell't, O villainy!
I thought so then. I'll kill myself for grief.
O villainy, villainy!

IAGO: What, are you mad? I charge you, get you home.

EMILIA: Good gentlemen, let me have leave to speak;
'Tis proper I obey him, but not now.
Perchance, Iago, I will ne'er go home.

OTHELLO: O! O! O! *Falls on the bed.*

EMILIA: Nay, lay thee down and roar;
For thou hast kill'd the sweetest innocent
That e'er did lift up eye.

OTHELLO: *Rises.* O, she was foul!
I scarce did know you, uncle; there lies your niece,
Whose breath indeed these hands have newly stopp'd.
I know this act shows horrible and grim.

GRATIANO: Poor Desdemon! I am glad thy father's dead.
Thy match was mortal to him, and pure grief
Shore his old thread in twain; did he live now,
This sight would make him do a desperate turn,
Yea, curse his better angel from his side,

And fall to reprobation.

OTHELLO: 'Tis pitiful, but yet Iago knows
That she with Cassio hath the act of shame
A thousand times committed. Cassio confess'd it,
And she did gratify his amorous works
With that recognizance and pledge of love
Which I first gave her. I saw it in his hand,
It was a handkerchief, an antique token
My father gave my mother.

EMILIA: O heaven! O heavenly powers!

IAGO: 'Zounds! Hold your peace.

EMILIA: 'Twill out, 'twill. I peace?
No, I will speak as liberal as the north;
Let heaven and men and devils, let them all,
All, all, cry shame against me, yet I'll speak.

IAGO: Be wise, and get you home.

EMILIA: I will not.
   Iago Offers to Stab Emilia.

GRATIANO: Fie!
Your sword upon a woman?

EMILIA: O thou dull Moor! That handkerchief thou speak'st of
I found by fortune and did give my husband,
For often with a solemn earnestness,
More than indeed belong'd to such a trifle,
He begg'd of me to steal it.

IAGO: Villainous whore!

EMILIA: She give it Cassio? No, alas, I found it,

And I did give't my husband.

IAGO: Filth, thou liest!

EMILIA: By heaven, I do not, I do not, gentlemen.
O murtherous coxcomb! What should such a fool
Do with so good a wife?

OTHELLO: Are there not stones in heaven
But what serve for thunder? Precious villain!
  He Runs at Iago, but Montano Disarms Him. Iago Stabs Emilia.

GRATIANO: The woman falls; sure, he hath kill'd his wife.

EMILIA: Ay, ay! O, lay me by my mistress' side.
  Exit Iago.

GRATIANO: He's gone, but his wife's kill'd.

MONTANO: 'Tis a notorious villain. Take you this weapon,
Which I have here recover'd from the Moor.
Come, guard the door without; let him not pass,
But kill him rather. I'll after that same villain,
For 'tis a damned slave.
  Exeunt All but Othello and Emilia.

OTHELLO: I am not valiant neither,
But every puny whipster gets my sword.
But why should honor outlive honesty?
Let it go all.

EMILIA: What did thy song bode, lady?
Hark, canst thou hear me? I will play the swan,
And die in music. *Sings.* "Willow, willow, willow."
Moor, she was chaste; she loved thee, cruel Moor;
So come my soul to bliss, as I speak true;
So speaking as I think, I die, I die. *Dies.*

OTHELLO: I have another weapon in this chamber;
It is a sword of Spain, the ice-brook's temper-
O, here it is. Uncle, I must come forth.

GRATIANO: *Within.* If thou attempt it, it will cost thee dear.
Thou hast no weapon, and perforce must suffer.

OTHELLO: Look in upon me then, and speak with me,
Or, naked as I am, I will assault thee.
   Re-enter Gratiano.

GRATIANO: What is the matter?

OTHELLO: Behold, I have a weapon;
A better never did itself sustain
Upon a soldier's thigh. I have seen the day
That with this little arm and this good sword
I have made my way through more impediments
Than twenty times your stop. But, O vain boast!
Who can control his fate? 'Tis not so now.
Be not afraid, though you do see me weapon'd;
Here is my journey's end, here is my butt
And very sea-mark of my utmost sail.
Do you go back dismay'd? 'Tis a lost fear.
Man but a rush against Othello's breast,
And he retires. Where should Othello go?
Now, how dost thou look now? O ill-starr'd wench!
Pale as thy smock! When we shall meet at compt,
This look of thine will hurl my soul from heaven,
And fiends will snatch at it. Cold, cold, my girl?
Even like thy chastity. O cursed, cursed slave!
Whip me, ye devils,
From the possession of this heavenly sight!
Blow me about in winds! Roast me in sulphur!
Wash me in steep-down gulfs of liquid fire!
O Desdemon! dead, Desdemon! dead!
O! O! O!

Enter Lodovico, Montano, Cassio Carried in a Chair, and Officers with Iago, Prisoner.

LODOVICO: Where is this rash and most unfortunate man?

OTHELLO: That's he that was Othello. Here I am.

LODOVICO: Where is that viper? Bring the villain forth.

OTHELLO: I look down towards his feet; but that's a fable.
If that thou be'st a devil, I cannot kill thee. *Wounds Iago.*

LODOVICO: Wrench his sword from him.

IAGO: I bleed, sir, but not kill'd.

OTHELLO: I am not sorry neither. I'ld have thee live,
For, in my sense, 'tis happiness to die.

LODOVICO: O thou Othello, that wert once so good,
Fall'n in the practice of a damned slave,
What shall be said to thee?

OTHELLO: Why, anything;
An honorable murtherer, if you will,
For nought did I in hate, but all in honor.

LODOVICO: This wretch hath part confess'd his villainy.
Did you and he consent in Cassio's death?

OTHELLO: Ay.

CASSIO: Dear general, I never gave you cause.

OTHELLO: I do believe it, and I ask your pardon.
Will you, I pray, demand that demi-devil
Why he hath thus ensnared my soul and body?

IAGO: Demand me nothing; what you know, you know.
From this time forth I never will speak word.

LODOVICO: What, not to pray?

GRATIANO: Torments will ope your lips.

OTHELLO: Well, thou dost best.

LODOVICO: Sir, you shall understand what hath befall'n,
Which, as I think, you know not. Here is a letter
Found in the pocket of the slain Roderigo,
And here another. The one of them imports
The death of Cassio to be undertook
By Roderigo.

OTHELLO: O villain!

CASSIO: Most heathenish and most gross!

LODOVICO: Now here's another discontented paper,
Found in his pocket too; and this, it seems,
Roderigo meant to have sent this damned villain;
But that, belike, Iago in the interim
Came in and satisfied him.

OTHELLO: O the pernicious caitiff!
How came you, Cassio, by that handkerchief
That was my wife's?

CASSIO: I found it in my chamber;
And he himself confess'd but even now
That there he dropp'd it for a special purpose
Which wrought to his desire.

OTHELLO: O fool! fool! fool!

CASSIO: There is besides in Roderigo's letter,
How he upbraids Iago, that he made him
Brave me upon the watch, whereon it came
That I was cast. And even but now he spake
After long seeming dead, Iago hurt him,
Iago set him on.

LODOVICO: You must forsake this room, and go with us.
Your power and your command is taken off,
And Cassio rules in Cyprus. For this slave,
If there be any cunning cruelty
That can torment him much and hold him long,
It shall be his. You shall close prisoner rest,
Till that the nature of your fault be known
To the Venetian state. Come, bring away.

OTHELLO: Soft you; a word or two before you go.
I have done the state some service, and they know't.
No more of that. I pray you, in your letters,
When you shall these unlucky deeds relate,
Speak of me as I am; nothing extenuate,
Nor set down aught in malice. Then must you speak
Of one that loved not wisely but too well;
Of one not easily jealous, but, being wrought,
Perplex'd in the extreme; of one whose hand,
Like the base Indian, threw a pearl away
Richer than all his tribe; of one whose subdued eyes,
Albeit unused to the melting mood,
Drop tears as fast as the Arabian trees
Their medicinal gum. Set you down this;
And say besides, that in Aleppo once,
Where a malignant and a turban'd Turk
Beat a Venetian and traduced the state,
I took by the throat the circumcised dog
And smote him, thus. *Stabs himself.*

LODOVICO: O bloody period!

GRATIANO: All that's spoke is marr'd.

OTHELLO: I kiss'd thee ere I kill'd thee. No way but this,
Killing myself, to die upon a kiss.
   Falls on the Bed, and Dies.

CASSIO: This did I fear, but thought he had no weapon;
For he was great of heart.

LODOVICO: *To Iago.* O Spartan dog,
More fell than anguish, hunger, or the sea!
Look on the tragic loading of this bed;
This is thy work. The object poisons sight;
Let it be hid. Gratiano, keep the house,
And seize upon the fortunes of the Moor,
For they succeed on you. To you, Lord Governor,
Remains the censure of this hellish villain,
The time, the place, the torture. O, enforce it!
Myself will straight aboard, and to the state
This heavy act with heavy heart relate. *Exeunt.*

END

King Lear

Dramatis Personae

LEAR, King of Britain.
KING OF FRANCE.
DUKE OF BURGUNDY.
DUKE OF CORNWALL.
DUKE OF ALBANY.
EARL OF KENT.
EARL OF GLOUCESTER.
EDGAR, son of Gloucester.
EDMUND, bastard son to Gloucester.
CURAN, a courtier.
OLD MAN, tenant to Gloucester.
DOCTOR.
LEAR'S FOOL.
OSWALD, steward to Goneril.
A CAPTAIN UNDER EDMUND'S COMMAND.
GENTLEMEN
A Herald.
SERVANTS TO CORNWALL.
GONERIL, daughter to Lear.
REGAN, daughter to Lear.
CORDELIA, daughter to Lear.
Knights attending on Lear, Officers, Messengers, Soldiers, Attendants.

SCENE: Britain.

ACT I. SCENE I. King Lear's Palace.

Enter Kent, Gloucester, and Edmund. Kent and Glouceste Converse. Edmund Stands Back.

KENT: I thought the King had more affected the Duke of Albany than Cornwall.

GLOUCESTER: It did always seem so to us; but now, in the division of the kingdom, it appears not which of the Dukes he values most, for equalities are so weigh'd that curiosity in neither can make choice of either's moiety.

KENT: Is not this your son, my lord?

GLOUCESTER: His breeding, sir, hath been at my charge. I have so often blush'd to acknowledge him that now I am braz'd to't.

KENT: I cannot conceive you.

GLOUCESTER: Sir, this young fellow's mother could; whereupon she grew round-womb'd, and had indeed, sir, a son for her cradle ere she had a husband for her bed. Do you smell a fault?

KENT: I cannot wish the fault undone, the issue of it being so proper.

GLOUCESTER: But I have, sir, a son by order of law, some year elder than this, who yet is no dearer in my account. Though this knave came something saucily into the world before he was sent for, yet was his mother fair, there was good sport at his making, and the whoreson must be acknowledged.- Do you know this noble gentleman, Edmund?

EDMUND: *Comes Forward* No, my lord.

GLOUCESTER: My Lord of Kent. Remember him hereafter as my honourable friend.

EDMUND: My services to your lordship.

KENT: I must love you, and sue to know you better.

EDMUND: Sir, I shall study deserving.

GLOUCESTER: He hath been out nine years, and away he shall again.
Sound a Sennet.
The King is coming.
Enter One Bearing a Coronet; Then Lear; Then the Dukes of Albany and Cornwall; Next, Goneril, Regan, Cordelia, with Followers.

LEAR: Attend the lords of France and Burgundy, Gloucester.

GLOUCESTER: I shall, my liege.
Exeunt Gloucester and Edmund.

LEAR: Meantime we shall express our darker purpose.
Give me the map there. Know we have divided
In three our kingdom; and 'tis our fast intent
To shake all cares and business from our age,
Conferring them on younger strengths while we
Unburthen'd crawl toward death. Our son of Cornwall,
And you, our no less loving son of Albany,
We have this hour a constant will to publish
Our daughters' several dowers, that future strife
May be prevented now. The princes, France and Burgundy,
Great rivals in our youngest daughter's love,
Long in our court have made their amorous sojourn,
And here are to be answer'd. Tell me, my daughters
(Since now we will divest us both of rule,
Interest of territory, cares of state),
Which of you shall we say doth love us most?
That we our largest bounty may extend

Where nature doth with merit challenge. Goneril,
Our eldest-born, speak first.

GONERIL: Sir, I love you more than words can wield the matter;
Dearer than eyesight, space, and liberty;
Beyond what can be valued, rich or rare;
No less than life, with grace, health, beauty, honour;
As much as child e'er lov'd, or father found;
A love that makes breath poor, and speech unable.
Beyond all manner of so much I love you.

CORDELIA: *Aside* What shall Cordelia speak? Love, and be silent.

LEAR: Of all these bounds, even from this line to this,
With shadowy forests and with champains rich'd,
With plenteous rivers and wide-skirted meads,
We make thee lady. To thine and Albany's issue
Be this perpetual.- What says our second daughter,
Our dearest Regan, wife to Cornwall? Speak.

REGAN: Sir, I am made
Of the selfsame metal that my sister is,
And prize me at her worth. In my true heart
I find she names my very deed of love;
Only she comes too short, that I profess
Myself an enemy to all other joys
Which the most precious square of sense possesses,
And find I am alone felicitate
In your dear Highness' love.

CORDELIA: *Aside* Then poor Cordelia!
And yet not so; since I am sure my love's
More richer than my tongue.

LEAR: To thee and thine hereditary ever
Remain this ample third of our fair kingdom,
No less in space, validity, and pleasure

Than that conferr'd on Goneril.- Now, our joy,
Although the last, not least; to whose young love
The vines of France and milk of Burgundy
Strive to be interest; what can you say to draw
A third more opulent than your sisters? Speak.

CORDELIA: Nothing, my lord.

LEAR: Nothing?

CORDELIA: Nothing.

LEAR: Nothing can come of nothing. Speak again.

CORDELIA: Unhappy that I am, I cannot heave
My heart into my mouth. I love your Majesty
According to my bond; no more nor less.

LEAR: How, how, Cordelia? Mend your speech a little,
Lest it may mar your fortunes.

CORDELIA: Good my lord,
You have begot me, bred me, lov'd me; I
Return those duties back as are right fit,
Obey you, love you, and most honour you.
Why have my sisters husbands, if they say
They love you all? Haply, when I shall wed,
That lord whose hand must take my plight shall carry
Half my love with him, half my care and duty.
Sure I shall never marry like my sisters,
To love my father all.

LEAR: But goes thy heart with this?

CORDELIA: Ay, good my lord.

LEAR: So young, and so untender?

CORDELIA: So young, my lord, and true.

LEAR: Let it be so! thy truth then be thy dower!
For, by the sacred radiance of the sun,
The mysteries of Hecate and the night;
By all the operation of the orbs
From whom we do exist and cease to be;
Here I disclaim all my paternal care,
Propinquity and property of blood,
And as a stranger to my heart and me
Hold thee from this for ever. The barbarous Scythian,
Or he that makes his generation messes
To gorge his appetite, shall to my bosom
Be as well neighbour'd, pitied, and reliev'd,
As thou my sometime daughter.

KENT: Good my liege-

LEAR: Peace, Kent!
Come not between the dragon and his wrath.
I lov'd her most, and thought to set my rest
On her kind nursery.- Hence and avoid my sight!-
So be my grave my peace as here I give
Her father's heart from her! Call France! Who stirs?
Call Burgundy! Cornwall and Albany,
With my two daughters' dowers digest this third;
Let pride, which she calls plainness, marry her.
I do invest you jointly in my power,
Preeminence, and all the large effects
That troop with majesty. Ourself, by monthly course,
With reservation of an hundred knights,
By you to be sustain'd, shall our abode
Make with you by due turns. Only we still retain
The name, and all th' additions to a king. The sway,
Revenue, execution of the rest,
Beloved sons, be yours; which to confirm,
This coronet part betwixt you.

William Shakespeare

KENT: Royal Lear,
Whom I have ever honour'd as my king,
Lov'd as my father, as my master follow'd,
As my great patron thought on in my prayers-

LEAR: The bow is bent and drawn; make from the shaft.

KENT: Let it fall rather, though the fork invade
The region of my heart! Be Kent unmannerly
When Lear is mad. What wouldst thou do, old man?
Think'st thou that duty shall have dread to speak
When power to flattery bows? To plainness honour's bound
When majesty falls to folly. Reverse thy doom;
And in thy best consideration check
This hideous rashness. Answer my life my judgment,
Thy youngest daughter does not love thee least,
Nor are those empty-hearted whose low sound
Reverbs no hollowness.

LEAR: Kent, on thy life, no more!

KENT: My life I never held but as a pawn
To wage against thine enemies; nor fear to lose it,
Thy safety being the motive.

LEAR: Out of my sight!

KENT: See better, Lear, and let me still remain
The true blank of thine eye.

LEAR: Now by Apollo-

KENT: Now by Apollo, King,
Thou swear'st thy gods in vain.

LEAR: O vassal! miscreant!
Lays His Hand on His Sword.

ALBANY: Corn. Dear sir, forbear!

KENT: Do!
Kill thy physician, and the fee bestow
Upon the foul disease. Revoke thy gift,
Or, whilst I can vent clamour from my throat,
I'll tell thee thou dost evil.

LEAR: Hear me, recreant!
On thine allegiance, hear me!
Since thou hast sought to make us break our vow-
Which we durst never yet- and with strain'd pride
To come between our sentence and our power,-
Which nor our nature nor our place can bear,-
Our potency made good, take thy reward.
Five days we do allot thee for provision
To shield thee from diseases of the world,
And on the sixth to turn thy hated back
Upon our kingdom. If, on the tenth day following,
Thy banish'd trunk be found in our dominions,
The moment is thy death. Away! By Jupiter,
This shall not be revok'd.

KENT: Fare thee well, King. Since thus thou wilt appear,
Freedom lives hence, and banishment is here.
To Cordelia The gods to their dear shelter take thee, maid,
That justly think'st and hast most rightly said!
To Regan and Goneril And your large speeches may your deeds approve,
That good effects may spring from words of love.
Thus Kent, O princes, bids you all adieu;
He'll shape his old course in a country new.
   Exit.
   Flourish. Enter Gloucester, with France and Burgundy; Attendants.

GLOUCESTER: Here's France and Burgundy, my noble lord.

LEAR: My Lord of Burgundy,
We first address toward you, who with this king
Hath rivall'd for our daughter. What in the least
Will you require in present dower with her,
Or cease your quest of love?

BURGUNDY: Most royal Majesty,
I crave no more than hath your Highness offer'd,
Nor will you tender less.

LEAR: Right noble Burgundy,
When she was dear to us, we did hold her so;
But now her price is fall'n. Sir, there she stands.
If aught within that little seeming substance,
Or all of it, with our displeasure piec'd,
And nothing more, may fitly like your Grace,
She's there, and she is yours.

BURGUNDY: I know no answer.

LEAR: Will you, with those infirmities she owes,
Unfriended, new adopted to our hate,
Dow'r'd with our curse, and stranger'd with our oath,
Take her, or leave her?

BURGUNDY: Pardon me, royal sir.
Election makes not up on such conditions.

LEAR: Then leave her, sir; for, by the pow'r that made me,
I tell you all her wealth. *To France* For you, great King,
I would not from your love make such a stray
To match you where I hate; therefore beseech you
T' avert your liking a more worthier way
Than on a wretch whom nature is asham'd
Almost t' acknowledge hers.

KING OF FRANCE: This is most strange,

That she that even but now was your best object,
The argument of your praise, balm of your age,
Most best, most dearest, should in this trice of time
Commit a thing so monstrous to dismantle
So many folds of favour. Sure her offence
Must be of such unnatural degree
That monsters it, or your fore-vouch'd affection
Fall'n into taint; which to believe of her
Must be a faith that reason without miracle
Should never plant in me.

CORDELIA: I yet beseech your Majesty,
If for I want that glib and oily art
To speak and purpose not, since what I well intend,
I'll do't before I speak- that you make known
It is no vicious blot, murther, or foulness,
No unchaste action or dishonoured step,
That hath depriv'd me of your grace and favour;
But even for want of that for which I am richer-
A still-soliciting eye, and such a tongue
As I am glad I have not, though not to have it
Hath lost me in your liking.

LEAR: Better thou
Hadst not been born than not t' have pleas'd me better.

KING OF FRANCE: Is it but this- a tardiness in nature
Which often leaves the history unspoke
That it intends to do? My Lord of Burgundy,
What say you to the lady? Love's not love
When it is mingled with regards that stands
Aloof from th' entire point. Will you have her?
She is herself a dowry.

BURGUNDY: Royal Lear,
Give but that portion which yourself propos'd,
And here I take Cordelia by the hand,
Duchess of Burgundy.

LEAR: Nothing! I have sworn; I am firm.

BURGUNDY: I am sorry then you have so lost a father
That you must lose a husband.

CORDELIA: Peace be with Burgundy!
Since that respects of fortune are his love,
I shall not be his wife.

KING OF FRANCE: Fairest Cordelia, that art most rich, being poor;
Most choice, forsaken; and most lov'd, despis'd!
Thee and thy virtues here I seize upon.
Be it lawful I take up what's cast away.
Gods, gods! 'tis strange that from their cold'st neglect
My love should kindle to inflam'd respect.
Thy dow'rless daughter, King, thrown to my chance,
Is queen of us, of ours, and our fair France.
Not all the dukes in wat'rish Burgundy
Can buy this unpriz'd precious maid of me.
Bid them farewell, Cordelia, though unkind.
Thou losest here, a better where to find.

LEAR: Thou hast her, France; let her be thine; for we
Have no such daughter, nor shall ever see
That face of hers again. Therefore be gone
Without our grace, our love, our benison.
Come, noble Burgundy.
   Flourish. Exeunt Lear, Burgundy, Cornwall, Albany, Gloucester, and Attendants.

KING OF FRANCE: Bid farewell to your sisters.

CORDELIA: The jewels of our father, with wash'd eyes
Cordelia leaves you. I know you what you are;
And, like a sister, am most loath to call
Your faults as they are nam'd. Use well our father.
To your professed bosoms I commit him;

But yet, alas, stood I within his grace,
I would prefer him to a better place!
So farewell to you both.

GONERIL: Prescribe not us our duties.

REGAN: Let your study
Be to content your lord, who hath receiv'd you
At fortune's alms. You have obedience scanted,
And well are worth the want that you have wanted.

CORDELIA: Time shall unfold what plighted cunning hides.
Who cover faults, at last shame them derides.
Well may you prosper!

KING OF FRANCE: Come, my fair Cordelia.
 Exeunt France and Cordelia.

GONERIL: Sister, it is not little I have to say of what most nearly appertains to us both. I think our father will hence to-night.

REGAN: That's most certain, and with you; next month with us.

GONERIL: You see how full of changes his age is. The observation we have made of it hath not been little. He always lov'd our sister most, and with what poor judgment he hath now cast her off appears too grossly.

REGAN: 'Tis the infirmity of his age; yet he hath ever but slenderly known himself.

GONERIL: The best and soundest of his time hath been but rash; then must we look to receive from his age, not alone the imperfections of long-ingraffed condition, but therewithal the unruly waywardness that infirm and choleric years bring with them.

REGAN: Such unconstant starts are we like to have from him as this of Kent's banishment.

GONERIL: There is further compliment of leave-taking between France and him. Pray you let's hit together. If our father carry authority with such dispositions as he bears, this last surrender of his will but offend us.

REGAN: We shall further think on't.

GONERIL: We must do something, and i' th' heat.
Exeunt.

ACT I. SCENE II. The Earl of Gloucester's Castle.
Enter Edmund the Bastard Solus, with a Letter.

EDMUND: Thou, Nature, art my goddess; to thy law
My services are bound. Wherefore should I
Stand in the plague of custom, and permit
The curiosity of nations to deprive me,
For that I am some twelve or fourteen moonshines
Lag of a brother? Why bastard? wherefore base?
When my dimensions are as well compact,
My mind as generous, and my shape as true,
As honest madam's issue? Why brand they us
With base? with baseness? bastardy? base, base?
Who, in the lusty stealth of nature, take
More composition and fierce quality
Than doth, within a dull, stale, tired bed,
Go to th' creating a whole tribe of fops
Got 'tween asleep and wake? Well then,
Legitimate Edgar, I must have your land.
Our father's love is to the bastard Edmund
As to th' legitimate. Fine word- 'legitimate'!
Well, my legitimate, if this letter speed,
And my invention thrive, Edmund the base
Shall top th' legitimate. I grow; I prosper.
Now, gods, stand up for bastards!
Enter Gloucester.

GLOUCESTER: Kent banish'd thus? and France in choler parted?
And the King gone to-night? subscrib'd his pow'r?
Confin'd to exhibition? All this done
Upon the gad? Edmund, how now? What news?

EDMUND: So please your lordship, none.
   Puts up the Letter.

GLOUCESTER: Why so earnestly seek you to put up that letter?

EDMUND: I know no news, my lord.

GLOUCESTER: What paper were you reading?

EDMUND: Nothing, my lord.

GLOUCESTER: No? What needed then that terrible dispatch of it into your pocket? The quality of nothing hath not such need to hide itself. Let's see. Come, if it be nothing, I shall not need spectacles.

EDMUND: I beseech you, sir, pardon me. It is a letter from my brother that I have not all o'er-read; and for so much as I have perus'd, I find it not fit for your o'erlooking.

GLOUCESTER: Give me the letter, sir.

EDMUND: I shall offend, either to detain or give it. The contents, as in part I understand them, are to blame.

GLOUCESTER: Let's see, let's see!

EDMUND: I hope, for my brother's justification, he wrote this but as an essay or taste of my virtue.

GLOUCESTER: *reads* 'This policy and reverence of age makes the world bitter to the best of our times; keeps our fortunes from us till our oldness cannot relish them. I begin to find an idle and fond bondage in the oppression of aged tyranny, who sways, not as it hath power, but as it is suffer'd. Come to me, that of this I may speak more. If our father would sleep till I wak'd him, you should enjoy half his revenue for ever, and live the beloved of your brother, 'Edgar.'

Hum! Conspiracy? 'Sleep till I wak'd him, you should enjoy half his revenue.' My son Edgar! Had he a hand to write this? a heart and brain to breed it in? When came this to you? Who brought it?

EDMUND: It was not brought me, my lord: there's the cunning of it. I found it thrown in at the casement of my closet.

GLOUCESTER: You know the character to be your brother's?

EDMUND: If the matter were good, my lord, I durst swear it were his; but in respect of that, I would fain think it were not.

GLOUCESTER: It is his.

EDMUND: It is his hand, my lord; but I hope his heart is not in the contents.

GLOUCESTER: Hath he never before sounded you in this business?

EDMUND: Never, my lord. But I have heard him oft maintain it to be fit that, sons at perfect age, and fathers declining, the father should be as ward to the son, and the son manage his revenue.

GLOUCESTER: O villain, villain! His very opinion in the letter! Abhorred villain! Unnatural, detested, brutish villain! worse than brutish! Go, sirrah, seek him. I'll apprehend him. Abominable villain! Where is he?

EDMUND: I do not well know, my lord. If it shall please you to suspend your indignation against my brother till you can derive from him better testimony of his intent, you should run a certain course; where, if you violently proceed against him, mistaking his purpose, it would make a great gap in your own honour and shake in pieces the heart of his obedience. I dare pawn down my life for him that he hath writ this to feel my affection to your honour, and to no other pretence of danger.

GLOUCESTER: Think you so?

EDMUND: If your honour judge it meet, I will place you where you shall hear us confer of this and by an auricular assurance have your satisfaction, and that without any further delay than this very evening.

GLOUCESTER: He cannot be such a monster.

EDMUND: Nor is not, sure.

GLOUCESTER: To his father, that so tenderly and entirely loves him. Heaven and earth! Edmund, seek him out; wind me into him, I pray you; frame the business after your own wisdom. I would unstate myself to be in a due resolution.

EDMUND: I will seek him, sir, presently; convey the business as I shall find means, and acquaint you withal.

GLOUCESTER: These late eclipses in the sun and moon portend no good to us. Though the wisdom of nature can reason it thus and thus, yet nature finds itself scourg'd by the sequent effects. Love cools, friendship falls off, brothers divide. In cities, mutinies; in countries, discord; in palaces, treason; and the bond crack'd 'twixt son and father. This villain of mine comes under the prediction; there's son against father: the King falls from bias of nature; there's father against child. We have seen the best of our time. Machinations, hollowness, treachery, and all ruinous disorders follow us disquietly to our graves. Find out this villain, Edmund; it shall lose thee nothing; do it carefully. And the noble and true-hearted Kent banish'd! his offence, honesty! 'Tis strange.
   Exit.

EDMUND: This is the excellent foppery of the world, that, when we are sick in fortune, often the surfeit of our own behaviour, we make guilty of our disasters the sun, the moon, and the stars; as if we were villains on necessity; fools by heavenly compulsion; knaves, thieves, and treachers by spherical pre-dominance; drunkards, liars, and adulterers by an enforc'd obedience of planetary influence; and all that we are evil in, by a divine thrusting on. An admirable evasion of whore-master man, to lay his goatish disposition to the charge of a star! My father compounded with my mother under the Dragon's Tail, and my nativity was under Ursa Major, so that it follows I am rough and lecherous. Fut! I should have been that I am, had the maidenliest star in the firmament twinkled on my bastardizing. Edgar-
Enter Edgar.
and pat! he comes, like the catastrophe of the old comedy. My cue is villainous melancholy, with a sigh like Tom o' Bedlam. O, these eclipses do portend these divisions! Fa, sol, la, mi.

EDGAR: How now, brother Edmund? What serious contemplation are you in?

EDMUND: I am thinking, brother, of a prediction I read this other day, what should follow these eclipses.

EDGAR: Do you busy yourself with that?

EDMUND: I promise you, the effects he writes of succeed unhappily: as of unnaturalness between the child and the parent; death, dearth, dissolutions of ancient amities; divisions in state, menaces and maledictions against king and nobles; needless diffidences, banishment of friends, dissipation of cohorts, nuptial breaches, and I know not what.

EDGAR: How long have you been a sectary astronomical?

EDMUND: Come, come! When saw you my father last?

EDGAR: The night gone by.

EDMUND: Spake you with him?

EDGAR: Ay, two hours together.

EDMUND: Parted you in good terms? Found you no displeasure in him by word or countenance

EDGAR: None at all.

EDMUND: Bethink yourself wherein you may have offended him; and at my entreaty forbear his presence until some little time hath qualified the heat of his displeasure, which at this instant so rageth in him that with the mischief of your person it would scarcely allay.

EDGAR: Some villain hath done me wrong.

EDMUND: That's my fear. I pray you have a continent forbearance till the speed of his rage goes slower; and, as I say, retire with me to my lodging, from whence I will fitly bring you to hear my lord speak. Pray ye, go! There's my key. If you do stir abroad, go arm'd.

EDGAR: Arm'd, brother?

EDMUND: Brother, I advise you to the best. Go arm'd. I am no honest man if there be any good meaning toward you. I have told you what I have seen and heard; but faintly, nothing like the image and horror of it. Pray you, away!

EDGAR: Shall I hear from you anon?

EDMUND: I do serve you in this business.
  Exit Edgar.
A credulous father! and a brother noble,
Whose nature is so far from doing harms
That he suspects none; on whose foolish honesty

My practices ride easy! I see the business.
Let me, if not by birth, have lands by wit;
All with me's meet that I can fashion fit.
   Exit.

ACT I. SCENE III. The Duke of Albany's Palace.
Enter Goneril and Her Steward Oswald.

GONERIL: Did my father strike my gentleman for chiding of his fool?

OSWALD: Ay, madam.

GONERIL: By day and night, he wrongs me! Every hour
He flashes into one gross crime or other
That sets us all at odds. I'll not endure it.
His knights grow riotous, and himself upbraids us
On every trifle. When he returns from hunting,
I will not speak with him. Say I am sick.
If you come slack of former services,
You shall do well; the fault of it I'll answer.
   Horns Within.

OSWALD: He's coming, madam; I hear him.

GONERIL: Put on what weary negligence you please,
You and your fellows. I'd have it come to question.
If he distaste it, let him to our sister,
Whose mind and mine I know in that are one,
Not to be overrul'd. Idle old man,
That still would manage those authorities
That he hath given away! Now, by my life,
Old fools are babes again, and must be us'd
With checks as flatteries, when they are seen abus'd.
Remember what I have said.

OSWALD: Very well, madam.

GONERIL: And let his knights have colder looks among you.
What grows of it, no matter. Advise your fellows so.
I would breed from hence occasions, and I shall,
That I may speak. I'll write straight to my sister
To hold my very course. Prepare for dinner.
   Exeunt.

ACT I. SCENE IV. The Duke of Albany's Palace.
Enter Kent, Disguised.

KENT: If but as well I other accents borrow,
That can my speech defuse, my good intent
May carry through itself to that full issue
For which I raz'd my likeness. Now, banish'd Kent,
If thou canst serve where thou dost stand condemn'd,
So may it come, thy master, whom thou lov'st,
Shall find thee full of labours.
   Horns within. Enter Lear, Knights, and Attendants.

LEAR: Let me not stay a jot for dinner; go get it ready.
   Exit an Attendant.
How now? What art thou?

KENT: A man, sir.

LEAR: What dost thou profess? What wouldst thou with us?

KENT: I do profess to be no less than I seem, to serve him truly that will put me in trust, to love him that is honest, to converse with him that is wise and says little, to fear judgment, to fight when I cannot choose, and to eat no fish.

LEAR: What art thou?

KENT: A very honest-hearted fellow, and as poor as the King.

LEAR: If thou be'st as poor for a subject as he's for a king, thou art poor enough. What wouldst thou?

KENT: Service.

LEAR: Who wouldst thou serve?

KENT: You.

LEAR: Dost thou know me, fellow?

KENT: No, sir; but you have that in your countenance which I would fain call master.

LEAR: What's that?

KENT: Authority.

LEAR: What services canst thou do?

KENT: I can keep honest counsel, ride, run, mar a curious tale in telling it and deliver a plain message bluntly. That which ordinary men are fit for, I am qualified in, and the best of me is diligence.

LEAR: How old art thou?

KENT: Not so young, sir, to love a woman for singing, nor so old to dote on her for anything. I have years on my back forty-eight.

LEAR: Follow me; thou shalt serve me. If I like thee no worse after dinner, I will not part from thee yet. Dinner, ho, dinner! Where's my knave? my fool? Go you and call my fool hither.
   Exit an Attendant.
   Enter Oswald the Steward.
You, you, sirrah, where's my daughter?

OSWALD: So please you—

Exit.

LEAR: What says the fellow there? Call the clotpoll back.
Exit a Knight. Where's my fool, ho? I think the world's asleep.
   Enter Knight
How now? Where's that mongrel?

KNIGHT: He says, my lord, your daughter is not well.

LEAR: Why came not the slave back to me when I call'd him?

KNIGHT: Sir, he answered me in the roundest manner, he would not.

LEAR: He would not?

KNIGHT: My lord, I know not what the matter is; but to my judgment your Highness is not entertain'd with that ceremonious affection as you were wont. There's a great abatement of kindness appears as well in the general dependants as in the Duke himself also and your daughter.

LEAR: Ha! say'st thou so?

KNIGHT: I beseech you pardon me, my lord, if I be mistaken; for my duty cannot be silent when I think your Highness wrong'd.

LEAR: Thou but rememb'rest me of mine own conception. I have perceived a most faint neglect of late, which I have rather blamed as mine own jealous curiosity than as a very pretence and purpose of unkindness. I will look further into't. But where's my fool? I have not seen him this two days.

KNIGHT: Since my young lady's going into France, sir, the fool hath much pined away.

LEAR: No more of that; I have noted it well. Go you and tell my daughter I would speak with her.

Exit Knight.
Go you, call hither my fool.
Exit an Attendant.
Enter Oswald the Steward.
O, you, sir, you! Come you hither, sir. Who am I, sir?

OSWALD: My lady's father.

LEAR: 'My lady's father'? My lord's knave! You whoreson dog! you slave! you cur!

OSWALD: I am none of these, my lord; I beseech your pardon.

LEAR: Do you bandy looks with me, you rascal?
Strikes Him.

OSWALD: I'll not be strucken, my lord.

KENT: Nor tripp'd neither, you base football player?
Trips up His Heels.

LEAR: I thank thee, fellow. Thou serv'st me, and I'll love thee.

KENT: Come, sir, arise, away! I'll teach you differences. Away, away! If you will measure your lubber's length again, tarry; but away! Go to! Have you wisdom? So.
Pushes Him Out.

LEAR: Now, my friendly knave, I thank thee. There's earnest of thy service.
Gives Money.
Enter Fool.

FOOL: Let me hire him too. Here's my coxcomb.
Offers Kent His Cap.

LEAR: How now, my pretty knave? How dost thou?

FOOL: Sirrah, you were best take my coxcomb.

KENT: Why, fool?

FOOL: Why? For taking one's part that's out of favour. Nay, an thou canst not smile as the wind sits, thou'lt catch cold shortly. There, take my coxcomb! Why, this fellow hath banish'd two on's daughters, and did the third a blessing against his will. If thou follow him, thou must needs wear my coxcomb.- How now, nuncle? Would I had two coxcombs and two daughters!

LEAR: Why, my boy?

FOOL: If I gave them all my living, I'ld keep my coxcombs myself. There's mine! beg another of thy daughters.

LEAR: Take heed, sirrah- the whip.

FOOL: Truth's a dog must to kennel; he must be whipp'd out, when Lady the brach may stand by th' fire and stink.

LEAR: A pestilent gall to me!

FOOL: Sirrah, I'll teach thee a speech.

LEAR: Do.

FOOL: Mark it, nuncle.
　　Have more than thou showest,
　　Speak less than thou knowest,
　　Lend less than thou owest,
　　Ride more than thou goest,
　　Learn more than thou trowest,
　　Set less than thou throwest;
　　Leave thy drink and thy whore,
　　And keep in-a-door,
　　And thou shalt have more

Than two tens to a score.

KENT: This is nothing, fool.

FOOL: Then 'tis like the breath of an unfeed lawyer- you gave me nothing for't. Can you make no use of nothing, nuncle?

LEAR: Why, no, boy. Nothing can be made out of nothing.

FOOL: *To Kent* Prithee tell him, so much the rent of his land comes to. He will not believe a fool.

LEAR: A bitter fool!

FOOL: Dost thou know the difference, my boy, between a bitter fool and a sweet fool?

LEAR: No, lad; teach me.

FOOL: That lord that counsell'd thee
    To give away thy land,
  Come place him here by me-
    Do thou for him stand.
  The sweet and bitter fool
    Will presently appear;
  The one in motley here,
    The other found out there.

LEAR: Dost thou call me fool, boy?

FOOL: All thy other titles thou hast given away; that thou wast born with.

KENT: This is not altogether fool, my lord.

FOOL: No, faith; lords and great men will not let me. If I had a monopoly out, they would have part on't. And ladies too, they will not let me have all the fool to myself; they'll be snatching. Give me an egg, nuncle, and I'll give thee two crowns.

LEAR: What two crowns shall they be?

FOOL: Why, after I have cut the egg i' th' middle and eat up the meat, the two crowns of the egg. When thou clovest thy crown i' th' middle and gav'st away both parts, thou bor'st thine ass on thy back o'er the dirt. Thou hadst little wit in thy bald crown when thou gav'st thy golden one away. If I speak like myself in this, let him be whipp'd that first finds it so.
Sings Fools had ne'er less grace in a year,
    For wise men are grown foppish;
   They know not how their wits to wear,
    Their manners are so apish.

LEAR: When were you wont to be so full of songs, sirrah?

FOOL: I have us'd it, nuncle, ever since thou mad'st thy daughters thy mother; for when thou gav'st them the rod, and put'st down thine own breeches,
Sings Then they for sudden joy did weep,
    And I for sorrow sung,
   That such a king should play bo-peep
    And go the fools among.
Prithee, nuncle, keep a schoolmaster that can teach thy fool to lie. I would fain learn to lie.

LEAR: An you lie, sirrah, we'll have you whipp'd.

FOOL: I marvel what kin thou and thy daughters are. They'll have me whipp'd for speaking true; thou'lt have me whipp'd for lying; and sometimes I am whipp'd for holding my peace. I had rather be any kind o' thing than a fool! And yet I would not be thee, nuncle. Thou hast pared thy wit o' both sides and left nothing i' th' middle. Here comes one o' the parings.
   Enter Goneril.

LEAR: How now, daughter? What makes that frontlet on? Methinks you are too much o' late i' th' frown.

FOOL: Thou wast a pretty fellow when thou hadst no need to care for her frowning. Now thou art an O without a figure. I am better than thou art now: I am a fool, thou art nothing.
To Goneril Yes, forsooth, I will hold my tongue. So your face bids me, though you say nothing. Mum, mum!

> He that keeps nor crust nor crum,
> Weary of all, shall want some.-

Points at Lear That's a sheal'd peascod.

GONERIL: Not only, sir, this your all-licens'd fool,
But other of your insolent retinue
Do hourly carp and quarrel, breaking forth
In rank and not-to-be-endured riots. Sir,
I had thought, by making this well known unto you,
To have found a safe redress, but now grow fearful,
By what yourself, too, late have spoke and done,
That you protect this course, and put it on
By your allowance; which if you should, the fault
Would not scape censure, nor the redresses sleep,
Which, in the tender of a wholesome weal,
Might in their working do you that offence
Which else were shame, that then necessity
Must call discreet proceeding.

FOOL: For you know, nuncle,
> The hedge-sparrow fed the cuckoo so long
> That it had it head bit off by it young.

So out went the candle, and we were left darkling.

LEAR: Are you our daughter?

GONERIL: Come, sir,
I would you would make use of that good wisdom
Whereof I know you are fraught, and put away

These dispositions that of late transform you
From what you rightly are.

FOOL: May not an ass know when the cart draws the horse?
Whoop, Jug, I love thee!

LEAR: Doth any here know me? This is not Lear.
Doth Lear walk thus? speak thus? Where are his eyes?
Either his notion weakens, his discernings
Are lethargied- Ha! waking? 'Tis not so!
Who is it that can tell me who I am?

FOOL: Lear's shadow.

LEAR: I would learn that; for, by the marks of sovereignty,
Knowledge, and reason, I should be false persuaded
I had daughters.

FOOL: Which they will make an obedient father.

LEAR: Your name, fair gentlewoman?

GONERIL: This admiration, sir, is much o' th' savour
Of other your new pranks. I do beseech you
To understand my purposes aright.
As you are old and reverend, you should be wise.
Here do you keep a hundred knights and squires;
Men so disorder'd, so debosh'd, and bold
That this our court, infected with their manners,
Shows like a riotous inn. Epicurism and lust
Make it more like a tavern or a brothel
Than a grac'd palace. The shame itself doth speak
For instant remedy. Be then desir'd
By her that else will take the thing she begs
A little to disquantity your train,
And the remainder that shall still depend
To be such men as may besort your age,

Which know themselves, and you.

LEAR: Darkness and devils!
Saddle my horses! Call my train together!
Degenerate bastard, I'll not trouble thee;
Yet have I left a daughter.

GONERIL: You strike my people, and your disorder'd rabble
Make servants of their betters.
   Enter Albany.

LEAR: Woe that too late repents!- O, sir, are you come?
Is it your will? Speak, sir!- Prepare my horses.
Ingratitude, thou marble-hearted fiend,
More hideous when thou show'st thee in a child
Than the sea-monster!

ALBANY: Pray, sir, be patient.

LEAR: *To Goneril* Detested kite, thou liest!
My train are men of choice and rarest parts,
That all particulars of duty know
And in the most exact regard support
The worships of their name.- O most small fault,
How ugly didst thou in Cordelia show!
Which, like an engine, wrench'd my frame of nature
From the fix'd place; drew from my heart all love
And added to the gall. O Lear, Lear, Lear!
Beat at this gate that let thy folly in
   Strikes His Head.
And thy dear judgment out! Go, go, my people.

ALBANY: My lord, I am guiltless, as I am ignorant
Of what hath mov'd you.

LEAR: It may be so, my lord.
Hear, Nature, hear! dear goddess, hear!

Suspend thy purpose, if thou didst intend
To make this creature fruitful.
Into her womb convey sterility;
Dry up in her the organs of increase;
And from her derogate body never spring
A babe to honour her! If she must teem,
Create her child of spleen, that it may live
And be a thwart disnatur'd torment to her.
Let it stamp wrinkles in her brow of youth,
With cadent tears fret channels in her cheeks,
Turn all her mother's pains and benefits
To laughter and contempt, that she may feel
How sharper than a serpent's tooth it is
To have a thankless child! Away, away!
   Exit.

ALBANY: Now, gods that we adore, whereof comes this?

GONERIL: Never afflict yourself to know the cause;
But let his disposition have that scope
That dotage gives it.
   Enter Lear.

LEAR: What, fifty of my followers at a clap?
Within a fortnight?

ALBANY: What's the matter, sir?

LEAR: I'll tell thee. *To Goneril* Life and death! I am asham'd
That thou hast power to shake my manhood thus;
That these hot tears, which break from me perforce,
Should make thee worth them. Blasts and fogs upon thee!
Th' untented woundings of a father's curse
Pierce every sense about thee!- Old fond eyes,
Beweep this cause again, I'll pluck ye out,
And cast you, with the waters that you lose,
To temper clay. Yea, is it come to this?
Let it be so. Yet have I left a daughter,

Who I am sure is kind and comfortable.
When she shall hear this of thee, with her nails
She'll flay thy wolvish visage. Thou shalt find
That I'll resume the shape which thou dost think
I have cast off for ever; thou shalt, I warrant thee.
Exeunt Lear, Kent, and Attendants.

GONERIL: Do you mark that, my lord?

ALBANY: I cannot be so partial, Goneril,
To the great love I bear you -

GONERIL: Pray you, content.- What, Oswald, ho!
To the Fool You, sir, more knave than fool, after your master!

FOOL: Nuncle Lear, nuncle Lear, tarry! Take the fool with thee.
    A fox when one has caught her,
    And such a daughter,
    Should sure to the slaughter,
    If my cap would buy a halter.
    So the fool follows after.
Exit.

GONERIL: This man hath had good counsel! A hundred knights?
'Tis politic and safe to let him keep
At point a hundred knights; yes, that on every dream,
Each buzz, each fancy, each complaint, dislike,
He may enguard his dotage with their pow'rs
And hold our lives in mercy.- Oswald, I say!

ALBANY: Well, you may fear too far.

GONERIL: Safer than trust too far.
Let me still take away the harms I fear,
Not fear still to be taken. I know his heart.
What he hath utter'd I have writ my sister.
If she sustain him and his hundred knights,

When I have show'd th' unfitness—
   Enter Oswald the Steward.
How now, Oswald?
What, have you writ that letter to my sister?

OSWALD: Yes, madam.

GONERIL: Take you some company, and away to horse!
Inform her full of my particular fear,
And thereto add such reasons of your own
As may compact it more. Get you gone,
And hasten your return.
   Exit Oswald.
No, no, my lord!
This milky gentleness and course of yours,
Though I condemn it not, yet, under pardon,
You are much more at task for want of wisdom
Than prais'd for harmful mildness.

ALBANY: How far your eyes may pierce I cannot tell.
Striving to better, oft we mar what's well.

GONERIL: Nay then—

ALBANY: Well, well; th' event.
   Exeunt.

   ACT I. SCENE V. *Court Before the Duke of Albany's Palace.*
Enter Lear, Kent, and Fool.

LEAR: Go you before to Gloucester with these letters. Acquaint my daughter no further with anything you know than comes from her demand out of the letter. If your diligence be not speedy, I shall be there afore you.

KENT: I will not sleep, my lord, till I have delivered your letter.
   Exit.

FOOL: If a man's brains were in's heels, were't not in danger of kibes?

LEAR: Ay, boy.

FOOL: Then I prithee be merry. Thy wit shall ne'er go slip-shod.

LEAR: Ha, ha, ha!

FOOL: Shalt see thy other daughter will use thee kindly; for though she's as like this as a crab's like an apple, yet I can tell what I can tell.

LEAR: What canst tell, boy?

FOOL: She'll taste as like this as a crab does to a crab. Thou canst tell why one's nose stands i' th' middle on's face?

LEAR: No.

FOOL: Why, to keep one's eyes of either side's nose, that what a man cannot smell out, 'a may spy into.

LEAR: I did her wrong.

FOOL: Canst tell how an oyster makes his shell?

LEAR: No.

FOOL: Nor I neither; but I can tell why a snail has a house.

LEAR: Why?

FOOL: Why, to put's head in; not to give it away to his daughters, and leave his horns without a case.

LEAR: I will forget my nature. So kind a father!- Be my horses ready?

FOOL: Thy asses are gone about 'em. The reason why the seven stars are no moe than seven is a pretty reason.

LEAR: Because they are not eight?

FOOL: Yes indeed. Thou wouldst make a good fool.

LEAR: To tak't again perforce! Monster ingratitude!

FOOL: If thou wert my fool, nuncle, I'ld have thee beaten for being old before thy time.

LEAR: How's that?

FOOL: Thou shouldst not have been old till thou hadst been wise.

LEAR: O, let me not be mad, not mad, sweet heaven!
Keep me in temper; I would not be mad!
 Enter a Gentleman.
How now? Are the horses ready?

GENTLEMEN: Ready, my lord.

LEAR: Come, boy.

FOOL: She that's a maid now, and laughs at my departure,
Shall not be a maid long, unless things be cut shorter
 Exeunt.

ACT II. SCENE I. A Court Within the Castle of the Earl of Gloucester.

Enter Edmund the Bastard and Curan, Meeting.

EDMUND: Save thee, Curan.

CURAN: And you, sir. I have been with your father, and given him notice that the Duke of Cornwall and Regan his Duchess will be here with him this night.

EDMUND: How comes that?

CURAN: Nay, I know not. You have heard of the news abroad- I mean the whisper'd ones, for they are yet but ear-kissing arguments?

EDMUND: Not I. Pray you, what are they?

CURAN: Have you heard of no likely wars toward 'twixt the two Dukes of Cornwall and Albany?

EDMUND: Not a word.

CURAN: You may do, then, in time. Fare you well, sir.
   Exit.

EDMUND: The Duke be here to-night? The better! best!
This weaves itself perforce into my business.
My father hath set guard to take my brother;
And I have one thing, of a queasy question,
Which I must act. Briefness and fortune, work!
Brother, a word! Descend! Brother, I say!
   Enter Edgar.
My father watches. O sir, fly this place!
Intelligence is given where you are hid.
You have now the good advantage of the night.
Have you not spoken 'gainst the Duke of Cornwall?
He's coming hither; now, i' th' night, i' th' haste,
And Regan with him. Have you nothing said
Upon his party 'gainst the Duke of Albany?
Advise yourself.

EDGAR: I am sure on't, not a word.

EDMUND: I hear my father coming. Pardon me!
In cunning I must draw my sword upon you.

Draw, seem to defend yourself; now quit you well.-
Yield! Come before my father. Light, ho, here!
Fly, brother.- Torches, torches!- So farewell.
  Exit Edgar.
Some blood drawn on me would beget opinion
Of my more fierce endeavour. *Stabs His Arm.* I have seen drunkards
Do more than this in sport.- Father, father!-
Stop, stop! No help?
  Enter Gloucester, and Servants with Torches.

GLOUCESTER: Now, Edmund, where's the villain?

EDMUND: Here stood he in the dark, his sharp sword out,
Mumbling of wicked charms, conjuring the moon
To stand 's auspicious mistress.

GLOUCESTER: But where is he?

EDMUND: Look, sir, I bleed.

GLOUCESTER: Where is the villain, Edmund?

EDMUND: Fled this way, sir. When by no means he could-

GLOUCESTER: Pursue him, ho! Go after.
  Exeunt some Servants.
By no means what?

EDMUND: Persuade me to the murther of your lordship;
But that I told him the revenging gods
'Gainst parricides did all their thunders bend;
Spoke with how manifold and strong a bond
The child was bound to th' father- sir, in fine,
Seeing how loathly opposite I stood
To his unnatural purpose, in fell motion
With his prepared sword he charges home
My unprovided body, lanch'd mine arm;

But when he saw my best alarum'd spirits,
Bold in the quarrel's right, rous'd to th' encounter,
Or whether gasted by the noise I made,
Full suddenly he fled.

GLOUCESTER: Let him fly far.
Not in this land shall he remain uncaught;
And found- dispatch. The noble Duke my master,
My worthy arch and patron, comes to-night.
By his authority I will proclaim it
That he which find, him shall deserve our thanks,
Bringing the murderous caitiff to the stake;
He that conceals him, death.

EDMUND: When I dissuaded him from his intent
And found him pight to do it, with curst speech
I threaten'd to discover him. He replied,
'Thou unpossessing bastard, dost thou think,
If I would stand against thee, would the reposal
Of any trust, virtue, or worth in thee
Make thy words faith'd? No. What I should deny
(As this I would; ay, though thou didst produce
My very character), I'ld turn it all
To thy suggestion, plot, and damned practice;
And thou must make a dullard of the world,
If they not thought the profits of my death
Were very pregnant and potential spurs
To make thee seek it.'

GLOUCESTER: Strong and fast'ned villain!
Would he deny his letter? I never got him.
   Tucket Within.
Hark, the Duke's trumpets! I know not why he comes.
All ports I'll bar; the villain shall not scape;
The Duke must grant me that. Besides, his picture
I will send far and near, that all the kingdom
May have due note of him, and of my land,
Loyal and natural boy, I'll work the means

To make thee capable.
   Enter Cornwall, Regan, and Attendants.

CORNWALL: How now, my noble friend? Since I came hither
Which I can call but now. I have heard strange news.

REGAN: If it be true, all vengeance comes too short
Which can pursue th' offender. How dost, my lord?

GLOUCESTER: O madam, my old heart is crack'd, it's crack'd!

REGAN: What, did my father's godson seek your life?
He whom my father nam'd? Your Edgar?

GLOUCESTER: O lady, lady, shame would have it hid!

REGAN: Was he not companion with the riotous knights
That tend upon my father?

GLOUCESTER: I know not, madam. 'Tis too bad, too bad!

EDMUND: Yes, madam, he was of that consort.

REGAN: No marvel then though he were ill affected.
'Tis they have put him on the old man's death,
To have th' expense and waste of his revenues.
I have this present evening from my sister
Been well inform'd of them, and with such cautions
That, if they come to sojourn at my house,
I'll not be there.

CORNWALL: Nor I, assure thee, Regan.
Edmund, I hear that you have shown your father
A childlike office.

EDMUND: 'Twas my duty, sir.

GLOUCESTER: He did bewray his practice, and receiv'd
This hurt you see, striving to apprehend him.

CORNWALL: Is he pursued?

GLOUCESTER: Ay, my good lord.

CORNWALL: If he be taken, he shall never more
Be fear'd of doing harm. Make your own purpose,
How in my strength you please. For you, Edmund,
Whose virtue and obedience doth this instant
So much commend itself, you shall be ours.
Natures of such deep trust we shall much need;
You we first seize on.

EDMUND: I shall serve you, sir,
Truly, however else.

GLOUCESTER: For him I thank your Grace.

CORNWALL: You know not why we came to visit you—

REGAN: Thus out of season, threading dark-ey'd night.
Occasions, noble Gloucester, of some poise,
Wherein we must have use of your advice.
Our father he hath writ, so hath our sister,
Of differences, which I best thought it fit
To answer from our home. The several messengers
From hence attend dispatch. Our good old friend,
Lay comforts to your bosom, and bestow
Your needful counsel to our business,
Which craves the instant use.

GLOUCESTER: I serve you, madam.
Your Graces are right welcome.
   Exeunt. Flourish.

ACT II. SCENE II. Before Gloucester's Castle.

Enter Kent and Oswald the Steward, Severally.

OSWALD: Good dawning to thee, friend. Art of this house?

KENT: Ay.

OSWALD: Where may we set our horses?

KENT: I' th' mire.

OSWALD: Prithee, if thou lov'st me, tell me.

KENT: I love thee not.

OSWALD: Why then, I care not for thee.

KENT: If I had thee in Lipsbury Pinfold, I would make thee care for me.

OSWALD: Why dost thou use me thus? I know thee not.

KENT: Fellow, I know thee.

OSWALD: What dost thou know me for?

KENT: A knave; a rascal; an eater of broken meats; a base, proud, shallow, beggarly, three-suited, hundred-pound, filthy, worsted-stocking knave; a lily-liver'd, action-taking, whoreson, glass-gazing, superserviceable, finical rogue; one-trunk-inheriting slave; one that wouldst be a bawd in way of good service, and art nothing but the composition of a knave, beggar, coward, pander, and the son and heir of a mongrel bitch; one whom I will beat into clamorous whining, if thou deny the least syllable of thy addition.

OSWALD: Why, what a monstrous fellow art thou, thus to rail on one that's neither known of thee nor knows thee!

KENT: What a brazen-fac'd varlet art thou, to deny thou knowest me! Is it two days ago since I beat thee and tripp'd up thy heels before the King?
Draws His Sword.
Draw, you rogue! for, though it be night, yet the moon shines. I'll make a sop o' th' moonshine o' you. Draw, you whoreson cullionly barbermonger! draw!

OSWALD: Away! I have nothing to do with thee.

KENT: Draw, you rascal! You come with letters against the King, and take Vanity the puppet's part against the royalty of her father. Draw, you rogue, or I'll so carbonado your shanks! Draw, you rascal! Come your ways!

OSWALD: Help, ho! murther! help!

KENT: Strike, you slave! Stand, rogue! Stand, you neat slave! Strike!
Beats Him.

OSWALD: Help, ho! murther! murther!
Enter Edmund, with His Rapier Drawn, Gloucester, Cornwall, Regan, Servants.

EDMUND: How now? What's the matter?
Parts Them.

KENT: With you, goodman boy, an you please! Come, I'll flesh ye! Come on, young master!

GLOUCESTER: Weapons? arms? What's the matter here?

CORNWALL: Keep peace, upon your lives! He dies that strikes again. What is the matter?

REGAN: The messengers from our sister and the King

CORNWALL: What is your difference? Speak.

OSWALD: I am scarce in breath, my lord.

KENT: No marvel, you have so bestirr'd your valour. You cowardly rascal, nature disclaims in thee; a tailor made thee.

CORNWALL: Thou art a strange fellow. A tailor make a man?

KENT: Ay, a tailor, sir. A stonecutter or a painter could not have made him so ill, though he had been but two hours at the trade.

CORNWALL: Speak yet, how grew your quarrel?

OSWALD: This ancient ruffian, sir, whose life I have spar'd
At suit of his grey beard-

KENT: Thou whoreson zed! thou unnecessary letter! My lord, if you'll give me leave, I will tread this unbolted villain into mortar and daub the walls of a jakes with him. 'Spare my grey beard,' you wagtail?

CORNWALL: Peace, sirrah!
You beastly knave, know you no reverence?

KENT: Yes, sir, but anger hath a privilege.

CORNWALL: Why art thou angry?

KENT: That such a slave as this should wear a sword,
Who wears no honesty. Such smiling rogues as these,
Like rats, oft bite the holy cords atwain
Which are too intrinse t' unloose; smooth every passion
That in the natures of their lords rebel,
Bring oil to fire, snow to their colder moods;
Renege, affirm, and turn their halcyon beaks
With every gale and vary of their masters,

Knowing naught (like dogs) but following.
A plague upon your epileptic visage!
Smile you my speeches, as I were a fool?
Goose, an I had you upon Sarum Plain,
I'd drive ye cackling home to Camelot.

CORNWALL: What, art thou mad, old fellow?

GLOUCESTER: How fell you out? Say that.

KENT: No contraries hold more antipathy
Than I and such a knave.

CORNWALL: Why dost thou call him knave? What is his fault?

KENT: His countenance likes me not.

CORNWALL: No more perchance does mine, or his, or hers.

KENT: Sir, 'tis my occupation to be plain.
I have seen better faces in my time
Than stands on any shoulder that I see
Before me at this instant.

CORNWALL: This is some fellow
Who, having been prais'd for bluntness, doth affect
A saucy roughness, and constrains the garb
Quite from his nature. He cannot flatter, he!
An honest mind and plain- he must speak truth!
An they will take it, so; if not, he's plain.
These kind of knaves I know which in this plainness
Harbour more craft and more corrupter ends
Than twenty silly-ducking observants
That stretch their duties nicely.

KENT: Sir, in good faith, in sincere verity,
Under th' allowance of your great aspect,

Whose influence, like the wreath of radiant fire
On flickering Phoebus' front-

CORNWALL: What mean'st by this?

KENT: To go out of my dialect, which you discommend so much. I know, sir, I am no flatterer. He that beguil'd you in a plain accent was a plain knave, which, for my part, I will not be, though I should win your displeasure to entreat me to't.

CORNWALL: What was th' offence you gave him?

OSWALD: I never gave him any.
It pleas'd the King his master very late
To strike at me, upon his misconstruction;
When he, conjunct, and flattering his displeasure,
Tripp'd me behind; being down, insulted, rail'd
And put upon him such a deal of man
That worthied him, got praises of the King
For him attempting who was self-subdu'd;
And, in the fleshment of this dread exploit,
Drew on me here again.

KENT: None of these rogues and cowards
But Ajax is their fool.

CORNWALL: Fetch forth the stocks!
You stubborn ancient knave, you reverent braggart, we'll teach you-

KENT: Sir, I am too old to learn.
Call not your stocks for me. I serve the King;
On whose employment I was sent to you.
You shall do small respect, show too bold malice
Against the grace and person of my master,
Stocking his messenger.

CORNWALL: Fetch forth the stocks! As I have life and honour,

There shall he sit till noon.

REGAN: Till noon? Till night, my lord, and all night too!

KENT: Why, madam, if I were your father's dog,
You should not use me so.

REGAN: Sir, being his knave, I will.

CORNWALL: This is a fellow of the selfsame colour
Our sister speaks of. Come, bring away the stocks!
   Stocks Brought Out.

GLOUCESTER: Let me beseech your Grace not to do so.
His fault is much, and the good King his master
Will check him for't. Your purpos'd low correction
Is such as basest and contemn'dest wretches
For pilf'rings and most common trespasses
Are punish'd with. The King must take it ill
That he, so slightly valued in his messenger,
Should have him thus restrain'd.

CORNWALL: I'll answer that.

REGAN: My sister may receive it much more worse,
To have her gentleman abus'd, assaulted,
For following her affairs. Put in his legs.-
   Kent Is Put in the Stocks.
Come, my good lord, away.
   Exeunt All but Gloucester and Kent.

GLOUCESTER: I am sorry for thee, friend. 'Tis the Duke's pleasure,
Whose disposition, all the world well knows,
Will not be rubb'd nor stopp'd. I'll entreat for thee.

KENT: Pray do not, sir. I have watch'd and travell'd hard.
Some time I shall sleep out, the rest I'll whistle.

A good man's fortune may grow out at heels.
Give you good morrow!

GLOUCESTER: The Duke 's to blame in this; 'twill be ill taken.
Exit.

KENT: Good King, that must approve the common saw,
Thou out of heaven's benediction com'st
To the warm sun!
Approach, thou beacon to this under globe,
That by thy comfortable beams I may
Peruse this letter. Nothing almost sees miracles
But misery. I know 'tis from Cordelia,
Who hath most fortunately been inform'd
Of my obscured course- and *Reads* 'shall find time
From this enormous state, seeking to give
Losses their remedies'- All weary and o'erwatch'd,
Take vantage, heavy eyes, not to behold
This shameful lodging.
Fortune, good night; smile once more, turn thy wheel.
Sleeps.

ACT II. SCENE III. The Open Country.

Enter Edgar.

EDGAR: I heard myself proclaim'd,
And by the happy hollow of a tree
Escap'd the hunt. No port is free, no place
That guard and most unusual vigilance
Does not attend my taking. Whiles I may scape,
I will preserve myself; and am bethought
To take the basest and most poorest shape
That ever penury, in contempt of man,
Brought near to beast. My face I'll grime with filth,
Blanket my loins, elf all my hair in knots,
And with presented nakedness outface
The winds and persecutions of the sky.
The country gives me proof and precedent

Of Bedlam beggars, who, with roaring voices,
Strike in their numb'd and mortified bare arms
Pins, wooden pricks, nails, sprigs of rosemary;
And with this horrible object, from low farms,
Poor pelting villages, sheepcotes, and mills,
Sometime with lunatic bans, sometime with prayers,
Enforce their charity. 'Poor Turlygod! poor Tom!'
That's something yet! Edgar I nothing am.
   Exit.

ACT II. SCENE IV. Before Gloucester's Castle; Kent in the Stocks.
Enter Lear, Fool, and Gentleman.

LEAR: 'Tis strange that they should so depart from home,
And not send back my messenger.

GENTLEMEN: As I learn'd,
The night before there was no purpose in them
Of this remove.

KENT: Hail to thee, noble master!

LEAR: Ha! Mak'st thou this shame thy pastime?

KENT: No, my lord.
FOOL: Ha, ha! look! he wears cruel garters. Horses are tied by the head, dogs and bears by th' neck, monkeys by th' loins, and men by th' legs. When a man's over-lusty at legs, then he wears wooden nether-stocks.

LEAR: What's he that hath so much thy place mistook
To set thee here?

KENT: It is both he and she-
Your son and daughter.

LEAR: No.

KENT: Yes.

LEAR: No, I say.

KENT: I say yea.

LEAR: No, no, they would not!

KENT: Yes, they have.

LEAR: By Jupiter, I swear no!

KENT: By Juno, I swear ay!

LEAR: They durst not do't;
They would not, could not do't. 'Tis worse than murther
To do upon respect such violent outrage.
Resolve me with all modest haste which way
Thou mightst deserve or they impose this usage,
Coming from us.

KENT: My lord, when at their home
I did commend your Highness' letters to them,
Ere I was risen from the place that show'd
My duty kneeling, came there a reeking post,
Stew'd in his haste, half breathless, panting forth
From Goneril his mistress salutations;
Deliver'd letters, spite of intermission,
Which presently they read; on whose contents,
They summon'd up their meiny, straight took horse,
Commanded me to follow and attend
The leisure of their answer, gave me cold looks,
And meeting here the other messenger,
Whose welcome I perceiv'd had poison'd mine-
Being the very fellow which of late
Display'd so saucily against your Highness-
Having more man than wit about me, drew.

He rais'd the house with loud and coward cries.
Your son and daughter found this trespass worth
The shame which here it suffers.

FOOL: Winter's not gone yet, if the wild geese fly that way.
    Fathers that wear rags
      Do make their children blind;
    But fathers that bear bags
      Shall see their children kind.
    Fortune, that arrant whore,
    Ne'er turns the key to th' poor.
But for all this, thou shalt have as many dolours for thy
daughters as thou canst tell in a year.

LEAR: O, how this mother swells up toward my heart!
Hysterica passio! Down, thou climbing sorrow!
Thy element's below! Where is this daughter?

KENT: With the Earl, sir, here within.

LEAR: Follow me not; stay here.
    Exit.

GENTLEMEN: Made you no more offence but what you speak of?

KENT: None.
How chance the King comes with so small a number?

FOOL: An thou hadst been set i' th' stocks for that question, thou'dst well deserv'd it.

KENT: Why, fool?

FOOL: We'll set thee to school to an ant, to teach thee there's no labouring i' th' winter. All that follow their noses are led by their eyes but blind men, and there's not a nose among twenty but can smell him that's stinking. Let go thy hold when a great wheel runs down a hill, lest it break thy neck with following it; but the great one that goes upward, let him draw thee after. When a wise man gives thee better counsel, give me mine again. I would have none but knaves follow it, since a fool gives it.

    That sir which serves and seeks for gain,
        And follows but for form,
    Will pack when it begins to rain
        And leave thee in the storm.
    But I will tarry; the fool will stay,
        And let the wise man fly.
    The knave turns fool that runs away;
        The fool no knave, perdy.

KENT: Where learn'd you this, fool?

FOOL: Not i' th' stocks, fool.
    Enter Lear and Gloucester

LEAR: Deny to speak with me? They are sick? they are weary?
They have travell'd all the night? Mere fetches-
The images of revolt and flying off!
Fetch me a better answer.

GLOUCESTER: My dear lord,
You know the fiery quality of the Duke,
How unremovable and fix'd he is
In his own course.

LEAR: Vengeance! plague! death! confusion!
Fiery? What quality? Why, Gloucester, Gloucester,
I'ld speak with the Duke of Cornwall and his wife.

GLOUCESTER: Well, my good lord, I have inform'd them so.

LEAR: Inform'd them? Dost thou understand me, man?

GLOUCESTER: Ay, my good lord.

LEAR: The King would speak with Cornwall; the dear father
Would with his daughter speak, commands her service.
Are they inform'd of this? My breath and blood!
Fiery? the fiery Duke? Tell the hot Duke that-
No, but not yet! May be he is not well.
Infirmity doth still neglect all office
Whereto our health is bound. We are not ourselves
When nature, being oppress'd, commands the mind
To suffer with the body. I'll forbear;
And am fallen out with my more headier will,
To take the indispos'd and sickly fit
For the sound man.- Death on my state! Wherefore
Should he sit here? This act persuades me
That this remotion of the Duke and her
Is practice only. Give me my servant forth.
Go tell the Duke and 's wife I'ld speak with them-
Now, presently. Bid them come forth and hear me,
Or at their chamber door I'll beat the drum
Till it cry sleep to death.

GLOUCESTER: I would have all well betwixt you.
Exit.

LEAR: O me, my heart, my rising heart! But down!

FOOL: Cry to it, nuncle, as the cockney did to the eels when she put 'em i' th' paste alive. She knapp'd 'em o' th' coxcombs with a stick and cried 'Down, wantons, down!' 'Twas her brother that, in pure kindness to his horse, buttered his hay.
Enter Cornwall, Regan, Gloucester, Servants.

LEAR: Good morrow to you both.

CORNWALL: Hail to your Grace!
Kent Here Set at Liberty.

REGAN: I am glad to see your Highness.

LEAR: Regan, I think you are; I know what reason
I have to think so. If thou shouldst not be glad,
I would divorce me from thy mother's tomb,
Sepulchring an adultress. *To Kent* O, are you free?
Some other time for that.- Beloved Regan,
Thy sister's naught. O Regan, she hath tied
Sharp-tooth'd unkindness, like a vulture, here!
   Lays His Hand on His Heart.
I can scarce speak to thee. Thou'lt not believe
With how deprav'd a quality- O Regan!

REGAN: I pray you, sir, take patience. I have hope
You less know how to value her desert
Than she to scant her duty.

LEAR: Say, how is that?

REGAN: I cannot think my sister in the least
Would fail her obligation. If, sir, perchance
She have restrain'd the riots of your followers,
'Tis on such ground, and to such wholesome end,
As clears her from all blame.

LEAR: My curses on her!

REGAN: O, sir, you are old!
Nature in you stands on the very verge
Of her confine. You should be rul'd, and led
By some discretion that discerns your state
Better than you yourself. Therefore I pray you
That to our sister you do make return;
Say you have wrong'd her, sir.

LEAR: Ask her forgiveness?
Do you but mark how this becomes the house:
'Dear daughter, I confess that I am old. *Kneels.*
Age is unnecessary. On my knees I beg

That you'll vouchsafe me raiment, bed, and food.'

REGAN: Good sir, no more! These are unsightly tricks.
Return you to my sister.

LEAR: *Rises* Never, Regan!
She hath abated me of half my train;
Look'd black upon me; struck me with her tongue,
Most serpent-like, upon the very heart.
All the stor'd vengeances of heaven fall
On her ingrateful top! Strike her young bones,
You taking airs, with lameness!

CORNWALL: Fie, sir, fie!

LEAR: You nimble lightnings, dart your blinding flames
Into her scornful eyes! Infect her beauty,
You fen-suck'd fogs, drawn by the pow'rful sun,
To fall and blast her pride!

REGAN: O the blest gods! so will you wish on me
When the rash mood is on.

LEAR: No, Regan, thou shalt never have my curse.
Thy tender-hefted nature shall not give
Thee o'er to harshness. Her eyes are fierce; but thine
Do comfort, and not burn. 'Tis not in thee
To grudge my pleasures, to cut off my train,
To bandy hasty words, to scant my sizes,
And, in conclusion, to oppose the bolt
Against my coming in. Thou better know'st
The offices of nature, bond of childhood,
Effects of courtesy, dues of gratitude.
Thy half o' th' kingdom hast thou not forgot,
Wherein I thee endow'd.

REGAN: Good sir, to th' purpose.

Tucket Within.

LEAR: Who put my man i' th' stocks?

CORNWALL: What trumpet's that?

REGAN: I know't- my sister's. This approves her letter,
That she would soon be here.
  Enter Oswald the Steward.
Is your lady come?

LEAR: This is a slave, whose easy-borrowed pride
Dwells in the fickle grace of her he follows.
Out, varlet, from my sight!

CORNWALL: What means your Grace?
  Enter Goneril.

LEAR: Who stock'd my servant? Regan, I have good hope
Thou didst not know on't.- Who comes here? O heavens!
If you do love old men, if your sweet sway
Allow obedience- if yourselves are old,
Make it your cause! Send down, and take my part!
To Goneril Art not asham'd to look upon this beard?-
O Regan, wilt thou take her by the hand?

GONERIL: Why not by th' hand, sir? How have I offended?
All's not offence that indiscretion finds
And dotage terms so.

LEAR: O sides, you are too tough!
Will you yet hold? How came my man i' th' stocks?

CORNWALL: I set him there, sir; but his own disorders
Deserv'd much less advancement.

LEAR: You? Did you?

REGAN: I pray you, father, being weak, seem so.
If, till the expiration of your month,
You will return and sojourn with my sister,
Dismissing half your train, come then to me.
I am now from home, and out of that provision
Which shall be needful for your entertainment.

LEAR: Return to her, and fifty men dismiss'd?
No, rather I abjure all roofs, and choose
To wage against the enmity o' th' air,
To be a comrade with the wolf and owl-
Necessity's sharp pinch! Return with her?
Why, the hot-blooded France, that dowerless took
Our youngest born, I could as well be brought
To knee his throne, and, squire-like, pension beg
To keep base life afoot. Return with her?
Persuade me rather to be slave and sumpter
To this detested groom.
   Points at Oswald.

GONERIL: At your choice, sir.

LEAR: I prithee, daughter, do not make me mad.
I will not trouble thee, my child; farewell.
We'll no more meet, no more see one another.
But yet thou art my flesh, my blood, my daughter;
Or rather a disease that's in my flesh,
Which I must needs call mine. Thou art a boil,
A plague sore, an embossed carbuncle
In my corrupted blood. But I'll not chide thee.
Let shame come when it will, I do not call it.
I do not bid the Thunder-bearer shoot
Nor tell tales of thee to high-judging Jove.
Mend when thou canst; be better at thy leisure;
I can be patient, I can stay with Regan,
I and my hundred knights.

REGAN: Not altogether so.

I look'd not for you yet, nor am provided
For your fit welcome. Give ear, sir, to my sister;
For those that mingle reason with your passion
Must be content to think you old, and so-
But she knows what she does.

LEAR: Is this well spoken?

REGAN: I dare avouch it, sir. What, fifty followers?
Is it not well? What should you need of more?
Yea, or so many, sith that both charge and danger
Speak 'gainst so great a number? How in one house
Should many people, under two commands,
Hold amity? 'Tis hard; almost impossible.

GONERIL: Why might not you, my lord, receive attendance
From those that she calls servants, or from mine?

REGAN: Why not, my lord? If then they chanc'd to slack ye,
We could control them. If you will come to me
(For now I spy a danger), I entreat you
To bring but five-and-twenty. To no more
Will I give place or notice.

LEAR: I gave you all-

REGAN: And in good time you gave it!

LEAR: Made you my guardians, my depositaries;
But kept a reservation to be followed
With such a number. What, must I come to you
With five-and-twenty, Regan? Said you so?

REGAN: And speak't again my lord. No more with me.

LEAR: Those wicked creatures yet do look well-favour'd
When others are more wicked; not being the worst

Stands in some rank of praise. *To Goneril* I'll go with thee.
Thy fifty yet doth double five-and-twenty,
And thou art twice her love.

GONERIL: Hear, me, my lord.
What need you five-and-twenty, ten, or five,
To follow in a house where twice so many
Have a command to tend you?

REGAN: What need one?

LEAR: O, reason not the need! Our basest beggars
Are in the poorest thing superfluous.
Allow not nature more than nature needs,
Man's life is cheap as beast's. Thou art a lady:
If only to go warm were gorgeous,
Why, nature needs not what thou gorgeous wear'st
Which scarcely keeps thee warm. But, for true need-
You heavens, give me that patience, patience I need!
You see me here, you gods, a poor old man,
As full of grief as age; wretched in both.
If it be you that stirs these daughters' hearts
Against their father, fool me not so much
To bear it tamely; touch me with noble anger,
And let not women's weapons, water drops,
Stain my man's cheeks! No, you unnatural hags!
I will have such revenges on you both
That all the world shall- I will do such things-
What they are yet, I know not; but they shall be
The terrors of the earth! You think I'll weep.
No, I'll not weep.
I have full cause of weeping, but this heart
Shall break into a hundred thousand flaws
Or ere I'll weep. O fool, I shall go mad!
   Exeunt Lear, Gloucester, Kent, and Fool. Storm and Tempest.

CORNWALL: Let us withdraw; 'twill be a storm.

REGAN: This house is little; the old man and 's people
Cannot be well bestow'd.

GONERIL: 'Tis his own blame; hath put himself from rest
And must needs taste his folly.

REGAN: For his particular, I'll receive him gladly,
But not one follower.

GONERIL: So am I purpos'd.
Where is my Lord of Gloucester?

CORNWALL: Followed the old man forth.
  Enter Gloucester.
He is return'd.

GLOUCESTER: The King is in high rage.

CORNWALL: Whither is he going?

GLOUCESTER: He calls to horse, but will I know not whither.

CORNWALL: 'Tis best to give him way; he leads himself.

GONERIL: My lord, entreat him by no means to stay.

GLOUCESTER: Alack, the night comes on, and the bleak winds
Do sorely ruffle. For many miles about
There's scarce a bush.

REGAN: O, sir, to wilful men
The injuries that they themselves procure
Must be their schoolmasters. Shut up your doors.
He is attended with a desperate train,
And what they may incense him to, being apt
To have his ear abus'd, wisdom bids fear.

CORNWALL: Shut up your doors, my lord: 'tis a wild night.
My Regan counsels well. Come out o' th' storm.
Exeunt.

ACT III. SCENE I. A Heath.

Storm Still. Enter Kent and a Gentleman at Several Doors.

KENT: Who's there, besides foul weather?

GENTLEMEN: One minded like the weather, most unquietly.

KENT: I know you. Where's the King?

GENTLEMEN: Contending with the fretful elements;
Bids the wind blow the earth into the sea,
Or swell the curled waters 'bove the main,
That things might change or cease; tears his white hair,
Which the impetuous blasts, with eyeless rage,
Catch in their fury and make nothing of;
Strives in his little world of man to outscorn
The to-and-fro-conflicting wind and rain.
This night, wherein the cub-drawn bear would couch,
The lion and the belly-pinched wolf
Keep their fur dry, unbonneted he runs,
And bids what will take all.

KENT: But who is with him?

GENTLEMEN: None but the fool, who labours to outjest
His heart-struck injuries.

KENT: Sir, I do know you,
And dare upon the warrant of my note
Commend a dear thing to you. There is division
(Although as yet the face of it be cover'd
With mutual cunning) 'twixt Albany and Cornwall;
Who have (as who have not, that their great stars

Thron'd and set high?) servants, who seem no less,
Which are to France the spies and speculations
Intelligent of our state. What hath been seen,
Either in snuffs and packings of the Dukes,
Or the hard rein which both of them have borne
Against the old kind King, or something deeper,
Whereof, perchance, these are but furnishings-
But, true it is, from France there comes a power
Into this scattered kingdom, who already,
Wise in our negligence, have secret feet
In some of our best ports and are at point
To show their open banner. Now to you:
If on my credit you dare build so far
To make your speed to Dover, you shall find
Some that will thank you, making just report
Of how unnatural and bemadding sorrow
The King hath cause to plain.
I am a gentleman of blood and breeding,
And from some knowledge and assurance offer
This office to you.

GENTLEMEN: I will talk further with you.

KENT: No, do not.
For confirmation that I am much more
Than my out-wall, open this purse and take
What it contains. If you shall see Cordelia
(As fear not but you shall), show her this ring,
And she will tell you who your fellow is
That yet you do not know. Fie on this storm!
I will go seek the King.

GENTLEMEN: Give me your hand. Have you no more to say?

KENT: Few words, but, to effect, more than all yet:
That, when we have found the King (in which your pain
That way, I'll this), he that first lights on him
Holla the other.

Exeunt Severally

ACT III. SCENE II. Another Part of the Heath.
Storm Still. Enter Lear and Fool.

LEAR: Blow, winds, and crack your cheeks! rage! blow!
You cataracts and hurricanoes, spout
Till you have drench'd our steeples, drown'd the cocks!
You sulph'rous and thought-executing fires,
Vaunt-couriers to oak-cleaving thunderbolts,
Singe my white head! And thou, all-shaking thunder,
Strike flat the thick rotundity o' th' world,
Crack Nature's moulds, all germains spill at once,
That makes ingrateful man!

FOOL: O nuncle, court holy water in a dry house is better than this rain water out o' door. Good nuncle, in, and ask thy daughters blessing! Here's a night pities nether wise men nor fools.

LEAR: Rumble thy bellyful! Spit, fire! spout, rain!
Nor rain, wind, thunder, fire are my daughters.
I tax not you, you elements, with unkindness.
I never gave you kingdom, call'd you children,
You owe me no subscription. Then let fall
Your horrible pleasure. Here I stand your slave,
A poor, infirm, weak, and despis'd old man.
But yet I call you servile ministers,
That will with two pernicious daughters join
Your high-engender'd battles 'gainst a head
So old and white as this! O! O! 'tis foul!

FOOL: He that has a house to put 's head in has a good head-piece.
   The codpiece that will house
      Before the head has any,
   The head and he shall louse:
      So beggars marry many.
   The man that makes his toe
      What he his heart should make

Shall of a corn cry woe,
    And turn his sleep to wake.
For there was never yet fair woman but she made mouths in a glass.
    Enter Kent.

LEAR: No, I will be the pattern of all patience;
I will say nothing.

KENT: Who's there?

FOOL: Marry, here's grace and a codpiece; that's a wise man and a fool.

KENT: Alas, sir, are you here? Things that love night
Love not such nights as these. The wrathful skies
Gallow the very wanderers of the dark
And make them keep their caves. Since I was man,
Such sheets of fire, such bursts of horrid thunder,
Such groans of roaring wind and rain, I never
Remember to have heard. Man's nature cannot carry
Th' affliction nor the fear.

LEAR: Let the great gods,
That keep this dreadful pudder o'er our heads,
Find out their enemies now. Tremble, thou wretch,
That hast within thee undivulged crimes
Unwhipp'd of justice. Hide thee, thou bloody hand;
Thou perjur'd, and thou simular man of virtue
That art incestuous. Caitiff, in pieces shake
That under covert and convenient seeming
Hast practis'd on man's life. Close pent-up guilts,
Rive your concealing continents, and cry
These dreadful summoners grace. I am a man
More sinn'd against than sinning.

KENT: Alack, bareheaded?
Gracious my lord, hard by here is a hovel;
Some friendship will it lend you 'gainst the tempest.
Repose you there, whilst I to this hard house

(More harder than the stones whereof 'tis rais'd,
Which even but now, demanding after you,
Denied me to come in) return, and force
Their scanted courtesy.

LEAR: My wits begin to turn.
Come on, my boy. How dost, my boy? Art cold?
I am cold myself. Where is this straw, my fellow?
The art of our necessities is strange,
That can make vile things precious. Come, your hovel.
Poor fool and knave, I have one part in my heart
That's sorry yet for thee.

FOOL: *Sings*
    He that has and a little tiny wit-
      With hey, ho, the wind and the rain-
    Must make content with his fortunes fit,
      For the rain it raineth every day.

LEAR: True, my good boy. Come, bring us to this hovel.
    Exeunt Lear and Kent.

FOOL: This is a brave night to cool a courtesan. I'll speak a prophecy ere I go:
    When priests are more in word than matter;
    When brewers mar their malt with water;
    When nobles are their tailors' tutors,
    No heretics burn'd, but wenches' suitors;
    When every case in law is right,
    No squire in debt nor no poor knight;
    When slanders do not live in tongues,
    Nor cutpurses come not to throngs;
    When usurers tell their gold i' th' field,
    And bawds and whores do churches build:
    Then shall the realm of Albion
    Come to great confusion.
    Then comes the time, who lives to see't,
    That going shall be us'd with feet.

This prophecy Merlin shall make, for I live before his time.
Exit.

ACT III. SCENE III. Gloucester's Castle.
Enter Gloucester and Edmund.

GLOUCESTER: Alack, alack, Edmund, I like not this unnatural dealing! When I desir'd their leave that I might pity him, they took from me the use of mine own house, charg'd me on pain of perpetual displeasure neither to speak of him, entreat for him, nor any way sustain him.
EDMUND: Most savage and unnatural!

GLOUCESTER: Go to; say you nothing. There is division betwixt the Dukes, and a worse matter than that. I have received a letter this night- 'tis dangerous to be spoken- I have lock'd the letter in my closet. These injuries the King now bears will be revenged home; there's part of a power already footed; we must incline to the King. I will seek him and privily relieve him. Go you and maintain talk with the Duke, that my charity be not of him perceived. If he ask for me, I am ill and gone to bed. Though I die for't, as no less is threat'ned me, the King my old master must be relieved. There is some strange thing toward, Edmund. Pray you be careful.
Exit.

EDMUND: This courtesy, forbid thee, shall the Duke
Instantly know, and of that letter too.
This seems a fair deserving, and must draw me
That which my father loses- no less than all.
The younger rises when the old doth fall.
Exit.

ACT III. SCENE IV. The Heath. Before a Hovel.
Storm still. Enter Lear, Kent, and Fool.

KENT: Here is the place, my lord. Good my lord, enter.

The tyranny of the open night 's too rough
For nature to endure.

LEAR: Let me alone.

KENT: Good my lord, enter here.

LEAR: Wilt break my heart?

KENT: I had rather break mine own. Good my lord, enter.

LEAR: Thou think'st 'tis much that this contentious storm
Invades us to the skin. So 'tis to thee;
But where the greater malady is fix'd,
The lesser is scarce felt. Thou'dst shun a bear;
But if thy flight lay toward the raging sea,
Thou'dst meet the bear i' th' mouth. When the mind's free,
The body's delicate. The tempest in my mind
Doth from my senses take all feeling else
Save what beats there. Filial ingratitude!
Is it not as this mouth should tear this hand
For lifting food to't? But I will punish home!
No, I will weep no more. In such a night
'To shut me out! Pour on; I will endure.
In such a night as this! O Regan, Goneril!
Your old kind father, whose frank heart gave all!
O, that way madness lies; let me shun that!
No more of that.

KENT: Good my lord, enter here.

LEAR: Prithee go in thyself; seek thine own ease.
This tempest will not give me leave to ponder
On things would hurt me more. But I'll go in.
To the Fool In, boy; go first.- You houseless poverty-
Nay, get thee in. I'll pray, and then I'll sleep.
  Exit Fool.

Poor naked wretches, wheresoe'er you are,
That bide the pelting of this pitiless storm,
How shall your houseless heads and unfed sides,
Your loop'd and window'd raggedness, defend you
From seasons such as these? O, I have ta'en
Too little care of this! Take physic, pomp;
Expose thyself to feel what wretches feel,
That thou mayst shake the superflux to them
And show the heavens more just.

EDGAR: *Within* Fathom and half, fathom and half! Poor Tom!
  Enter Fool From the Hovel.

FOOL: Come not in here, nuncle, here's a spirit. Help me, help me!

KENT: Give me thy hand. Who's there?

FOOL: A spirit, a spirit! He says his name's poor Tom.

KENT: What art thou that dost grumble there i' th' straw? Come forth.
  Enter Edgar Disguised as a Madman.

EDGAR: Away! the foul fiend follows me! Through the sharp hawthorn blows the cold wind. Humh! go to thy cold bed, and warm thee.

LEAR: Hast thou given all to thy two daughters, and art thou come to this?

EDGAR: Who gives anything to poor Tom? whom the foul fiend hath led through fire and through flame, through ford and whirlpool, o'er bog and quagmire; that hath laid knives under his pillow and halters in his pew, set ratsbane by his porridge, made him proud of heart, to ride on a bay trotting horse over four-inch'd bridges, to course his own shadow for a traitor. Bless thy five wits! Tom 's acold. O, do de, do de, do de. Bless thee from whirlwinds, star-blasting, and taking! Do poor Tom some charity, whom the foul fiend vexes. There could I have him now- and there- and there again- and there!

Storm Still.

LEAR: What, have his daughters brought him to this pass?
Couldst thou save nothing? Didst thou give 'em all?

FOOL: Nay, he reserv'd a blanket, else we had been all sham'd.

LEAR: Now all the plagues that in the pendulous air
Hang fated o'er men's faults light on thy daughters!

KENT: He hath no daughters, sir.

LEAR: Death, traitor! nothing could have subdu'd nature
To such a lowness but his unkind daughters.
Is it the fashion that discarded fathers
Should have thus little mercy on their flesh?
Judicious punishment! 'Twas this flesh begot
Those pelican daughters.

EDGAR: Pillicock sat on Pillicock's Hill. 'Allow, 'allow, loo, loo!

FOOL: This cold night will turn us all to fools and madmen.

EDGAR: Take heed o' th' foul fiend; obey thy parents: keep thy word justly; swear not; commit not with man's sworn spouse; set not thy sweet heart on proud array. Tom 's acold.

LEAR: What hast thou been?

EDGAR: A servingman, proud in heart and mind; that curl'd my hair, wore gloves in my cap; serv'd the lust of my mistress' heart and did the act of darkness with her; swore as many oaths as I spake words, and broke them in the sweet face of heaven; one that slept in the contriving of lust, and wak'd to do it. Wine lov'd I deeply, dice dearly; and in woman out-paramour'd the Turk. False of heart, light of ear, bloody of hand; hog in sloth, fox in stealth, wolf in greediness, dog in madness, lion in prey.

Let not the creaking of shoes nor the rustling of silks betray
thy poor heart to woman. Keep thy foot out of brothel, thy hand
out of placket, thy pen from lender's book, and defy the foul
fiend. Still through the hawthorn blows the cold wind; says
suum, mun, hey, no, nonny. Dolphin my boy, my boy, sessa! let
him trot by.

Storm Still.

LEAR: Why, thou wert better in thy grave than to answer with thy
uncover'd body this extremity of the skies. Is man no more than
this? Consider him well. Thou ow'st the worm no silk, the beast
no hide, the sheep no wool, the cat no perfume. Ha! Here's three
on's are sophisticated! Thou art the thing itself;
unaccommodated man is no more but such a poor, bare, forked
animal as thou art. Off, off, you lendings! Come, unbutton here.

Tears at His Clothes.

FOOL: Prithee, nuncle, be contented! 'Tis a naughty night to swim
in. Now a little fire in a wild field were like an old lecher's
heart- a small spark, all the rest on's body cold. Look, here
comes a walking fire.

Enter Gloucester with a Torch.

EDGAR: This is the foul fiend Flibbertigibbet.
He begins at curfew, and walks till the first cock.
He gives the web and the pin, squints the eye,
and makes the harelip; mildews the white wheat,
and hurts the poor creature of earth.

> Saint Withold footed thrice the 'old;
> He met the nightmare, and her nine fold;
>   Bid her alight
>   And her troth plight,
> And aroint thee, witch, aroint thee!

KENT: How fares your Grace?

LEAR: What's he?

KENT: Who's there? What is't you seek?

GLOUCESTER: What are you there? Your names?

EDGAR: Poor Tom, that eats the swimming frog, the toad, the todpole, the wall-newt and the water; that in the fury of his heart, when the foul fiend rages, eats cow-dung for sallets, swallows the old rat and the ditch-dog, drinks the green mantle of the standing pool; who is whipp'd from tithing to tithing, and stock-punish'd and imprison'd; who hath had three suits to his back, six shirts to his body, horse to ride, and weapons to wear;
    But mice and rats, and such small deer,
    Have been Tom's food for seven long year.
Beware my follower. Peace, Smulkin! peace, thou fiend!

GLOUCESTER: What, hath your Grace no better company?

EDGAR: The prince of darkness is a gentleman!
Modo he's call'd, and Mahu.

GLOUCESTER: Our flesh and blood is grown so vile, my lord,
That it doth hate what gets it.

EDGAR: Poor Tom 's acold.

GLOUCESTER: Go in with me. My duty cannot suffer
T' obey in all your daughters' hard commands.
Though their injunction be to bar my doors
And let this tyrannous night take hold upon you,
Yet have I ventur'd to come seek you out
And bring you where both fire and food is ready.

LEAR: First let me talk with this philosopher.
What is the cause of thunder?

KENT: Good my lord, take his offer; go into th' house.

LEAR: I'll talk a word with this same learned Theban.
What is your study?

EDGAR: How to prevent the fiend and to kill vermin.

LEAR: Let me ask you one word in private.

KENT: Importune him once more to go, my lord.
His wits begin t' unsettle.

GLOUCESTER: Canst thou blame him?
   Storm Still.
His daughters seek his death. Ah, that good Kent!
He said it would be thus- poor banish'd man!
Thou say'st the King grows mad: I'll tell thee, friend,
I am almost mad myself. I had a son,
Now outlaw'd from my blood. He sought my life
But lately, very late. I lov'd him, friend-
No father his son dearer. True to tell thee,
The grief hath craz'd my wits. What a night 's this!
I do beseech your Grace-

LEAR: O, cry you mercy, sir.
Noble philosopher, your company.

EDGAR: Tom's acold.

GLOUCESTER: In, fellow, there, into th' hovel; keep thee warm.

LEAR: Come, let's in all.

KENT: This way, my lord.

LEAR: With him!
I will keep still with my philosopher.

KENT: Good my lord, soothe him; let him take the fellow.

GLOUCESTER: Take him you on.

KENT: Sirrah, come on; go along with us.

LEAR: Come, good Athenian.

GLOUCESTER: No words, no words! hush.

EDGAR: Child Rowland to the dark tower came;
His word was still
   Fie, foh, and fum!
   I smell the blood of a British man.
Exeunt.

ACT III. SCENE V. Gloucester's Castle.
Enter Cornwall and Edmund.

CORNWALL: I will have my revenge ere I depart his house.

EDMUND: How, my lord, I may be censured, that nature thus gives way to loyalty, something fears me to think of.

CORNWALL: I now perceive it was not altogether your brother's evil disposition made him seek his death; but a provoking merit, set awork by a reproveable badness in himself.

EDMUND: How malicious is my fortune that I must repent to be just! This is the letter he spoke of, which approves him an intelligent party to the advantages of France. O heavens! that this treason were not- or not I the detector!

CORNWALL: Go with me to the Duchess.

EDMUND: If the matter of this paper be certain, you have mighty business in hand.

CORNWALL: True or false, it hath made thee Earl of Gloucester. Seek out where thy father is, that he may be ready for our apprehension.

EDMUND: *Aside* If I find him comforting the King, it will stuff his suspicion more fully.- I will persever in my course of loyalty, though the conflict be sore between that and my blood.

CORNWALL: I will lay trust upon thee, and thou shalt find a dearer father in my love.
Exeunt.

ACT III. SCENE VI. A Farmhouse near Gloucester's Castle.
Enter Gloucester, Lear, Kent, Fool, and Edgar.

GLOUCESTER: Here is better than the open air; take it thankfully. I will piece out the comfort with what addition I can. I will not be long from you.

KENT: All the power of his wits have given way to his impatience. The gods reward your kindness!
Exit Gloucester.

EDGAR: Frateretto calls me, and tells me Nero is an angler in the lake of darkness. Pray, innocent, and beware the foul fiend.

FOOL: Prithee, nuncle, tell me whether a madman be a gentleman or a yeoman.

LEAR: A king, a king!

FOOL: No, he's a yeoman that has a gentleman to his son; for he's a mad yeoman that sees his son a gentleman before him.

LEAR: To have a thousand with red burning spits
Come hizzing in upon 'em-

EDGAR: The foul fiend bites my back.

FOOL: He's mad that trusts in the tameness of a wolf, a horse's health, a boy's love, or a whore's oath.

LEAR: It shall be done; I will arraign them straight.
To Edgar Come, sit thou here, most learned justicer.
To the Fool Thou, sapient sir, sit here. Now, you she-foxes!

EDGAR: Look, where he stands and glares!
Want'st thou eyes at trial, madam?
Come o'er the bourn, Bessy, to me.

FOOL: Her boat hath a leak,
    And she must not speak
      Why she dares not come over to thee.

EDGAR: The foul fiend haunts poor Tom in the voice of a nightingale. Hoppedance cries in Tom's belly for two white herring. Croak not, black angel; I have no food for thee.

KENT: How do you, sir? Stand you not so amaz'd.
Will you lie down and rest upon the cushions?

LEAR: I'll see their trial first. Bring in their evidence.
To Edgar Thou, robed man of justice, take thy place.
To the Fool And thou, his yokefellow of equity,
Bench by his side.
To Kent You are o' th' commission, sit you too.

EDGAR: Let us deal justly.
    Sleepest or wakest thou, jolly shepherd?
      Thy sheep be in the corn;
    And for one blast of thy minikin mouth
      Thy sheep shall take no harm.
Purr! the cat is gray.

LEAR: Arraign her first. 'Tis Goneril. I here take my oath before this honourable assembly, she kicked the poor King her father.

FOOL: Come hither, mistress. Is your name Goneril?

LEAR: She cannot deny it.

FOOL: Cry you mercy, I took you for a joint-stool.

LEAR: And here's another, whose warp'd looks proclaim
What store her heart is made on. Stop her there!
Arms, arms! sword! fire! Corruption in the place!
False justicer, why hast thou let her scape?

EDGAR: Bless thy five wits!

KENT: O pity! Sir, where is the patience now
That you so oft have boasted to retain?
EDGAR: *Aside* My tears begin to take his part so much
They'll mar my counterfeiting.

LEAR: The little dogs and all,
Tray, Blanch, and Sweetheart, see, they bark at me.

EDGAR: Tom will throw his head at them. Avaunt, you curs!
    Be thy mouth or black or white,
    Tooth that poisons if it bite;
    Mastiff, greyhound, mongrel grim,
    Hound or spaniel, brach or lym,
    Bobtail tyke or trundle-tall-
    Tom will make them weep and wail;
    For, with throwing thus my head,
    Dogs leap the hatch, and all are fled.
Do de, de, de. Sessa! Come, march to wakes and fairs and market towns. Poor Tom, thy horn is dry.

LEAR: Then let them anatomize Regan. See what breeds about her

heart. Is there any cause in nature that makes these hard
hearts? *To Edgar* You, sir- I entertain you for one of my
hundred; only I do not like the fashion of your garments. You'll
say they are Persian attire; but let them be chang'd.

KENT: Now, good my lord, lie here and rest awhile.

LEAR: Make no noise, make no noise; draw the curtains.
So, so, so. We'll go to supper i' th' morning. So, so, so.

FOOL: And I'll go to bed at noon.
   Enter Gloucester.

GLOUCESTER: Come hither, friend. Where is the King my master?

KENT: Here, sir; but trouble him not; his wits are gone.

GLOUCESTER: Good friend, I prithee take him in thy arms.
I have o'erheard a plot of death upon him.
There is a litter ready; lay him in't
And drive towards Dover, friend, where thou shalt meet
Both welcome and protection. Take up thy master.
If thou shouldst dally half an hour, his life,
With thine, and all that offer to defend him,
Stand in assured loss. Take up, take up!
And follow me, that will to some provision
Give thee quick conduct.

KENT: Oppressed nature sleeps.
This rest might yet have balm'd thy broken senses,
Which, if convenience will not allow,
Stand in hard cure.
To the Fool Come, help to bear thy master.
Thou must not stay behind.

GLOUCESTER: Come, come, away!
   Exeunt all but Edgar.

EDGAR: When we our betters see bearing our woes,
We scarcely think our miseries our foes.
Who alone suffers suffers most i' th' mind,
Leaving free things and happy shows behind;
But then the mind much sufferance doth o'erskip
When grief hath mates, and bearing fellowship.
How light and portable my pain seems now,
When that which makes me bend makes the King bow,
He childed as I fathered! Tom, away!
Mark the high noises, and thyself bewray
When false opinion, whose wrong thought defiles thee,
In thy just proof repeals and reconciles thee.
What will hap more to-night, safe scape the King!
Lurk, lurk.
  Exit.

ACT III. SCENE VII. Gloucester's Castle.
Enter Cornwall, Regan, Goneril, Edmund The Bastard, and Servants.

CORNWALL: *To Goneril* Post speedily to my lord your husband, show him this letter. The army of France is landed.- Seek out the traitor

GLOUCESTER:
  Exeunt some of the Servants.

REGAN: Hang him instantly.

GONERIL: Pluck out his eyes.

CORNWALL: Leave him to my displeasure. Edmund, keep you our sister company. The revenges we are bound to take upon your traitorous father are not fit for your beholding. Advise the Duke where you are going, to a most festinate preparation. We are bound to the like. Our posts shall be swift and intelligent betwixt us. Farewell, dear sister; farewell, my Lord of Gloucester.
  Enter Oswald the Steward.

How now? Where's the King?

OSWALD: My Lord of Gloucester hath convey'd him hence.
Some five or six and thirty of his knights,
Hot questrists after him, met him at gate;
Who, with some other of the lord's dependants,
Are gone with him towards Dover, where they boast
To have well-armed friends.

CORNWALL: Get horses for your mistress.

GONERIL: Farewell, sweet lord, and sister.

CORNWALL: Edmund, farewell.
　Exeunt Goneril, Edmund, and Oswald.
Go seek the traitor Gloucester,
Pinion him like a thief, bring him before us.
　Exeunt other Servants.
Though well we may not pass upon his life
Without the form of justice, yet our power
Shall do a court'sy to our wrath, which men
May blame, but not control.
　Enter Gloucester, Brought in by Two or Three.
Who's there? the traitor?

REGAN: Ingrateful fox! 'tis he.

CORNWALL: Bind fast his corky arms.

GLOUCESTER: What mean, your Graces? Good my friends, consider
You are my guests. Do me no foul play, friends.

CORNWALL: Bind him, I say.
　Servants Bind Him.

REGAN: Hard, hard. O filthy traitor!

GLOUCESTER: Unmerciful lady as you are, I am none.

CORNWALL: To this chair bind him. Villain, thou shalt find-
Regan Plucks His Beard.

GLOUCESTER: By the kind gods, 'tis most ignobly done
To pluck me by the beard.

REGAN: So white, and such a traitor!

GLOUCESTER: Naughty lady,
These hairs which thou dost ravish from my chin
Will quicken, and accuse thee. I am your host.
With robber's hands my hospitable favours
You should not ruffle thus. What will you do?

CORNWALL: Come, sir, what letters had you late from France?

REGAN: Be simple-answer'd, for we know the truth.

CORNWALL: And what confederacy have you with the traitors
Late footed in the kingdom?

REGAN: To whose hands have you sent the lunatic King?
Speak.

GLOUCESTER: I have a letter guessingly set down,
Which came from one that's of a neutral heart,
And not from one oppos'd.

CORNWALL: Cunning.

REGAN: And false.

CORNWALL: Where hast thou sent the King?

GLOUCESTER: To Dover.

REGAN: Wherefore to Dover? Wast thou not charg'd at peril-

CORNWALL: Wherefore to Dover? Let him first answer that.

GLOUCESTER: I am tied to th' stake, and I must stand the course.

REGAN: Wherefore to Dover, sir?

GLOUCESTER: Because I would not see thy cruel nails
Pluck out his poor old eyes; nor thy fierce sister
In his anointed flesh stick boarish fangs.
The sea, with such a storm as his bare head
In hell-black night endur'd, would have buoy'd up
And quench'd the steeled fires.
Yet, poor old heart, he holp the heavens to rain.
If wolves had at thy gate howl'd that stern time,
Thou shouldst have said, 'Good porter, turn the key.'
All cruels else subscrib'd. But I shall see
The winged vengeance overtake such children.

CORNWALL: See't shalt thou never. Fellows, hold the chair.
Upon these eyes of thine I'll set my foot.

GLOUCESTER: He that will think to live till he be old,
Give me some help!- O cruel! O ye gods!

REGAN: One side will mock another. Th' other too!

CORNWALL: If you see vengeance-

FIRST SERVANT: Hold your hand, my lord!
I have serv'd you ever since I was a child;
But better service have I never done you
Than now to bid you hold.

REGAN: How now, you dog?

FIRST SERVANT: If you did wear a beard upon your chin,
I'd shake it on this quarrel.

REGAN: What do you mean?

CORNWALL: My villain! Draw and fight.

FIRST SERVANT: Nay, then, come on, and take the chance of anger.

REGAN: Give me thy sword. A peasant stand up thus?
  She Takes a Sword and Runs at Him Behind.

FIRST SERVANT: O, I am slain! My lord, you have one eye left
To see some mischief on him. O! He dies.

CORNWALL: Lest it see more, prevent it. Out, vile jelly!
Where is thy lustre now?

GLOUCESTER: All dark and comfortless! Where's my son Edmund?
Edmund, enkindle all the sparks of nature
To quit this horrid act.

REGAN: Out, treacherous villain!
Thou call'st on him that hates thee. It was he
That made the overture of thy treasons to us;
Who is too good to pity thee.

GLOUCESTER: O my follies! Then Edgar was abus'd.
Kind gods, forgive me that, and prosper him!

REGAN: Go thrust him out at gates, and let him smell
His way to Dover.
  Exit one with Gloucester.
How is't, my lord? How look you?

CORNWALL: I have receiv'd a hurt. Follow me, lady.
Turn out that eyeless villain. Throw this slave

Upon the dunghill. Regan, I bleed apace.
Untimely comes this hurt. Give me your arm.
  Exit Cornwall, led by Regan.

SECOND SERVANT: I'll never care what wickedness I do,
If this man come to good.

THIRD SERVANT: If she live long,
And in the end meet the old course of death,
Women will all turn monsters.

SECOND SERVANT: Let's follow the old Earl, and get the bedlam
To lead him where he would. His roguish madness
Allows itself to anything.

THIRD SERVANT: Go thou. I'll fetch some flax and whites of eggs
To apply to his bleeding face. Now heaven help him!
  Exeunt.

ACT IV. SCENE I. The Heath.

Enter Edgar.

EDGAR: Yet better thus, and known to be contemn'd,
Than still contemn'd and flatter'd. To be worst,
The lowest and most dejected thing of fortune,
Stands still in esperance, lives not in fear.
The lamentable change is from the best;
The worst returns to laughter. Welcome then,
Thou unsubstantial air that I embrace!
The wretch that thou hast blown unto the worst
Owes nothing to thy blasts.
  Enter Gloucester, Led by an Old Man.
But who comes here?
My father, poorly led? World, world, O world!
But that thy strange mutations make us hate thee,
Life would not yield to age.

OLD MAN: O my good lord,
I have been your tenant, and your father's tenant,
These fourscore years.

GLOUCESTER: Away, get thee away! Good friend, be gone.
Thy comforts can do me no good at all;
Thee they may hurt.

OLD MAN:: You cannot see your way.

GLOUCESTER: I have no way, and therefore want no eyes;
I stumbled when I saw. Full oft 'tis seen
Our means secure us, and our mere defects
Prove our commodities. Ah dear son Edgar,
The food of thy abused father's wrath!
Might I but live to see thee in my touch,
I'ld say I had eyes again!

OLD MAN: How now? Who's there?

EDGAR: *Aside* O gods! Who is't can say 'I am at the worst'?
I am worse than e'er I was.

OLD MAN: 'Tis poor mad Tom.

EDGAR: *Aside* And worse I may be yet. The worst is not
So long as we can say 'This is the worst.'

OLD MAN: Fellow, where goest?

GLOUCESTER: Is it a beggarman?

OLD MAN: Madman and beggar too.

GLOUCESTER: He has some reason, else he could not beg.
I' th' last night's storm I such a fellow saw,
Which made me think a man a worm. My son

Came then into my mind, and yet my mind
Was then scarce friends with him. I have heard more since.
As flies to wanton boys are we to th' gods.
They kill us for their sport.

EDGAR: *Aside* How should this be?
Bad is the trade that must play fool to sorrow,
Ang'ring itself and others.- Bless thee, master!

GLOUCESTER: Is that the naked fellow?

OLD MAN: Ay, my lord.

GLOUCESTER: Then prithee get thee gone. If for my sake
Thou wilt o'ertake us hence a mile or twain
I' th' way toward Dover, do it for ancient love;
And bring some covering for this naked soul,
Who I'll entreat to lead me.

OLD MAN: Alack, sir, he is mad!

GLOUCESTER: 'Tis the time's plague when madmen lead the blind.
Do as I bid thee, or rather do thy pleasure.
Above the rest, be gone.

OLD MAN: I'll bring him the best 'parel that I have,
Come on't what will.
   Exit.

GLOUCESTER: Sirrah naked fellow-

EDGAR: Poor Tom's acold. *Aside* I cannot daub it further.

GLOUCESTER: Come hither, fellow.

EDGAR: *Aside* And yet I must.- Bless thy sweet eyes, they bleed.

GLOUCESTER: Know'st thou the way to Dover?

EDGAR: Both stile and gate, horseway and footpath. Poor Tom hath been scar'd out of his good wits. Bless thee, good man's son, from the foul fiend! Five fiends have been in poor Tom at once: of lust, as Obidicut; Hobbididence, prince of dumbness; Mahu, of stealing; Modo, of murder; Flibbertigibbet, of mopping and mowing, who since possesses chambermaids and waiting women. So, bless thee, master!

GLOUCESTER: Here, take this Purse, thou whom the heavens' plagues
Have humbled to all strokes. That I am wretched
Makes thee the happier. Heavens, deal so still!
Let the superfluous and lust-dieted man,
That slaves your ordinance, that will not see
Because he does not feel, feel your pow'r quickly;
So distribution should undo excess,
And each man have enough. Dost thou know Dover?

EDGAR: Ay, master.

GLOUCESTER: There is a cliff, whose high and bending head
Looks fearfully in the confined deep.
Bring me but to the very brim of it,
And I'll repair the misery thou dost bear
With something rich about me. From that place
I shall no leading need.

EDGAR: Give me thy arm.
Poor Tom shall lead thee.
   Exeunt.

ACT IV. SCENE II. Before the Duke of Albany's Palace.
Enter Goneril and Edmund The Bastard.

GONERIL: Welcome, my lord. I marvel our mild husband
Not met us on the way.

Enter Oswald The Steward.
Now, where's your master?

OSWALD: Madam, within, but never man so chang'd.
I told him of the army that was landed:
He smil'd at it. I told him you were coming:
His answer was, 'The worse.' Of Gloucester's treachery
And of the loyal service of his son
When I inform'd him, then he call'd me sot
And told me I had turn'd the wrong side out.
What most he should dislike seems pleasant to him;
What like, offensive.

GONERIL: *To Edmund* Then shall you go no further.
It is the cowish terror of his spirit,
That dares not undertake. He'll not feel wrongs
Which tie him to an answer. Our wishes on the way
May prove effects. Back, Edmund, to my brother.
Hasten his musters and conduct his pow'rs.
I must change arms at home and give the distaff
Into my husband's hands. This trusty servant
Shall pass between us. Ere long you are like to hear
(If you dare venture in your own behalf)
A mistress's command. Wear this. *Gives a Favour.*
Spare speech.
Decline your head. This kiss, if it durst speak,
Would stretch thy spirits up into the air.
Conceive, and fare thee well.

EDMUND: Yours in the ranks of death!
   Exit.

GONERIL: My most dear Gloucester!
O, the difference of man and man!
To thee a woman's services are due;
My fool usurps my body.

OSWALD: Madam, here comes my lord.

Exit.
Enter Albany.

GONERIL: I have been worth the whistle.

ALBANY: O Goneril,
You are not worth the dust which the rude wind
Blows in your face! I fear your disposition.
That nature which contemns it origin
Cannot be bordered certain in itself.
She that herself will sliver and disbranch
From her material sap, perforce must wither
And come to deadly use.

GONERIL: No more! The text is foolish.

ALBANY: Wisdom and goodness to the vile seem vile;
Filths savour but themselves. What have you done?
Tigers, not daughters, what have you perform'd?
A father, and a gracious aged man,
Whose reverence even the head-lugg'd bear would lick,
Most barbarous, most degenerate, have you madded.
Could my good brother suffer you to do it?
A man, a prince, by him so benefited!
If that the heavens do not their visible spirits
Send quickly down to tame these vile offences,
It will come,
Humanity must perforce prey on itself,
Like monsters of the deep.

GONERIL: Milk-liver'd man!
That bear'st a cheek for blows, a head for wrongs;
Who hast not in thy brows an eye discerning
Thine honour from thy suffering; that not know'st
Fools do those villains pity who are punish'd
Ere they have done their mischief. Where's thy drum?
France spreads his banners in our noiseless land,
With plumed helm thy state begins to threat,

Whiles thou, a moral fool, sit'st still, and criest
'Alack, why does he so?'

ALBANY: See thyself, devil!
Proper deformity seems not in the fiend
So horrid as in woman.

GONERIL: O vain fool!

ALBANY: Thou changed and self-cover'd thing, for shame!
Bemonster not thy feature! Were't my fitness
To let these hands obey my blood,
They are apt enough to dislocate and tear
Thy flesh and bones. Howe'er thou art a fiend,
A woman's shape doth shield thee.

GONERIL: Marry, your manhood mew!
Enter a Gentleman.

ALBANY: What news?

GENTLEMEN: O, my good lord, the Duke of Cornwall 's dead,
Slain by his servant, going to put out
The other eye of Gloucester.

ALBANY: Gloucester's eyes?

GENTLEMEN: A servant that he bred, thrill'd with remorse,
Oppos'd against the act, bending his sword
To his great master; who, thereat enrag'd,
Flew on him, and amongst them fell'd him dead;
But not without that harmful stroke which since
Hath pluck'd him after.

ALBANY: This shows you are above,
You justicers, that these our nether crimes
So speedily can venge! But O poor Gloucester!

Lose he his other eye?

GENTLEMEN: Both, both, my lord.
This letter, madam, craves a speedy answer.
'Tis from your sister.

GONERIL: *Aside* One way I like this well;
But being widow, and my Gloucester with her,
May all the building in my fancy pluck
Upon my hateful life. Another way
The news is not so tart.- I'll read, and answer.
  Exit.

ALBANY: Where was his son when they did take his eyes?

GENTLEMEN: Come with my lady hither.

ALBANY: He is not here.

GENTLEMEN: No, my good lord; I met him back again.

ALBANY: Knows he the wickedness?

GENTLEMEN: Ay, my good lord. 'Twas he inform'd against him,
And quit the house on purpose, that their punishment
Might have the freer course.

ALBANY: Gloucester, I live
To thank thee for the love thou show'dst the King,
And to revenge thine eyes. Come hither, friend.
Tell me what more thou know'st.
  Exeunt.

ACT IV. SCENE III. The French Camp near Dover.
Enter Kent and a Gentleman.

KENT: Why the King of France is so suddenly gone back know you the reason?

GENTLEMEN: Something he left imperfect in the state, which since his coming forth is thought of, which imports to the kingdom so much fear and danger that his personal return was most required and necessary.

KENT: Who hath he left behind him general?

GENTLEMEN: The Marshal of France, Monsieur La Far.

KENT: Did your letters pierce the Queen to any demonstration of grief?

GENTLEMEN: Ay, sir. She took them, read them in my presence,
And now and then an ample tear trill'd down
Her delicate cheek. It seem'd she was a queen
Over her passion, who, most rebel-like,
Sought to be king o'er her.

KENT: O, then it mov'd her?

GENTLEMEN: Not to a rage. Patience and sorrow strove
Who should express her goodliest. You have seen
Sunshine and rain at once: her smiles and tears
Were like, a better way. Those happy smilets
That play'd on her ripe lip seem'd not to know
What guests were in her eyes, which parted thence
As pearls from diamonds dropp'd. In brief,
Sorrow would be a rarity most belov'd,
If all could so become it.

KENT: Made she no verbal question?

GENTLEMEN: Faith, once or twice she heav'd the name of father
Pantingly forth, as if it press'd her heart;
Cried 'Sisters, sisters! Shame of ladies! Sisters!
Kent! father! sisters! What, i' th' storm? i' th' night?

Let pity not be believ'd!' There she shook
The holy water from her heavenly eyes,
And clamour moisten'd. Then away she started
To deal with grief alone.

KENT: It is the stars,
The stars above us, govern our conditions;
Else one self mate and mate could not beget
Such different issues. You spoke not with her since?

GENTLEMEN: No.

KENT: Was this before the King return'd?

GENTLEMEN: No, since.

KENT: Well, sir, the poor distressed Lear's i' th' town;
Who sometime, in his better tune, remembers
What we are come about, and by no means
Will yield to see his daughter.

GENTLEMEN: Why, good sir?

KENT: A sovereign shame so elbows him; his own unkindness,
That stripp'd her from his benediction, turn'd her
To foreign casualties, gave her dear rights
To his dog-hearted daughters- these things sting
His mind so venomously that burning shame
Detains him from Cordelia.

GENTLEMEN: Alack, poor gentleman!

KENT: Of Albany's and Cornwall's powers you heard not?

GENTLEMEN: 'Tis so; they are afoot.

KENT: Well, sir, I'll bring you to our master Lear

And leave you to attend him. Some dear cause
Will in concealment wrap me up awhile.
When I am known aright, you shall not grieve
Lending me this acquaintance. I pray you go
Along with me.
   Exeunt.

ACT IV. SCENE IV. The French Camp.
Enter, with Drum and Colours, Cordelia, Doctor, and Soldiers.

CORDELIA: Alack, 'tis he! Why, he was met even now
As mad as the vex'd sea, singing aloud,
Crown'd with rank fumiter and furrow weeds,
With hardocks, hemlock, nettles, cuckoo flow'rs,
Darnel, and all the idle weeds that grow
In our sustaining corn. A century send forth.
Search every acre in the high-grown field
And bring him to our eye.
   Exit an Officer.
What can man's wisdom
In the restoring his bereaved sense?
He that helps him take all my outward worth.

DOCTOR: There is means, madam.
Our foster nurse of nature is repose,
The which he lacks. That to provoke in him
Are many simples operative, whose power
Will close the eye of anguish.

CORDELIA: All blest secrets,
All you unpublish'd virtues of the earth,
Spring with my tears! be aidant and remediate
In the good man's distress! Seek, seek for him!
Lest his ungovern'd rage dissolve the life
That wants the means to lead it.
   Enter Messenger.

MESSENGER: News, madam.

The British pow'rs are marching hitherward.

CORDELIA: 'Tis known before. Our preparation stands
In expectation of them. O dear father,
It is thy business that I go about.
Therefore great France
My mourning and important tears hath pitied.
No blown ambition doth our arms incite,
But love, dear love, and our ag'd father's right.
Soon may I hear and see him!
  Exeunt.

ACT IV. SCENE V. Gloucester's Castle.
Enter Regan and Oswald The Steward.

REGAN: But are my brother's pow'rs set forth?

OSWALD: Ay, madam.

REGAN: Himself in person there?

OSWALD: Madam, with much ado.
Your sister is the better soldier.

REGAN: Lord Edmund spake not with your lord at home?

OSWALD: No, madam.

REGAN: What might import my sister's letter to him?

OSWALD: I know not, lady.

REGAN: Faith, he is posted hence on serious matter.
It was great ignorance, Gloucester's eyes being out,
To let him live. Where he arrives he moves
All hearts against us. Edmund, I think, is gone,
In pity of his misery, to dispatch

His nighted life; moreover, to descry
The strength o' th' enemy.

OSWALD: I must needs after him, madam, with my letter.

REGAN: Our troops set forth to-morrow. Stay with us.
The ways are dangerous.

OSWALD: I may not, madam.
My lady charg'd my duty in this business.

REGAN: Why should she write to Edmund? Might not you
Transport her purposes by word? Belike,
Something- I know not what- I'll love thee much-
Let me unseal the letter.

OSWALD: Madam, I had rather-

REGAN: I know your lady does not love her husband;
I am sure of that; and at her late being here
She gave strange eliads and most speaking looks
To noble Edmund. I know you are of her bosom.

OSWALD: I, madam?

REGAN: I speak in understanding. Y'are! I know't.
Therefore I do advise you take this note.
My lord is dead; Edmund and I have talk'd,
And more convenient is he for my hand
Than for your lady's. You may gather more.
If you do find him, pray you give him this;
And when your mistress hears thus much from you,
I pray desire her call her wisdom to her.
So farewell.
If you do chance to hear of that blind traitor,
Preferment falls on him that cuts him off.

OSWALD: Would I could meet him, madam! I should show
What party I do follow.

REGAN: Fare thee well.
Exeunt.

ACT IV. SCENE VI. The Country near Dover.
Enter Gloucester, and Edgar Like a Peasant.

GLOUCESTER: When shall I come to th' top of that same hill?

EDGAR: You do climb up it now. Look how we labour.

GLOUCESTER: Methinks the ground is even.

EDGAR: Horrible steep.
Hark, do you hear the sea?

GLOUCESTER: No, truly.

EDGAR: Why, then, your other senses grow imperfect
By your eyes' anguish.

GLOUCESTER: So may it be indeed.
Methinks thy voice is alter'd, and thou speak'st
In better phrase and matter than thou didst.

EDGAR: Y'are much deceiv'd. In nothing am I chang'd
But in my garments.

GLOUCESTER: Methinks y'are better spoken.

EDGAR: Come on, sir; here's the place. Stand still. How fearful
And dizzy 'tis to cast one's eyes so low!
The crows and choughs that wing the midway air
Show scarce so gross as beetles. Halfway down
Hangs one that gathers sampire- dreadful trade!

Methinks he seems no bigger than his head.
The fishermen that walk upon the beach
Appear like mice; and yond tall anchoring bark,
Diminish'd to her cock; her cock, a buoy
Almost too small for sight. The murmuring surge
That on th' unnumb'red idle pebble chafes
Cannot be heard so high. I'll look no more,
Lest my brain turn, and the deficient sight
Topple down headlong.

GLOUCESTER: Set me where you stand.

EDGAR: Give me your hand. You are now within a foot
Of th' extreme verge. For all beneath the moon
Would I not leap upright.

GLOUCESTER: Let go my hand.
Here, friend, is another purse; in it a jewel
Well worth a poor man's taking. Fairies and gods
Prosper it with thee! Go thou further off;
Bid me farewell, and let me hear thee going.

EDGAR: Now fare ye well, good sir.

GLOUCESTER: With all my heart.

EDGAR: *Aside.* Why I do trifle thus with his despair
Is done to cure it.

GLOUCESTER: O you mighty gods! He kneels.
This world I do renounce, and, in your sights,
Shake patiently my great affliction off.
If I could bear it longer and not fall
To quarrel with your great opposeless wills,
My snuff and loathed part of nature should
Burn itself out. If Edgar live, O, bless him!
Now, fellow, fare thee well.

He Falls Forward and Swoons.

EDGAR: Gone, sir, farewell.-
And yet I know not how conceit may rob
The treasury of life when life itself
Yields to the theft. Had he been where he thought,
By this had thought been past.- Alive or dead?
Ho you, sir! friend! Hear you, sir? Speak!-
Thus might he pass indeed. Yet he revives.
What are you, sir?

GLOUCESTER: Away, and let me die.

EDGAR: Hadst thou been aught but gossamer, feathers, air,
So many fadom down precipitating,
Thou'dst shiver'd like an egg; but thou dost breathe;
Hast heavy substance; bleed'st not; speak'st; art sound.
Ten masts at each make not the altitude
Which thou hast perpendicularly fell.
Thy life is a miracle. Speak yet again.

GLOUCESTER: But have I fall'n, or no?

EDGAR: From the dread summit of this chalky bourn.
Look up a-height. The shrill-gorg'd lark so far
Cannot be seen or heard. Do but look up.

GLOUCESTER: Alack, I have no eyes!
Is wretchedness depriv'd that benefit
To end itself by death? 'Twas yet some comfort
When misery could beguile the tyrant's rage
And frustrate his proud will.

EDGAR: Give me your arm.
Up- so. How is't? Feel you your legs? You stand.

GLOUCESTER: Too well, too well.

EDGAR: This is above all strangeness.
Upon the crown o' th' cliff what thing was that
Which parted from you?

GLOUCESTER: A poor unfortunate beggar.

EDGAR: As I stood here below, methought his eyes
Were two full moons; he had a thousand noses,
Horns whelk'd and wav'd like the enridged sea.
It was some fiend. Therefore, thou happy father,
Think that the clearest gods, who make them honours
Of men's impossibility, have preserv'd thee.

GLOUCESTER: I do remember now. Henceforth I'll bear
Affliction till it do cry out itself
'Enough, enough,' and die. That thing you speak of,
I took it for a man. Often 'twould say
'The fiend, the fiend'- he led me to that place.

EDGAR: Bear free and patient thoughts.
   Enter Lear, Mad, Fantastically Dressed with Weeds.
But who comes here?
The safer sense will ne'er accommodate
His master thus.

LEAR: No, they cannot touch me for coming;
I am the King himself.

EDGAR: O thou side-piercing sight!

LEAR: Nature 's above art in that respect. There's your press money. That fellow handles his bow like a crow-keeper. Draw me a clothier's yard. Look, look, a mouse! Peace, peace; this piece of toasted cheese will do't. There's my gauntlet; I'll prove it on a giant. Bring up the brown bills. O, well flown, bird! i' th' clout, i' th' clout! Hewgh! Give the word.

EDGAR: Sweet marjoram.

LEAR: Pass.

GLOUCESTER: I know that voice.

LEAR: Ha! Goneril with a white beard? They flatter'd me like a dog, and told me I had white hairs in my beard ere the black ones were there. To say 'ay' and 'no' to everything I said! 'Ay' and 'no' too was no good divinity. When the rain came to wet me once, and the wind to make me chatter; when the thunder would not peace at my bidding; there I found 'em, there I smelt 'em out. Go to, they are not men o' their words! They told me I was everything. 'Tis a lie- I am not ague-proof.

GLOUCESTER: The trick of that voice I do well remember. Is't not the King?

LEAR: Ay, every inch a king!
When I do stare, see how the subject quakes.
I pardon that man's life. What was thy cause? Adultery?
Thou shalt not die. Die for adultery? No.
The wren goes to't, and the small gilded fly
Does lecher in my sight.
Let copulation thrive; for Gloucester's bastard son
Was kinder to his father than my daughters
Got 'tween the lawful sheets.
To't, luxury, pell-mell! for I lack soldiers.
Behold yond simp'ring dame,
Whose face between her forks presageth snow,
That minces virtue, and does shake the head
To hear of pleasure's name.
The fitchew nor the soiled horse goes to't
With a more riotous appetite.
Down from the waist they are Centaurs,
Though women all above.
But to the girdle do the gods inherit,
Beneath is all the fiend's.

There's hell, there's darkness, there's the sulphurous pit;
burning, scalding, stench, consumption. Fie, fie, fie! pah, pah!
Give me an ounce of civet, good apothecary, to sweeten my
imagination. There's money for thee.

GLOUCESTER: O, let me kiss that hand!

LEAR: Let me wipe it first; it smells of mortality.

GLOUCESTER: O ruin'd piece of nature! This great world
Shall so wear out to naught. Dost thou know me?

LEAR: I remember thine eyes well enough. Dost thou squiny at me?
No, do thy worst, blind Cupid! I'll not love. Read thou this
challenge; mark but the penning of it.

GLOUCESTER: Were all the letters suns, I could not see one.

EDGAR: *Aside* I would not take this from report. It is,
And my heart breaks at it.

LEAR: Read.

GLOUCESTER: What, with the case of eyes?

LEAR: O, ho, are you there with me? No eyes in your head, nor no
money in your purse? Your eyes are in a heavy case, your purse
in a light. Yet you see how this world goes.

GLOUCESTER: I see it feelingly.

LEAR: What, art mad? A man may see how the world goes with no eyes.
Look with thine ears. See how yond justice rails upon yond
simple thief. Hark in thine ear. Change places and, handy-dandy,
which is the justice, which is the thief? Thou hast seen a
farmer's dog bark at a beggar?

GLOUCESTER: Ay, sir.

LEAR: And the creature run from the cur? There thou mightst behold
the great image of authority: a dog's obeyed in office.
Thou rascal beadle, hold thy bloody hand!
Why dost thou lash that whore? Strip thine own back.
Thou hotly lusts to use her in that kind
For which thou whip'st her. The usurer hangs the cozener.
Through tatter'd clothes small vices do appear;
Robes and furr'd gowns hide all. Plate sin with gold,
And the strong lance of justice hurtless breaks;
Arm it in rags, a pygmy's straw does pierce it.
None does offend, none- I say none! I'll able 'em.
Take that of me, my friend, who have the power
To seal th' accuser's lips. Get thee glass eyes
And, like a scurvy politician, seem
To see the things thou dost not. Now, now, now, now!
Pull off my boots. Harder, harder! So.

EDGAR: O, matter and impertinency mix'd!
Reason, in madness!

LEAR: If thou wilt weep my fortunes, take my eyes.
I know thee well enough; thy name is Gloucester.
Thou must be patient. We came crying hither;
Thou know'st, the first time that we smell the air
We wawl and cry. I will preach to thee. Mark.

GLOUCESTER: Alack, alack the day!

LEAR: When we are born, we cry that we are come
To this great stage of fools. This' a good block.
It were a delicate stratagem to shoe
A troop of horse with felt. I'll put't in proof,
And when I have stol'n upon these sons-in-law,
Then kill, kill, kill, kill, kill, kill!
   Enter a Gentleman With Attendants.

GENTLEMEN: O, here he is! Lay hand upon him.- Sir,
Your most dear daughter-

LEAR: No rescue? What, a prisoner? I am even
The natural fool of fortune. Use me well;
You shall have ransom. Let me have a surgeon;
I am cut to th' brains.

GENTLEMEN: You shall have anything.

LEAR: No seconds? All myself?
Why, this would make a man a man of salt,
To use his eyes for garden waterpots,
Ay, and laying autumn's dust.

GENTLEMEN: Good sir-

LEAR: I will die bravely, like a smug bridegroom. What!
I will be jovial. Come, come, I am a king;
My masters, know you that?

GENTLEMEN: You are a royal one, and we obey you.

LEAR: Then there's life in't. Nay, an you get it, you shall get it
by running. Sa, sa, sa, sa!
   Exit Running. Attendants Follow.

GENTLEMEN: A sight most pitiful in the meanest wretch,
Past speaking of in a king! Thou hast one daughter
Who redeems nature from the general curse
Which twain have brought her to.

EDGAR: Hail, gentle sir.

GENTLEMEN: Sir, speed you. What's your will?

EDGAR: Do you hear aught, sir, of a battle toward?

GENTLEMEN: Most sure and vulgar. Every one hears that
Which can distinguish sound.

EDGAR: But, by your favour,
How near's the other army?

GENTLEMEN: Near and on speedy foot. The main descry
Stands on the hourly thought.

EDGAR: I thank you sir. That's all.

GENTLEMEN: Though that the Queen on special cause is here,
Her army is mov'd on.

EDGAR: I thank you, sir
  Exit Gentleman.

GLOUCESTER: You ever-gentle gods, take my breath from me;
Let not my worser spirit tempt me again
To die before you please!

EDGAR: Well pray you, father.

GLOUCESTER: Now, good sir, what are you?

EDGAR: A most poor man, made tame to fortune's blows,
Who, by the art of known and feeling sorrows,
Am pregnant to good pity. Give me your hand;
I'll lead you to some biding.

GLOUCESTER: Hearty thanks.
The bounty and the benison of heaven
To boot, and boot!
  Enter Oswald the Steward.

OSWALD: A proclaim'd prize! Most happy!
That eyeless head of thine was first fram'd flesh

To raise my fortunes. Thou old unhappy traitor,
Briefly thyself remember. The sword is out
That must destroy thee.

GLOUCESTER: Now let thy friendly hand
Put strength enough to't.
   Edgar Interposes.

OSWALD: Wherefore, bold peasant,
Dar'st thou support a publish'd traitor? Hence!
Lest that th' infection of his fortune take
Like hold on thee. Let go his arm.

EDGAR: Chill not let go, zir, without vurther 'cagion.

OSWALD: Let go, slave, or thou diest!

EDGAR: Good gentleman, go your gait, and let poor voke pass. An chud ha' bin zwagger'd out of my life, 'twould not ha' bin zo long as 'tis by a vortnight. Nay, come not near th' old man. Keep out, che vore ye, or Ise try whether your costard or my ballow be the harder. Chill be plain with you.

OSWALD: Out, dunghill!
   They Fight.

EDGAR: Chill pick your teeth, zir. Come! No matter vor your foins.
   Oswald Falls.

OSWALD: Slave, thou hast slain me. Villain, take my purse.
If ever thou wilt thrive, bury my body,
And give the letters which thou find'st about me
To Edmund Earl of Gloucester. Seek him out
Upon the British party. O, untimely death! Death!
   He Dies.

EDGAR: I know thee well. A serviceable villain,

As duteous to the vices of thy mistress
As badness would desire.

GLOUCESTER: What, is he dead?

EDGAR: Sit you down, father; rest you.
Let's see his pockets; these letters that he speaks of
May be my friends. He's dead. I am only sorry
He had no other deathsman. Let us see.
Leave, gentle wax; and, manners, blame us not.
To know our enemies' minds, we'ld rip their hearts;
Their papers, is more lawful. Reads the letter.
  'Let our reciprocal vows be rememb'red. You have many
opportunities to cut him off. If your will want not, time and
place will be fruitfully offer'd. There is nothing done, if he
return the conqueror. Then am I the prisoner, and his bed my
jail; from the loathed warmth whereof deliver me, and supply the
place for your labour.
    'Your (wife, so I would say) affectionate servant,
                              'Goneril.'
O indistinguish'd space of woman's will!
A plot upon her virtuous husband's life,
And the exchange my brother! Here in the sands
Thee I'll rake up, the post unsanctified
Of murtherous lechers; and in the mature time
With this ungracious paper strike the sight
Of the death-practis'd Duke, For him 'tis well
That of thy death and business I can tell.

GLOUCESTER: The King is mad. How stiff is my vile sense,
That I stand up, and have ingenious feeling
Of my huge sorrows! Better I were distract.
So should my thoughts be sever'd from my griefs,
And woes by wrong imaginations lose
The knowledge of themselves.
  A Drum Afar Off.

EDGAR: Give me your hand.

Far off methinks I hear the beaten drum.
Come, father, I'll bestow you with a friend. *Exeunt.*

ACT IV. SCENE VII. A Tent in the French Camp.
Enter Cordelia, Kent, Doctor, and Gentleman.

CORDELIA: O thou good Kent, how shall I live and work
To match thy goodness? My life will be too short
And every measure fail me.

KENT: To be acknowledg'd, madam, is o'erpaid.
All my reports go with the modest truth;
Nor more nor clipp'd, but so.

CORDELIA: Be better suited.
These weeds are memories of those worser hours.
I prithee put them off.

KENT: Pardon, dear madam.
Yet to be known shortens my made intent.
My boon I make it that you know me not
Till time and I think meet.
CORDELIA: Then be't so, my good lord.
To the Doctor How, does the King?

DOCTOR: Madam, sleeps still.

CORDELIA: O you kind gods,
Cure this great breach in his abused nature!
Th' untun'd and jarring senses, O, wind up
Of this child-changed father!

DOCTOR: So please your Majesty
That we may wake the King? He hath slept long.

CORDELIA: Be govern'd by your knowledge, and proceed
I' th' sway of your own will. Is he array'd?

Enter Lear in a Chair Carried by Servants.

GENTLEMEN: Ay, madam. In the heaviness of sleep
We put fresh garments on him.

DOCTOR: Be by, good madam, when we do awake him.
I doubt not of his temperance.

CORDELIA: Very well.
Music.

DOCTOR: Please you draw near. Louder the music there!

CORDELIA: O my dear father, restoration hang
Thy medicine on my lips, and let this kiss
Repair those violent harms that my two sisters
Have in thy reverence made!

KENT: Kind and dear princess!

CORDELIA: Had you not been their father, these white flakes
Had challeng'd pity of them. Was this a face
To be oppos'd against the warring winds?
To stand against the deep dread-bolted thunder?
In the most terrible and nimble stroke
Of quick cross lightning? to watch- poor perdu!-
With this thin helm? Mine enemy's dog,
Though he had bit me, should have stood that night
Against my fire; and wast thou fain, poor father,
To hovel thee with swine and rogues forlorn,
In short and musty straw? Alack, alack!
'Tis wonder that thy life and wits at once
Had not concluded all.- He wakes. Speak to him.

DOCTOR: Madam, do you; 'tis fittest.

CORDELIA: How does my royal lord? How fares your Majesty?

LEAR: You do me wrong to take me out o' th' grave.
Thou art a soul in bliss; but I am bound
Upon a wheel of fire, that mine own tears
Do scald like molten lead.

CORDELIA: Sir, do you know me?

LEAR: You are a spirit, I know. When did you die?

CORDELIA: Still, still, far wide!

DOCTOR: He's scarce awake. Let him alone awhile.

LEAR: Where have I been? Where am I? Fair daylight,
I am mightily abus'd. I should e'en die with pity,
To see another thus. I know not what to say.
I will not swear these are my hands. Let's see.
I feel this pin prick. Would I were assur'd
Of my condition!

CORDELIA: O, look upon me, sir,
And hold your hands in benediction o'er me.
No, sir, you must not kneel.

LEAR: Pray, do not mock me.
I am a very foolish fond old man,
Fourscore and upward, not an hour more nor less;
And, to deal plainly,
I fear I am not in my perfect mind.
Methinks I should know you, and know this man;
Yet I am doubtful; for I am mainly ignorant
What place this is; and all the skill I have
Remembers not these garments; nor I know not
Where I did lodge last night. Do not laugh at me;
For (as I am a man) I think this lady
To be my child Cordelia.

CORDELIA: And so I am! I am!

LEAR: Be your tears wet? Yes, faith. I pray weep not.
If you have poison for me, I will drink it.
I know you do not love me; for your sisters
Have, as I do remember, done me wrong.
You have some cause, they have not.

CORDELIA: No cause, no cause.

LEAR: Am I in France?

KENT: In your own kingdom, sir.

LEAR: Do not abuse me.

DOCTOR: Be comforted, good madam. The great rage
You see is kill'd in him; and yet it is danger
To make him even o'er the time he has lost.
Desire him to go in. Trouble him no more
Till further settling.

CORDELIA: Will't please your Highness walk?

LEAR: You must bear with me.
Pray you now, forget and forgive. I am old and foolish.
   Exeunt. Manent Kent and Gentleman.

GENTLEMEN: Holds it true, sir, that the Duke of Cornwall was so slain?

KENT: Most certain, sir.

GENTLEMEN: Who is conductor of his people?

KENT: As 'tis said, the bastard son of Gloucester.

GENTLEMEN: They say Edgar, his banish'd son, is with the Earl of Kent in Germany.

KENT: Report is changeable. 'Tis time to look about; the powers of the kingdom approach apace.

GENTLEMEN: The arbitrement is like to be bloody.
Fare you well, sir.
  Exit.

KENT: My point and period will be throughly wrought,
Or well or ill, as this day's battle's fought.
  Exit.

ACT V. SCENE I. The British Camp near Dover.

Enter, with Drum and Colours, Edmund, Regan, Gentleman, and Soldiers.

EDMUND: Know of the Duke if his last purpose hold,
Or whether since he is advis'd by aught
To change the course. He's full of alteration
And self-reproving. Bring his constant pleasure.
  Exit an Officer.

REGAN: Our sister's man is certainly miscarried.

EDMUND: Tis to be doubted, madam.

REGAN: Now, sweet lord,
You know the goodness I intend upon you.
Tell me- but truly- but then speak the truth-
Do you not love my sister?

EDMUND: In honour'd love.

REGAN: But have you never found my brother's way
To the forfended place?

EDMUND: That thought abuses you.

REGAN: I am doubtful that you have been conjunct
And bosom'd with her, as far as we call hers.

EDMUND: No, by mine honour, madam.

REGAN: I never shall endure her. Dear my lord,
Be not familiar with her.

EDMUND: Fear me not.
She and the Duke her husband!
 Enter, with Drum and Colours, Albany, Goneril, Soldiers.

GONERIL: *Aside* I had rather lose the battle than that sister
Should loosen him and me.

ALBANY: Our very loving sister, well bemet.
Sir, this I hear: the King is come to his daughter,
With others whom the rigour of our state
Forc'd to cry out. Where I could not be honest,
I never yet was valiant. For this business,
It toucheth us as France invades our land,
Not bolds the King, with others whom, I fear,
Most just and heavy causes make oppose.

EDMUND: Sir, you speak nobly.

REGAN: Why is this reason'd?

GONERIL: Combine together 'gainst the enemy;
For these domestic and particular broils
Are not the question here.

ALBANY: Let's then determine
With th' ancient of war on our proceeding.

EDMUND: I shall attend you presently at your tent.

REGAN: Sister, you'll go with us?

GONERIL: No.

REGAN: 'Tis most convenient. Pray you go with us.

GONERIL: *Aside* O, ho, I know the riddle.- I will go.
  As They Are Going Out, Enter Edgar Disguised.

EDGAR: If e'er your Grace had speech with man so poor,
Hear me one word.

ALBANY: I'll overtake you.- Speak.
  Exeunt all but Albany and Edgar.

EDGAR: Before you fight the battle, ope this letter.
If you have victory, let the trumpet sound
For him that brought it. Wretched though I seem,
I can produce a champion that will prove
What is avouched there. If you miscarry,
Your business of the world hath so an end,
And machination ceases. Fortune love you!

ALBANY: Stay till I have read the letter.

EDGAR: I was forbid it.
When time shall serve, let but the herald cry,
And I'll appear again.

ALBANY: Why, fare thee well. I will o'erlook thy paper.
  Exit Edgar.
  Enter Edmund.

EDMUND: The enemy 's in view; draw up your powers.
Here is the guess of their true strength and forces
By diligent discovery; but your haste
Is now urg'd on you.

ALBANY: We will greet the time.
Exit.

EDMUND: To both these sisters have I sworn my love;
Each jealous of the other, as the stung
Are of the adder. Which of them shall I take?
Both? one? or neither? Neither can be enjoy'd,
If both remain alive. To take the widow
Exasperates, makes mad her sister Goneril;
And hardly shall I carry out my side,
Her husband being alive. Now then, we'll use
His countenance for the battle, which being done,
Let her who would be rid of him devise
His speedy taking off. As for the mercy
Which he intends to Lear and to Cordelia-
The battle done, and they within our power,
Shall never see his pardon; for my state
Stands on me to defend, not to debate.
Exit.

ACT V. SCENE II. A Field Between the Two Camps.

Alarum Within. Enter, with Drum and Colours, the Powers of France over the Stage, Cordelia with Her Father in Her Hand, and Exeunt.
Enter Edgar and Gloucester.

EDGAR: Here, father, take the shadow of this tree
For your good host. Pray that the right may thrive.
If ever I return to you again,
I'll bring you comfort.

GLOUCESTER: Grace go with you, sir!
Exit Edgar.
Alarum and Retreat Within. Enter Edgar,

EDGAR: Away, old man! give me thy hand! away!
King Lear hath lost, he and his daughter ta'en.
Give me thy hand! come on!

GLOUCESTER: No further, sir. A man may rot even here.

EDGAR: What, in ill thoughts again? Men must endure
Their going hence, even as their coming hither;
Ripeness is all. Come on.

GLOUCESTER: And that's true too.
Exeunt.

ACT V. SCENE III. The British Camp, near Dover.
Enter, in Conquest, with Drum and Colours, Edmund; Lear and Cordelia as Prisoners; Soldiers, Captain.

EDMUND: Some officers take them away. Good guard
Until their greater pleasures first be known
That are to censure them.

CORDELIA: We are not the first
Who with best meaning have incurr'd the worst.
For thee, oppressed king, am I cast down;
Myself could else outfrown false Fortune's frown.
Shall we not see these daughters and these sisters?

LEAR: No, no, no, no! Come, let's away to prison.
We two alone will sing like birds i' th' cage.
When thou dost ask me blessing, I'll kneel down
And ask of thee forgiveness. So we'll live,
And pray, and sing, and tell old tales, and laugh
At gilded butterflies, and hear poor rogues
Talk of court news; and we'll talk with them too-
Who loses and who wins; who's in, who's out-
And take upon 's the mystery of things,
As if we were God's spies; and we'll wear out,
In a wall'd prison, packs and sects of great ones
That ebb and flow by th' moon.

EDMUND: Take them away.

LEAR: Upon such sacrifices, my Cordelia,
The gods themselves throw incense. Have I caught thee?
He that parts us shall bring a brand from heaven
And fire us hence like foxes. Wipe thine eyes.
The goodyears shall devour 'em, flesh and fell,
Ere they shall make us weep! We'll see 'em starv'd first.
Come.
   Exeunt Lear and Cordelia, Guarded.

EDMUND: Come hither, Captain; hark.
Take thou this note *Gives a Paper*. Go follow them to prison.
One step I have advanc'd thee. If thou dost
As this instructs thee, thou dost make thy way
To noble fortunes. Know thou this, that men
Are as the time is. To be tender-minded
Does not become a sword. Thy great employment
Will not bear question. Either say thou'lt do't,
Or thrive by other means.

CAPTAIN: I'll do't, my lord.

EDMUND: About it! and write happy when th' hast done.
Mark- I say, instantly; and carry it so
As I have set it down.

CAPTAIN: I cannot draw a cart, nor eat dried oats;
If it be man's work, I'll do't.
   Exit.
   Flourish. Enter Albany, Goneril, Regan, Soldiers.

ALBANY: Sir, you have show'd to-day your valiant strain,
And fortune led you well. You have the captives
Who were the opposites of this day's strife.
We do require them of you, so to use them
As we shall find their merits and our safety
May equally determine.

EDMUND: Sir, I thought it fit
To send the old and miserable King
To some retention and appointed guard;
Whose age has charms in it, whose title more,
To pluck the common bosom on his side
And turn our impress'd lances in our eyes
Which do command them. With him I sent the Queen,
My reason all the same; and they are ready
To-morrow, or at further space, t' appear
Where you shall hold your session. At this time
We sweat and bleed: the friend hath lost his friend;
And the best quarrels, in the heat, are curs'd
By those that feel their sharpness.
The question of Cordelia and her father
Requires a fitter place.

ALBANY: Sir, by your patience,
I hold you but a subject of this war,
Not as a brother.

REGAN: That's as we list to grace him.
Methinks our pleasure might have been demanded
Ere you had spoke so far. He led our powers,
Bore the commission of my place and person,
The which immediacy may well stand up
And call itself your brother.

GONERIL: Not so hot!
In his own grace he doth exalt himself
More than in your addition.

REGAN: In my rights
By me invested, he compeers the best.

GONERIL: That were the most if he should husband you.

REGAN: Jesters do oft prove prophets.

GONERIL: Holla, holla!
That eye that told you so look'd but asquint.

REGAN: Lady, I am not well; else I should answer
From a full-flowing stomach. General,
Take thou my soldiers, prisoners, patrimony;
Dispose of them, of me; the walls are thine.
Witness the world that I create thee here
My lord and master.

GONERIL: Mean you to enjoy him?

ALBANY: The let-alone lies not in your good will.

EDMUND: Nor in thine, lord.

ALBANY: Half-blooded fellow, yes.

REGAN: *To Edmund* Let the drum strike, and prove my title thine.

ALBANY: Stay yet; hear reason. Edmund, I arrest thee
On capital treason; and, in thine attaint,
This gilded serpent *Points to Goneril.* For your claim, fair sister,
I bar it in the interest of my wife.
'Tis she is subcontracted to this lord,
And I, her husband, contradict your banes.
If you will marry, make your loves to me;
My lady is bespoke.

GONERIL: An interlude!

ALBANY: Thou art arm'd, Gloucester. Let the trumpet sound.
If none appear to prove upon thy person
Thy heinous, manifest, and many treasons,
There is my pledge *Throws down a Glove!* I'll prove it on thy heart,
Ere I taste bread, thou art in nothing less
Than I have here proclaim'd thee.

REGAN: Sick, O, sick!

GONERIL: *Aside* If not, I'll ne'er trust medicine.

EDMUND: There's my exchange
Throws down a Glove. What in the world he is
That names me traitor, villain-like he lies.
Call by thy trumpet. He that dares approach,
On him, on you, who not? I will maintain
My truth and honour firmly.

ALBANY: A herald, ho!

EDMUND: A herald, ho, a herald!

ALBANY: Trust to thy single virtue; for thy soldiers,
All levied in my name, have in my name
Took their discharge.

REGAN: My sickness grows upon me.

ALBANY: She is not well. Convey her to my tent.
  Exit Regan, Led.
  Enter a Herald.
Come hither, herald. Let the trumpet sound,
And read out this.

CAPTAIN: Sound, trumpet! A trumpet sounds.

HERALD: (reads) 'If any man of quality or degree within the lists of the army will maintain upon Edmund, supposed Earl of Gloucester, that he is a manifold traitor, let him appear by the third sound of the trumpet. He is bold in his defence.'

EDMUND: Sound! First trumpet.

DOCTOR: Again! Second trumpet.

HERALD: Again! Third trumpet.
Trumpet Answers Within.
Enter Edgar, Armed, at the Third Sound, a Trumpet Before Him.

ALBANY: Ask him his purposes, why he appears
Upon this call o' th' trumpet.

HERALD: What are you?
Your name, your quality? and why you answer
This present summons?

EDGAR: Know my name is lost;
By treason's tooth bare-gnawn and canker-bit.
Yet am I noble as the adversary
I come to cope.

ALBANY: Which is that adversary?

EDGAR: What's he that speaks for Edmund Earl of Gloucester?

EDMUND: Himself. What say'st thou to him?

EDGAR: Draw thy sword,
That, if my speech offend a noble heart,
Thy arm may do thee justice. Here is mine.
Behold, it is the privilege of mine honours,
My oath, and my profession. I protest-
Maugre thy strength, youth, place, and eminence,
Despite thy victor sword and fire-new fortune,
Thy valour and thy heart- thou art a traitor;
False to thy gods, thy brother, and thy father;
Conspirant 'gainst this high illustrious prince;
And from th' extremest upward of thy head
To the descent and dust beneath thy foot,
A most toad-spotted traitor. Say thou 'no,'
This sword, this arm, and my best spirits are bent
To prove upon thy heart, whereto I speak,

Thou liest.

EDMUND: In wisdom I should ask thy name;
But since thy outside looks so fair and warlike,
And that thy tongue some say of breeding breathes,
What safe and nicely I might well delay
By rule of knighthood, I disdain and spurn.
Back do I toss those treasons to thy head;
With the hell-hated lie o'erwhelm thy heart;
Which- for they yet glance by and scarcely bruise-
This sword of mine shall give them instant way
Where they shall rest for ever. Trumpets, speak!
Alarums. Fight. Edmund Falls.

ALBANY: Save him, save him!

GONERIL: This is mere practice, Gloucester.
By th' law of arms thou wast not bound to answer
An unknown opposite. Thou art not vanquish'd,
But cozen'd and beguil'd.

ALBANY: Shut your mouth, dame,
Or with this paper shall I stop it. *Shows Her Her Letter to Edmund.-*
To Edmund. Hold, sir.
To Goneril Thou worse than any name, read thine own evil.
No tearing, lady! I perceive you know it.

GONERIL: Say if I do- the laws are mine, not thine.
Who can arraign me for't?

ALBANY: Most monstrous!
Know'st thou this paper?

GONERIL: Ask me not what I know.
Exit.

ALBANY: Go after her. She's desperate; govern her.

Exit an Officer.

EDMUND: What, you have charg'd me with, that have I done,
And more, much more. The time will bring it out.
'Tis past, and so am I.- But what art thou
That hast this fortune on me? If thou'rt noble,
I do forgive thee.

EDGAR: Let's exchange charity.
I am no less in blood than thou art, Edmund;
If more, the more th' hast wrong'd me.
My name is Edgar and thy father's son.
The gods are just, and of our pleasant vices
Make instruments to scourge us.
The dark and vicious place where thee he got
Cost him his eyes.

EDMUND: Th' hast spoken right; 'tis true.
The wheel is come full circle; I am here.

ALBANY: Methought thy very gait did prophesy
A royal nobleness. I must embrace thee.
Let sorrow split my heart if ever I
Did hate thee, or thy father!

EDGAR: Worthy prince, I know't.

ALBANY: Where have you hid yourself?
How have you known the miseries of your father?

EDGAR: By nursing them, my lord. List a brief tale;
And when 'tis told, O that my heart would burst!
The bloody proclamation to escape
That follow'd me so near (O, our lives' sweetness!
That with the pain of death would hourly die
Rather than die at once!) taught me to shift
Into a madman's rags, t' assume a semblance

That very dogs disdain'd; and in this habit
Met I my father with his bleeding rings,
Their precious stones new lost; became his guide,
Led him, begg'd for him, sav'd him from despair;
Never (O fault!) reveal'd myself unto him
Until some half hour past, when I was arm'd,
Not sure, though hoping of this good success,
I ask'd his blessing, and from first to last
Told him my pilgrimage. But his flaw'd heart
(Alack, too weak the conflict to support!)
'Twixt two extremes of passion, joy and grief,
Burst smilingly.

EDMUND: This speech of yours hath mov'd me,
And shall perchance do good; but speak you on;
You look as you had something more to say.

ALBANY: If there be more, more woful, hold it in;
For I am almost ready to dissolve,
Hearing of this.

EDGAR: This would have seem'd a period
To such as love not sorrow; but another,
To amplify too much, would make much more,
And top extremity.
Whilst I was big in clamour, came there a man,
Who, having seen me in my worst estate,
Shunn'd my abhorr'd society; but then, finding
Who 'twas that so endur'd, with his strong arms
He fastened on my neck, and bellowed out
As he'd burst heaven; threw him on my father;
Told the most piteous tale of Lear and him
That ever ear receiv'd; which in recounting
His grief grew puissant, and the strings of life
Began to crack. Twice then the trumpets sounded,
And there I left him tranc'd.

ALBANY: But who was this?

EDGAR: Kent, sir, the banish'd Kent; who in disguise
Followed his enemy king and did him service
Improper for a slave.
  Enter a Gentleman with a Bloody Knife.

GENTLEMEN: Help, help! O, help!

EDGAR: What kind of help?

ALBANY: Speak, man.

EDGAR: What means that bloody knife?

GENTLEMEN: 'Tis hot, it smokes.
It came even from the heart of- O! she's dead!

ALBANY: Who dead? Speak, man.

GENTLEMEN: Your lady, sir, your lady! and her sister
By her is poisoned; she hath confess'd it.

EDMUND: I was contracted to them both. All three
Now marry in an instant.
  Enter Kent.

EDGAR: Here comes Kent.

ALBANY: Produce their bodies, be they alive or dead.
  Exit Gentleman.
This judgement of the heavens, that makes us tremble
Touches us not with pity. O, is this he?
The time will not allow the compliment
That very manners urges.

KENT: I am come
To bid my king and master aye good night.
Is he not here?

ALBANY: Great thing of us forgot!
Speak, Edmund, where's the King? and where's Cordelia?
      The bodies of Goneril and Regan are brought in.
Seest thou this object, Kent?

KENT: Alack, why thus?

EDMUND: Yet Edmund was belov'd.
The one the other poisoned for my sake,
And after slew herself.

ALBANY: Even so. Cover their faces.

EDMUND: I pant for life. Some good I mean to do,
Despite of mine own nature. Quickly send
(Be brief in't) to the castle; for my writ
Is on the life of Lear and on Cordelia.
Nay, send in time.

ALBANY: Run, run, O, run!

EDGAR: To who, my lord? Who has the office? Send
Thy token of reprieve.

EDMUND: Well thought on. Take my sword;
Give it the Captain.

ALBANY: Haste thee for thy life.
  Exit Edgar.

EDMUND: He hath commission from thy wife and me
To hang Cordelia in the prison and
To lay the blame upon her own despair
That she fordid herself.

ALBANY: The gods defend her! Bear him hence awhile.
  Edmund Is Borne Off.

Enter Lear, with Cordelia Dead in His Arms, Edgar, Captain, and Others Following.

LEAR: Howl, howl, howl, howl! O, you are men of stone.
Had I your tongues and eyes, I'd use them so
That heaven's vault should crack. She's gone for ever!
I know when one is dead, and when one lives.
She's dead as earth. Lend me a looking glass.
If that her breath will mist or stain the stone,
Why, then she lives.

KENT: Is this the promis'd end?

EDGAR: Or image of that horror?

ALBANY: Fall and cease!

LEAR: This feather stirs; she lives! If it be so,
It is a chance which does redeem all sorrows
That ever I have felt.

KENT: O my good master!

LEAR: Prithee away!

EDGAR: 'Tis noble Kent, your friend.

LEAR: A plague upon you, murderers, traitors all!
I might have sav'd her; now she's gone for ever!
Cordelia, Cordelia! stay a little. Ha!
What is't thou say'st, Her voice was ever soft,
Gentle, and low- an excellent thing in woman.
I kill'd the slave that was a-hanging thee.

CAPTAIN: 'Tis true, my lords, he did.

LEAR: Did I not, fellow?

I have seen the day, with my good biting falchion
I would have made them skip. I am old now,
And these same crosses spoil me. Who are you?
Mine eyes are not o' th' best. I'll tell you straight.

KENT: If fortune brag of two she lov'd and hated,
One of them we behold.

LEAR: This' a dull sight. Are you not Kent?

KENT: The same-
Your servant Kent. Where is your servant Caius?

LEAR: He's a good fellow, I can tell you that.
He'll strike, and quickly too. He's dead and rotten.

KENT: No, my good lord; I am the very man-

LEAR: I'll see that straight.

KENT: That from your first of difference and decay
Have followed your sad steps.

LEAR: You're welcome hither.

KENT: Nor no man else! All's cheerless, dark, and deadly.
Your eldest daughters have fordone themselves,
And desperately are dead.

LEAR: Ay, so I think.

ALBANY: He knows not what he says; and vain is it
That we present us to him.

EDGAR: Very bootless.
Enter a Captain.

CAPTAIN: Edmund is dead, my lord.

ALBANY: That's but a trifle here.
You lords and noble friends, know our intent.
What comfort to this great decay may come
Shall be applied. For us, we will resign,
During the life of this old Majesty,
To him our absolute power;
To Edgar and Kent you to your rights;
With boot, and Such addition as your honours
Have more than merited.- All friends shall taste
The wages of their virtue, and all foes
The cup of their deservings.- O, see, see!

LEAR: And my poor fool is hang'd! No, no, no life!
Why should a dog, a horse, a rat, have life,
And thou no breath at all? Thou'lt come no more,
Never, never, never, never, never!
Pray you undo this button. Thank you, sir.
Do you see this? Look on her! look! her lips!
Look there, look there! He dies.

EDGAR: He faints! My lord, my lord!

KENT: Break, heart; I prithee break!

EDGAR: Look up, my lord.

KENT: Vex not his ghost. O, let him pass! He hates him
That would upon the rack of this tough world
Stretch him out longer.

EDGAR: He is gone indeed.

KENT: The wonder is, he hath endur'd so long.
He but usurp'd his life.

ALBANY: Bear them from hence. Our present business is general woe.
To Kent and Edgar Friends of my soul, you twain
Rule in this realm, and the gor'd state sustain.

KENT: I have a journey, sir, shortly to go.
My master calls me; I must not say no.

ALBANY: The weight of this sad time we must obey,
Speak what we feel, not what we ought to say.
The oldest have borne most; we that are young
Shall never see so much, nor live so long.
   Exeunt with a Dead March.

END

www.ingramcontent.com/pod-product-compliance
Lightning Source LLC
Chambersburg PA
CBHW031357160426
42813CB00081B/237